KARL MARX

·A POLITICAL BIOGRAPHY·

KARL MARX

·A POLITICAL BIOGRAPHY·

BY
FRITZ J. RADDATZ

TRANSLATED FROM THE GERMAN BY
RICHARD BARRY

LITTLE, BROWN AND COMPANY   BOSTON · TORONTO

FIRST ENGLISH LANGUAGE EDITION

T 02/79

LIBRARY OF CONGRESS CATALOGING IN PUBLICATION DATA

Raddatz, Fritz Joachim.
  Karl Marx: a political biography.

  Bibliography: p.
  Includes index.
  1. Marx, Karl, 1818–1883. 2. Communists—Biography
HX39.5.R26313 1978   335.4'092'4 [B]   78-23341
ISBN 0-316-73210-9

  The author and publishers are grateful to Lawrence & Wishart Ltd. for permission to reproduce passages from *The Collected Works of Marx and Engels.*

AUTHOR'S
· ACKNOWLEDGMENTS ·

My thanks for help in research are due to the Instituto Giangiacomo Feltrinelli, Milan; to the Foundation of the Student Library for the History of the Workers Movement, Zurich; to the Internationaal Instituut voor Sociale Geschiedenes, Amsterdam; and to the Karl-Marx-Haus, Trier–Friedrich Ebert Foundation. My thanks are also due to Regine Stützner, without whose assistance the manuscript would never have reached book form.

F.J.R.

·CONTENTS·

KARL MARX

·A POLITICAL BIOGRAPHY·

·CHAPTER ONE·

EARLY YEARS

A DESCENDANT OF JEWISH RABBIS BECOMES A
PROTESTANT SCHOOLBOY IN CATHOLIC TRIER

The baptism was performed at home. The sun shone on that August 26, 1824; Carl Heinrich Marx, already at school, was six and a half years old. The baptismal register of the Evangelical parish of Trier shows that his five sisters and his brother Hermann were also baptized at the same time;[1] it also notes that the children's mother had not yet turned Christian, out of respect for her parents' feelings. The subsequent great family celebration, of which there are several accounts,[2] consisted of a gala dinner attended by the ten godparents, almost all of whom were upper class. Even such authorities as Friedrich Engels and Franz Mehring assume that Carl's father, Heinrich Marx, a lawyer, also changed his religion in 1824, but this is not correct.[3] He was actually baptized several years earlier, before the birth of his son Carl.

In this important matter the family went different ways. Heinrich Marx, the father, came of a traditionally rabbinical family; his brother was chief rabbi of Trier (population 15,000) but he was baptized as a Christian at the age of thirty-five. The mother, on the other hand, whose family was scattered all over Europe and included numerous rabbis and men of learning, did not turn Christian with her husband nor with her seven children when they were baptized seven years later; Henriette Marx, née Presburg, did not make up her mind to take the plunge until a year later, on November 20, 1825, after receiving "preliminary instruction in Christianity." Did she ever actually take it?

The family history was unusual, though not extraordinary. Henriette Marx had come to Trier from Nijmegen and all her life she never fully mastered the German language; her ancestors can be traced back through complex peregrinations to the early fifteenth century and include the famous Rabbi Jehuda ben Eliezer ha Levy Minz, professor at Padua University. The family tree also contains names shared with that of Heinrich Heine; Heinrich Heine's great-great-grandparents were Karl Marx's great-great-great-grandparents.[4]

Heinrich Marx, known as Herschel or Hirschel until his baptism, had a family tree reading like an extract from an almanac of Jewish aristocracy:

Marx-Levy, his grandfather, known simply as "Marx," was Rabbi in Trier until his death in 1789. He married Eva Moses Lvov (1737–1823) whose family came from Hesse and emigrated to Poland where they took the name of their town Lvov (Lemberg). The family returned to Germany in the 17th century and settled in Trier. Among Eva Moses Lvov's ancestors were famous rabbis such as Meier Katzellenbogen, Rector of the Talmudic University in Padua (died 1565), Josef ben Gerson ha Cohen (died 1591) and Professor Josua Heschel Lvov (1693–1771).
   This couple had three sons of whom the eldest, Samuel (died 1827) was rabbi in Trier and the youngest Hirschel, Karl Marx's father, was a lawyer, also in Trier. . . .
   Karl Marx's parents had nine children, four sons and five daughters. Little is known of the other eight and they played no great part in Karl's life. Moritz David, the eldest brother, died shortly after Karl was born; four others died of consumption comparatively young, Eduard at the age of eleven, Hermann and Caroline at twenty-three, and Henriette at thirty-six. Sophie, the eldest daughter and the closest to Karl, married Schmalhausen, an attorney from Maastricht; Louise married a Dutch businessman named Juta and emigrated with him to South Africa; Emilie married an engineer named Conradi and lived in Trier until her death.[5]

No date can be established for the father's conversion to Christianity — the baptismal register in the Evangelical parish of Trier only starts at March 1, 1818, and includes no entry on the subject; it may be assumed to have taken place between 1816 and 1819. The change was undoubtedly connected with his professional and social position. We shall see later the effect of this break with Jewry on Karl Marx's habits of thought and phraseology. There were good reasons, however, for the father to "emancipate himself" — if that, rather than "alienating himself," is what he did.

Until the end of the eighteenth century the Jews were still outcasts in German society. They could not own land; they could not pursue a trade; they could not follow any of the liberal professions. They were confined to money-lending and so-called unauthorized emergency business which the mercantile guilds would not touch.[6] They were subjected to a poll tax, an annual tax, lodging increment, and a registration levy. Although by mid–nineteenth century the most powerful financial speculators were quite clearly Christians,[7] the "Jewish usurer" was still the stereotype; both the market economy and capitalism were regarded as manifestations of the morbidly materialistic Jewish spirit, while the corporations were regarded as "truly Christian." As late as 1848 a craftsmen's petition to the Frankfurt National

Assembly stated that "our German nature, our inmost soul" revolted against Jewish emancipation.[8]

In 1793 there were no more than twenty Jewish traders in Trier offering their wares at fairs or in marketplaces; by 1817 there were some two hundred, but even then they were still a minority. By that time Grattenauer, the Commissioner of Justice in Berlin, had already proposed that Jews be compelled to wear a yellow ribbon — which Berlin Professor Friedrich Rühs referred to in 1815 as a "noose round the neck of a people."

The legal position of Jews was obscure and confused. After his conquest of the German states, Napoleon emancipated them almost overnight. In the successor Federal States and Free Cities, however, many laws were evaded; Jews were expelled from Lübeck, for instance. Policy was not consistent: a decree of September 28, 1791, by the French National Assembly, revoked all specifically anti-Jewish legislation, granting Jews the rights and obligations of French citizens, and these provisions were extended to the areas annexed by France on the left bank of the Rhine. As against this, a decree of March 17, 1808, setting up a strictly regimented system of parishes, once more restricted the civil rights of Jews. When reports reached Napoleon about real estate speculation or shady financial dealings, he turned primarily on the Jews; their freedom of movement was restricted once more and permission to engage in a trade or profession was made dependent on a license from the Prefect, for which a certificate of good character was required.

In Prussia itself the "Edict concerning the civil position of Jews in the Prussian State" issued on March 11, 1812, was still in force; this prescribed cancellation of special taxation, freedom of choice of a profession and marriage, and admission to official positions in schools and colleges. The edict was never revoked but it was interpreted: Jewish lawyers were refused permission to practice; widows of Jewish soldiers killed in action had their pensions withheld, their husbands' religion being given as the reason. In 1816 some 125,000 Jews were living in Prussia and some 300,000 in Germany as a whole; they represented about 1.25 percent of the total population of 24,000,000.

The reasons for Heinrich Marx's conversion to Christianity are not, therefore, far to seek. His object was not simply to be called Heinrich instead of Herschel; it was to see his family integrated into society, to ensure his livelihood or even advancement, and to preserve a modest standard of living.

The two things went together. Heinrich Marx's relationships with upper-class families were bound up with his professional contacts; the godparents were drawn almost exclusively from the legal profession. The house which he acquired in 1819 had previously belonged to *Justizrat* (public attorney)

Schwarz, President of a Chamber of the High Court of Appeal in Köln.[9] Dr. Lion Berncastle, whom he later recommended to his son as medical adviser,[10] was co-owner of one of his vineyards.[11]

Undoubtedly he had had a long hard row to hoe — there is no pathos in the reference to this fact in a subsequent letter to his son in Berlin. It is not even clear where Heinrich Marx studied but it may well have been in France; the predominantly French literature in his library, his use of the Christian name "Henry" in 1814, and the fact that he is shown as "*avoué*" in the birth certificate of his niece Caroline indicate as much.[12] In the Trier *Taschenkalendar* (almanac) for 1816 he is shown as "lawyer"; the roll of barristers accredited to the Rhineland Court of Appeal gives 1815 as the year when he began to practice; a report of 1816 records that the President and Attorney General of the Appeal Court had given him a "glowing testimonial"; lastly, as barrister or attorney, Heinrich Marx was Dean of the Trier Bar for years.[13]

His conversion to the Protestant faith — and its timing — were therefore connected with the obstacles in the way of a professional career for a Jew; the 1812 edict had barred Jews from official positions or entry into "other public services," a really oppressive measure instituted by reactionary Prussia. In 1815 King Friedrich Wilhelm III of Prussia banned Jews from all public office under Article 16 of the German Federation's constitution and in 1822 he extended the ban even to the liberal professions.

This is only half the truth, however. Heinrich Marx should not simply be labeled a time-serving renegade from the Jewish faith. He was also a man who drew the logical conclusions from an enlightened view of emancipation. Heinrich Marx's step was not merely a change of allegiance from Jehovah to God (the Evangelical parish register shows that he only received communion once, at Whitsun 1827), nor did it signify merely a change of residence from the ghetto to the rich quarter; it was a deliberate act by a disciple of Voltaire and Rousseau. It is known that Karl Marx was well acquainted with Voltaire and Racine through his father,[14] that Rousseau was favorite reading in the house at 8 Simeonsgasse,[15] and that Heinrich Marx was well versed in the writings of Locke, Lessing, and Leibniz.[16] He did not, however, sever his ties with the Jewish community in Trier, certainly not with his rabbi brother nor with the Jewish population,[17] for whom he continued to act in legal matters.[18]

So Heinrich Marx's decision represented both a break with the past and a step forward; it undoubtedly carried with it the germ of dissension with his adolescent eldest son but at the same time it opened up possibilities of development for "dear beloved Carl."

There are hardly any photographs and very few descriptions of Karl Marx as a child. One wonders what he looked like — swarthy, uncouth, bumptious? His sisters say that he was invariably the domineering leader in their games together: for instance he would force them to run down the Weinberg near Trier as fast as their legs would carry them; he would also insist that they ate with apparent enjoyment the mud pies that his grubby hands had "cooked" for them.[19]

At any rate, in 1819 the family was able to move into a highly respectable house of their own, bought for nearly 12,000 francs;* this does not imply, however, that their previous rented house at 664 Brückengasse — now the "Karl Marx House" — was not in good upper-middle-class style; it was in fact almost a town mansion. In addition the family owned property, primarily a number of vineyards of considerable size. Decades later, in one of his remarkable "matchmaking" letters to François Lafargue of Bordeaux, father of his son-in-law Paul Lafargue, Karl Marx described himself as a "former vineyard proprietor."[20] The family fortune was therefore considerable; it ensured not only an expensive education for "dear Carl" but the necessary allowance for the "unintelligent" son, Hermann,[21] and adequate dowries for the daughters. More important still it enabled Henriette Marx to enjoy a comfortable old age as a widow, bitterly envied by her son Karl; she was even able to lend money.[22] Her papers contained details of sums owed, surprising in the case of a woman who had economized even on night attire during her lifetime, for:

In 1853 Louise, one of the daughters, asked her aunt Sophie Phllips to have six night-dresses and six petticoats made for her in Bommel. She said that she was sorry to trouble her aunt with this but that "Mummy wants me to, since she thinks that I would not get them so cheaply here. . . ." A later letter said: "Mummy thinks . . . that if you have not yet bought the night-dresses, you had better have shifts made since they are not so expensive and night-dresses are not so essential in a warmer climate. Also would you be so good as to have the petticoats made less wide than usual since width is not necessary and is more expensive."[23]

This high standard of living was not achieved during a period or in a society characterized by general prosperity. When a public issue of shares in a fund for puchase of cereals for the poor of the town was made, Heinrich Marx was able to subscribe for two shares (the Burgomaster subscribed ten and the Bishop twenty),[24] but this merely shows that private wealth existed amid general poverty.

In fact the end of Napoleonic rule in the Rhineland marked the beginning of political, social, and economic decline. When Prussian troops marched unopposed into Trier during the night January 5/6, 1814, they were by no means welcomed with enthusiasm (they were succeeded by Austrians in May). The decision of the Congress of Vienna whereby Prussia acquired the Rhineland and the greater part of Westphalia initially threw the administra-

* Figures of currencies given throughout the book are explained in the Appendix.

tion into confusion; by virtue of the declaration of April 5, 1815 "concerning occupation of the Grand Duchy of the Lower Rhine" the *Regierungsbezirk* (governmental district) of which Trier was the capital was finally incorporated into Prussia. The mayor became Burgomaster, City Commissar and District President of the borough, which included the surrounding area; he and his *Stadtrat* (Chairman of City Council) were subordinate to the Governor. For the citizenry, who had hitherto enjoyed the benefits of the Napoleonic *Code Civil,* this was a retrograde step; only property owners, for instance, could be members of the provincial Chamber (in other words, of the decision-making administrative organization).

Economic recession set in at once. In 1816 the harvest failed; in 1817 prices rose and there were food shortages; trade declined owing to loss of markets to British competition, the iron industry in the Eifel being particularly hard hit. In 1816, thirty thousand fewer wagonloads of iron ore were exported than in previous years; in the same year blast-furnace production was only 357,427 kilos whereas the annual average between 1808 and 1813 had been 844,700 kilos. To the misery of the working class was added that of the Moselle farmers, who were unable to sell their products in Prussia. In 1817 Clausewitz, Chief of Staff of III Army Corps, reported from Koblenz that distress in the Trier area had "reached an incredible level; for weeks the poorer sections of the population have been without bread and have been living on frozen potatoes which have been lying out in the fields since last year."[25]

The city of Trier was in ruins. The outer wall was still intact and inside it ran an avenue of poplars and walnut trees; the eight gates were open to traffic, but inside, instead of the glitter of a capital city, there was nothing but desolation; the spaces between monasteries, churches, and public places were occupied by pastureland rather than houses. As late as 1837 there were still only 1184 habitable dwellings in the city.

Apart from two or three exceptions the city streets were narrow and rough. Traffic on the streets was impeded by numerous itinerant traders and the craftsmen's habit of doing their work largely on the street in front of their houses. Butchers allowed their dogs to chase calves through the streets and slaughtered pigs in the open. Many middle-class houses stood empty; all had lost in value. Some thirty of the best houses, previously occupied by Frenchmen, were up for sale but there were no takers. A number of houses in the town were in danger of collapse. Arguments about thatch which owners could not afford to replace went on for years. . . . Orders from the municipal police dated 31 July 1818 give a picture of what life in the town was like, at least up to that year. They laid down that new houses must in future be built on a definite alignment and facing on to the street; chimneys and stove-pipes must not give on to the street. Water was to be drained from roofs by gutters; kitchens, stables and workshops must not drain on to the street. It was forbidden to throw dirty water, contents of chamber pots or other filth from houses into the street by day or night. Restrictions were placed on work carried on in front of houses and sale of goods on the streets.[26]

Various factors contributed to produce not exactly solidarity but at least some form of alliance between the poverty-stricken people and the dispirited bourgeoisie who had lost their privileges if nothing else. Hatred of Prussia, far distant both culturally and geographically, led not only to a predilection for French habits of thought but also to a genuine process of liberalization; an example was the administration of justice. Poaching and wood-stealing — the culprits were known as "timber-farmers" — were punished leniently or not at all. The Burgomaster intervened personally on behalf of certain defendants, pointing out that they were very poor people who could barely feed themselves and their numerous families and would not survive the winter cold; it was difficult to convince them that thieving from a state forest was a crime. At times the Minister of Justice was forced to call attention to the fact that mercy and forbearance were the prerogatives of the rulers and to take action against overlenient sentences; he also had to issue instructions against laxity in the treatment of persons under detention. It was made known that proceedings would be taken against officials of the Justice Department who showed themselves too easygoing, even in political cases. This was bitterly resented by the Rhineland judges, who felt their independence threatened; all classes of society seethed with indignation.

Various incidents in the life of Heinrich Marx, the lawyer, show that his position, both socially and morally, was equivocal, if not double faced. On the one hand he was loyal to the monarchy and an obedient servant of Prussia, on the other he was liberal and Francophile; politically he zigzagged. He refused an invitation to the farewell banquet for Prussian Lieutenant General von Ryssel on December 29, 1830; in the same year, however, his name appears on a list of citizens charged with maintenance of law and order.[27] He was not even invited to the ball for the Princess of Prussia on August 2, 1835, but he did receive an invitation, which he accepted, to the City Ball on January 20, 1836.[28] His position is highlighted by the famous "Case of the Casino Society."

The Casino Society was the most exclusive club in Trier, frequented by officers, officials, and the most distinguished men in town. People were not simply members but owned shares in the form of bonds. Naturally, Heinrich Marx belonged to the Society; he owned bonds to the value of 60 taler. On January 12, 1834, the Society gave a "ceremonial banquet" in honor of the deputies to the Rhineland Provincial Legislature (*Landtag*). The overall plan for this feast was drawn up by forty members, of whom five were in charge of the detailed arrangements and one of these was to make the speech of welcome. Heinrich Marx was one of the five and he it was who made the speech.

The "unbalanced assimilated Jew"[29] gave further proof of his own blend of servility, reverential respect for the monarchy, and a shrewd admixture of reserve; this set the tone of his speech, as it had in an earlier petition to von Sack, the Governor General.

As before, Heinrich must have been suffering on this occasion from fear of being platitudinous. At any rate, although the King's hatred of Jews was common knowledge, he referred to Friedrich Wilhelm III as a benevolent father and just king, whose noble heart would always be open and receptive to right and reasonable desires on the part of his people. Or was there a touch of sarcasm here?

In any case, after the speech opposition songs were sung and an officer accused Heinrich Marx of having joined in them. Although it read like a declaration of loyalty, the Prussian government was displeased with the speech. The anniversary celebration of the Casino Society held in the same month, moreover, turned into a real demonstration: homage was paid to the French tricolor; the Marseillaise and other revolutionary songs were sung; Brixius, one of Heinrich Marx's fellow-lawyers, even went so far as to proclaim that, unless there was a revolution, people would go on eating grass like sheep. He was promptly arrested.

Evidence about Heinrich Marx's participation in this "demonstration" is contradictory.[30] Some say that he had left beforehand and "in good time"; the interrogation report on Schneemann, Karl Marx's schoolmaster, says that Heinrich did not leave the room until the third verse of the Marseillaise was being sung. There is no proof that he "recanted," a matter which apparently adversely affected the relationship between father and son. The fact remains that on other occasions subservience to authority was the keynote of his utterances; for instance he defended an absolute monarch's right to infringe the common law in the interests of state security.[31] Later correspondence with his son proves that Heinrich Marx's emancipation was a private matter aimed at personal advancement; it was in no way political or motivated by concern for the res publica. The question was soon to become pressing, however.

The school that Karl Marx, now baptized (and confirmed at the age of sixteen), attended from 1830 onwards provided a good illustration of the problem. He entered school in the third form and so had obviously been coached privately (direct transition from elementary school to high school was possible only after 1835). The Trier High School had been founded by Jesuits in the sixteenth century; it had opened as a secondary school in 1804 with Wyttenbach as newly appointed headmaster; it was subsequently renamed Collège de Trèves and became a state school in 1815. The tone of the school was clearly set by two mutually complementary societies: first there were the pupils, mostly sons of small farmers or craftsmen, certainly not drawn from the upper levels of society; then there were the teachers, whose leanings were mostly liberal, in fact democratic. Only eight of the thirty-two boys in Karl Marx's school-leaving year (1835) came from academic families (and significantly, seven of these were Protestants). The fathers of most of the boys — later described by Marx as "country bumpkins"[32] — were farmers, vine-growers or craftsmen. Equally indicative of their social position (in other words, of their prospects of rising in the social scale) was the fact that twelve of the boys chose theology as their main subject; eleven of them in fact became parish priests and one a curate.[33] The previous senior year had been taught by Matthias Eberhard, subsequently Bishop of Trier. At the same time, however, the establishment was not a cloistered one. In 1833, for instance, a report reached Berlin that banned literature was circulating among the boys, including even a copy of the seditious speech made at the Hambach Rally; worse still, some of the boys were composing political poetry.

Here was a scandal. The school was searched and the speech found, also some of the poems. One boy was arrested. In the next year something even worse occurred: two of the masters were involved in the Casino Society affair and were charged with materialism and atheism; one of them, Schneemann, was even "interrogated by the authorities" for singing revolutionary songs. Wyttenbach, the headmaster, was removed on November 1, 1835, and replaced by his deputy, a reactionary to whom Karl Marx refused to pay the statutory farewell visit on matriculating.

Wyttenbach's ideal as a schoolmaster was "the best for all"; he had edited a collection of poems entitled *Lieder für Freie* (Songs for the Free) and had written a school textbook, *Handbuch für den Unterricht in den Pflichten und Rechten des Menschen und des Bürgers* (Handbook of Instruction in the Rights and Duties of a Man and Citizen). Clear echoes of the address with which he sent his boys out into the world are to be found in Karl Marx's school-leaving essay.

Karl Marx left school at the age of seventeen with a final report that referred to "good moral behavior" and results leading his principals to hope that "he will fulfill the favorable expectations which his aptitudes justify." His final essay on the subject "Reflections of a Young Man on the Choice of a Profession" is written with disconcerting depth of feeling. It marks both the conclusion of a phase and at the same time the initiation of a new one — echo of the past, threat of the future; it is the product of what has been and a prophecy of what is to come. His religious essay "The Union of Believers with Christ" reads like a complementary document; both essays[34] testify to a secularized ethos, high ambition, and great self-esteem. His main theme, "the chief guide which must direct us in the choice of a profession is the welfare of mankind and our own perfection," juxtaposes two things that do not necessarily hang together. In the eyes of this seventeen-year-old, a profession and a calling are one and the same thing; attainment of "worth" for oneself coincides with general attainments and therefore of course with the "happiness of millions" — "our happiness will belong to millions, our deeds will live on quietly but perpetually at work, and over our ashes will be shed the hot tears of noble people."

His message of salvation on earth is contained in the word he uses with greatest frequency, "worth" — "worth is what primarily uplifts a man, imparts a higher nobility to his actions and all his endeavors, makes him invulnerable, admired by the crowd and raised above it." Such a gospel had to have a prophet, a leader, a lone figure both divorced from and admired by the crowd. Karl Marx was in no doubt that he was that man. It was his "God-given" task; if he failed, his life was a failure and "we see our whole existence in ruins." Man had the ability to choose, the privilege of decision to pursue some great purpose, but also the ability to fail; this was what differentiated him from the animal, with its predetermined sphere of activity, outside of which it might not trespass. One of the most striking passages in *Capital* took up this idea and redefined it. "The Deity" who had selected a man for this purpose was taken to task; in the religious essay "our hearts, reason, history, the Word of Christ" are listed, as if in arithmetical progression, as factors of equivalent value in determining who the great officiating individual should be. In his essay on choice of profession Marx gives no indication of *what* profession he has in mind, nor does the religious essay give any concrete explanation of the "union" that he seeks; it is all a question of enlightenment, a special mission, a calling.

We shall see later how Karl Marx's whole scheme of life bore the imprint of this concept of the Sovereign Being, the supreme Jupiter-like, Jehovah-like Judge who creates laws valid for *him,* to which others must conform, though the "others" are generally treated with scorn whether they have conformed or not. "Follow your path and let the people say what they will" stands as the motto of his main work, *Capital.* "We had received our appointment as representatives of the proletarian party from nobody but ourselves," he wrote to Engels in 1859,[35] in the same letter in which he referred to the workers as "*Knoten.*"* Son of God?

In these "Early Writings" (the *Frühschriften*) two ingredients can already be seen merging: first, Karl Marx, now no longer a Jew, had the Jewish predisposition to self-hate, the contempt for self which he himself recognized as bordering on misanthropy; second, historical determinism, which emerges with astonishing clarity in this passage, classic for a seventeen-year-old: "But we cannot always attain the position to which we believe we are called; our

* Craftsman, journeyman, or artisan — implying a person of backward, narrow mentality. — TR.

relations in society have to some extent already begun to be established before we are in a position to determine them. Our physical constitution itself is often a threatening obstacle, and let no one scoff at its rights."

Both the phraseology and the train of thought are striking. The word "we" is used throughout the essay. True to the concept of classical Hassidism, "Man" means *every* man, a member of a species rather than an individual. The word "relations" carries an implication of "behavior." Years later, in his sixth "Thesis on Feuerbach," he elaborated on the idea that private and personal "relations" do not exist: "The human essence is no abstraction inherent in each single individual. In its reality it is the ensemble of the social relations."[36] A decade after the school-leaving essay he wrote in "The German Ideology": "Where there exists a relationship, it exists for me; the animal does not enter into 'relations' with anything; it does not enter into any relations at all. For the animal its relation to others does not exist as a relation."[37]

When still only twenty-one, Karl Marx was setting his sights on the "ruling power" of knowledge. In the writings of Plato, one of his favorite authors, are to be found passages foreshadowing with truly terrifying accuracy what was to be Marx's concept of his career and his purpose in life: that "to rule is the due of the wise," that the people of a state "must be forced to recognize what we, as the greatest intellects, set before them, in other words to perceive what is the common good" — in other words the ideal Platonic state where "cultivated philosophers must rule."[38]

The motive impelling young Marx toward sociology, therefore, did not derive from the enlightening literature in his father's library or from the moral code instilled into him by Wyttenbach; the mainspring was a highly domineering requirement for self-fulfillment. Here was a young man who knew precisely what his career had to be and was determined to let no one stand in his way. It was not *a* rule of life that Marx made for himself — Paul Lafargue, his son-in-law, recalled that "working for the world was one of his favourite sayings"[39] — it was *his* rule of life.

Analysis of young Marx's handwriting at the time the school-leaving essay was written shows that certain definite characteristics were already established: marked self-esteem, outstanding intellectual ability, a considerable degree of self-will, distinct susceptibility to criticism. Throughout his life Karl Marx's calligraphy never actually *changed;* its characteristics merely became accentuated. Examination of his early handwriting shows a certain capacity for sympathetic perception within the limits of a clearly defined, circumscribed subjective conviction; on the other hand it also shows a tendency to dogmatic inflexibility, an obduracy impervious to argument and more potent than any capacity for sympathy — the writer does not see or does not perceive what he does not wish to see or perceive. The development of the thinker, the fighter, of the man who delighted in aggression is in fact detectable in the development of his handwriting, the increasing illegibility of which made it of decreasing value as a means of communication. An expert writes:

As time went on these conflicts and tensions had to find some outlet into the outside world from the closed world of his personality; it was a sort of internal cleansing process which inevitably had an adverse effect upon much of the world outside. As this development progressed it increasingly reflected an egocentric, self-willed, cynical personality to which the susceptibility already mentioned and the fact that he was temperamentally inclined to irritable reaction made their contribution.[40]

No sooner had Karl entered Bonn University than his high-flown ideas and overbearing ways became the keynote of the entire correspondence between father and son. Karl seldom wrote, and when he did, it was illegible; alternatively he sent poems of which his father could not make head or tail:

More than three weeks have passed since you went away and there is no sign of you! You should know your mother and how anxious she is and yet you show this boundless negligence! That, unfortunately, only too strongly confirms the opinion, which I hold in spite of your many good qualities, that in your heart egoism is predominant. . . . I have read your poem word by word. I quite frankly confess, dear Karl, that I do not understand it, neither its true meaning nor its tendency. In ordinary life it is an undisputed proposition that with the fulfilment of one's most ardent wishes the value of what one wished is very much diminished and often disappears altogether. That is surely not what you wanted to say. That would be worth consideration at most as a moral principle because, guided by this idea, one avoids immoral enjoyments and even puts off what is permissible in order, by the postponement, to retain the desire or even secure a heightened enjoyment. Kant felicitously says something of this sort in his anthropology.

Do you want to find happiness only in abstract idealising (somewhat analogous to fanciful reverie)? In short give me the key. I admit that is beyond me.[41]

The father's letters, often running to several pages, are touching, almost humble. He says quite frankly that this son of his is "the only" one for him, that in him he wishes to see realized everything that he himself was denied, that he is doing his best to spare him the difficulties and depressing experiences of his own young days. The letters show clearly that the father felt subordinate to the son — and to a son who simply accepted his parents' devotion, declarations of affection, and avowals of loyalty without any attempt to meet their wishes.

His mother also openly declared that she felt that he was someone special:

Much beloved, dear Carl. . . . Now you must not regard it as a weakness of our sex if I am curious to know how you arrange your little household, whether economy really plays the main role, which is an absolute necessity for both big and small households. Here allow me to note, dear Carl, that you must never regard cleanliness and order as something secondary, for health and cheerfulness depend on them. Insist strictly that your rooms are scrubbed frequently and fix a definite time for it — and you, my dear Carl, have a weekly scrub with sponge and soap. How do you get on about coffee, do you make it, or how is it? Please let me know everything about your household. Your amiable Muse will surely not feel insulted by your mother's prose, tell her that the higher and better is achieved through the lower. So good-bye now. If you have any wish to express for Christmas that I can satisfy, I am ready to do so with pleasure. Farewell, my dear beloved Carl, be upright and good and always keep God and your parents before your eyes. Adieu, your loving mother Henriette Marx.

P.S. All the children send you greetings and kisses, and as usual you are the kindest and best.[42]

The much beloved dear Carl, the kindest and best, wanted one thing above all — money. He attended many courses of lectures, for instance "Mythology of the Greeks and Romans" and "Elegiacs of Propertius," in addition to five courses on law — so many that his father warned him: "Do not study more than your health can bear."[43] His demands for money were so large, however, that his excessively careful father asked for a reckoning, saying: "If you have somewhat overstepped the bounds, let it be glossed over, since it must."[44]

Heinrich Marx commented:

As regards your letter containing the accounts, I already told you at the time that I could not make head or tail of them. Thus much I did see, that you need money and therefore I sent you 50 talers. With what you took with you that makes 160 talers. You have been away five months in all, and now you do not even say *what* you need. That, at all events, is strange. . . . Please, dear Karl, write at once, but write frankly, without reserve and truthfully. Calm me and your dear, kind mother, and we will soon forget the little monetary sacrifice.[45]

Loyal though he might be, Karl's father was quite right; the student had overstepped the bounds. The Certificate of Release from Bonn University, dated August 22, 1836, noted that "Herr Carl Heinrich Marx . . . has incurred a punishment of one day's detention for disturbing the peace by rowdiness and drunkenness at night. . . . Subsequently he was accused of having carried prohibited weapons in Köln. The investigation is still pending."[46]

There is here a murky, unexplained incident in the life of Karl Marx. Clearly in Köln, though not in Bonn, he had been involved in a duel, not using the normal student weapons, the foil or saber, but something more deadly, such as pistols. His father must have known about it since in the summer he asked, somewhat incredulously but casually, whether dueling had much to do with philosophy. It is not known whom Karl Marx fought, or why, or whether he or his opponent were wounded. Heinrich Marx quite rightly regarded dueling as evidence of fear of other people's opinion. The student, however, considered imprisonment and dueling as gentlemanly peccadilloes that were all "part of the game." Through Christian Heinrich Wienenbrugge, his roommate in Bonn, Karl Marx had become a member of the Men of Trier Society; by summer 1836 he had become one of the five Presidents of the Bar Club in Trier; Levy-Elkan, a student artist, painted a picture of him outside the White Horse Inn in Godesberg. Nights spent in prison were passed in beer-drinking, payment of fines in beer, cardplaying, wearing of student caps and colored scarves, and battles with a fellow-student from the Borussia Corps, in which Marx received a cut over the left eye; it was all a source of great amusement since, although behind bars, the jailbirds could be visited by their friends.

All his life Karl Marx adopted a curiously ambivalent attitude to dueling, this "gentleman's way of obtaining satisfaction"; he challenged an opponent in London as late as 1852[47] and in 1858 wrote to Lassalle: "The duel depends entirely on circumstances and as an exceptional emergency resort may be adopted in exceptional circumstances."[48]

In autumn 1836 Marx went to Berlin, once more supported by his father without whose authorization he could not have entered the university: "I not only grant my son Karl Marx permission, but it is my will that he should enter the University of Berlin next term for the purpose of continuing there his studies . . . which he began in Bonn. Trier, 1 July 1836"[49]

Karl Marx's search for lodgings ended in typical fashion; in the Leipziger-strasse, in the middle of this huge unfamiliar city, he noticed a house with a plaque announcing that "Lessing lived here." There Karl Marx took up residence.[50]

THE STUDENT FALLS IN LOVE WITH TRIER'S "QUEEN OF THE BALL" AND GOES TO BERLIN

While a student in Berlin Karl Marx had no fewer than eight addresses but only one house still stands: No. 60 Luisenstrasse (then No. 45). A bronze plaque proclaims that here "the greatest son of the German people" lived in 1838 and 1839. At the time the house belonged to the "medicos' quarter," a cheap new housing estate outside the city gates; the great hospital of the Charité stood in the canal meadows just behind the house. After his father's death our student, who was always in debt — the leaving certificate from the university states that "on several occasions he has been the object of proceedings for debt"[51] — moved into the area, a favorite one for students.

During the autumn of 1837, on doctor's advice, Marx temporarily moved out "into the country"; he selected the little village of Stralau, which had only twenty houses, romantically situated on a narrow tongue of land between the right bank of the River Spree and the left bank of Lake Rummelsburg. He took lodgings in No. 4, near the water and the church which was surrounded by tall trees, his host being Gottlieb Köhler, fisherman and innkeeper. He would sit around among the lime trees of the inn garden with his friends of the Doctors' Club who had introduced him, in some obscure tavern in the Französischestrasse, Berlin, to the other would-be philosophers and world reformers, Wilhelm Wolfsohn, Moritz Carrière, and Heinrich Bernard Oppenheim. Through the good offices of some of the more wealthy students such as the von Behr brothers, friends of Heine and Börne, a sort of circle or salon took shape. Here Marx not only met one of his lecturers, Professor Gans, but on numerous evenings listened to Devrient and Seidelmann, both leading actors, reading Shakespeare's plays, dividing the parts between them. Years later Wilhelm Liebknecht was to hear Marx imitating Seidelmann in the role of Mephistopheles.

He matriculated on October 22, 1836. The first courses of lectures he attended were given by Professors Savigny and Gans: "Jurisprudence was my special subject of study but I pursued it only as a secondary discipline after philosophy and history."[52] This is a curious statement in the light of the list of twelve courses of lectures attended by Marx over a period of nine terms; all were connected with law, only one with philosophy and not a single one with history. These last two subjects he must therefore have studied on his own, using his typical method of voracious nighttime reading, bringing him warnings from his father, whose letters became increasingly apprehensive. The father commented on his son's every whim as regards a profession — theater critic, writer, philosopher — never laying down the law but putting forward sound, solid suggestions and warning against ending as a penniless well-read librarian like Lessing. The student was probably either bored or amused by homely advice from his mother — "make you for the autumn woollen jackets which will protect you from catching cold"[53] — or his father's remarkably prosaic ideas; at one moment, for instance, the straitlaced Prussian lawyer advised against dramatic composition as a career, saying that the big city theaters were hotbeds of intrigue and petty jealousy; instead he urged his son to write poetry:

The subject should be a period taken from the history of Prussia, not one so prolonged as to call for an epic, but a crowded moment of time where, however, the future hung in the balance. It should redound to the honour of Prussia and afford the opportunity of allotting a role to the genius of the monarchy — if need be through the mind of the very noble Queen Louise. Such a moment was the great battle at La Belle Alliance — Waterloo.[54]

The main theme of his parents' letters, however, is anxiety about something quite different — their son's character and human feelings. The same letter, among others, contains this:

And yet at times I cannot rid myself of ideas which arouse in me sad forebodings and fear, when I am struck as if by lightning by the thought: is your heart in accord with your head, your talents? Has it room for the earthly but gentler sentiments which in this vale of sorrow are so essentially consoling for a man of feeling? And since that heart is obviously animated and governed by a demon not granted to all men, is that demon heavenly or Faustian? Will you ever — and that is not the least painful doubt of my heart — will you ever be capable of truly human, domestic happiness.[55]

This thread runs through all the letters. His mother, for instance, wrote: "I let feeling go before reason and I regret, dear Carl, that you are too reasonable."[56] His father referred to his son's appalling egoism, frigidity, and plaintiveness, saying that at the smallest setback he gave way to grief, agony, heartbreak, fantastic gloomy ideas, and morbid sensitivity: "God protect us from the most beautiful of all nature's gifts if that is its immediate effect. No, it is only weakness, over-indulgence, self-love and conceit which reduce everything to their own measure in this way and force even those we love most into the background."[57]

Marx was in fact adopting an attitude that was to become increasingly marked: he simply took no notice of things he did not like; if some reaction was unavoidable, then it was as anodyne as possible, as his attitude to his father's complaints about the illegibility of his handwriting was later to show. Years afterward when Marx made the only effort of his life to obtain a professional post, his application was written in so slovenly a fashion that it was turned down. The two great letters exchanged between father and son in November 1837 show how far apart they were:

An address, however, is form, and precisely that seems to be your weak side. Things may well be different as regards material? . . . after an interval of two months, the second of which caused me some unpleasant hours full of anxiety, I received a letter without form or content, a torn fragment saying nothing, which stood in no relation to what went before it and had no connection with the future!

If a correspondence is to be of interest and value, it must have consistency, and the writer must necessarily have *his* last letter before his eyes, as also the last reply. Your last letter but one contained much that excited my expectation. I had written a number of letters which asked for information on my points. And instead of all that I received a letter of bits and fragments and, what is much worse, an *embittered* letter.

Frankly speaking, my dear Karl, I do not like this modern word, which all weaklings use to cloak their feelings when they quarrel with the world because they do not possess, without labour or trouble, well-furnished palaces with vast sums of money and elegant carriages. This embitterment disgusts me and you are the last person from whom I would expect it.[58]

Heinrich Marx had never written in such explicit, even forceful, terms. Though himself prone to weakness and sentimentality, here he was putting his finger on a particularly sensitive sore spot: his son clearly had a tendency to employ sentiment when in fact he had no feelings; whenever he "swore" to do something or adopted a plaintive pose, then skepticism was the order of the day — he was within a hairbreadth of cynicism. At certain major turning points in his life Marx withdrew into this shell of cynical unconcern — on the "old man's" death, for instance, or that of Engels's wife, or the sudden demise of Georg Weerth. The poems that Marx wrote for his father and occasionally sent him also testify to this "second-hand sentiment."

Naturally too much store should not be set by the poetic frolics of an eighteen-year-old;[59] the complete crudity and banality of his rhymes, however, are appalling. It is almost inconceivable that a young man in love could express himself so vapidly:

NOCTURNAL LOVE

Frantic, he holds her near
Darkly he looks in her eye.
"Pain so burns you, dear,
And at my breath you sigh.

"Oh, you have drunk my soul.
Mine is your glow, in truth.
My jewel, shine your fill.
Glow, blood of youth."

"Sweetest, so pale your face,
So wondrous strange your words
See, rich in music's grace
The lofty gliding worlds."

"Gliding, dearest, gliding,
Glowing, stars, glowing.

Let us go heavenwards riding,
Our souls together flowing."

His voice is muffled, low.
Desperate he looks about.
Glances of crackling flame
His hollow eyes shoot out.

"You have drunk poison, Love.
With me you must away.
The sky is dark above,
No more I see the day."

Shuddering he pulls her close to him.
Death in the breast doth hover.
Pain stabs her, piercing deep within,
And eyes are closed forever.[60]

Franz Mehring has aptly characterized these early efforts:

Did we not know the period in which they originated, no one would suspect that they were written one year after Platen's death and nine years after Heine's Book of Songs. . . . There is romantic harping, a song of the elfs, a song of the gnomes, a siren song, songs to the stars, the song of the bell-ringers, the singer's last song, the pale maiden or the boy and the little girl, a string of ballads about Alboin and Rosamund; there even appears the brave knight who does mighty deeds of valour in far-off lands and returns just as his faithless bride goes to the altar with another.[61]

More detailed study of this poetry, however, shows something else as well: through all the verbiage about flowery groves, beetling cliffs, and windswept oceans can be detected the burgeoning of the worship of "fulfillment." The metaphors used show a penchant for the titanic — laurel wreaths, godlike creatures, life-giving breasts, and sweet dreams are all instruments to be employed in the struggle toward higher things.

Never can I do in peace
That with which my Soul's obsessed,
Never take things at my ease;
I must press on without rest.

All things I would strive to win,
All the blessings Gods impart,

Grasp all knowledge deep within,
Plumb the depths of Song and Art.

Therefore let us risk our all,
Never resting, never tiring;
Not in silence dismal, dull,
Without action or desiring;

Not in brooding introspection
Bowed beneath a yoke of pain,
So that yearning, dream and action
Unfulfilled to us remain.[62]

The general tone is the same, no matter to whom the poems are addressed —
and by no means all of them were for his father; the majority were dedicated
to Jenny von Westphalen.

Karl Marx was in love. He had chosen "the loveliest girl in Trier, the queen
of the ball,"[63] and turned her against her fiancé, Second Lieutenant Karl von
Pannewitz; before he left for Berlin they were secretly engaged. This secrecy
was surprising, for Government Councillor Ludwig von Westphalen, Jenny's
father, was a broad-minded man whose son Edgar had been Karl Marx's
classmate at school (Marx christened his favorite son Edgar), and Karl had
been a frequent visitor to the house.

Ludwig von Westphalen had been sent to Trier by Hardenberg in 1816 as
an official of the Royal Prussian Provincial Government; with an annual
salary of 1,800 taler he was one of the highest-paid civil servants in the
Justice Department.[64] Like Heinrich Marx he was a member of the Casino
Society, and their political views must have been very similar — in favor of
the monarchy, antirepublican even, but hoping that good sense and good
order would produce "real" freedom. Both he and his wife occasionally
remarked on the people's misery but more as a criticism of conditions in
general; at the end of an "outspoken" letter to a cousin, however, Caroline,
Jenny's mother (she was Ludwig's second wife), asked that the letter be
burned after reading, saying: "I don't know but I have an innate dread of
written statements."[65] The family had no private means but were reckoned
among the upper class because of their aristocratic lineage. Jenny's grandfather had been private secretary to the Duke of Brunswick; later, during the
Seven Years War, he became Chief of the General Staff and was given a title
by the King of England. He married the British commanding general's niece
and so was related to a famous family of the Scottish nobility, the Dukes of
Argylle, one of whom was the Presbyterian rebel publicly beheaded on orders

of King James II, in the Edinburgh marketplace. One result of these complex family relationships is that even today certain inheritances have not been cleared up; in 1972 a legacy of £50,000 was registered as "unclaimed" in London.

Ludwig von Westphalen had four children by his first marriage and three by his second. Ferdinand, one of the elder sons, later a reactionary Minister of the Interior in Prussia, and Edgar, the youngest, were both destined to play a part in Karl Marx's life in the future.

Two things brought the families together: in the first place, on the prosaic professional level Heinrich Marx had to deal with Ludwig von Westphalen in the course of legal business; second, the children went to the same school. Jenny was one of Karl's playmates and Edgar grew up in the Marx house as if he were a child of the family.

Karl Marx became particularly attached to Ludwig von Westphalen; in the young man's eyes he must have represented the acme of what a personality and a father should be. The acquaintanceship marked a turning point in Karl's development. He admired the older man's culture, his bearing, and his family. He was never admonished in that house, never had caution urged upon him, was never encouraged to write poems in praise of the government; he was simply accepted. Ludwig von Westphalen, who was about sixty, used to take the young son of his friend Heinrich Marx for long walks, would quote Homer or Shakespeare to him, fired his enthusiasm for romantic literature, and also talked of something hitherto quite unknown — socialism. From him Karl Marx first learned of the doctrines of Saint-Simon.[66] They were an oddly assorted couple — the nobleman attracted to an idealistic youth as his pupil, the young man's admiration, indeed affection, for "an old man with the strength of youth," a masculine intellect, a *seigneur*. In Ludwig von Westphalen he saw a man who was what he himself wished to be. The dedication with which Karl Marx, then aged twenty-three, headed his doctoral dissertation — which would normally have been dedicated to his father or his parents — has a ring of veneration about it: "To his dear fatherly friend . . . as a token of filial love."[67] A draft of the dedication, which he did not use, referred to his highly erudite treatise as a "messenger of love" which he hoped soon to follow in person so that he might "roam again . . . through our wonderfully picturesque mountains and forests" at the side of the "old man with the strength of youth."[68]

It is therefore puzzling why engagement to his daughter had to be kept secret from this man. Admittedly many of the Westphalen family were opposed to it; there were aristocratic pietists among the relatives, of whom Marx later said to Ruge that they placed the "Lord in heaven" on a level with the "Lord in Berlin." The most determined opponents were Jenny's stepbrother and his wife, who wrote vicious, scheming letters to Jenny's mother.

One would have thought, however, that this would be all the more reason for Marx to confide in his "fatherly friend," whose assent was not eventually given until 1837.

Heinrich Marx, on the other hand, the feeble, despised, compromising father, was turned, to his increasing discomfort, into a go-between for the lovers. Once more he is to be seen as the indefatigable giver of advice: the anxious, almost maternal parent, worried about his son's happiness, about the health of his soul, about his capacity to maintain a binding relationship with another human being:

But I repeat, you have undertaken great duties and, dear Karl, at the risk of irritating your sensitivity, I express my opinion somewhat prosaically after my fashion: with all the exaggerations and exaltations of love in a poetic mind you cannot restore the tranquillity of a being to whom you have wholly devoted yourself; on the contrary, you run the risk of destroying it. Only by the most exemplary behaviour, by manly, firm efforts which, however, win people's good-will and favour, can you ensure that the situation is straightened out and that she is exalted in her own eyes and the eyes of the world, and comforted.

I have spoken with Jenny and I should have liked to be able to set her mind at rest completely. I did all I could but it is not possible to argue everything away. She still does not know how her parents will take the relationship. Nor is the judgment of relatives and the world a trifling matter. I am afraid of your not always just sensitivity and therefore leave it to you to appreciate this situation. . . . Unfortunately, however, I am weak in every respect.

She is making a priceless sacrifice for you. She is showing a self-denial which can only be fully appreciated in the light of cold reason. Woe to you if ever in your life you could forget this![69]

Karl Marx sent poems to Jenny but the correspondence was later destroyed by his daughter Laura. Three folios, entitled "Book of Love I and II" and "Book of Songs," have also vanished. In 1911 Franz Mehring and the Russian expert Ryazanoff actually handled them but in 1925, when Ryazanoff asked Jean Longuet where they were, he said that he had lent them to someone (he could not remember to whom) and that they had not been returned. A visit paid to Robert Jean Longuet, great-great-grandson of Karl Marx and his last direct descendant, in Paris yielded little; his house was crammed with mementos of Marx and reference was made to a packet of family letters that was still lying around "somewhere" but no one knew where. There is a thin folder of photostats in the Internationaal Instituut voor sociale Geschiedenes in Amsterdam containing original letters from Jenny von Westphalen to Karl Marx; the actual originals are in Moscow and remarkably enough have not been copied as has almost all other material; the photostats that reached Amsterdam had been rendered almost illegible. The little that can be deciphered shows that, almost from the outset, the relationship between Karl and Jenny was a highly complex one; Jenny's early letters are written in a shrill, almost hysterical tone. Remarks such as "base girl" or "you are not keen on me" clearly refer to letters from her fiancé. Evidently there were serious quarrels: "At your glance . . . it seemed as if my heart would break. . . . It was not just a penetrating glance; you wanted to crush me. . . . If you can do that in a moment of passion, what can I expect when love has cooled? One . . . would be suicide but things must be still worse for that. . . . Another time it would be the death of me."[70] An album of poems dedicated "to my sweetheart Jenny" has been preserved; it is a fat octavo volume, handsomely bound in cream-white with a gold-engraved pattern of green wreaths and red roses, a vase of grapes, and flowers in the middle, and gilt edging.

Poetry, however, led him into something else. On January 23, 1841, his two "Wild Songs" were published in the Berlin weekly *Athenäum* — the only literary effort to be published in his lifetime. Not only did *Athenäum* subsequently print Friedrich Engels's "Wanderings in Lombardy," but it was the center of the circle of "Athenians," forming a sort of connecting link between the Doctors' Club of 1837–1840 and the Society of "The Free" of 1842. From this circle came the staff of the *Rheinische Zeitung,* first published on January 1, 1842 — a staff that included Adolf Rutenberg, the man who summoned Marx to be chief editor of the newspaper.

Marx's long letter of November 10, 1837, to his father, six months before the latter's death, reads like a compendium of this entire period of his life — and the start of a new one. The opening sentence explicitly says: "There are moments in one's life which are like frontier posts marking the completion of a period but at the same time clearly indicating a new direction."[71]

It is an audit of account testifying to a literally vast amount of hard thinking; it includes extracts from Lessing, Winckelmann, and Solger, translations of Tacitus, Aristotle, and Ovid; it refers to study of the English and Italian languages, poems, an unfinished treatise, "a new system of metaphysical principles," study of Savigny and Feuerbach, of criminal law and the *"Doctrina Pandectorum,"* of Gratian's *Concordia discordantium canonum.* The letter is a mixture of eccentricity and insecurity, exaltation, megalomania, and contrition:

At the end of the term, I again sought the dances of the Muses and the music of the Satyrs. Already in the last exercise book that I sent you idealism pervades forced humour (*Scorpion and Felix*) and an unsuccessful, fantastic drama (*Oulanem*), until it finally undergoes a complete transformation and becomes mere formal art, mostly without objects that inspire it and without any impassioned train of thought.

And yet these last poems are the only ones in which suddenly, as if by a magic touch — oh, the touch was at first a shattering blow — I caught sight of the glittering realm of true poetry like a distant fairy palace, and all my creations tumbled into nothing.

Busy with these various occupations, during my first term I spent many a sleepless night, fought many a battle, and endured much internal and external excitement. . . .

A curtain had fallen, my holy of holies was rent asunder, and new gods had to be installed.

From the idealism which, by the way, I had compared and nourished with the idealism of Kant and Fichte, I arrived at the point of seeking the idea in reality itself. If previously the gods had dwelt above the earth, now they became its centre.

I had read fragments of Hegel's philosophy, the grotesque craggy method of which did not appeal to me. Once more I wanted to dive into the sea, but with the definite intention of establishing that the nature of the mind is just as necessary, concrete and firmly based as the nature of the body. My aim was no longer to practise tricks of swordsmanship, but to bring genuine pearls into the light of day.

I wrote a dialogue of about 24 pages: "Cleanthes, or the Starting Point and Necessary Continuation of Philosophy". Here art and science, which had become completely divorced from each other, were to some extent united, and like a vigorous traveller I set about the task itself, a philosophical-dialectical account of divinity, as it manifests itself as the idea-in-itself, as religion, as nature, and as history.[72]

A start down some fresh path can hardly be detected from all this nebulous verbiage. Or can it? The names of Hegel and Feuerbach are mentioned; the Doctors' Club, Rutenberg, and Bruno Bauer are referred to — the Young Hegelians in other words. These were the academic elite of the rising generation and Marx had quickly thrown in his lot with them. Discussion continuously revolved round Hegel, who had died in 1831. The left-wing disciples of Hegel — David Strauss, Bruno and Edgar Bauer, Arnold Ruge, Ludwig Feuerbach — were concerned primarily with criticism of religion. Strauss's *Das Leben Jesu* (Life of Jesus), published in 1835, was the first to proclaim the antireligious dogma; Feuerbach's *Wesen des Christentums* (Essence of Christianity), published in 1841, was the culmination of a near-revolution in thought. Engels later said: "Enthusiasm was general; we all became at once Feuerbachians."[73]

The Young Hegelian circle in Berlin, the Doctors' Club, was led by Bruno Bauer, a freelance lecturer from Bonn. There are various indications of the influence and position of Karl Marx in this circle while he was still only a student: he used the familiar "*du*" with Bauer; Karl Friedrich Köppen dedicated his book *Friedrich der Grosse und seine Widersacher* (Frederick the Great and his Detractors) to him; Moses Hess wrote to his friend Berthold Auerbach:

Here is a phenomenon who has made an enormous impression on me although I work in the same field. In short prepare to meet the greatest, perhaps the *only genuine philosopher* now living who will soon have the eyes of all Germany upon him wherever he may appear in public, whether in print or on the rostrum.

Dr. Marx, as my idol is called, is still quite a young man (aged about 24 at the most) and it is he who will give mediaeval religion and politics their *coup de grâce*; he combines a biting wit with deeply serious philosophical thinking. Imagine Rousseau, Voltaire, Holbach, Lessing, Heine and Hegel combined into one person — and I say *combined*, not blended — and there you have Dr. Marx. Yours ever   Hess.[74]

In May 1838 Karl Marx's father died — in the spring his mother had exhorted him: "I cannot impress on you too strongly to be most affectionate in your letters; then your good father will read them several times over."[75] It seemed almost ordained as part of the process of cutting loose. From now on Karl Marx had nothing in common with his home and he went his own way intellectually as in other matters. The conflict with Hegel had begun.

On this subject there were as many views as there were people; there was no system, not even that ultimately constructed by Hegel — history as a continuous evolutionary process toward a higher state of things, toward the Absolute Idea, the significance, the soul and the purpose of the world. This idealistic systematization of the spirit of the world ultimately stood opposed to Hegel's own method of the dialectical development of history.

At this point the Berlin circle came on the scene, the tone being set, not surprisingly, by Köppen, the historian commended by Schopenhauer. His criticism of contemporary historians such as Ranke and Schlosser, like his articles in the *Hallische Jahrbücher* (Halle Annals) showed the inconsistency, the inherent contradiction, in the position of the Young Hegelians: on the one hand they were trying to "extend" eighteenth-century enlightenment, on the other — in Köppen's book on Frederick the Great, for instance — was their concept of history as the product of great intellects — not Frederick II the despot but Frederick the Great, a great philosopher's spirit reincarnate. This was both reactionary and progressive, for Frederick as the "Apostle of Enlightenment" was loathed by the collection of romantic reactionaries described by Köppen as mouthpieces of "a horrible caterwauling, Old and New Testament trumpets, moral Jew's harps, edifying and historical bagpipes and other horrible instruments and in the middle of it all hymns of freedom boomed out in a beery teutonic bass."[76]

Strauss's *Leben Jesu,* published five years earlier, suffered from a similar defect, casting doubt on the gospels as historical accounts of Jesus' life and on Jesus as a historical personality. Therein lay its repugnancy — and its inconsistency. It was a criticism of the history of religion rather than a criticism of religion.

Here Bruno Bauer, intellectual leader of the Doctors' Club and Marx's closest associate during his years in Berlin, took a hand. Bauer went further than anyone in criticizing the gospels and proving that they were without historical substance, mere exercises in authorship on the part of the evangelists. With his consistency of theory he was indubitably the spearhead of the "philosophical mountaineers," as Arnold Ruge dubbed the circle. At the same time he was excessively loyal to King and Country, swore by the hereditary intelligence of the House of Hohenzollern and the inherent good sense of the State (at this point unfortunately; on Altenstein's death the new king, Friedrich Wilhelm IV, appointed the reactionary Eichhorn as Minister of Culture and the good sense of King and State led straight to the refusal of a professorship to Bruno Bauer, the freelance lecturer from Bonn). In a series of pining letters written from Bonn to Marx in Berlin, Bauer made much of his hope that together they could turn the university upside down and publish a radical newspaper to compete with the unsuccessful *Hallische Jahrbücher* owned by the "intellectual tycoon" Arnold Ruge. But that was now all over and done with. Franz Mehring says that Bruno Bauer's "political shortsightedness was the reverse side of his philosophical acumen"[77] because he ascribed to philosophy a revolutionary force similar to that which had enabled the Christian religion to dominate education in the ancient world.

All these emergent theories with their laudable motives and tangled results must be borne in mind if the gigantic intellectual tour de force with which Marx forced his way out of this *circulus vitiosus* is to be given its due. The direction in which previous lines of thought needed to be changed was clear; they had to be turned upside down and set on their feet. But what were the feet?

This mind-clearing process had a bearing on the length of time Marx took to complete his doctoral dissertation. In autumn 1838 "your loving mother Henriette Marx" sent him "the sum of 160 taler which you need in order to take your degree."[78] Yet eighteen months later Bruno Bauer was writing to him urgently: "Do at last stop temporising and being so dilatory about the nonsensical farce which this examination is."[79]

Karl Marx was not simply being dilatory over his work, however. In his study of Epicurean, Stoic, and Skeptic philosophy he was wrestling with himself, with the standpoint of the Young Hegelians. He was not occupied merely with the philosophers of self-consciousness, as the Epicureans, Stoics, and Skeptics had called themselves, though it was a school of philosophy that had exerted much influence on Christian thinking, placing the individual in antithesis to the world and enjoining upon him internal happiness and independence of material things. Even in his preparatory work for his doctoral dissertation, the seven "Notebooks on Epicurean, Stoic and Skeptic Philosophy," he had insisted on the potential of philosophy for progress and action;

he was trying in fact to produce a new concept of philosophy's role: "like Prometheus who stole fire from heaven and began to build houses and populate the earth, so philosophy, which has so evolved as to impinge on the world, turns itself against the world that it finds."[80]

The comprehensive treatise on "The Difference between the Democritean and Epicurean Philosophy of Nature" with which Marx ultimately graduated in Jena on April 15, 1841, was a grand-scale apotheosis of Epicurus's doctrine of freedom. The theme, or rather the challenge, is that, in a world of folly, ethics, morality, and philosophy are active factors of change. Even a foretaste of the style that marked so many of his subsequent works is to be found, that of the philosophically oriented pamphlet containing many a memorable epigram such as: "The result is that, as the world becomes philosophical, philosophy also becomes worldly, that its realisation is also its loss."[81]

Even in this very first work Marx showed himself as an "anti" writer, an author who defined his own position as a result of polemic and criticism. His most important productions have as their title or subtitle the word "Critique"; his less important polemical writings are attempts to pick a quarrel or to counterattack. This particular treatise illustrates, with a degree of brilliance unusual for a doctoral dissertation, this basic dialectical framework whereby a position is reached as a result of a negative approach.

Marx's central theme is Epicurus's concept of human freedom; this he wishes to preserve in face of Democritus's materialist and determinist philosophy of nature — subjectivity, even sensuality, against the immutability of the atom. Has Marx not yet become Marx? Is this still the "young man choosing a profession," to whom individuality, the mind, and elitism mean more than anything else?

Epicurus's *Voluptas* is eulogized as liberation of the human spirit, the liberated individual as liberated man — historical eschatology as it were. There is no mention yet of the "new man."

Marx worked himself into this position primarily through his dismissal of Plutarch's religious and moral philosophy. With gay abandon, but also with considerable erudition, he produced a devastating criticism of Plutarch delivered with some pride as from a higher plane of thought.

Marx treated the actual process of obtaining his degree with characteristic negligence. The main reason was the appointment as the new Minister of Culture of Eichhorn, who had vetoed Bruno Bauer's nomination to Bonn and his appointment to Halle despite a petition from the students to the King asking for him. Instead, old Schelling had been summoned to Berlin. Marx accordingly tried to take his degree *in absentia* at some "foreign" university. (Schelling's appointment to Hegel's chair was generally considered as a measure of exorcism.) Marx's covering letter was not even couched in normal academic form:

The specimen testifies to intelligence and perspicacity as much as to erudition for which reason I regard the candidate as preeminently worthy. Since, according to his German letter, he desires to receive only the degree of Doctor, it is clear that it is merely an error due to lack of acquaintance with the statutes of the faculty that in the Latin letter he speaks of the degree of Magister. He probably thought that the two belong together.[82]

Only one incomplete version of the dissertation is extant, and it is presumably a copy;[83] oddly there is no copy in Jena University archives and so this must be the copy that was actually handed in and then reclaimed for publication. It includes various amendments in Marx's handwriting in two different colors of ink and therefore clearly made at two different periods. Some are corrections of spelling or grammar, others are insertions, addenda, or stylistic improvements; there is a comment critical of Schelling (an obvious tilt at his appointment) and the draft of a new preface. The amendments to the new preface, clearly made in view of a planned publication of the treatise (which never took place) include two vital words. The paragraph reads:

The treatise that I hereby submit to the public is an old piece of work and was originally intended as part of a comprehensive exposition of Epicurean, Stoic and Sceptic philosophy. At present, however, political and philosophical arrangements of an entirely different kind prevent me from bringing such a task to completion. Only now the time has come in which the systems of the Epicureans, Stoics and Sceptics can be understood. They are the *philosophers of self-consciousness.*[84]

Instead of the words "political and philosophical arrangements," the original version read "professional affairs and activities."

But Marx had no profession. He no longer had any family, for his father had died on May 10, 1838, without ever seeing his beloved son again, and Marx was so far out of touch with his mother that even her explicit request — "I want to know whether you have taken your degree"[85] — remained unanswered. He wanted nothing from her but money. As late as 1842 he was still complaining bitterly to Arnold Ruge:

From April to the present day I have been able to work for a total of perhaps only four weeks at the most, and that not without interruption. I had to spend six weeks in connection with another death. The rest of the time was split up and poisoned by the most unpleasant family controversies. My family laid obstacles in my way which, despite the prosperity of the family, put me for the moment in very serious straits. I cannot possibly burden you with the story of these private scandals; it is truly fortunate that scandals of a public nature make it impossible for a man of character to be irritated over private ones.[86]

Even his relationship to the von Westphalen family seemed more distant and somewhat complex. Two years after his father's death came a curious wail from his mother:

For six weeks after your dear father was taken from us no one of the Westphalen family put in an appearance here; no one from there came to comfort me or show friendship; it was as if they had never seen us. . . . For a time Jenny came every 4–5 weeks but only to weep and wail instead of comforting us. . . . I had always feared that she wanted to break off your relationship and that might make you unhappy. This excessive mother love, which I have allowed to torture and persecute me, is unforgivable. I ought to have said: Do what your feelings and your heart tell you; I don't care. But every family has a basic attitude which [illegible] remains constant like its circumstances. That of the Westphalen family is an exaggerated one; there is no happy mean; either they are in the seventh heaven or they must make do with the depths.[87]

Marx had not even gone to Trier when his father died. Now, however, he was there "in connection with another death," that of his future father-in-law. But he lived neither in his fiancée's house nor with his mother; his address was Gasthof zu Venedig.

Marx was in low water. He was in love but his loved one seemed farther from him than ever. He was the cherished infant prodigy of the Berlin Doctors' Club but not a line of his writings had been published apart from two insignificant poems; typically he insisted on spending his time in quarrels and trivialities. Bruno Bauer wrote complainingly from Bonn:

What is this berserk rage which has taken control of you once more? What is driving you and unsettling you? What has impelled you yet again to say things that are true before writing them down; afterwards you can say them as softly as a babe in arms or a thousand-fold more furiously than you have already done. What's the matter with you? Stop this nonsense and snap out of it.[88]

Marx had in fact offered his mentor books which did not exist at all:

My dear Marx: The letter which you gave me for Marcus was so bad that I could not possibly pass it on to him. You can write like that to your washerwoman but not to a publisher whom you want to get on your side. . . . You must now write and tell me what you ought to have told Marcus long ago — whether the book exists, whether it is ready. . . .[89]

Although the family was well off, Marx had no income since his mother had inherited everything. In the last analysis his academic career depended on the fate of Bruno Bauer — who had not been appointed to his expected chair and so could not summon Marx to Bonn.

Then came the chance to work on a newspaper.

CHIEF EDITOR IN NAPOLEONIC-PRUSSIAN KÖLN AT
THE AGE OF TWENTY-FOUR

A new newspaper, the *Rheinische Zeitung,* had been founded in Köln on January 1, 1842. Prosperous liberal-minded citizens were anxious to show that Augsburg and Berlin were not the only places where progressive ideas could be publicized; anti-Prussianism was also a good selling point. Nevertheless, insofar as they themselves were concerned, the Rhineland bourgeoisie had little to complain of regarding economic progress under Prussian rule. Vested interests — including those of the newly formed newspaper — were therefore varied; driving uphill with the brakes on was the order of the day.

The men commissioned to form the editorial staff were Georg Jung, a barrister, and Dagobert Oppenheim, a clerk of the court; both were enthusiastic Young Hegelians, and this was the milieu in which they looked for personnel. Moses Hess drew their attention to Berlin. Marx recommended his friend Rutenberg. He himself then moved to Bonn and his first articles appeared; they dealt with the Rhineland *Landtag* (Provincial Assembly), with parliamentary proceedings therefore, and with freedom of the press ("The primary freedom of the press lies in not being a trade").[90]

Georg Jung had been a close friend of Marx's since 1841; he was one of the leading members of the "Köln Circle," though initially Marx did not know this; the "Circle," however, included among its sympathizers influential personalities such as Camphausen and Hansemann, together with a number of well-read liberals. Camphausen, one of the two chairmen of the *Rheinische Zeitung* and later Minister President of Prussia, passed word to Marx in the spring of 1848 that he would gladly have him on his staff in Berlin — which Marx had referred to as an "insinuation."[91]

Marx first appeared in print in a series of six major articles published between May 5 and May 19, 1842; like all his contributions to the newspaper they were unsigned. Subsequent articles soon brought him up against Dolleschall, the censor who became the plague of his life as editor (Dolleschall had already deleted an advertisement for a translation of Dante's *Divine Comedy* in the *Kölnische Zeitung* with the comment: "Divine matters should not be turned into comedy").[92]

The attention of the censorship authorities was soon drawn also to articles for which Rutenberg was responsible as "German copy editor." The new paper seemed to find space for all sorts of heresies; for instance, it compared the "have-nots'" covetousness for the riches of the middle class with the latter's struggle against the nobility in 1789.

The paper had only been granted a provisional license for a year. On October 1, 1842, its horrified backers appointed Marx to the editorial office, clearly hoping that he would bring it down to earth and also increase its circulation. So his situation changed almost overnight. At the age of twenty-four Karl Marx was chief editor of a newspaper.

He was not given the formal title. Financially the newspaper was well assured by the "Köln Circle" (the Rheinische Zeitung Company Ltd. had capital of 30,000 taler), so even though Marx was shown in the table of organization only as "actual editor," he was given a considerable salary, 600 taler per annum. His name did not appear in the newspaper heading.

A kaleidoscopic interplay of forces now began. Marx's first articles demonstrated his marked sense of practical politics; as Franz Mehring aptly says, he still retained "his incomparable ability to take things as they were and make petrified conditions dance by singing them their own melody."[93]

His articles caused a stir but not a scandal; they were censorious but not inflammatory; where there was injustice they said so but did not call in question the basis of the law. They were articles of the type now published in Der Spiegel.

The new editor's first major contribution, for which he was asked as early as October 15, 1842, was his series dealing with the debates on wood stealing; this was much on the increase, producing thirty times more cases than normal theft and causing the government to table a special law at the 6th Rhineland Landtag. Like any adroit journalist Marx brought his theoretical knowledge into discussion of current problems. He did not embark on theoretical argument, however, or try to rock the foundations of the State. He scored a resounding success. On November 21 one of the correspondents of the Leipziger Allgemeine Zeitung was reporting that "the Rheinische Zeitung was previously far more troublesome to the government than it has been recently."[94] Even the minister responsible for censorship reported to the King that the newspaper was far calmer in tone than it had been[95] and Moses Hess wrote to his friend Auerbach that "the position of the newspaper is now assured vis-à-vis both the public and the government."[96]

What had happened?

Dr. Rutenberg, who had meanwhile been made "desk officer" for German politics and for France — in other words, who was in charge of two subjects which were of major importance both theoretically and politically — had become increasingly difficult. Von Schaper, the Oberpräsident (Provincial Governor) demanded his removal on pain of closure of the newspaper. The shareholders were worried about renewal of their license. Marx's reaction was that of any chief editor: he wrote a sarcastically worded letter to the Oberpräsident — and dismissed Rutenberg.

He went further still. He gave an assurance that under no circumstances would he try to arouse sympathy for France or propagate superficially

French ideas in the Rhineland; he wished instead, he said, to publicize the Prussian path of progress and assist a German form of liberalism to make its voice heard, "which can surely not be disagreeable to the government of Friedrich Wilhelm IV."[97]

Franz Mehring refers to the letter as being drafted "with a diplomatic caution of which the life of its author offers no other example."[98]

Marx was temporizing in order to save his newspaper, accepting the fact that this entailed a breach with his Berlin friends who had meanwhile re-christened themselves the Society of "The Free." There was more in this than a mere change of name, however; in Berlin "emancipation" had suddenly become the watchword of ostensibly antiphilistine, but in fact simply ordinary publicity-seeking, maneuvers. There were begging processions through the streets, scandals in brothels, brawls in bars, and top-hatted demonstrations. The "revolution" in fact was degenerating into a fashionable occupation. Even Bruno Bauer took part in all this; for instance he handed the parson who married Max Stirner two brass rings acquired through his crooked money-market, saying that they would do as well as anything else for wedding rings.

Marx would not tolerate such antics, verbal or otherwise. Nor would he tolerate the public insults of a competing newspaper, the great *Augsburger Allgemeine* which published Heine's poems and attacked Marx with every form of derisive comment, making jokes about young gentlemen from rich well-bred families playing with communistic ideas as a pastime. Marx counterattacked — he not only rejected the suggestion that he was merely playing with the ideas of communism, but he rejected the whole idea of communism as such. Marx referred to it as the real threat, which he proposed to present to his readers "in all its unwashed nakedness"; he stated that it was not a theoretical reality, nor was its practical realization desirable; he considered the undeniable conflict between rich and poor to be capable of solution by peaceful means. He promised a fundamental critique of these ideas in his newspaper.[99]

He promoted to the leading page of number 333 of the paper some correspondence with Berlin dated November 25, 1842, which implied a breach with the Berliners — and with Bruno Bauer too. He then set out his position in a letter to Arnold Ruge, with whom he wished to continue to collaborate both as author and editor, first ridiculing Rutenberg as stupid, "no danger to anyone but the *Rheinische Zeitung* and himself" and barely capable of inserting punctuation marks. Ruge had just paid a visit to their former friends in Berlin in company with Georg Herwegh, who had just made his debut with Friedrich Engels in Gutzkow's *Telegraph für Deutschland* and to whom Heine later referred as the "iron-willed songster of the revolution." The letter to Ruge is a clear rejection of the ideas current in Berlin:

I stated that I regard it as inappropriate, even immoral, to smuggle communist and socialist doctrines, hence a new world outlook, into incidental theatrical criticisms etc. and that I demand a quite different and more thorough discussion of communism, if it should be discussed at all. . . . Finally I desired that, if there is to be talk about philosophy, there should be less trifling with the *label* "atheism" (which reminds one of children assuring everyone who is ready to listen to them that they are not afraid of the bogy man) and that instead the content of philosophy should be brought to the people. *Voilà tout.*[100]

Marx did not even await the instructions of the censor specially appointed to the newspaper; he made deletions himself and he refused to accept the "watery torrent of words"[101] from "The Free." Nevertheless the paper remained suspect and a second censor was appointed. Marx's own articles became increasingly polemical. First reports on the plight of the Moselle farmers were more explosive than any philosophizing. *Oberpräsident* von Schaper compelled the paper to make corrections and produce proof of its assertions. The result was "cheerful acceptance" of the cabinet order on the part of the editors, the "political monks" as Bruno Bauer called them; they welcomed the "calm dignity" with which "the authorities have demanded publication of fuller details of the case against them so that they may either defend themselves or redress grievances."[102] This sounded conciliatory rather than revolutionary. Shortly thereafter, however, appeared a series of five articles giving further details of the misery on the Moselle. On January 21, 1843, the Prussian Council of Ministers, which had just banned the *Leipziger Allgemeine Zeitung* for printing an insulting open letter from Herwegh, decided, with the King present, to withdraw forthwith the license from the "sister harlot on the Rhine."

Marx's reaction was once more curiously "two-edged." His flagship was apparently sinking but at least the captain should remain visible on deck, erect and responsible. To save the paper he asked his deputy, Heinzen, to insert an article in some newspaper showing that he, Karl Marx, alone was the principal responsible party. Heinzen did not even have to write the article — it was all ready; Marx had already drafted it: "I therefore propose to you that in some newspaper for which you write you should explain that everything risky that has appeared in the *Rheinische Zeitung* is my exclusive and personal responsibility."[103]

Heinzen refused but found a journalist on the *Mannheimer Abendzeitung* who was prepared to do it. He was named Karl Grün and his services were not forgotten. The article by Marx about Marx appeared on February 28, 1843. It reminded readers of "the piercing incisive reasoning, the truly admirable dialectic, with which the author had dissected the empty utterances of parliamentary deputies and then demolished them from within; the faculty of criticism has seldom been seen in such destructive virtuosity, has never more brilliantly demonstrated its abhorrence of the so-called positive which is caught and stifled in its own toils . . . a remarkable gift and a rare versatility of talent."[104]

Karl Heinzen, who later emigrated to the United States, had less pleasant memories of the time when he and Marx worked together on the *Rheinische Zeitung*. He recalled nightly rounds of taverns with his boss who, though amazingly quick-witted, was also extremely egoistic, mendacious, and an intriguer; he was consumed by envy of others' achievements, even more than by his own ambition. Marx liked to quote his friend Georg Weerth's couplet: "There is nothing nicer in the world than foes of his to bite on."[105]

One of the scenes of that Köln period, vividly pictured by Heinzen, is both revealing and sinister. The chief editor and his colleagues often sat over a glass of wine in the evenings, and if the row of empty glasses was becoming noticeably long, Marx would look round the company with the angry flashing eye of the autocrat. One of his friends would be taken aback by a finger suddenly pointed at him, accompanied with the words "I will destroy you."[106]

Three decades later Marx was to use these very words with Bakunin as the target. A full century later Stalin said: "I only have to move my little finger and there will be no more Tito. He will fall."[107]

Marx was not to know that at the same time "competent authorities" had made a report on him in terms similar to those of Heinzen and that it had found its way into secret government files in Berlin; one of the censors, later dismissed for carousing with "The Free" in Berlin and brawling outside brothels in Köln, reported to Berlin:

Dr. Marx is in any case the focus of doctrine here and the active source of the newspaper's theories; I have made his acquaintance; he is dead set on his views which have turned into convictions; he is determined to leave Prussia and, whatever happens, sever all connection with the *Rheinische Zeitung*. For the moment he has gone to Trier to bring back his bride.[108]

That was it. Jenny von Westphalen had waited seven years. Karl had gone to Bonn, then to Berlin, and then back to Bonn. His "two fathers" had died meanwhile. He had studied, taken his degree, and run a newspaper. Now he was back, with nothing in view. His plans for a profession were vague in the extreme and his prospects of earning a living even more so. Jenny was now his only tie: "I can assure you, without the slightest romanticism," he wrote to Ruge, "that I am head over heels in love and indeed in the most serious way. I have been engaged for more than seven years and for my sake my fiancée has fought the most violent battles, which almost undermined her health."[109]

For about a year she had been living with her mother in Bad Kreuznach. Oddly, Marx had seldom visited her there and, when he did go, he preferred to go about with Bettina von Arnim, who was also in the town. Betty Lucas, Jenny's long-standing friend, says that Jenny used to bemoan the fact that those two wandered about together from early morning till late at night, when Karl was only in Bad Kreuznach for a week and he and Jenny had not seen each other for six months.[110]

Be that as it may, the banns were called on May 21 and May 28, 1843, and the civil wedding, followed by the religious wedding in the Pauluskirche Kreuznach, took place on June 19. Before this, for a fee of 6 taler 15 groschen, a marriage contract had been drawn up in Jenny's mother's house. Therein common ownership of property was agreed upon, subject, however, to a saving clause: "Each spouse shall for his or her own part pay the debts he or she has made or contracted, inherited or otherwise incurred before marriage; in consequence whereof these debts shall be excluded from the common ownership of property."[111]

It is quite possible that this "businesslike reservation" stemmed from Jenny, who was a capable girl. When she had been confirmed in the Evangelical church in Trier on March 30, 1828, the family had selected as her text St. Paul's selfless words from the Epistle to the Galatians: "Nevertheless I live; yet not I, but Christ liveth in me." At the same time, however, her father had listed every present received by his daughter — "second gift of 500 taler to Jenny on Nov. 8, 1836."[112] Jenny managed such gifts of money well; she had her own shares in the wine trade, for instance.

So Marx's prolonged wooing was now happily concluded. It was to be a long time before he wrote "*beatus ille* who has no family."[113] The immediate future was the pressing problem, and Marx could no longer see a future in Germany; on the very day the ban on the *Rheinische Zeitung* had been announced he had written to Ruge: "I have become tired of hypocrisy, stupidity, gross arbitrariness, and of our bowing and scraping, dodging and hair-splitting over words. Consequently the government has given me back my freedom. . . . I can do nothing more in Germany. Here one makes a counterfeit of oneself."[114]

Ruge was the last friend Marx now had; his *Hallische Jahrbücher* followed by *Deutsche Jahrbücher* (German Annals) had been rallying points for the Young Hegelians for years. The *Rheinische Zeitung,* which had increased its circulation from 800 to 1,800 under Marx's direction, had been regarded as an "offshoot" of the *Deutsche Jahrbücher.* Bruno Bauer even referred to a sort of symbiosis between "the poet and the editor," in other words between Herwegh and Ruge, both united in the "new religion of the *Deutsche Jahrbücher.*"[115]

Ruge's was not a creative mind; he was, however, a cultured, versatile man with ambition, knowledge, and drive, a literary stage-manager. Having private means, he was in a position to put plans into practice, and he was now planning a new paper, which he discussed with Marx, who was only too happy to be involved. Early in March 1843 Ruge produced in Zurich his *Anekdota zur neuesten deutschen Philosophie und Publizistik* (Anecdotes on the Most Recent German Philosophy and Journalism), a collection of articles unpublishable elsewhere, and in this appeared Marx's first really comprehensive political treatise. In late May, after the banns had been called, but before the wedding, he had gone to Dresden for a few days to talk over the new newspaper with Ruge; pleasant as the months in Kreuznach were, he was temperamentally unsuited to studing for studying's sake. He wanted to awaken echoes, provoke reaction, produce some effect. He turned the honeymoon home into a workroom but that was not enough for him. The "Kreuznach Notebooks" show how wide and varied was his reading of history.[116] The thirty-nine manuscript sheets of his "Contribution to the Critique of Hegel's Philosophy of Law" (first published in Moscow in 1927) show that he not only devoured but also produced; the mere volume of all this labor sheds a curious light on the first few months of his long-awaited married bliss. But none of this could rouse Marx's enthusiasm, which was devoted entirely to Ruge's new plan: "Even if the publication of the *Deutsche Jahrbücher* were again permitted, at the very best we could achieve a poor copy of the deceased publication, and nowadays that is no longer enough. On the other hand *Deutsch-Französische Jahrbücher* [Franco-German Annals] — that would be a principle, an event of consequence, an undertaking over which one can be enthusiastic."[117]

Marx envisaged a comprehensive philosophical critique starting from new premises and produced with the cooperation primarily of leading French socialists such as Louis Blanc, Etienne Cabet, and Proudhon. His last extant letter written from Germany was to Ludwig Feuerbach asking for his cooperation:

You would therefore be doing a great service to our enterprise, but even more to truth, if you were to contribute a characterization of Schelling to the very first issue. You are just the man for this because you are *Schelling in reverse.* . . . Schelling is therefore an *anticipated caricature* of you, and as soon as reality confronts the caricature the latter must dissolve into thin air. I therefore regard you as the necessary, natural — that is nominated by Their Majesties Nature and History — opponent of Schelling. Your struggle with him is the struggle of the imagination of philosophy with philosophy itself. Yours very truly   Dr Marx.[118]

Feuerbach refused, but his answer did not find Marx at home.[119] His new address was 38 Rue Vaneau, Paris VII. Karl Marx, now aged twenty-five, had left Germany — forever; he never lived there again.

Once more an exchange of letters marks a turning point in the life of Karl Marx. The great letter to his father had distilled the experiences of his teenage years, gathering into perspective his school-leaving essay and his doctoral dissertation; at the same time, however, it heralded a fresh start. Similarly, the exchange of letters between Marx, Ruge, Feuerbach, and Bakunin initiating the *Deutsch-Französische Jahrbücher* marks the end of one chapter and the start of the next.

Ruge later claimed authorship of this "fictitious exchange of letters" and even reproduced the texts in his *Sämtliche Werke* (Collected Works). Nevertheless it is clear beyond all doubt that Marx's letters were written by Marx. In considered detail they develop a program for the newspaper, while at the same time developing his own program; in other words they are part of a great process of self-discovery. Marx is the one who sets out the political arguments, rejecting Ruge's jeremiads with haughty scorn: "Your letter, my dear friend, is a fine elegy, a funeral song that takes one's breath away; but there is absolutely nothing political about it."[120]

What was "political" in Marx's eyes? Two things stand out in these letters: first, the eschatological outline of a new human being; second, the endeavor to include politics in the category of practical rather than philosophical activity — as the "Theses on Feuerbach" were to show even more clearly a year later. The two are complementary, though both are self-contradictory. Marx's language is almost Christian, or at least religious in tone: "The monarchical principle . . . is . . . the dehumanized man."[121] A foretaste. One day he would be using the word "capitalism" instead of "monarchy" and "alienated," instead of "dehumanized." Marx was on the way to Marx. The strongly worded conclusion of this introductory letter setting out his program refers to critical philosophy and self-clarification as "confessions" — "in order to secure remission of its sins, mankind has only to declare them for what they actually are."[122] He even uses typical Talmudic dialectic hyperbole — here speaks the son of Jehovah, the prophet, the seer, the leader; *he* will lead his people out of the desert; *he* will outline the plan. One of Marx's great pregnant, explosively poetic sentences is to be found here — conclusive — prophetic and revolutionary — the word of Moses: "It will then become evident that the world has long dreamed of possessing something of which it has only to be conscious in order to possess it in reality."[123]

"Then." When? That was not yet established, nor even were the principles — ". . . we do not confront the world in a doctrinaire way with a new principle — here is the truth, kneel down before it!"[124] For the moment "ruthless criticism of all that exists"[125] was the important point; the new world, the dawning world, was still in the melting pot:

Therefore I am not in favour of raising any dogmatic banner. On the contrary, we must try to help the dogmatists to clarify their propositions for themselves. Thus communism, in particular, is a dogmatic abstraction; in which connection, however, I am not thinking of some imaginary and possible communism, but actually existing communism as taught by Cabet, Dezamy, Weitling etc. This communism is itself only a special expression of the humanistic principle, an expression which is still infected by its antithesis — the private system. Hence the abolition of private property and communism are by no means identical, and it is not accidental but inevitable that communism has seen other socialist doctrines — such as those of Fourier, Proudhon etc. — arising to confront it because it is itself only a special, one-sided realisation of the socialist principle.[126]

Criticism of that which exists. To Marx this meant at this time criticism of religion, or to be more precise criticism of the belief that religion makes man and not vice versa.

The tone of this first — and only — series issued by the *Deutsch-Französische Jahrbücher* was set by two of Marx's studies, *Contribution to the Critique of Hegel's Philosophy of Law* and *On the Jewish Question*. The first is so intellectually persuasive, so lucid, and so brilliant that its enormous effect can well be imagined. Religion is presented as "the sigh of the oppressed creature, the heart of a heartless world." At this point comes the famous sentence: "Religion is the opium of the people."[127] No one had ever argued like this before and no one had ever expressed his views so well. His language had the force of Luther's. His target, however, was not some castle chapel but a fortress, all fortresses.

Marx's eloquence is such that the mere reading of him is a pleasure. It is not surprising that a number of the "winged words" that everyone today associates with Marx come from this short essay. "Theory becomes a material force as soon as it has gripped the masses," or "To be radical is to grasp the root of the matter. But for man the root is man himself."[128] Marx's élan and pathos are born of his grand design. Here lies the mainspring of what Ernst Bloch later called the "concrete utopia"; here is what invades the lives of men and reaches out beyond them — beyond them but riding roughshod over them too.

We shall be reverting to these early studies when dealing with the life and career of the mature Marx and searching for the answer to the question: Is man "utopia-worthy"? Marx himself was determined to set forth down the straight and narrow path, on the assumption that man's nature was characterized by backbone and brain, morality and intellect: that for him was man. For the first time there emerged his preoccupation with that class which he called "*la plus labourieuse et la plus miserable,*" the proletariat.

The second study, "On the Jewish Question," is the more difficult since it is full of cross-currents of thought; it clearly stemmed from Kreuznach. Its starting point is the same: secular questions should not be turned into theological ones but theological questions should be turned into secular ones; history has hitherto been merged in superstition but superstition should now be merged in history. Man, who, in his "most immediate reality," regards himself as a real individual and is so regarded by others, is a "fictitious phenomenon."[129] The Christian state is not only an imperfect state but a hypocritical state. It is based on "human rubbish,"[130] an expression not of disdain but of pity.

This study, which criticizes two essays by his former associate Bruno Bauer, is entitled "On the Jewish Question." So Karl Marx, the Jew, the descendant of famous rabbinical families, but baptized, confirmed, and married in church, was venturing into a field full of explosive material for him, explosive not merely in theory. Here something remarkable occurred: Marx aimed too low. For him "the Jew" was the "huckstering" Jew, and Jewish consciousness aimed solely at profit-making. All his arguments are founded on this basis and this basis alone: he lays down a one-way street. He concedes no separate existence to consciousness, religion, or the manifold patterns of behavior stemming from differences in psychology or character. Once again his language is brilliant but it is often no more than verbiage or epigram: "Hence man was not freed from religion, he received religious freedom. He was not freed from property, he received freedom to own property. He was not freed from the egoism of business, he received freedom to engage in business."[131]

Such statements, devoid of real meaning, sound precious; they could just as well be turned back to front. Only flat statements, not logical conclusions, can emerge from a process of thought circumscribed by the assumption that men are molded solely by their economic situation:

Let us consider the actual worldly Jew, not the Sabbath Jew, as Bauer does, but the everyday Jew.

Let us not look for the secret of the Jew in his religion, but let us look for the secret of his religion in the real Jew.

What is the secular basis of Judaism? Practical need, self-interest.

What is the worldly religion of the Jew? Huckstering. What is his worldly God? Money.

Very well then! Emancipation from huckstering and money, consequently from practical real Judaism would be the self-emancipation of our time.[132]

This is not correct even sociologically. For instance in 1844, when this treatise was written, there were some ten thousand Jews resident and employed in Bavaria and over half of them were craftsmen and farmers; of the five thousand Jews living in Breslau and Oppeln only a thousand were engaged in trade and the remainder were craftsmen, domestic servants, mechanics, doctors, teachers, or farmers; in 1808 there were only four moneylenders among more than twenty-five hundred Jews in Paris.[133]

Marx's theory was without foundation. It was not, as is often maintained, anti-Semitic per se. The resounding final sentence, "The social emancipation of the Jew is the emancipation of society from Judaism,"[134] would undoubtedly have been suitable for *Der Stürmer* if quoted out of context. The context, however, shows that Marx was using the words "Jew" and "Judaism" in a "quasi-non-Jewish" sense. This is the point: he makes use of a meaningless idea, remolds and typifies it, and attributes to it an exclusively economic meaning.

But this very point proves that nothing is explicable by this line of argument. The unmistakable intolerance of this disquisition and its apodictic rather than enlightening severity, in other words the absence of analysis, show this with complete clarity. What emerges here is not an ideology of the leader and redeemer but a blueprint for violent change with emphasis on the negative. Marx clearly intends to force the egoistic individual (the Jew) to develop into the true human being (the citizen).

This is presumption and its basis is precarious. The fact that Marx takes refuge in invective — in those days phrases like "little Jew," "Izzy," "aroma of garlic," "Jewish hook-nose," or "no renting" provided ammunition for carping and ill will — indicates astonishing ignorance.

Marx never worked on the problem of Jewry. The excerpts he made on the subject as a student in Berlin are small, usually only a few lines; he noted down some nine and half lines about it from Wachsmuth's *Allgemeine Kulturgeschichte* (General History of Culture) compared to fifteen pages from the same author's chapter on India.[135] There is nothing to show that he ever busied himself with the problem of Judaism apart from reading Bruno Bauer's pamphlets. There is not a single recorded utterance by him about Jewish socialism. When a social-revolutionary "Society of Jewish Workers" was formed in London in 1876, although fully informed, he took as little notice of it as he did of the existence of a Jewish proletariat, to whose misery Engels drew attention.

Throughout, however, contempt for everything Jewish stands out. It runs through all Karl Marx's writings, observations, polemics, and letters. Did it stem from a sense of superiority or the typical Jewish self-hate? The speed of passages on the subject and the combination of explosive and suffocating material have a defensive, if not self-justifying, ring about them. If his phraseology be stripped of its economic veneer and transposed into the language of "heaven or hell," if "guilt" be substituted for "usury" and "redemption" for "emancipation," Karl Marx's self-appointed mission can be deduced: not to take man's guilt upon himself but to eradicate it. Rage at his probable inability to fulfill his mission turned into rage against his own race.[136]

CHAPTER TWO

EXILE IN PARIS

FRIENDSHIP WITH HEINRICH HEINE

Karl Marx had left Germany.

He was now aged twenty-five, a well-built slender man with the first streaks of gray in his hair and a jet-black beard. Photographs of this period show him as an elegantly dressed gentleman, mature for his years, with a morose, in fact melancholy, look in his eye. His "personal details" are variously described.[1] Passport entries generally agree on a height of 5'6"; his contemporaries often refer to him as "small and rather skinny." Paul Lafargue, who was a doctor, said that his back was too long for his legs; when sitting, therefore, he seemed a large man. His nose is sometimes described as thick, sometimes as average, and sometimes as large; his skin as light, dark, or brown, sometimes simply as "healthy"; his forehead sometimes as straight, sometimes oval; and his face also sometimes oval and sometimes round. Passport details vary particularly on color of eyes and hair, the eyes being "dark," "brown," "somewhat dull," or "piercing, fiery, devilishly sinister." In his young days his hair and beard were jet-black, but a "personal description" filed by the police in 1861 gives only the mustache as jet-black, the hair being "white," the beard "snowy," and the eyebrows "blond." A report of 1872, however, gives hair and beard as handsome, gray, and curly. Innumerable other details of real or supposed characteristics are given elsewhere — accent and features indicative of his Jewish ancestry, for instance; Prussian police files describe him as "sly, cold and determined"; other writers rave about his distinguished exterior, the elegance of his dress, and the fiery enthusiasm of a bold spirit concealed beneath discreet modesty. It is difficult to be definite about Marx's appearance at this period of his life since, apart from the lithograph by Levy-Elkans from the student days of 1836, few photographs of him exist prior to 1861. Marx did not like being photographed; the best studio portraits — of the mature man — are those of the well-known Mayall who took the world-famous portraits of Disraeli, Palmerston, and Queen Victoria.[2]

In Paris, however, he was still a young man, married and with a wife expecting a child. The Rue Vaneau in the well-to-do VIIme Arrondissement was not *his* address alone — Arnold Ruge and Georg Herwegh lived there too. In the heading of the first issue of the *Deutsch-Französische Jahrbücher* it is also given as the location of the editorial office. A period of important personal encounters and political contacts then began, together with — as always — quarrels with his friends. This was also a period of highly concentrated work, disorderly but not purposeless; Ruge describes it thus:

He is a strange character with a pronounced bent towards scholarship and authorship but totally incompetent as a journalist. He reads a great deal; he works at extraordinary pressure and has a talent for criticism which sometimes develops into presumptuous and discourteous dialectics; he never completes anything, is always breaking off and plunging back again into an endless welter of books.[3]

The names of those working on the *Deutsch-Französische Jahrbücher* indicate the circle in which Marx moved — and from which he moved on; they include Ruge, Herwegh, Moses Hess, Bakunin, Engels, and Heinrich Heine.

Heine, who had just returned from his first trip to Germany since 1831, lived in the Faubourg Poissonière. A month later the two men met and a close friendship developed; they were together almost daily — Heine would read some new poem and Marx would listen, criticize, and suggest amendments. They composed numerous poems in concert after hours of polishing, rearranging, and erasing. Heine's conversion to political lyrics was due to Marx's influence; Arnold Ruge recalls how he and Marx led Heine on, saying: "Give up these everlasting laments about love and show the lyric poets how it should be done — with the lash."[4]

Heine was morbidly sensitive to criticism and Marx had to be most careful. Though acid and scornful when engaged in polemics, Heine would come running to Marx literally in tears when some attack had been made on him, however unfounded or trivial. On these occasions Marx was somewhat at a loss and Jenny would be summoned to comfort and soothe. Heine was charmed by her humor, grace, and occasional deliberate reserve; he respected her and felt at home in her house. Heine became so much part of the Marx family that one evening when he found them all standing, desperate and helpless, watching baby Jenny writhing in convulsions, he said at once: "Give the child a bath." He prepared the bath, put the child into it, and so, as Marx later said, saved little Jenny's life.[5]

Poles apart though they were, the two men were always on intimate terms; neither was competing with the other. Marx remained fond of Heine all his life, and admired his poetry. Heine's "Weavers Song" and "Germany, A Winter's Tale" both stemmed from his friendship with Marx. Marx was invariably most cautious in his condemnation of Heine's political "improprieties"; Heine had the privileged status of a poet — poets were "queer fish" not to be judged by ordinary or even "otherwise" extraordinary standards.

Even Heine's supplication to the "living God" found by Marx in his friend's will, and his "apology to God and mankind for anything immoral he may have written" drew only good-natured derision from Marx.[6] He passed over in charitable silence the fact that Heine, a German émigré though highly appreciated by the French, accepted a secret pension from Louis Philippe for years — a piece of dishonesty for which Marx would have forgiven hardly anyone else.

This friendship, however, passed through a number of phases and at times there was a lack of reciprocity. It is a subject worth pursuing. For instance, there is no truth in the legend that Heine was converted to communism by Marx nor in the converse story that Heine's defensive forebodings in the prologue to his *Lutetia,* written in 1855, were the result of an encounter with Marx. The background was more complex.

Even before moving to Paris in 1829 Heine had studied Saint-Simon and had bought the first bound volumes of his paper *Le Globe.*[7] In Paris he visited the editorial office and was often to be seen with Michel Chevalier, the chief editor, and Barthélemy-Prosper Enfantin, spokesman of the Saint-Simonists, to whom he dedicated the French edition of his essays on Germany.[8] Heine's knowledge of the organization and basic theoretical principles of communism came either from the antigovernment secret societies of the early 1830s — the "Friends of the People" society or the "Human Rights" society — or from the leaders of the neo-Babouvist movement; he had listened to Auguste Blanqui, the republican demagogue, and reported on the relevant meeting in the *Augsburger Allgemeine Zeitung.*[9] The first secret society designed to implement Gracchus Babeuf's program was the "Societé des Saisons" formed in 1837.

When Heine uses the word communism he is referring to Babeuf,[10] the head of the "Conspiracy of Levellers" executed on May 28, 1797, and referred to by Marx as "the first manifestation of a truly effective communist party."[11] The title "Conspiracy of Levellers" indicates the general trend of his doctrine — an "egalitarian frenzy" and "iconoclastic fury" that made Heine shudder. It is no accident that Babeuf's name appears in Heine's passage bemoaning "mankind's disaster."[12] Heine was also familiar with the book *Conspiration pour l'égalité dite de Babeuf* written by Filippo Buonarroti, Babeuf's fellow conspirator, and published in Brussels in 1828. The results he could see when he visited the Faubourg Saint Marceau in Paris and certain "workshops" in the working-class quarter; he reported in the *Augsburger Allgemeine* that pamphlets circulating among the workers smelled of blood.[13] Babeuf's "equality of pleasures" was anathema to Heine; he even quotes verbatim a phrase about "communal pleasures" from Buonarroti's pamphlet *"Analyse der Lehre Babeuf's"* (Analysis of Babeuf's Doctrine), published in Paris in 1796 and subsequently repeated in his book — "nature has given every man an equal right to the enjoyment of all good things."[14] Heine gave vent to his horror of communism in numerous passages referring to a brood of frogs creeping out of hedges and marshes and to the fact that republican croaking carried more weight than his nightingale songs.[15] Even in his *Letters from Germany,* written in his later years, he quoted from his own book *On Germany:* "You demand simple costumes, austere manners and cheap unseasoned pleasures; we, on the contrary, demand nectar and ambrosia, purple garments, costly perfumes, luxury and splendour, dances of laughing nymphs, music and comedies."[16]

Heine's apprehensions were understandable in the light of Article 3 of the "Draft of a Police Law," a paper produced by Buonarroti; this showed what might be expected after a victory by the "Levellers." "Useful occupations" were given as farming and fishing, navigation, and the art of war; education and science came at the bottom of the list and were only classified as "useful" if those engaged in them could furnish proof of "civic reliability."

"When Heine says 'communism' he means babouvism"[17] — this incisive statement reveals the difference in time-scale between the views of Heine and those of Marx; Heine's encounter with Marx did not lead him to Marx; he did not accompany his friend on the march toward the "Communist Manifesto." What Marx and Engels regarded as a transitional phase through which one must pass, in Heine's eyes was and remained the goal, the appalling ultimate end:

In very truth is is only with dread and horror that I think of the time when these gloomy iconoclasts will attain power; when their heavy hands will break without pity all the marble statues of beauty which are so dear to my heart. They will crush into dust all the fantastic play and baubles of Art which are so dear to the poet; they will fell my groves of laurel and plant potatoes in their place and the lilies of the field, which toil not neither do they spin and yet are more magnificently arrayed than Solomon in all his glory, will be rooted up from the soil of society unless they will take distaff in hand. The roses, those idle brides of the nightingales, must suffer the same fate; the nightingales themselves will be driven away as useless singers and ah! my book of songs will be used by the grocers to make paper cornets in which to put coffee or snuff for the old women of the future.

Yes, I foresee all this and nameless grief comes over me when I think of the destruction with which the victorious proletariat threatens my verses, which will sink into the grave with the whole ancient romantic world. Yet despite this I publicly confess that this communism, which is so inimical to all my interests and inclinations, exerts a magic influence on my soul from which I cannot defend myself.[18]

This was written by the émigré decried as a revolutionary and trouble-maker, a poet, the reading of whose verses in Russian was the dying wish of a certain twenty-one-year-old before his execution on May 8, 1887 — Alexander Ilyich Ulyanov, Lenin's beloved and admired elder brother. Heine wrote this, moreover, years *after* he had met Marx. Ten years had passed and at least seven since the revolution — and here was Heine reverting to his old skepticism. Backsliding? Betrayal?

Neither this nor many other passages in Heine's later works should be regarded merely as a reversion to his earlier antipathy to Babeuf's theories. He saw danger *also* in Marxist communism. For him this was still an open question, undecided. Even minor details testify to his uncertainty. In the first impression of his *Confessions*, which appeared in *Revue des deux Mondes* in Paris on September 15, 1854, he says: "The more or less clandestine leaders of the German communists are great logicians, the most powerful among them having come from the Hegelian school; they are undoubtedly the most capable brains and most energetic characters in Germany. These doctors of revolution and their relentlessly determined pupils are the only men in Germany with some life in them and the future belongs to them, I fear."[19] In the bound edition he omitted the words "I fear."

Intellectually, therefore, there can be no question of intimate friendship between Heine and Marx; Marx was too busy with his own affairs. These few months in Paris covered the period of his conversion from Feuerbachian to anti-Feuerbachian. During this transitional period too he perfected his method of reasoning — polemics as his natural method of attacking a problem, the destructive approach as a means of establishing views of his own. A year later he was to write the famous eleven "Theses" in his scribbling book.

Initially Marx had no material anxieties. Friends in Germany had collected over 1,000 taler for him and shortly thereafter another 800 francs arrived; so all in all he had well over 6,000 francs, enough for several years.[20] The house was comfortable. His mother-in-law had sent her daughter a very big "present" in the shape of a capable young maid, a peasant girl who had worked in the von Westphalen household. Her name was Lenchen Demuth and she was to become a highly important member of the family for decades to come. In May came the first addition to the family, a daughter christened Jenny after her mother who displayed her proudly to relatives in Germany, entailing a long expensive journey which Marx could clearly afford. The Marx family's standard of living was therefore good middle class. The "doctors of revolution" came from a prosperous, well-to-do background.

THE PLEASURES OF LIFE WITH GEORG HERWEGH

In his own way Marx enjoyed life in Paris; he worked and looked for political contacts. He also took his fill of the capital's social life; he was certainly not referring to the impecunious Bakunin when he later remarked that the Russian aristocracy in Paris had cosseted him. An even more intimate friend than

Heine was Herwegh (his was the house in which Jenny and her little daughter took refuge when the family had to leave Paris in a hurry in February 1845), and Herwegh had totally succumbed to the delights of Paris — "the shops, the carriages, the rich people's lovely rooms, the flower stalls, the girls."[21] Ruge's comment on Marx at this period was that he had become "a genius, in other words a fool"[22] and he was referring to his association with Herwegh. Ruge was shocked by the vulgar profligacy of a certain Countess d'Agoult, Herwegh's mistress — "100-taler dresses, new gloves every day, flowers at three golden louis apiece."[23] Referring to Marx: "His wife gave him for his birthday a riding switch costing 100 francs and the poor devil cannot ride nor has he a horse. Everything he sees he wants to 'have' — a carriage, smart clothes, a flower garden, new furniture from the Exhibition, in fact the moon."[24]

Ruge's comment that Marx was spending more time with Herwegh than before and, although despising him, was up to all sorts of youthful pranks leads one to suspect that Marx not only had a high regard for the poet Herwegh but also participated with him to the full in the pleasures of life in Paris. Marx defended Herwegh against Heine's ridicule and Herwegh was the cause of his ultimate breach with Ruge. Marx was in any case extremely angry with Ruge because he would not invest further money in the newspaper idea (something which he himself later did unreservedly in a similar situation). In fact the Prussian government had entered the lists against the *Deutsch-Französische Jahrbücher;* a circular of April 18, 1844, warned all provincial governors that here was a case of attempted treason and lèse majesté and if Ruge, Marx, Heine, or Bernays set foot on Prussian soil they were to be arrested. Worse still, a boycott of the paper was instituted; Prussia's frontiers were closed to a newspaper! A hundred copies were confiscated on a Rhine steamer and another two hundred on the Franco-Palatinate frontier. Commercially the enterprise was ruined. The "literary counting-house" in Zurich owned by Ruge and Julius Fröbel could no longer carry it. Marx's salary, for instance, consisted solely of free copies!

In fact there was no agreement as regards the general, in other words political, line of the paper. This had been clear from the prepublication exchange of letters, which had shown that Marx was aiming at revolution and Ruge at reform. The vehemence of Marx's arguments carried the ring of a call to humanity; he was setting out to show that "the world has long dreamed of possessing something of which it has only to be conscious in order to possess it in reality."[25] With impressive pathos Marx fulminated against incapacity to feel shame:

You look at me with a smile and ask: What is gained by that? No revolution is made out of shame. I reply: Shame is already a revolution of a kind; shame is actually the victory of the French Revolution over the German patriotism that defeated it in 1813. Shame is a kind of anger that is turned inward. And if a whole nation really experienced a sense of shame, it would be like a lion crouching ready to spring.[26]

Marx's aim was to overcome this spiritual lethargy — both in action and in politics and so he was led to produce for the first time the idea of "practice" that he later expressed with such poignancy in his "Theses on Feuerbach"; his demands for secularization of philosophy and for political criticism concerning *real* issues sound as if they were preparatory studies, but the goal which he puts before his readers is far more than the program for a newspaper: "This is a work for the world and for us. It can only be the work of united forces. It is a matter of a confession and nothing more. In order to secure remission of its sins, mankind has only to declare them for what they are."[27]

Shame, sins, confession, mankind — Marx's reasoning is based on emotion; both the phraseology and general approach of The Preacher are clearly governed by sympathy and mercy. Marx is not here presenting some ready-made system, some *una sancta* which has only to be entered to find complete salvation: "We do not confront the world in a doctrinaire way with a new principle: Here is the truth, kneel down before it! We develop new principles for the world out of the world's own principles."[28]

Despite this "open-mindedness," however, the breach with Ruge, which he calls sad though entirely unconnected with politics, was on the horizon. The "publishing quarrel" was a further factor. Yet little more than a year earlier Ruge had written to everybody recommending Marx either as the new co-editor or as a staff member now that he had been released from the *Rheinische Zeitung*. One of the most pressing letters, dated March 8, 1843, had been dispatched to Switzerland from Dresden; it was addressed to Herwegh.

BREACH WITH ARNOLD RUGE

Herwegh was the cause of the final breach between Marx and Ruge. They were sitting over a glass of wine in Paris one evening and discussing the future progress or rather the salvage of the *Jahrbücher* when Ruge began to ridicule Herwegh's indolence and debauchery, even calling him a blackguard. Marx said nothing and embraced Ruge warmly as they parted. Next morning, however, a letter arrived saying that Herwegh was a genius with a great future, that he, Marx, had been scandalized to hear him stigmatized as a blackguard, that Ruge was narrow-minded and inhuman. The two never met again. From that moment Ruge was the enemy. Ruge wrote a generous letter saying that they must not part like puppets in a Punch-and-Judy show but could do so politely like well brought-up people. He would be happy, he went on, if Marx's principles proved correct and practicable; his remarks about Herwegh, moreover, had only been made in passing and were no harsher than many of Marx's own expressed views. But no further word came from Marx.

Marx's abrupt changes of attitude, this rapid transition from friendly companionship to indignant enmity — caresses one minute, claws out the next — were clearly incomprehensible to Ruge. For him, political differences were still matters to be settled between gentlemen. He remained courteous. Though the surface might be ruffled, so to speak, the deeper waters remained undisturbed; parliamentary courtesies were still the rule. Men like Ruge remain unruffled and self-possessed like present-day liberals; basically they are nonpolitical.

Here lies the difference: to the last fiber of his being Marx was a politician; he was like lava, a revolutionary natural element; for him politics were the essence of all things; nothing else motivated him. This explains his explosive lack of the normal courtesies. To him, the rules of political good manners were just as incomprehensible as they were self-evident to Ruge. His disregard of them was to be painfully self-destructive. From this too stemmed his errors: there were men who had no right to be right, and there were men who were right even if they were wrong. So the "misunderstanding" about Herwegh was characteristic of Marx; he was definitely in the wrong; his picture of Herwegh was a piece of wishful thinking. His error was as honest as it was dangerous and it provides a further illustration of one of the main flaws in his thinking — he expected from men and their history more than they were able or willing to achieve. His vast overestimation of the Silesian weavers' rising and its historical significance is in the same category; in fact, as we shall see, almost without exception all Marx's and Engels's historic prognoses were to this extent "wrong"; their "historical materialism" might well be termed "historical utopianism" — certainly when they projected into the future their diagnoses of past conditions. So what remains — an attempt to set standards untempered by moderation, "vehement" in other words.

This word is used and emphasized by Marx in an article disputing Ruge's contemptuous estimate of the political and intellectual capabilities of the German working man and he uses it deliberately:

Where among the bourgeoisie — including its philosophers and learned writers — is to be found a book about the emancipation of the bourgeoisie — *political emancipation* — similar to Weitling's work: *Garantien der Harmonie und Freiheit* [Guarantees of Harmony and Freedom]? It is enough to compare the petty, fainthearted mediocrity of German political literature with this *vehement* and brilliant literary debut of the German workers; it is enough to compare these gigantic *infant shoes* of the proletariat with the dwarfish, worn-out political shoes of the German bourgeoisie and one is bound to prophesy that the *German Cinderella* will one day have the *figure of an athlete*.[29]

DISPUTE WITH LUDWIG FEUERBACH —
THE "ECONOMIC AND PHILOSOPHIC MANUSCRIPTS"

The "Prophet" in Paris now exerted himself in two ways to "bring heaven down to earth": he embarked upon a gigantic reading marathon and he made his first contacts with proletarian associations.

At the outset, however, came a curious "diversion." In fact Marx had initially been interested primarily in the French Revolution; while still in Kreuznach he had studied the memoirs of Jean-Baptiste Louvet, the Girondist and member of the Convention, Montgaillard's *Révolutions en France et Brabant*, and Saint-Just's and Robespierre's speeches. He was fascinated by the Convention, which he regarded as "the maximum of political energy, political power and political understanding."[30] During his early days in Paris he read further memoirs of members of the Convention, such as Levasseur de la Sarthe, the writings of Babeuf, and the official minutes of the Convention debates. He wanted to write a history of the Convention while at the same time working on a critique of Hegel's *Phenomenology of Mind*.

At this point there appeared in the Paris *Vorwärts* a series of articles on the situation in England. The author was a man who had already made the only nonphilosophical, nontheoretical contribution to the *Deutsch-Französische Jahrbücher* with his *Outlines of a Critique of Political Economy*. He was a manufacturer's son, two years younger than Marx, who had given him a very cool reception when he visited the editorial office of the *Rheinische Zeitung*. His name was Friedrich Engels. Earlier than all the others he had grasped the fact that economics was the root of all things, earlier above all than Marx, the philosophic and religious critic.

In September 1844, while his series in *Vorwärts* was still coming out, Engels visited Paris and there followed ten days of intimate contact and exchange of ideas between the two men; Engels later said of this period: ". . . our complete agreement in all theoretical fields became evident and our joint work dates from that time."[31]

From now on Marx laid more emphasis on his economic studies. Problems of political economy were somewhat new to him; when Franz Mehring asked Engels what were the results of Marx's early reading, he replied: "He knew absolutely nothing of economics; a phrase like 'form of industry' meant nothing to him."[32] There now appeared Marx's famous "Economic and Philosophic Manuscripts" — consisting largely of extracts from Adam Smith, David Ricardo, Jean-Baptiste Say, and John Stuart Mill, all of whom he had read either in the original or in French translation. In this outline he adopted a very humanist line of argument, but already there appears as the heading of one of the sections the word "Capital."

This, the most significant of Marx's *Frühschriften* (Early Writings) is a preparatory study for his "Critique of Hegel's Philosophy of Law," announced for publication in the *Deutsch-Französische Jahrbücher* but which never progressed further than the introduction; Marx realized that he could not set out the relationship of political economy to the state, the law, morality, and bourgeois existence in a *single* systematized treatise and he planned a number of independent brochures. They never appeared.

The "Economic and Philosophic Manuscripts" served both to outline his ideas and assemble material. There are four manuscripts. The first consists of nine folio sheets of extracts and reflections on wage labor, ground rents, and profits — the extracts show how much Marx was indebted in questions of political economy to the liberal German journalist Wilhelm Schulz. The second manuscript has only one folio sheet and is clearly the conclusion of another manuscript which has been lost; it deals with the problem of private property. The third manuscript is of seventeen folio pages and again examines Hegel's dialectic and philosophy; it also deals with questions of money, production, and division of labor. The fourth manuscript consists exclusively of extracts from Hegel. The manuscripts were missing for a long time.[33] Even Franz Mehring does not mention them. Parts of them appeared for the first time in 1927 in a Russian translation entitled "Preparatory Studies for 'The Holy Family' "; two years later further parts were published in the Paris *Revue Marxiste;* in January 1931 J. P. Mayer gave an account in the Zurich *Rote Revue* of the discovery of a notebook-type Marx manuscript and finally they were published in full in *Karl Marx Friedrich Engels — Historisch-kritische Gesamtausgabe.* One of the earliest critiques was published by Herbert Marcuse, whose now well-known theory of the 1960s, "the great negation," owes much to Marx's early ideas.

The notion around which the manuscripts revolve is "alienation." From critical examination of Hegel's phenomenology and Feuerbach's philosophy on the one hand and from Engels's articles "Outlines of a Critique of Political Economy" (which he describes as an "inspired sketch") together with certain less apposite writings (by Moses Hess[34] for example) on the other, Marx distilled the beginnings of a system of his own: critical analysis of the existing social order and the initial outline of a new one. The self-alienation — or "dehumanization" — of men in a bourgeois society is contrasted with the conquest of alienation, or "togetherness" as Hegel called it, of a communist society. For Marx, communism is the true solvent of the conflict between man and nature, the solution to the riddle of history.

His description of what exists, with its emotional mixture of hard fact and ethos, is convincing, but his projection into the future is terribly vague. These are "Economic and Philosophic Manuscripts" with emphasis on the "philosophic"; Marx is analyzing primarily Hegel's notion that the contradictions inherent in capitalism are capable of harmonization; in his eyes the central feature of Hegel's scheme of things, the subject-object relationship, could be reduced to the concept of "consciousness." For Hegel the dialectic between man and nature could be resolved in the realm of thought, through self-recognition of the mind in nature; for Marx this would take place in the realm of concrete, *active* living, nature being humanized rather than turned into an abstraction; he wanted action — in other words politics, in other words change — in place of an abstract world manifested in history.

Marx was fighting a two-front war — against Hegel's views and against Feuerbach's, who thought that alienation could be eliminated by religious criticism. This led Marx to argue in two directions, but one thing is clear: his basic emotion is sympathy and his basic motivation an ethical one. The degeneration of human relationships into business relationships, the alienated, indeed antithetical, relationship between the producing individual and his product, the devaluation of sensuality, morals and vitality, in short the reduction of man to the level of a social cypher — fetish commodities equal fetish man — all this Marx wished to eliminate through a colossal effort of the understanding and the emotions. This elimination meant to him the abolition of private property which, by transforming commodities for use into commodities for exchange, necessarily brought about increased production; men produce goods not merely to meet mutual needs but as a means of profit. A man, says Marx, proves himself — finds himself — as a man when he is employed as a man.

So what? The analysis may have been convincing but the panacea was not: the communist ideal demanded precise concrete details but these Marx did not provide. He knew that mere criticism of the existing order would change nothing, that wholesale abolition of private property implied radical upheaval of existing society, revolution in other words. And then what? Marx seizes on utopian socialism or "crude communism" and its idealistic concept of man; he knew that only a change of circumstances could produce a different type of mankind, humanity blossoming in free communal activity, in other words the true human community. But this was only a vague definition, little more than mere verbiage, a meaningless prescription despite certain sublime flashes of discovery. His attacks on so-called primitive communism, postulating equal distribution rather than abolition of private property, read like blistering criticism of present-day socialist states. Under this system, according to Marx, work was still a means to private profit rather than expression of man's creative activity, greater control over material advantages took the place of de-alienation; egalitarianism and drab simplicity would be the rule; culture would be doomed; talent, personality, and individuality would become abstractions.[35] Was this not exactly what Heinrich Heine had found so abhorrent?

True communism, however, which the world of human beings, not the material world, should regard as the aim of production and social intercourse — what did that look like? All Marx can offer are empty formulae — the rich man, rich human need, the man whose self-expression is a deep-rooted necessity, communism as practical humanism.[36] Marx gives no organizational pattern, no structural plan of this society, no details of division of political powers or checks and balances. He preaches, he demolishes, he summons to the promised land, but his goal is only the road to that land. He wanted to lead his people home without knowing whither — and he himself was an exile.

Marx's life in Paris was a restless one. He met Bakunin frequently and was to be found in the smart salons of liberal Russian nobility. He was present at a "democratic banquet" together wih Ruge and Louis Blanc, Bakunin and Grigori Michailovich Tolstoy, the Russian landowner to whom he introduced Engels early in September. Count Tolstoy lived in state; as well as his house he owned an *hôtel de ville* in the Rue Mathurin where he gave brilliant receptions for the diplomatic corps. Once more Marx's penchant for social gatherings and salons was in evidence. But he was also present at functions of the communist secret societies, though he was not a member of them.

Marx's labors were philosophic, economic, and literary. He read, and was enraged by, Bruno Bauer's *Allgemeine Literaturzeitung* (General Literary Newspaper); he also read the widely circulating current paper *Journal des Débats*, which published articles in series by trashy writers such as Eugène Sue and featured portraits by its editor, Bertin von Ingres. He wrote in *Vorwärts*, which was owned by Heinrich Börnstein, a theatrical agent, and was financed for publicity purposes by Meyerbeer, the composer; under the direction of F. C. Bernays, one of the staff of the *Deutsch-Französische Jahrbücher*, it turned into a democratic newspaper. In an emotional letter from Hamburg dated September 21, 1844, Heine asked Marx to intervene on his behalf — "we need only one or two indications in order to understand each other, your devoted . . ." — and eventually extracts from *Germany — A Winter's Tale* appeared. The grateful poet sent the proofs to Marx.

In *Vorwärts* Marx pursued his battle with Ruge. Issue number 60 carried an article entitled "Critical Marginal Notes," on the King of Prussia and social reform, signed misleadingly "a Prussian" — Ruge was a Saxon and Marx a Prussian citizen; a note stated that "Special reasons prompt me to state that the present article is the first which I have contributed to 'Vorwärts'."[37] It was nevertheless an attempt to define a political position both rejecting Blanquism and setting out its author's purpose: "Every revolution dissolves the old society and to that extent it is social. Every revolution overthrows the old power and to that extent it is political."[38]

His striving for utopia led Marx to the conviction that the "half-dozen laborers"[39] so scorned by Ruge constituted the force from which one day an organized workers' movement would develop. It is typical too that, though his theory visualized a centralized organization — and his theory was the product of polemics — he remained, as far as practical politics were concerned, an observer, not a participant. Engels was the first to tell him, for instance, of the Communist League's political doings and his own activities in London and Switzerland. Marx's own disordered labors enabled him to relate developments to theory, to see that the German proletariat was destined to provide the theorists of a European movement, the British its political economists, and the French its politicians. But he himself could not decide whether to become a theorist, an economist, or a politician.

Marx was still malleable — by people, by supposed intrigue, or by attacks made on him. Through defense against attack he developed his own positions; once he had an enemy "in his sights" he could define his own ideas.

SHOWDOWN WITH BRUNO BAUER

Bruno Bauer's extremely paltry newspaper, the *Literaturzeitung,* of which no one else took any notice, now became such a target. During his few days' stay in Paris with Marx, Engels had read their Berlin ex-ally's ill-humored potpourri with more amusement than irritation. He had had one or two sharp words for the nonsense about antithesis between mind and mass and Bakunin's childish criticism of Proudhon; he wrote a page or two against Bruno Bauer but more in the spirit of a standard after-dinner game following a happy, agreeable evening arguing with Marx than as serious polemics; he was not very interested in the "old woman" from Charlottenburg.

Marx, however, went full tilt at this windmill with malice and ferocity. On returning to Barmen, Engels found to his astonishment that his newfound friend was not working regularly on his major politicoeconomic treatise at all but for months past had been laboring at some disquisition several hundred pages long; it seemed like evasive action. Engels wrote: "Do ensure that the material you have assembled is loosed upon the world soon. It is damned well high time . . . so work hard and get into print quickly."[40] "Do your best to get finished; set yourself a time even though you may be dissatisfied with many things; ensure that you are in print soon."[41] And so it was to go on intermittently for decades.

Meanwhile Marx plodded on — and produced a mammoth treatise which was generally greeted with puzzled astonishment. Engels was taken aback by its size (twenty folios) and by the fact that Marx wished Engels's name to appear as co-author although he had contributed practically nothing, one and a half sheets at most.[42] This "great thing" seemed to him out of proportion;

lofty contempt was all that he thought necessary. Nevertheless he found a publisher, J. Rütten, who made an advance of 1,000 francs. Georg Jung found its "enumeration of trivialities horribly wearisome";[43] Ruge referred to "odious, vulgar sludge"[44] and made fun of "the simpleton Engels for whom Bruno Bauer was the oracle a few months ago" and who had now changed and become one of Bauer's dunces.[45] Even the selected publisher (Ruge had forbidden his Swiss partner Fröbel to publish further books by Marx)[46] wrote from Frankfurt that the book was too closely connected with another publication, the *Allgemeine Literaturzeitung,* that to many of the public it would not seem to stand on its own feet, and that it was "without absorbing interest."[47] Hardly any notice was taken of the "great thing," *The Holy Family or Critique of Critical Criticism.* In this book Marx jotted down haphazard his thoughts on politics and economics instead of systematizing them. Valuable passages on freedom and bourgeois privileges, private property, and the proletariat were buried rather than standing out clearly from their context. The lack of uniformity in *The Holy Family* reflects the lack of uniformity, one might almost say the jumble, of idealistic humanist ideas with which Marx had to wrestle, the "theoretical twaddle"[48] as Engels called it.

The year 1840 alone, however, had yielded a rich harvest of books with idealistic themes. Pierre-Joseph Proudhon, son of a bankrupt brewer, had answered the question in his own title *Qu'est-ce que la Propriété?* (What Is Property?) with "Property is stealing"; Louis Blanc, son of an impoverished ex-millionaire, produced his *Organisation du Travail,* intended to improve the lot of all men; Etienne Cabet, former Governor of Corsica, published his idyllic *Voyage en Icarie* picturing a distant fairyland of happiness and pleasure which Marx had ridiculed in the *Deutsch-Französische Jahrbücher;* in his articles published in *Vorwärts* Moses Hess was giving a preview of his *Europäische Triarchie.*

However, such idealism had been anticipated by others. Charles Fourier, who had squandered his father's legacy on the stock exchange, divided mankind into platoons each of 810 men and women, this being the number of different types of character; collective capital, collective ownership of land, and a collective "platoon palace" for each unit, he said, would solve mankind's problems. Then again Count Saint-Simon wanted "a new Christianity." In his *New Moral World* and *New View of Society* Robert Owen, the fabulously rich textile manufacturer, saw the formation of village and factory communities as the panacea. Owen — he was the first to use the word "communist," in 1827 — did more than all the others to practice what he preached; he sacrificed his vast fortune to form model village and factory communities in England and America.

Marx's contact with these ideas was also the start of his rejection of them, just as his association with people almost invariably carried with it the germ of a breach and a quarrel. He poured scorn on Bruno Bauer's concept of the French Revolution as a pure battle of ideas for liberty and equality; for him ideas were not a means of changing world conditions. They did, however, provide an opportunity of changing ideas about previous world conditions; this heralded his concept, soon to be set out in his "Theses on Feuerbach," of practical action, the use of actual force, as a possibility for putting ideas into practice. It is significant that the same notebook in which Marx wrote these famous "Theses," never published in his lifetime, also contained notes for a planned book on "The Origins of the Bourgeois State — History of the French Revolution."

REBUFF FOR PIERRE-JOSEPH PROUDHON

The major dispute, however, was with Proudhon. During the winter and spring of 1844 he was in Paris, living an extraordinary life of anarchist revolutionary activity, pursuit of fresh theories, and bohemianism. He stayed in bed till midday, lunch was at 6 P.M., and then he would sit in some café till three in the morning. An informer's report gives a whole list of German-named cafés as haunts of suspects — Café Scherger, Café Gaissler, Café Schiever, Restaurant Schreiber.[49] Börnstein, editor of *Vorwärts,* describes Bakunin's room, furnished with a camp bed, a trunk, and tin mugs; whole nights were spent there in smoking and in animated discussion.[50] Proudhon was attracted by this debauched libertinism in the Rue de Bourgogne; he became friendly with Bakunin and listened to him discoursing on Hegel or to Reichel playing his variations on Beethoven. Visitors often left early, bored with the interminable arguments on phenomenology. Karl Vogt describes an attempt to take Reichel for a morning walk in the Jardin des Plantes after one of these wild nights; Proudhon and Bakunin were still sitting in the same chairs in broad daylight, motionless in front of a dead fire, still involved in the same argument.

Young Marx belonged to this circle, as he had to the Doctors' Club in Berlin. Decades later he recalled the long nocturnal arguments during which he had "infected him [Proudhon], to his great injury, with Hegelianism which, owing to his lack of German, he could not study properly."[51] Marx himself both spoke and wrote French well; he even liked playing with words and making puns in French, as for instance: *"Napoleon le premier a eu génie — Napoleon le troisième a Eugénie"* (Napoleon I had genius — Napoleon III had Eugénie).[52]

Proudhon occasionally mentioned a number of Germans who admired his work but this particular young German does not seem to have made any special impression on him; the name Karl Marx does not figure either in his diary or his letters. In any case the great man was used to being admired; with complete self-assurance he refers to his own works as "incredible things such as the world of thinkers has never before produced."[53]

Marx's main criticism was that Proudhon's ideas were illogical. He did rate Proudhon as one of the best of French socialists[54] and in an article in *Vorwärts* referred to his book on property as "the best product of French socialism."[55] He concentrated, however on the philanthropic rather than militant aspects of Proudhon's thinking. Proudhon had no wish to abolish private property; he wanted to increase small holdings and guarantee enjoyment of this restricted right to property against abuse by the state. Proudhon wanted co-determination, Marx co-ownership. Proudhon wanted to retain capitalism but curb its excesses by popular shareholding; Marx already wanted to abolish capitalism, to change rather than improve class relations. Marx was soon in head-on collision with this "liberalist" concept of "everything for the people, nothing through the people." In Proudhon he saw someone who was doing his best to "defeat French phrase-mongering by phrases."[56] He wrote a voluminous letter in French to Annenkov, the liberal Russian landowner, which gives a preview of his later anti-Proudhon book.[57]

Annenkov, the Russian aristocrat, has given us a picture of the tempestuous young Marx striding down the Paris boulevards with his thick flowing black hair and his coat buttoned up askew, waving his hairy hands to emphasize his arguments and passing lapidary judgments on men and things in his penetrating metallic voice. A sharp biting note ran through everything he said: "It voiced his firm conviction that his mission was to guide people's thoughts, lay down their laws and direct them. Before me stood the embodiment of the democratic dictator."[58]

The guns were now turned on Proudhon. In Marx's eyes Proudhon's attempt to compose their differences made him a declared enemy of any political movement; he "mixed up ideas and things," causing Marx eventually to produce his great pamphlet (also written in French) contemptuously twisting Proudhon's "Philosophy of Poverty" into "Poverty of Philosophy":

M. Proudhon does not give us a false criticism of political economy because he is the possessor of an absurd philosophic theory, but he gives us an absurd philosophic theory because he fails to understand the social situation of today in its *engrenement* [concatenation] — to use a word which, like much else, M. Proudhon has borrowed from Fourier.[59]

This letter was written from the Rue Orléans, Brussels, in the smart Faubourg Namur, for Marx's tortuous life had taken another turn. By the time his book against Proudhon and his anti-Bauer polemics had been published by Rütten in Frankfurt (barely three years earlier Bauer had been supposed to be getting a professorship in Bonn for him), Marx was no longer living in Paris.

What had happened?

An abortive revolver attack on the King of Prussia had been welcomed by *Vorwärts* — actually, the paper had expressed sorrow that a better marksman had not been available. The Prussian government demanded that Guizot's ministry ban the paper. The French minister proposed instead that the staff of the paper be taken to law for incitement to murder, but this idea was not well received in Berlin — a lawsuit with interminable public argument centered round the King of Prussia? Agreement was reached on an expulsion order with which only one of those affected complied. Heine stayed, Bakunin stayed, and Ruge stayed, but Marx went to Brussels — in great distress.

His financial intake in Paris had been adequate. During the bare fourteen months of his stay there he had received 7,000 francs; he had obviously succeeded in supplementing his salary from the *Deutsch-Französische Jahrbücher* by selling his proof copies, bringing in nearly another 2,000 francs; his total receipts, therefore, should have been enough for several years. Moreover he had been far more occupied in studying than "instigating unrest"; his work on *Vorwärts* had been marginal and had attracted little notice; except in a single instance his articles had not even been signed.

But he had attended the meetings of those "half-dozen laborers" ridiculed by Ruge whom the Prussian government clearly found more disturbing than did the French; it had received the following secret police report:

It is a really lamentable situation . . . to see here how a few intriguers are misleading the impoverished German workers, not simply the laborers but also young tradesmen, clerks, etc., and attempting to attract them to communism. Every Sunday the German communists assemble outside the Barrière du Trone in a hall belonging to a wine merchant on the Chaussée; coming from the gate it is the second or third house on the right in the Avenue de Vincennes. Sometimes 30, sometimes 100 or 200 German communists collect here; they have rented the hall. Speeches are made openly advocating regicide, abolition of property, down with the rich, etc.; there is no longer any talk of religion; in short it is the crudest, most abominable nonsense. I could give names of young Germans who are taken there on Sundays by perfectly respectable parents and so perverted. The police must know that so many Germans assemble there every Sunday but they perhaps do not know what the political purpose is. I write you this in all haste to prevent such people as Marx, Hess, Herwegh, A. Weil and Börnstein continuing to lead young people to disaster.[60]

At any rate a police commissaire appeared at the door of the Marx house and produced an expulsion order; Karl Marx had to leave Paris within twenty-four hours! The personal description furnished "as a measure of assistance" by police headquarters in Berlin read: "22 years of age. 5 ft. 2 ins. tall. Straight forehead. Brown eyes. Oval face. Light-colored skin. Thick nose. Average mouth. Round chin."[61]

Jenny Marx was allowed a little more time

which I used to sell my furniture and part of my linen. It went at a knock-down price but I had to have money for the journey. The Herweghs took me in for two days. Then early in February, though I was sick and it was bitterly cold, I followed Karl to Brussels. We took lodgings in the "Bois Sauvage" where I first made the acquaintance of Heinzen and Freiligrath. In May we moved into a small house in the Rue de l'Alliance, Faubourg St. Louvain, which we rented from Dr Breuer.[62]

At first everything in Paris was at sixes and sevens: Bakunin visited the Herweghs and made dramatic rhetorical speeches as usual; Ewerbeck complained about Bürgers; Herwegh played with the child; Heine rushed off to the office of Ledru-Rollin, the politician, who promised to bring the whole matter up in the Chamber. Marx's last depressed letter, written on February 1, 1845, the very day he went to Brussels, was addressed to Heine: "Of all the people I leave behind here, I find the saddest thing is my leave-taking of Heine. I would like to pack you in my luggage."[63] In the very same letter, however, he is indefatigably discussing plans for the future — a newspaper of course. Leske, the publisher, was to produce a quarterly periodical: "I, Engels, Hess, Herwegh, Jung, etc. are working on it together."

These very plans made Marx an object of suspicion from the moment he arrived in Brussels.

·CHAPTER THREE·

STOP-OFF
IN BRUSSELS

LEADER OF THE PROLETARIAT AS
RESPECTABLE PHILOSOPHER

Immediately on arrival in Brussels on February 2, 1845, Marx addressed a missive to King Leopold I in which he "respectfully takes the liberty of humbly requesting Your Majesty to grant him permission to establish residence in Belgium — Your Majesty's most humble and obedient servant. . . ."[1] He was not destined to "serve" either humbly or obediently but first he had to surmount a number of embarrassing obstacles. Having been expelled from Paris, he was an object of suspicion to the Belgian authorities; an agent's report of February 14 imputed to him precisely the nefarious purpose that he had mentioned to Heine — that he proposed to publish a newspaper. The Minister of Justice warned police headquarters to keep watch on this "dangerous democrat and communist." The Chief of Police wrote to the Burgomaster of Brussels asking whether it could be established that Marx proposed to publish *Vorwärts* in Belgium. On March 3 the Head of the Police in Aachen asked the same Burgomaster whether is was correct that Marx (with Herwegh, Ruge and others) proposed to travel to Prussia. Marx was in the toils of a political Interpol.

Marx did not receive his residence permit until March 22, after giving an assurance in writing to the Administration de la Sûreté Publique that he would be working exclusively on philosophical matters — a complete farce given Marx's wide interpretation of the word "philosophy."[2] He lent verisimilitude to this promise by producing his contract with Leske, the publisher, but the Chief of Police nevertheless asked the Burgomaster to report immediately should the delinquent prove to have broken his word. The Belgians had no wish to annoy the Prussian government. Also in the same year Marx ceased to be a member of the Royal Prussian Subjects' Association; an exchange of letters with Görtz, the Burgomaster of Trier, gives the astonishing reason — Marx proposed to emigrate to America shortly.[3] Nowhere else is there any indication that he seriously intended to do this. When these letters were written Marx was heavily involved in all sorts of activities.

He also had to give some thought to his family; it now numbered four souls and his wife was two months pregnant. They had become accustomed to a middle-class standard of living, so a house was rented forthwith and in May they moved into another more comfortable one. Engels had collected money in Barmen and Elberfeld; he had also made over to Marx the fee for his book *The Condition of the Working Class in England,* published in May. Jung sent 750 francs from Köln (during his time in Paris Marx had received over 4,000 francs from Köln). In his three years in Brussels, during which time his family grew to a total of seven, Marx did not earn a single penny apart from an advance of 1,500 francs from Leske for a book that was never written. His first extant letter to Engels is a cry for financial assistance; it refers to money troubles and losses on the exchange and is almost an order: ". . . since the matter is very pressing, I expect you not to lose a single day in putting things to rights *and informing me.*"[4] He was the only one of the émigrés who made no effort to earn; all the others had taken up some profession. He was completely absorbed in his own business, which once again was threefold: an enormous quantity of polemics, very intensive philosophic and economic study, and party organization.

Initially polemics took up all his time. Bruno Bauer had been "dealt with"; his war of words with Proudhon had been terminated by the battle-cry borrowed from George Sand: "Struggle or death; bloody war or nothing. There is the inexorable question."[5] (Despite this Proudhon had by no means been "annihilated"; in the Latin countries he was in fact more celebrated and influential than ever.) Now, with exaggerated sarcasm, came the assault on the whole post-Hegelian philosophy — Feuerbach, Stirner, Bauer. Marx's *German Ideology* consigned to the depths everything to do with "German socialism" and its various prophets. Here were "two arrogant young men"[6] reveling in battle — they had discovered the fundamental law of life and history; anything which did not accord with it had no right to exist. The book is stupefying in its didactic inflexibility and censorious severity, best described by slightly adapting George Bernard Shaw's comment on the Jews: polemicists are like all other men only a little more so.

Early in April 1845 Engels moved to Brussels; together they concocted an ambitious plan for a "History of Socialism and Communism in France and England in the 18th Century," but it was turned down by Leske, the publisher, who was now suspicious. Marx had presented his ally with an "already fully developed materialist theory of history in its main features,"[7] so they amused themselves with these small-scale intellectual battles, playing the part of executioner. The spiteful tone of this shapeless pamphlet is reminiscent of the deadly turns of phrase in Shakespeare's verbal duels where ambiguous phrases are suggestive of the most ludicrous implications, or the incomprehensible and unsavory joke, for instance, which indicates on reflection what

Marlowe or Jones, Fletcher or Beaumont thought on a certain subject. Franz Mehring considers this crude saber-swiping to be "a still more discursive super-polemic than 'The Holy Family' even in its most arid chapters and the oases in the desert are still more rare, though they are by no means entirely absent, whilst even when trenchant dialectic does show itself, it soon degenerates into hair-splitting and quibbling, some of it of a rather puerile character."[8]

Admittedly it is stated that communism is not a state of affairs to be established as a precondition, an ideal to which reality must adjust itself;[9] the description of the new world, however, reads like a fairy tale: ". . . whereas in communist society, where nobody has one exclusive sphere of activity but each can become accomplished in any branch he wishes, society regulates the general production and thus makes it possible for me to do one thing today and another tomorrow, to hunt in the morning, fish in the afternoon, rear cattle in the evening, criticise after dinner, just as I want without ever becoming hunter, fisherman, shepherd or critic."[10]

The manuscript, two fat octavo folders containing over five hundred pages, never reached the printer and was consigned to the "gnawing criticism of the mice."[11]

Not until 1888, five years after Marx's death, did Engels publish the eleven "Theses on Feuerbach," dismissed by Mehring as "aphorisms"; they had been found in a notebook and clearly represented the essence of all Marx's pre-1848 theorizing; they were evidently a preliminary study for the *Communist Manifesto*. These two "Commandments" are undoubtedly the most important written material to emerge from the Brussels period.

After Feuerbach's first article, *"Zur Kritik der positiven Philosophie"* (A Criticism of positive Philosophy) had been published (partially censored) in Ruge's *Hallische Jahrbücher* in December 1838, Marx had become a "Feuerbachian"; he and Ruge urged the philosopher to join them on the *Deutsch-Französische Jahrbücher*. A request to contribute an article on Schelling was passed to Feuerbach but he refused, finding Schelling too "peripheral" and the newspaper too "loud."

This was not merely an excuse for procrastination; his reticence was all of a piece with his general hesitancy about putting theory into practice. The central feature of his philosophy, the most striking summary of which is to be found in his *Das Wesen des Christentums* (Essence of Christianity) published in 1841, is his criticism of Hegel and a consequential new picture of mankind. In Hegel's view matter and reality were merely illusory things; Feuerbach wished to bring mind and matter into synthesis and he took matter as his starting point rather than ideas. For him religion was a product of man who was in no way God's creature; instead man had created God to fit *his own* picture. Feuerbach also detected a "dichotomy" in man which he termed egoism, the governing factors of which were neither economic constraints nor class nor politics; if man was to be brought into harmony with himself, he must be harmonized with his species. For man the highest form of being was man, and so he it was who must be brought to reality. Egoism must be overcome by love, love of other men, not of God — "if human nature is the highest nature to man, then practically also the *highest and first law* must be *the love of man to man. Homo homini Deus est.*"[12]

This was indeed materialism, but of a metaphysical kind. Marx's criticism was soon aimed at this particular point: that although Feuerbach considered man in a concrete relationship to his environment, he did so in relation to nature rather than society. For Feuerbach the essence of man was his general human quality; for Marx it was his social qualities. For Feuerbach relationships between men were relationships between an individual and his species; for Marx they were a social activity. Feuerbach said that unity of thought and existence only acquired purpose and reality if it was realized that man was the basis, the subject, of this unity. Having read these theories in Ruge's *Anekdota*, Marx wrote to him in 1843 (a casual reference only, in the letter in which he told Ruge that he was "head over heels in love") that "Feuerbach's aphorisms seem to me incorrect only in one respect, that he refers too much to nature and too little to politics."[13]

It is noteworthy that Marx's relationship to Feuerbach was the only instance throughout his life when he "overcame" another man but retained his respect, even veneration, for him. Marx's career is strewn with the debris of broken or abandoned relationships — with his co-revolutionaries, co-émigrés, or co-communists; hardly one of them remained, Feuerbach, however, he revered, an attitude he never abandoned even though he soon rejected Feuerbach's theories.

In one of his first letters from Paris Marx endeavored to put his own concept before the famous man, then living in poverty:

I am glad to have an opportunity of assuring you of the great respect and — if I may use the word — love, which I feel for you. Your *"Philosophie der Zukunft"* and your *"Wesen des Glaubens"*, in spite of their small size, are certainly of greater weight than the whole of contemporary German literature put together.

In these writings you have provided — I don't know whether intentionally — a philosophical basis for socialism and the Communists have immediately understood them in this way. The unity of man with man, which is based on the real differences between men, the concept of the human species brought down from the heaven of abstraction to the real earth, what is this but the concept of society![14]

From the outset Feuerbach remained as reticent as he had been when he had refused to "direct my substance-starved mind to such an unreal, vain and transitory an apparition as Schelling. . . . I should have no object in view since I present no contrast to him."[15]

The fact that Marx did not publish his "Theses on Feuerbach" is certainly not accidental. They are clearly more than jottings in a notebook; they are thought out and expressed with great precision, a counterbarrage. Even Engels underestimated them when he published them in 1888 in an annex to his book on Feuerbach and referred to them as "notes hurriedly scribbled down . . . absolutely not intended for publication."[16] Marx did not want to hurt Feuerbach's feelings and in fact the "Theses" are written in an advisory tone. The phraseology is terse and striking, referring to "defects":

The chief defect of all hitherto existing materialism — that of Feurerbach included — is that the thing, reality, sensuousness, is conceived only in the form of the object or of contemplation, but not as human sensuous activity, practice, not subjectively. . . .

Feurerbach, not satisfied with abstract thinking, appeals to sensuous contemplation; but he does not conceive sensuousness as practical, human-sensuous activity. . . .

The philosophers have only interpreted the world in various ways; the point, however, is to change it.[17]

This is what Marx wanted to do. The remarkable fact is, however, that while interpreting a changed world in various ways, again and again Marx evaded his postulate of "practice," though here, as in numerous other passages in his writings, he proclaimed it as basic. The name of his "practice" was theory.

Karl Marx was contradictory to the very roots of his being. Letters, the reminiscences of his contemporaries, and documents demonstrate mainly one thing: these contradictions were entirely disconnected ingredients in his nature; they neither compensated nor complemented each other. One of his favorite sayings, for instance, recalled by Paul Lafargue, his son-in-law, was "working for the world"; at the same time, however, he wanted each discipline to be pursued for its own sake and thought that, in conducting scientific research, one should not be concerned with its possible consequences.[18] He rejected science as an egoistic pastime but said that his favorite occupation was "book-worming." This appears as one of his answers to his daughters' "Questionnaire,"[19] which was intended as a party game but which he completed with a lack of humor almost horrifying in its self-importance:

YOUR FAVORITE VIRTUE	Simplicity
YOUR FAVORITE VIRTUE IN MAN	Strength
YOUR FAVORITE VIRTUE IN WOMAN	Weakness
YOUR CHIEF CHARACTERISTIC	Singleness of purpose

YOUR IDEA OF HAPPINESS	To fight
YOUR IDEA OF MISERY	Submission
THE VICE YOU EXCUSE MOST	Gullibility
THE VICE YOU DETEST MOST	Servility
YOUR PET AVERSION	Martin Tupper
YOUR POET	Shakespeare, Aeschylus, Goethe
YOUR PROSE WRITER	Diderot
YOUR HERO	Spartacus, Kepler
YOUR HEROINE	Gretchen
YOUR FAVORITE FLOWER	Daphne
YOUR COLOUR	Red
YOUR FAVORITE NAME	Laura, Jenny
YOUR FAVORITE DISH	Fish
YOUR FAVORITE MAXIM	*Nihil humani a me alienum* [Nothing human is alien to me]
YOUR FAVORITE MOTTO	*De omnibus dubitandum* [Doubt everything]

The charming humor with which Engels answered the same questionnaire is highly characteristic: his idea of happiness was thoroughly unheroic (the bouquet of Chateau Margaux 1848), his chief characteristic was nothing solemn or gallant but an ironical "semi-knowledge of everything," and his heroine simply "too many."[20] Here is the light touch, elegance and humor as against portentous self-importance. Some of the high priests of Marxology such as Ryazanoff have tried to deduce entire philosophies from this party game, a process that Franz Mehring found highly entertaining. One thing is clear, however: Marx's list of answers is ponderous to the point of puerility; here was someone taking himself very seriously. Clearly he affected an attitude of conscience-laden concern on mundane matters, even in the kitchen. On one occasion Marx and his wife were at dinner with friends when the maid dropped a valuable cut-glass dish but fortunately did not cut herself; the hostess's relief at this outweighed any anger over the breakage. The following conversation, which may originate from Eugène Sue, then ensued:

Jenny embraced my mother saying: "And you have no thought for the loss of your dish?" "Oh, well," she replied, "there are lovely irreplaceable things around but people are more important to me than things." "If everyone thought like that, in matters both great and small" Marx said, "then we should achieve what we are striving for."[21]

No wonder the ill-intentioned insinuated that the bust of Jupiter later installed by Marx in his study in London was there to demonstrate that he belonged to the Olympians of mankind. In fact the bust had been given him by his friend Ludwig Kugelmann, who was recognized as an expert gynecologist and was also a correspondent of Virchov and Sammelweiss; he had been intrigued by the resemblance between his friend Marx and this Jupiter by

Otricoli. Wilhelm Blos, one of Marx's comrades-in-arms, found it incredible that anyone could make up rhymes about the proletariat's Zeus such as the following:

Oben dort an dem Orchester
Sass der Sozialisten-Nestor
Marx, bei dessen Namen schon
Jeden guten Bürgersohn
Uberläuft ein Grauen.

[High up there among the gods
The socialist Nestor sits —
Marx, the mention of whose name
Produces shuddering fits
In any honest citizen.][22]

Blos describes Marx as kindly, radiating good humor, tall, slender, dressed with elegance and distinction. Others of his contemporaries, however, paint a very different picture. James Guillaume, the historian of the International, says that his attitude was that of "a ruling sovereign."[23]

The most horrifying picture of Marx is that given by Lieutenant Techow, who fought with him during the 1848 revolution, met him again as an exile in London, and spent a long evening drinking with him. Marx's tongue had been loosened by alcohol, Techow says, but his head was clear and so he talked uninhibitedly; it became evident that all the good in him had been eaten away by the most dangerous personal ambition; he laughed at the fools who parroted his proletarian catechism and had real respect only for aristocrats: "I came away with the impression that the aim of all his endeavors was personal domination, that all his associates were far beneath him, lagging behind him, and that, if they should dare to forget it for a moment, he would put them back in their place with a shameless impudence worthy of a Napoleon."[24]

Such contradictory opinions about him were expressed throughout Marx's life; almost without exception all his contemporaries over a period of decades refer to similar characteristic features. Mazzini, the exiled Italian politician, called him "a destructive spirit whose heart was filled with hatred rather than love of mankind . . . extraordinarily sly, shifty and taciturn. Marx is very jealous of his authority as leader of the Party; against his political rivals and opponents he is vindictive and implacable; he does not rest until he has beaten them down; his overriding characteristic is boundless ambition and thirst for power. Despite the communist egalitarianism which he preaches he is the absolute ruler of his party; admittedly he does everything himself but he is also the only one to give orders and he tolerates no opposition."[25]

His upper-middle-class way of life with his tailor-made suits, eyeglass and choice wines contrasted oddly with his tendency to disappear into his world of books; they lay about in no order, quarto and octavo volumes or pamphlets all higgledy-piggledy, submerging everything else in the house. He would say of them: "They are my slaves and must do as I bid them." "He was at one with his study where the books and papers were as obedient to his will as were his own limbs. . . . To him books were intellectual tools, not luxuries. . . . He had scant respect for their form, their binding, the beauty of paper or printing; he would turn down the corners of pages, underline freely and cover the margins with pencil marks."[26]

One of Marx's favorite sayings, a further indication of the value he placed on any intellectual activity, was Hegel's remark that "even the criminal thought of a scoundrel is grander and more sublime than the wonders of the heavens."[27] Scholastic work and reading were a passion with him, so much so that he often forgot his surroundings, failed to appear for meals, or hardly noticed what he swallowed down in haste. He would generally read into the small hours, even as an old man at least until 2 or 3 A.M. but nevertheless he was always up at eight, when he would drink a cup of black coffee and study the newspapers. He made a break in this long working day either by taking a midday nap on the sofa or going for a walk; frequently, however, he would lie on the sofa and read novels. Fielding, Walter Scott, and Dumas were his favorites, but above all Balzac, of whom he was so fond that he planned to write a major book about him if he should ever finish his economic work. Occasionally Marx would read several novels simultaneously.

GEE-GEE TO THE CHILDREN — DOMESTIC TYRANT —
ROCKY MARRIAGE

The children were barely old enough when he began to read them passages from Homer, the *Nibelungenlied,* and *Don Quixote,* or repeat poetry and scenes from Shakespeare by heart; the youngest daughter, Eleanor, knew scenes from Shakespeare by heart when only six years old.[28] There are many stories of Marx's proverbial love of children — his wife called him "my big child." Even when quite elderly he would allow his grandchildren to use him as a "bus": with a child on the box — in other words, on his shoulders — and Engels and Liebknecht harnessed as "bus horses" he would chase madly through the garden. The children drove their perspiring grandfather along with the international jargon current in the Marx house — *Hü Hot,* go on, *plus vite.* If the "horses" went lame, the coachman's whip descended on Engels and Liebknecht with "You naughty horse, *en avant*" until Marx was exhausted.[29] Normally he would wave beggars sternly away, but begging children could take his last penny from him. When he had already become the dreaded "Head of the International" a ten-year-old youngster once accosted him on the street with "Swop knives." Marx uncomplainingly pulled out his pocket-knife, which had two blades to the boy's one, but the blades of which were very blunt. A prolonged haggle ended with a "fine" of one penny levied on the author of *Capital*.

The family increased in Brussels; a daughter, Laura, was born in 1845 and in 1847 the beloved son Edgar. Here too the family lived on a thoroughly middle-class standard; here too their house was definitely in the "smart quarter," in the Plaine St. Gudule close to the cathedral. Oddly enough, if one visits the house these days no one remembers its famous inhabitant. Such is perhaps the fate of great earthshaking spirits. Louis Fischer, Lenin's English biographer, tells of a visit to the British Museum when he asked an old curator: " 'Do you remember Lenin coming and reading here?' The curator looked puzzled. 'Do you remember a Mr Ulyanov coming in?' 'Of course I remember Mr Ulyanov, a very charming gentleman, short and with a pointed beard. Can you tell me what has become of him?' "[30]

The Marx household was ruled by two women, each of whom was a considerable personality in her own way. Jenny Marx was unusually beautiful and elegant to look at; she radiated regal dignity. She was capable of "running an establishment" even when the silver was in the pawnshop and shopkeepers demanding payment of their bills were on the doorstep. Her husband enjoyed teasing her about her relatives, which she did not like at all. She is said to have gone scarlet with anger when he said one day in front of their guests: "Your brother is so stupid that he's becoming a Prussian Minister again."[31] (Ferdinand von Westphalen was in fact Prussian Minister of the Interior.) The émigrés and associates of Marx who flowed in and out of the house as if it was a dovecote had the highest regard for this woman's "magic."[32] Her charm once led Wolff, who was a connoisseur of women, into temptation and acute embarrassment; one day in Paris he saw a beautiful veiled woman, accosted her, followed her, and circled around her, becoming increasingly daring; the unknown lady took no notice of him and he was very nearsighted; finally, as he told Liebknecht, he realized to his consternation: "The devil take me — it was Frau Marx." "Well, what did she say?" "Nothing. That's what makes it so infernally awkward." "What did you do? Did you beg her pardon?" "The devil take me — I did a bunk."[33]

Jenny's tireless activity was mirrored in Helene Demuth, the maid of all work, the "present" from Jenny's mother in Trier; she was five years younger than Marx, nine years younger than Jenny, and had joined the household at the age of twenty-one. No one could imagine the Marx establishment without "Lenchen"; she was its guardian angel — and a lot more besides. Jenny Marx looked on her as a sort of younger sister or at least an intimate friend. The children loved her like a mother — she was authority, majordomo, and housekeeper all rolled into one. She cooked, baked bread, and cut out dresses, which she and Jenny together then sewed; she would not allow Marx strong smoked fish, mixed pickles, caviar or heavy wine, all of which he liked but which did not agree with him, and he obeyed her without a murmur. In return Lenchen Demuth was totally devoted to the Marx family; no one was allowed to say a word against them, and anyone who became a member of their circle of friends was included as an object of her devotion. Anything Karl Marx did was good. And when he got angry with her over a game of chess — because he was losing — then they did not play chess any more.

From the outset, and even before the wedding, Marx's marriage was subject to exceptional strains and stresses — an engagement lasting seven years, intrigues by relatives, continuous house-moves and restlessness, Marx's obvious aversion even to considering adoption of a profession and the male egoism associated with frequent pregnancies . . . The glorious fairy story of untroubled matrimonial bliss from the altar to the grave certainly does not apply in this case. The reasons are by no means confined to external difficulties such as poverty (Marx was hardly ever really poor) or the miseries of the refugee. One may well wonder whether Marx's love of children, which led him to play "Gee-Gee" and dole out his last penny, was not balanced by sheer unadulterated egoism and — an additional trait that would fit well into this picture — contempt for everything feminine. Marx's correspondence with Friedrich Engels is full of passages indicating a certain expertise in obscenity — "cock" and "toss off," indecent rhymes, sex stories, tales about fit, strong young men being "ridden to death" in twenty-four hours in Russian nunneries[34] — just boys together perhaps. The emotional rubbish about "weakness" as his favorite quality in woman or "Gretchen" as his heroine is balanced by his disappointment when another daughter was born and his jubilation when grandchildren turned out to be boys.[35] There is no doubt at all that Jenny Marx was a wife with experience of terrible want and both physical and mental distress, that she endured periods of blackest misery; her description of the death of their little daughter Franziska is only one example out of many:

At Easter 1852 our little Franziska fell ill with severe bronchitis. For three days she was between life and death. She suffered terribly. When she died we left her lifeless little body in the back room, went into the front room and made our beds on the floor. Our three living children lay down by us and we all wept for the little angel whose livid lifeless body was in the next room. Our beloved child's death occurred at the time of the hardest privations. [There was no money for the child's funeral.] . . . I hurried to a French émigré who lived not far away and used to come and see us. . . . He immediately gave me £2 with the most friendly sympathy. That money was used to pay for the coffin in which my poor child rests in peace. She had no cradle when she came into the world and for a long time was refused a last resting-place. With what heavy hearts we saw her carried to her grave.[36]

It is clear, however, that under these manifold strains the marriage was slowly breaking up, that Jenny herself was at breaking point. A letter sent to Manchester reads like an SOS: "And meanwhile I sit here and go to pieces. Karl, it is now at its worst pitch. . . . I sit here and almost weep my eyes out and can find no help. . . . My head is splitting [?]. For a week I have kept my strength up [?] and now I can no more."[37]

A whole series of remarks by Marx could be listed full of gloomy skepticism, self-torturing lamentation, and self-pity: "I feel pity for my wife. Most of the pressure falls on her and *au fond* she is right. *Il faut que l'industrie soit plus productive que le mariage* [industry must be more productive than marriage]. In spite of everything you remember that by nature I am *peu endurant* [not very patient] and even *quelque peu dur* [somewhat hard] so that from time to time my equanimity disappears."[38]

"It will be the end of my wife"; "My wife is in a dangerous condition"; "My wife has been ill for the last few months"; "My wife's nerves are shattered"; "My wife is suffering more than she has done for months"; "My wife is confined to bed and almost entirely deaf"[39] — so it went on over the years. "For years now my wife has totally lost her good humor — understandable in the circumstances but no more agreeable for that; she plagues the children to death with her complaining, irritability and bad humor, though small children take everything in a more jolly way."[40]

In fact Jenny Marx complained comparatively little; she worked like a maniac for her husband, wrote almost all his correspondence, and transcribed almost all his manuscripts; she was engrossed in his work to the point of exhaustion, identifying herself completely with his ideas and his struggles. He, on the other hand, was soon saying "*beatus ille* who has no family," or, "Privately, I think I lead the most troubled life that can be imagined. Never mind! For those with great aspirations there can be no greater stupidity than to marry. . . ."[41]

He was no longer the merry father of the family playing the warhorse with a laughing little girl on his shoulders;[42] the household was no longer the cheerful home for dogs called Whisky, cats called Sambo, or birds called Calypso.[43] All too many of Marx's letters refer to lamentations at home, clashes in the house,[44] sickening caterwauling,[45] or a "most turbulent family life";[46] all too many remarks by Jenny are recorded registering deep depression, resignation and melancholy, "disappointed hopes," misery, or silent withdrawal into herself.[47] There are undoubtedly blots on the picture of untroubled marital bliss that devout disciples of Marx like to paint. It would even seem that at times Jenny Marx found a "substitute hero" for herself; there is no mistaking her admiration for Gustave Flourens, the ebullient young member of the International and follower of Blanqui who fell fighting for the Paris Commune at the age of thirty-three and who had previously been a frequent visitor to the Marx house. She wrote an obituary[48] phrased in almost fanatical language, referring to him as young, bold, chivalrous, tender, noble, rich, refined and courteous in manner, impulsive, tall and slender, interested in all things human — a knight in shining armor in contrast to her husband?

One of the few long extant letters from Karl Marx to his wife demonstrates the same somewhat curious intensity of emotion that led Jenny to write to Lassalle after Marx's visit to Berlin that on the evening of his return they had "sat up late chattering, telling each other everything, gazing into each other's eyes, happy, laughing, cuddling and kissing."[49] Marx's great letter to his father had been a ritual act of homage concealing the fact that there was a terrible gulf between them, a demonstration of an excess of affection when in fact there was none; similarly his surprising love letter to his wife, written in later life, reads like an avowal of desire but in imagination only. Perhaps, like many intellectual egocentric thoroughbreds, his "I love you" should really be translated into "I want to love you" — a yearning relationship which the presence of the loved one did not satisfy. Marx found his love overwhelming "as soon as you are away from me."

I have a vivid picture of you before my eyes and I carry you in my arms and I kiss you from head to foot and I fall on my knees before you and I groan: "Madame, I love you". . . .

Temporary absence is good since, when you are there, things seem too much the same to be distinguishable. . . . Little habits which become compulsive through proximity, disappear as soon as the eye cannot see the person who constitutes their object. Great passions become little habits through the proximity of their object but through the magical effect of distance they grow and reassume their natural intensity. So it is with my love. I have only to dream that you have been removed from me and I know at once that time has done to my love what sun and rain do to plants — made it grow. As soon as I am away from you my love for you appears as what it is, something gigantic in which is concentrated all the energy of my mind and all the temper of my heart. . . .

Man is made a man again by love, not love for Feuerbachian man, not love for Moleschott's metabolism, not love for the proletariat but love of my darling, in other words of you. . . .[50]

In this letter Marx set out something which one so often misses in his writings, the right of the individual to have his own world, his private anxieties and longings — but as a proposal, an idea, not as an active reality. Even in this letter there is no word of his wife's feelings although at the time she was at the bedside of her dying mother. One thing is indisputable: Karl Marx had the ability simply to deny the existence of facts which did not suit him and conversely to assert that things which he merely *wished* to be so were in fact so. Wilhelm Liebknecht tells a revealing story of a visitor who lit an expensive cigar with relish. Marx sniffed and said: "That smells glorious! A genuine Havana." The visitor then offered him a cigar, but it was one of the nastiest, cheapest brand such as could only be bought in Saint Giles, the most dismal working-class quarter of Brussels' West End. Marx lit it, puffed, savored it, and, rolling his eyes with delight, said that at first he had been suspicious since visitors from Germany usually brought the most appalling weeds with them but "this is really good."[51] All the other visitors nearly split their sides with laughter. Two days later he was told the story but he was not furious at all; he merely insisted that the incident had never taken place, asserting quite firmly that the cigar had been a genuine Havana. No one could dissuade him or in other words persuade him of the truth.

A revolutionary, after all, is not a man who wants to alter the truth but someone who wants to alter what exists. To dispense truth as *he* saw it, to act as the supreme judge, the High Priest, the dictator, in fact — this, in Marx's eyes, accorded with the precepts enunciated in his eleven "Theses on Feuerbach"; for him history's verdict was that, instead of placing different interpretations on the world, the world should be changed, and that *his* mission in life was to put *his* theory into practice. No other theory existed.

THE FIRST COMMUNIST PARTY'S CONFESSION OF FAITH — *The Communist Manifesto*

The Brussels period, culminating and ending with the drafting of the *Communist Manifesto,* was Marx's first period of Party activity. In Paris he had attended meetings of democratic workpeople, had listened to their speeches and written to Feuerbach that they were "remarkably responsive" to his ideas.[52] In his brochure entitled "Herr Vogt" he recalled that: "During my first stay in Paris I made it my business to keep in personal touch with the leaders of the League there and with leaders of most of the secret workers' associations, without, however, joining any of these associations."[53]

These "workers' associations" were in fact craftsmen's leagues. According to the custom of their guild the majority of craftsmen traveled; German tailors, the "central force of the League"[54] as Engels called them, were everywhere; they formed such powerful groups that German became the dominant language in this "line of business," so much so that Engels remembered a Norwegian tailor who had come to France by sea from Drontheim

(Trondheim) and who had hardly learned a word of French in eighteen months but could speak fluent German.[55] The men who forgathered in Paris (and in Switzerland) formed only a small group and they discussed their muddled ideology of love of all men, the dream of harmony and freedom as put forward primarily in the writings of Moses Hess and Wilhelm Weitling. In his "Economic and Philosophic Manuscripts" Marx had laid special emphasis on Hess, the "communist rabbi" whose *21 Bogen aus der Schweiz* had provided a natural forum for Feuerbach. Hess, a tall lean figure with head craning forward on his chicken-neck, had something of the missionary about him; it was he in fact who had "converted" the twenty-two-year-old Engels to socialism in the course of an afternoon. In their *German Ideology*, however, his two pupils had taken issue with his gospel of compassion for the poor.

In 1838 the tailor Wilhelm Weitling became a member of the central agency of the "League of the Just" (originally called "League of the Outlaws"). For years he was one of the leading lights of this first "cell" of a workers' movement; his dream was common ownership of property, which would turn the earth into a paradise, and he published the first important program document, printed in an issue of two thousand copies and entitled *Mankind As It Is and As It Should Be*. An expanded version, hailed by Marx as "an immeasurable and brilliant debut of the German workers,"[56] was entitled *Guarantees of Harmony and Freedom;* its motto, however, showed that it could not possibly accord with Marx's ideas: "We wish to be free as the birds in the sky; we wish to dart through life like them, carefree in joyful flight and sweet harmony!"[57]

This was aimed at people whom Ruge had scornfully referred to as "a half-dozen laborers — impossible that Marx should consider this business as politically important."[58] It matters little whether there were a couple of dozen workers who met secretly in back rooms of taverns in the suburb of Vincennes or whether there were two hundred who backed publication of the periodical *The Outlaws,* as Weitling says there were;[59] the fact remains that there was no question here of a militant organization with a clearly formulated program. There was no one with experience; even in the great cities the target of their hostility, the man to guard against, was the master craftsman who was himself a small man in straitened circumstances and with his own worries. Engels later put this very clearly:

On the one hand the exploiter of these artisans was a small master; on the other hand they all hoped ultimately to become small masters themselves. . . . And I do not believe that there was a single man in the whole League at that time who had ever read a book on political economy. But that mattered little; for the time being "equality," "brotherhood" and "justice" helped them to surmount every theoretical obstacle.[60]

This was, therefore, no organization with any very definite object, still less a party. The "League of Outlaws" was based on the theories of the early proletarian revolutionary Babeuf; it pursued antifeudal aims, in other words a German republic. Politics, social equality, and freedom took their place alongside demands for the civil virtues and popular unity.[61] The "League of the Just" did not go much further; neo-Babouvism, promoted by publication of Babeuf's associate Buonarroti's book, had played a considerable role in these early secret societies in France. The "League of the Just" was one among innumerable other groupings. It was the smallest but it had the strongest international links. Correspondence flowed between its leaders and innumerable local suboffices; a flood of publications, catechisms, articles of faith and creeds were amended in one place, rejected in another, and expanded in a third. According to the statutes of the "League of the Just" dated 1838, it was divided into communes, districts, and people's localities; acceptance into it entailed swearing an oath.

For a man like Karl Marx whose whole working life was devoted to demonstrating that the law of historical evolution could not be interpreted as demanding a change of morality in such matters as envy, self-seeking, or malice, phrases such as "The Dawn of Freedom," "All men are brothers," or "The tyrants will be driven into the shadows" were enough to make his hair stand on end, as can be imagined. The unctuous tone adopted by these lay preachers — "Dear brothers, your work for the good cause gives us much pleasure" — was totally at variance with his ideas of what a circular letter from a workers' organization should be; he equally disliked Weitling addressing him (and Engels) as "My dear young people."[62] Weitling's whole ideology became an increasing abomination to him — as did his idea of the purchase of a colony to which every worker would be moved at the age of fifty[63] and the concept of the bloodless revolution.[64]

Marx was pursuing a vision — or was it an illusion? He wanted to turn a "class as such" into a "class of its own," to make the proletariat conscious of itself — both of its present and its future. He wanted a tight-knit international organization, wanted his "people,"[65] and it was clear that *he* would be the leader of them.

In his "Introduction to the Critique of Hegel's Philosophy of Law" written in late 1843 / early 1844, Marx had pronounced that "The head of this emancipation is philosophy, its heart is the proletariat."[66] These are the words not of the politician, the philosopher, or the scientist but of the Pentateuch, of a prophet; the parallel between his vision of the proletariat's historic mission of salvation and biblical prophecy concerning that of the Children of Israel stands out even in the syntax and metaphor.[67] If the word "proletariat" be replaced by "Israel" and "class" by "people" the resemblance is striking. Eschatology rather than diagnosis of a state of affairs? In fact, as early as 1845 Marx in Brussels was faced with a letter from London which said: "My dear Marx, where are all these English workers whom Engels so adores?"[68]

At this point Marx joined the League in Brussels; he formed a "Communist Correspondence Bureau" and christened his group "Communist Party." It comprised seventeen members, all German. Fourteen of them were bourgeois men of letters, the best known being Ferdinand Freiligrath; two (Karl Wallau and Stephan Born) were compositors in the *Deutsche Brüsseler Zeitung*, which Engels says "we took over";[69] and lastly Weitling was the second senior dignitary — he was summoned to Brussels and the breach with him was not long in coming. Marx was, of course, Head of the Brussels "parish"; Engels "took over" Paris; Schapper was in London.

Much in this "infant's shoes" period of the proletariat is obscure. Documents are hard to come by and are contradictory. Engels himself quotes — sometimes erroneously, moreover — without references or from police reports. It is not clear who derived what authority from whom, which bureau corresponded or competed with which. One thing is clear, however: between the two "Communist League" Congresses and also before them, violent internecine battles took place. Marx gave proof of his political instinct in establishing the principle that his circulars, pamphlets, and hectographed newssheets were distributed simultaneously in translation to all conceivable circles and societies possessing socialist ideas; by this means he reached a far wider reading public than, for instance, the "Londoners," who confined themselves to German-speaking subscribers. Leopold Schwarzschild considers that this was the "real" moment at which the Communist Party was born:

His ideas on socialism had to become international ideas. The movement whose leader he aspired to be must weld together the workers of all countries into one single massive block, uniformly inspired, controlled from a single source. This was the far-reaching plan with which Karl Marx entered the competition of the socialist market. It was the idea of the International.[70]

The first essential was to make a clean sweep of the "sentimental love-dreaming" proclaimed in "corrupt Hegelian German"[71] and this meant a showdown with Weitling. He was now in Brussels, no longer the young journeyman-tailor surprised by his own talents but a "great man" scenting envious rivals and undercover enemies everywhere with almost hypochondriac suspicion. Marx's dealings with him hardly showed the "superhuman forbearance" mentioned by Engels;[72] Annenkov's account highlights the intolerance and malice characteristic of Marx's attacks on all his "comrades," whether the name was Freiligrath, Lassalle, or Bakunin.

The occasion was an evening in Marx's house when they had met to discuss a common plan of action. Weitling appeared, handsome and blond, in a fashionably tailored jacket and with a carefully trimmed little beard; their Russian visitor was astounded, finding him more like a commercial traveler than the clandestine workers' leader he had expected. Marx kept his leonine head bent over his paper and pencil while Engels opened the session with elegance and solemnity.

Engels had not yet finished his speech when Marx raised his head and addressed Weitling direct with the question: "Tell us, Weitling, you who have made such a noise in Germany with your communist preaching and have won over many workers who, as a result, have lost their work and their livelihood, on what grounds do you justify your revolutionary and social activity and on what do you propose to base it in future?" I remember quite well the form of this blunt question because it started a heated discussion in the small circle of those present, though, as will soon be apparent, it did not last long. Weitling apparently wanted to confine the meeting to the commonplace liberal talk. . . . Weitling would probably have gone on talking had not Marx, frowning and angry, interrupted him and started to reply. The burden of his sarcastic comments was that it was mere fraud to incite people without giving them some definite, well thought-out basis for their activity. . . . Weitling's pale cheeks colored and he talked animatedly and freely. His voice trembling with emotion, he began to explain that, in face of these attacks, he, Weitling, was comforted by the memory of the hundreds of letters and declarations of gratitude which he had received from all parts of Germany; perhaps, he went on, his modest preparatory work was of greater value to the common cause than criticism and arm-chair analyses based on doctrines divorced from the world of suffering and the afflicted people. At these last words Marx lost his temper completely and banged his fist on the table so hard that the lamp jingled and swayed; jumping up he shouted: "Ignorance never yet helped anybody!"[73]

Quarrels of this sort were treated with some skepticism in London and Paris. Weitling was internationally respected for many reasons, including his modest way of life — "a piece of board as a writing-desk and now and then a cup of black coffee."[74] Together with Marx and Engels he had recently signed the "Anti-Kriege Circular" dated May 17, 1846, protesting against the "Transformation of communism into love-dreaming" and officially condemning the "childish, pompous, visionary emotionalism"[75] of the "true socialist" Hermann Kriege, editor of the New York German-language newspaper *Der Volks-Tribun*. The sarcasm with which the authors of the circular listed Kriege's thirty-five forms of love may have been justified — and entertaining — as was their condemnation of his "metaphysical fanfares," but the ex cathedra tone adopted roused suspicions among members of the other groups, and it was Weitling who fell into disfavor again as a result. The London Communist Correspondence Bureau, which had developed from the

"League of the Just" under the direction of Schapper and Moll, voiced the suspicion that "you have it in mind to form a sort of learned aristocracy, to look down on the people and rule them from your new throne among the gods."[76] A month later came an even more explicit protest: "Your Brussels proletarian possesses a high degree of this damned intellectual arrogance; this is clear from your attack on Kriege. . . ."[77]

Engels warned against any official severance of relations with the Londoners; he thought that the tiny Brussels group could hardly do battle against an organization of several hundred men that had already attracted the attention of the German press as being anything but an impotent communist association. Obviously, however, there was no question of a common political purpose or agreement on theory. Marx nevertheless set out to weld together all these totally divergent views, philosophies, and concrete ideas; the way he did it testified to his outstanding political ability, fanaticism, and ruthlessness both with himself and those with whom he was directly or indirectly associated. It was an immense tour de force. During the honeymoon weeks in Kreuznach he had worked his way through twenty-four books comprising forty-five volumes and 20,000 pages in all; he had made extracts covering 250 pages. Now, an exile with a wife and young children, he devoted himself day and night to research and political activity. Think of it: here was this man maintaining a correspondence involving hundreds of letters and all this was happening thirty years before the first mass-produced typewriter had been invented, thirty years before the telephone had been invented, to say nothing of express trains, cars, photocopy machines or airplanes. He had no office, no "director's floor," no "personal assistant," no "intercom" such as any editor has today. His "secretary" was Jenny, his wife.

He went to Manchester with Engels. He went to Paris. He went to Holland to borrow money from rich relatives. He dispatched Engels to Paris. He had visitors in dozens — émigrés, revolutionaries, democrats, "true" or not-so-true socialists. He wrote major pamphlets, such as those attacking Proudhon and Bruno Bauer. He wrote regularly in the *Deutsche-Brüsseler-Zeitung*, edited by Adalbert von Bronstedt, who was later discovered to be an agent of the Prussian and Austrian governments (Marx may well have been aware of this but his idea of strategy and tactics allowed him to make pacts with the devil). It was better to do that than do nothing.

He spread the web of his League wider; by 1847 there were "lodges" in Altona, Berlin, Breslau, Hamburg, Köln, Königsberg, Leipzig, Magdeburg, Mainz, Mannheim, Munich, and Stuttgart.[78] He suffered certain setbacks. Proudhon, for example, refused to participate in any of these organizations; instead he warned Marx against falling into the same trap as his fellow-countryman Luther and setting himself up as the apostle of a new religion; the proletariat would take it amiss, he said, if offered nothing but blood to drink. At the same time all efforts to find a publisher for *The German Ideology* failed and Leske, the publisher, was demanding the return of the 1,500-franc advance for "Critique of Political Economy," which Marx had never delivered.

In addition Marx addressed the Brussels "lodges" (they were tiny) on political economy; in one of his more emotional lectures he referred in the same sentence to the 105 members and the "power" which German workers in Brussels now constituted.[79] During a house search on March 1, 1848, a manuscript list of members prepared by Wilhelm Wolff was found in the lodging of Adriens Wageman, the master shoemaker, in the Grande Rue de Baichers; it comprised ninety-one names. Once a week instructional evenings were held — "Comrade Engels gave an address in which he showed that economic crises arose through overproduction and that the stock exchanges were the main breeding grounds of proletarians.[80] On one occasion there was a "social gathering with ladies present." At these meetings Karl Marx held the stage and declaimed his political and economic theories, finding this "public activity immeasurably refreshing,[81] as he wrote in a letter to Herwegh. Reading the texts of these "lectures," however, one has the impression that they were training sessions, "instructional pieces" in Brecht's sense of the word, not so much rehearsals for civil disobedience as exercises in thinking aloud, debates with himself to clarify his mind.

After spending a fortnight's holdiay with Marx in Ostend in August 1846, Engels, who was a bachelor, moved to Paris where he had to "look after" the local lodge. The precise meaning of that we shall soon see. At the end of that year the crisis with the Londoners became more acute; Moll appeared in Brussels in January 1847 armed with full powers to negotiate. Marx and Engels now joined the League as members but their terms were — no other authorities![82] It was a question of victory or defeat, of acceptance or rejection of Marx's theory of "critical communism." The die was by no means cast yet, however; even in September 1847, for instance, Marx was not once given the floor at the Brussels Economic Congress.

Nevertheless all the omens were that victory was on the way. The First League Congress was planned for June 1847 in London. Marx could not go for lack of funds and was represented by his devoted Wilhelm Wolff. Engels, however, appeared as the French delegate; his move to Paris had paid off. His election had been a close thing, only three of the five lodges voting for him and the other two for a specially selected delegate, for which presumption they were expelled from the League. The outcome of the Congress was that the "League of the Just" decided on a complete reorganization and rechristened itself "League of Communists" (the Hamburg lodge among others protesting).[83] Weitling's adherents were expelled and, most important of all, a communist profession of faith was to be prepared for the next congress. In addition, publication of a specifically communist newspaper was planned and a small printing press was purchased as League property. The experimental issue of this paper (there was never any other) was the first to carry the heading, accepted by the Congress, "Proletarians of all countries, unite," which thenceforth is to be found heading the newspapers and periodicals of almost all communist parties. It originated from Friedrich Engels. An imprint destined to become historic now appeared: "Office of the '*Bildungsgesell-schaft für Arbeiter*,' G. E. Burghard, 46 Liverpool Street, Bishopsgate." This was the heading of a thin twenty-three-page brochure, five hundred copies of which appeared a year later. The author's name was not given; it was entitled "Manifesto of the Communist Party."

Recent research has established without doubt[84] that Engels played a far more decisive role in the drafting of the *Communist Manifesto* than has hitherto been thought. He had already played a large part in the drafting of the "Proposal for a Communist Profession of Faith," which had been ratified by the First Congress and had been dispatched all over the world, together with the draft statutes, as an official Congress document; it was distributed from Paris to Altona, from Denmark to New York. This was the most intensive piece of activity that the League had undertaken. The text contained the germ of the *Communist Manifesto.*

Other wordings are also to be found that follow almost verbatim passages in Marx's lectures on "Wage Labor and Capital," but these lectures were not given until six months later in Brussels. The anti-Proudhon pamphlet entitled *The Poverty of Philosophy* did not appear until *after* the First Congress, although some of its ideas are central to the draft program.

When Engels went to Paris from Brussels in October 1847 he found that certain different ideas, produced by Moses Hess, had been introduced into the draft. At the last moment, at a meeting of the district authorities on October 22, he managed to torpedo this draft by Hess, who "was making a devil of a fuss."[85] Even in these early days of the Communist Party these internecine battles were waged "somewhat outside the rules," the "apparat," the "system," being used to force through decisions behind the backs of suspected opponents. Marx and Engels were not merely the founders of the Communist Party; they were also the inventors of the strategy of manipulating a congress and of wily underhand maneuvering. This was their method of operation, the object being to remain on top or be deposed. Man being for them an eschatological notion, a being who did not yet *exist* but only *would exist*,[86] a prophet could perceive the truth and determine the path to the truth. The name of the prophet was "Central Committee," and Marx and Engels were their own first Central Committee, though there was still no Party beneath it:

Quite between ourselves I have played a devilish trick on Mosi. He had actually put through the most absurd revised confession of faith. Last Friday I went through this in the circle . . . and before I had got halfway people announced that they were satisfied. Without any opposition I got myself commissioned to draft a new one which will now be discussed in the circle next Friday and, behind the backs of the communes, sent to London. But of course not a soul must notice this or we shall all be deposed and there will be a deadly row.[87]

During October and November 1847, between the two congresses, Engels drafted the "Principles of Communism"; these were still in catechism form, more precise, more informative, and more generally understandable than that of the later manifesto. But Engels was unsure of himself. Marx clearly had not bothered his head about it; there can be no other explanation for the remarkable sentence in Engels's letter of November 24, 1847: "Think over the confession of faith a bit."[88] A bit! In the same letter Engels suggests that they drop the catechism form and draft a manifesto.

Today it is regarded as certain that, when Marx went to London in December 1847 for the Second Congress of the League, at which he and Engels were commissioned to work out a manifesto for the Communist Party, he had large sections of it ready in his pocket.[89]

This Congress did not pass off without sharp disagreements. Its length alone — at least ten days — testifies to the prolonged debates and the difficulty of keeping the proceedings orderly. Complete harmonious unity was evidently not achieved, for a ukase from London, received in Brussels in January 1848, shows all the old irritability and impatience:

The Central Agency hereby requests the District Agency Brussels to point out to K. Marx that, if the Manifesto of the Communist Party, the drafting of which he undertook at the last Congress, has not reached London by Tuesday 1 February this year, further measures against him will be taken. In the event that K. Marx has not completed the Manifesto the Central Agency demands that the documents made available to him at the Congress be returned forthwith.

IN THE NAME OF AND ON BEHALF OF ETC.
SIGNED: Schapper, Bauer, Moll[90]

Were the Londoners worried lest Marx carry out some extraordinary maneuver designed to turn Brussels into the "headquarters"? Or was he unable to make progress without Engels, who only stopped off in Brussels for a couple of days on his way back to Paris? The delay cannot altogether be explained. Eventually, however, his final draft, a brochure of twenty-three pages, was loosed upon the world; the profits from its first impression amounted to £2/3s/9d; today it has a wider circulation than the Bible. The 9,600 words of the *Communist Manifesto* were destined to have a greater effect than all previous prayers, commandments, and laws, greater than the

Lord's Prayer with its 56 words, than the Ten Commandments with 297, and the American Declaration of Independence with its 300.

The text opens with a threat and ends with a promise: "A spectre is haunting Europe — the spectre of communism. . . . Proletarians have nothing to lose but their chains. They have a world to win." The train of thought in Marx's creed is a logical one; his theses are a summary of earlier pronouncements; there is no new revelation here.[91] The dissolution of personal worth into exchange value, he says, has created a pauperized stratum of society. For this "stratum" to become a class it must acquire insight into historical conditions. Only the communists have this insight; in matters of theory they are ahead of the main mass of the proletariat, they form the "section which pushes forward" and their primary purpose is to abolish private property as being the source of exploitation, misery, and destruction of individuality. This can only be done by revolutionary methods. Socialization of the means of production will produce a new society: "In place of the old bourgeois society, with its classes and class antagonisms, we shall have an association in which the free development of each is the condition for the free development of all."[92]

In so far as plans instead of destructive criticism are concerned, however, the *Manifesto* remains indefinite and ultimately inapplicable. Nowhere is there a definition of what a "class" really is. It is certainly not accidental that in the English version of 1888 Engels added a note to the heading of Section I, "Bourgeois and Proletarians," explaining the meaning of the words.[93] Whenever Marx refers to the scum of the proletariat (which can easily be persuaded to participate in reactionary intrigues) or to bourgeois ideologists ("who have raised themselves to the level of comprehending theoretically the historical movement as a whole"), in other words whenever he is dealing not with mere economic mechanisms but with social (in other words, human) relationships, his theory fails. Was his concept of mankind an inaccurate one?

Perhaps this was what Marx and Engels were referring to when, in the preface to the new edition of 1872, they called the *Manifesto* "in some details antiquated" and said that, as far as practical application was concerned, it would "in many respects be differently worded today."[94] Or was it what Engels meant when he said later that the *Manifesto* had had "absolutely no effect upon the other peoples," although by then it had been translated into French, English, Flemish, Danish, and other languages.[95]

This exposes the very core of an unsolved contradiction, the most delicate problem of the whole Marxist debate even to the present day. First: why must there necessarily be revolution if the theory of the progressive pauperization of the working class under capitalism proves to be incorrect? Franz Mehring voiced cautious skepticism on the question whether it could be genuinely maintained that, with the advance of industry, the working man's living standard inevitably fell: "It is true that the capitalist mode of production has definitely this general tendency, but nevertheless broad sections of the working class have succeeded in securing for themselves, on the basis of capitalist society, an existence which raises them even above the level of existence of some petty-bourgeois strata."[96]

Second, and even more important: what precisely was the revolution to set in motion, what mechanisms should it either retain or abolish if it was not ultimately to remain a prisoner of capitalist methods of production under another name — as a result either of overhasty demolition or takeover? The problem was *not* simply to change production methods; there were far more complex questions. These are not answered by Marx. Rossana Rossanda, a long-standing member of the Italian Communist Party's Central Committee, co-founder of "Il Manifesto," the Italian neo-Marxist group, and co-editor of the newspaper of the same name, put the problem succinctly in December 1972:

The fact that this question is hard to answer stems from an ambiguity in Marx's thinking; he regarded socialist revolution both as the apotheosis and the reversal of capitalist development. . . . The socialist revolution should not be understood as mere transfer of property resulting in more equitable distribution of profits, as something divorced from all other material considerations.[97]

So then: Brezhnev drinking the first bottle of Pepsi Cola from a newly opened factory in the Soviet Union is not the solution. The problem can be reduced to the story of the Russian talking triumphantly to an American: "With you, you see, exploitation of one man by another is still the rule. With us it is precisely the other way round." In modern terms there is a danger that in modern socialist countries the proletariat may become the subject instead of the object of its own exploitation, that by its political hypostasis — Party or State — it is exploiting itself. There remains only the fact that this utopia is purely imaginary.

Of all Marxist historiographers Franz Mehring was the one who referred most frequently to Marx's "Speech at the Hague Congress." In this speech, made twenty-four years after the *Manifesto*, he admitted that in highly industrialized countries like England, Holland, or America these changes could be brought about by peaceful means.[98] This was the speech — made in French and German — with which Marx closed the First International, and the International had made its debut in Brussels. A recantation?

On January 23, 1848, Engels published an article in the *Deutsch-Brusseler-Zeitung* in which he listed the great developments of 1847 — the convocation of the provincial Estates as a "United *Landtag*" (Parliament) (which dictated its terms to the impoverished Friedrich Wilhelm IV), the constitution, the new radical parliament in England, growing unrest in France. The article ended with the prophetic sentence culled from Heine's "Sir Olaf": "The headsman stands in the doorway."

Four weeks later the February revolution broke out in Paris and in the same month the *Communist Manifesto* appeared in London. A further four weeks later revolution broke out in Germany.

·CHAPTER FOUR·

EUROPE'S THRONES TOTTER

ESCORTED COACH TO BARRICADED PARIS

At last. That which Marx had not only prophesied but tried to engineer both by word and deed seemed to be coming to pass: Europe's thrones were tottering. King Louis Philippe was forced to abdicate and flee the country and the (Second) Republic was proclaimed in France. King Leopold, his son-in-law, maneuvered with more circumspection; he offered to abdicate but nevertheless, on February 28, 1848, ordered demonstrating workers to be mowed down and mobilized the police, the military, and the Civil Guard. Wilhelm Wolff was arrested; the name Karl Marx topped a list of foreigners earmarked for expulsion — logically not an entirely unreasonable step in a country fighting for its existence. Marx really had no grounds for his indignation at the outrage perpetrated against him; his activities could hardly be classed as "modest, humble and obedient." Early in February he had received 6,000 francs from his mother as an advance on his inheritance, a sum so astonishing that it led the Belgian police to have his mother questioned through the Trier authorities; their polite assurance that this was merely a contribution for which her son had long been asking for the maintenance of his family did not entirely dispel the suspicion that the money would be used for revolutionary machinations. And this is precisely what happened: not only did Marx move house at once into the Bois Sauvage but he also donated money for arms for German workers (he did not know any Belgian ones). In her memoirs Jenny Marx registers indignation that the government should suspect the Marx household of plotting and conspiracy, but in the previous sentence she writes: "It seemed to the German workers that it was time to look round for weapons. Daggers, revolvers etc. were obtained. Karl gladly provided resources for this purpose since he had just come into property of his own."[1]

Marx had arranged for the powers of the central authorities of the League of Communists in London to be transferred to the Brussels agency, in other words to himself (in March the "seat" of the central authority went with him to Paris — wherever Pope or President resided there was the Vatican or

White House). He had also induced the Association Démocratique in Brussels to demand reinforcement of the regular Civil Guard by a second draft consisting of workers and craftsmen. For a revolutionary this may have been legitimate, but it was certainly not so for a foreigner with a residence permit based on his assurance that he intended to devote himself solely to philosophical studies. With his assistance the Association drafted a congratulatory address to the New French provisional government — with the result that Marx's mail on March 3, 1848, was remarkable. He received two very different letters on that day. The first read:

Good and loyal Marx: The soil of the French Republic is a field of refuge for all friends of liberty. Tyranny exiled you; now free France opens its doors to you . . . to you and to all those who are fighting for the holy cause, the fraternal cause of all the peoples. Every agent of the French government must interpret his mission in this sense. Fraternal Greetings. Ferdinand Flocon, Member of the Provisional Government[2]

The second letter brought him an order from the Belgian King to leave the country within twenty-four hours. And something else as well happened on this March 3, 1848: the *Communist Manifesto* made its first appearance in London in the *Deutsche Londoner Zeitung*.

Events now came thick and fast, not without a touch of farce. About 1 A.M. that same night ten policemen under a commissaire forced their way into Marx's house as he was getting ready to leave for Paris; they searched the house and arrested him. Although he could produce an adequate show of official papers, a residence permit, a deportation order, and the French government's invitation, the reason given was that he had no papers. Frau Marx ran off into the night to arouse "influential people," as she later recorded, but her odyssey was disastrous: on her return she was arrested outside her house, interrogated, and then incarcerated in the Town Hall prison on a charge of vagrancy; she was eventually taken before the examining magistrate under an escort of gendarmes. After two hours "under arrest" she was released, as was her husband a little later. Both extracted maximum publicity from this "scandalous occurrence," giving dramatic accounts of it, Karl Marx in an open letter printed a week later by the Paris *Réforme* and Jenny in her memoirs.[3] Both refer to solitary confinement and dark cells; Jenny Marx also says that she was locked up with prostitutes and subjected both to indecent comment on the part of the gendarmes and to the rigors of the weather. She registers hysterical horror as if she was on the way to Siberia — "it was a hard plank bed. I sank down on the bed . . . an ashen-pale face behind iron bars";[4] similarly Marx voices righteous indignation at this treatment of "a member of the Prussian aristocracy."[5] Seeing that they were under suspicion, supported by fact, of illegal arms trafficking, that they were quickly and correctly examined by a magistrate, and that the whole police action took place within a few hours, all this sounds disproportionately querulous. In any case their accounts are not factual and on numerous points of detail they contradict each other. Jenny refers to two "police sergeants," Karl Marx to ten; he says that he was arrested in the *hotel* and not at home. She says that she was arbitrarily arrested and carried off in a dark street by night after visiting various "influential people"; he refers to *one* visit, to L. Jottrand, President of the "Democratic Society," followed by arrest outside the house. There is, however, one witness whose recollection of these events is quite different — the prison jailer. According to his statement,[6] he was unable to accede to Madame Marx's desire for a cell of her own simply because at that moment several cells had to be opened and shut. He therefore had to put her in a communal cell for a quarter of an hour but immediately thereafter was able to arrange for her to sleep in a two-bed cell; he did not think that the substantial *pourboire* that he received from Madame Marx was an expression of her pain and misery.

Marx and his wife were just able to sell some of their household effects and store their silver and other valuables with friends. They were then taken under police guard to the French frontier, whence they journeyed on to Paris through the revolution-scarred country, by night and in bitter cold.

The long night of the barricades of February 24 had left its mark on the city — windows solidly shuttered with the plaster above them pockmarked by bullets, shops boarded up, overturned buses and carriages, tricolors and red flags everywhere. The words *Palais National* were chalked on the Palais Royal. The Tuileries windows had been blown in — and there Marx's friend Jacques Imbert was now installed as Governor, with Marc Caussidière, a close acquaintance, in the Prefecture of Police.

Marx took up residence near the Place de la Bastille, in a little side street off the Boulevard Beaumarchais. His next address, however, after the family had arrived in mid-March, sounds peculiar — Hôtel Manchester, 1 Rue Gramont. This housed the headquarters of a police district and there is no trace of a hotel. Had his friend Caussidière arranged a cover address for him? Marx plunged into the tumultuous activity of the capital — and purposefully pursued his own plans.

To implement these in the long term, he had brought with him a sort of outline summary entitled "Demands of the Communist Party in Germany"[7] and during the second half of March he reduced this to seventeen points. As before, his demands were radical-democratic rather than socialist; the word socialism does not appear. The document was a watered-down version of the *Communist Manifesto,* still largely unknown in Germany. Point 1 declared "the whole of Germany" to be "a single indivisible republic," the structure of which was set out as follows: nationalization of all means of transport, free access to the courts and free popular education, abolition of feudal taxes, universal military service, separation of church and state, restriction of the right of inheritance. These were demands to which the liberal wing of the Frankfurt National Assembly, soon to be constituted, could well subscribe. The most important demand, nationalization of private banks and issue of a universally valid paper currency, was explicitly explained as being in the interests of the bourgeoisie: "This measure is ultimately essential in order to weld the interests of the conservative bourgeoisie to the government."[8]

These were long-term aims, practicable only for a politician. Marx, the author and theorist, had, however, a more definite plan for the immediate propagation of his ideas: to find shareholders for a newspaper. Almost all his activities during these confused and hectic weeks of March revolved round this plan.

On the day he arrived Marx joined the "Société des droits de l'homme et du citoyen," the largest political organization in Paris, headed by Flocon and Ledru-Rollin; Marx founded the "German Workers Club" (every member was to wear a red armband); Marx constituted Paris as the seat of the central authority of the League; Marx paid out of his own pocket for the printing of a leaflet containing the seventeen "demands"; Marx negotiated with Harney and Jones, who were in Paris, as representatives of the "Fraternal democrats," with Schapper and Moll, Bauer and Wolff, who became co-signatories of the seventeen points, and with Flocon, who offered him funds for a newspaper.

This last Marx refused. He wanted to formulate *his own* aims, and for this purpose he had to be independent, to have "neutral" money. The decision by the "Democratic Association" to form a German legion from the various émigré groups and initiate an armed "invasion" of Germany had already brought him into conflict with the policy of the Provisional Government, of which Ledru-Rollin and Flocon were members. They were relieved at the prospect of thus ridding themselves of potential troublemakers and so placed accommodation at the disposal of the volunteers, soon numbered in thousands, allowed them to train on the Champs-de-Mars, and allocated 50 centimes per man per day for the march to the frontier. Bornstedt and even more Herwegh were in raptures, picturing themselves marching into Germany at the head of their victorious "troops" with colors flying, drums beating, and trumpets blaring. From the outset — before the outbreak of revolution in Germany — Marx bitterly opposed this adventurism. He also realized that the French authorities were only too willing to rid themselves of an "explosive potential" that could well change both the character and purposes of the revolution.

At this point a myth should be exploded or at least a misconception should be corrected: Karl Marx wanted no socialist revolution. He was no *gauchiste*.

The chant of the Paris students in May 1968, *"Imagination au pouvoir,"* would certainly have drawn from him a skeptical chuckle and he would have asked who or what then was now in power, pray. For Marx the "development of socialism from a utopia to a science" lay in distinguishing between the desirable and the possible, between hope and practicality. This is the fundamental rule of Marx's — and Marxists' — political thinking; the positive and negative aspects are closely intertwined. The reason: rational analysis of the existing situation precludes Herwegh-type slap-happy enthusiasm and flag-waving revolutionary marches; *at the same time* it also precludes any spontaneous activity — the masses, after all, are totally ignorant. Only a leader has knowledge, the man with a mission, the Chosen One, the man who can understand all the repercussions. From this follows the pattern of communist organization: it is not a mass party but a cadre party. By virtue of this law of history — a law not handed down by history but extracted by analysis of history — Marx knew when weapons should be distributed and when one should come to terms with the bourgeoisie, Lenin knew when the NEP was indicated and when the kulak was obnoxious, Stalin knew when Ribbentrop's signature was of value, Mao knew when to receive Franz Josef Strauss. It is a policy of single-minded pragmatism, men being disposable according to requirements and any tactics, any pact being permissible. This concept of policy undoubtedly conforms to reality. Is it equally compatible with truth?

Even as a youngster, in his school-leaving essay, Marx had rejected enthusiasm and precipitate action and had opted for examination of alternatives "in cold blood." And this attitude can be traced back to that remarkable ambivalence in values taught by the wise men of Hassidism — "Rabbi Bunam said to his pupils: 'Each of you must have two pockets so that you can reach into one or the other as occasion demands; in the right-hand pocket are the words "the world was created for me" and in the left-hand "I am dust and ashes." ' "[9]

Karl Marx's strategic plan was headed "Proletarian Revolution." An inherent component of the strategy, however, was the possibility of abrupt tactical change at any time. There was still no such thing as the proletariat; it had first to be created and led to consciousness of itself. Moreover tactics changed quickly. When Metternich was chased out of Vienna on March 19, 1848, and revolution broke out in Berlin on March 20, Marx concluded an agreement with Flocon providing money even for individual emissaries whom *he* sent to Germany. The first thousand copies of the *Communist Manifesto* had just arrived from London; he gave them and the revised seventeen demands to his emissaries, thus equipping them for any eventuality.

Marx himself went to Köln, which after all was the third largest Prussian city and where one quarter of the workers were unemployed. He did not, however, join the "Workers Association" which had already been formed there and was regarded by its founder Gottschalk as a sort of successor to the Communist League. Instead he dissolved the League[10] and took a hand in the formation of a "Köln Democratic Association," getting himself elected president; he raised no objection to the dispatch of the petit-bourgeois democrat Franz Raveaux as its representative to the Frankfurt parliament. The showdown with Gottschalk illustrated Marx's concept clearly; Gottschalk was too "left-wing" for him. Marx was as firmly opposed to Gottschalk's refusal to take part in elections for a bourgeois republic as he was to the "Workers' Union's" call for support of Herwegh's volunteers, who by this time were on the run.

HIS OWN PARTY — *The Neue Rheinische Zeitung*

Did Marx think that the "Communist Party's" demands might be detrimental to his own "Party"? For he had meanwhile created one. It was called the *Neue Rheinische Zeitung* (New Rhineland Newspaper). In it, moreover, he was the unfettered ruler and he controlled it with a calculated rigidity such as would be tolerated by no serious political newspaper today, from *Le Monde* to *The Times*. "The editorial constitution was simply the dictatorship of Marx. A big daily paper, which has to be ready at a definite hour, cannot observe a consistent policy with any other constitution."[11]

Marx and Engels had floated shares in this paper in Paris but nobody wanted them. A fishing expedition to Wuppertal did not produce much. Engels wrote in disillusionment that there was nothing to be extracted from his Old Man who had thought the *Kölnische Zeitung* to be simple agitation and would "rather send us 1,000 bullets than 1,000 taler."[12] Various concessions made to bourgeois patrons — acceptance of Heinrich Bürgers into the editorial office, for instance — resulted in renewed attacks from Gottschalk rather than more money; Gottschalk was editing the "Köln Workers Association" paper and was incensed not only at the failure of the newly arrived communists to work on his paper but at the fact that, by paying their printers low wages and banning strikes, they had contrived to create exceptionally favorable conditions for their own paper. The *Rheinische Zeitung*'s suspected nuptials with the financial aristocrats, however, did not in fact produce all that large a wedding gift — of the 30,000 taler required only 13,000 were collected. Half the shareholders took fright after the very first issue, which included Engels's attack on the Frankfurt National Assembly. Marx financed the newspaper out of his own pocket and in a short time it was his legal property.

The first number, dated June 1, 1848, reached the newsstands on the evening of May 31, four weeks before the planned opening date, since current events necessitated some rapid expression of opinion. Mainz was under siege and Camphausen, the Minister, recalled the fugitive Prince of Prussia (the Czar had offered the assistance of his army in reestablishing despotism — something which Marx could not know.)[13] The newspaper heading read impressively:

KARL MARX, EDITOR IN CHIEF: HEINRICH BÜRGERS, ERNST DRONKE, FRIEDRICH ENGELS, GEORG WEERTH, FERDINAND WOLFF, WILHELM WOLFF — EDITORS.

So the paper was two things — a newspaper and a party. In other words it proposed to follow, comment on, and attack day-to-day developments with varying violence and severity. This implies, however, that it was attempting to *bring about* developments. Marx himself clearly regarded this as his function. Engels hit the nail on the head when he lamented that Marx was not and never would be a journalist; he pored over papers, redrafting, polishing, and amending amendments, so thorough that he would never be finished, as if he was dealing not with an article but with the solution of some profound philosophical problem.[14] Marx was not interested in articles but in the solution of a philosophical problem, or rather a political one — a bourgeois revolution. Where to find starting points for the exertion of influence on its motivating forces, for the infiltration of proletarian or socialist elements? To what extent could an undeveloped, unorganized, inarticulate proletariat, at best only dimly conscious of its thralldom,[15] be molded into some sort of system for oppression? If for the present the proletariat could not appear upon the political stage other than as the extreme wing of an established democratic party, that line must be followed both strategically and tactically; it must become "the extreme democratic party." This implied that it must be directed and guided at every step; it must infuse energy into the bourgeois movement so as to drive it into the most extreme positions possible and, if feasible, a little further. Marx had no wish to be either possessor of a little out-of-the-way left-wing paper, a self-sufficient educational backwater, or to be a voice crying in the wilderness. He wanted not to think about politics but to *make* them. This meant that not a word must be said about socialist democracy, not a word about a proletarian republic; the workers must not be mentioned at all. These words are not to be found in the *Neue Rheinische Zeitung* of 1848. The main point in its program was proclaimed by Engels to be the single, indivisible, democratic German republic.[16] For these reasons the paper supported the "Köln Democratic Association" even though it had held aloof from the proletariat's June rising; for these reasons "views based on principle" took a backseat and "Citizen Marx" cast his vote against the "Workers Association" and its attempt to put up its own candidates for parliament; "simple democrats or even liberals were adequate" for opposition to absolutism, feudal rulers, and the existing government.[17]

The fourteen months in Köln — Marx was back in Paris almost a year to the day after the first number of the *Neue Rheinische Zeitung* appeared — were a period of finely balanced dual strategy. They were also a period of tireless activity. Initially Marx had lived in Köln by himself, lodging at 7 Apostelgasse. His family did not arrive until three months later, coming from Trier where they had been awaiting a residence permit. They took up residence in 7 Cecilienstrasse close to the editorial office, the address of which read "At St Agatha, No. 12." Was Marx living near his office or was he working only a couple of tiny alleyways away from his house?

During these weeks and months Marx had little time to spare for his family. Wherever there was a meeting, a committee, or a panel, wherever signatures were being collected for a petition, there the mane of graying hair appeared; he was aged just thirty. He had deliberately chosen Köln not only because he had previously had supporters there but because the tradition of the Code Napoleon was still valid in the city; there were no Prussian courts. Unrestricted freedom of the press was the rule and "we used it to the last drop."[18] Berlin, the *"Residenz"* which he anyway despised, could not hold a candle to this; in Berlin were to be found a timorous but loudmouthed petit bourgeoisie, an even more underdeveloped working class, the aristocracy, the palace scum, the bureaucrats — and Prussian law.[19] Political cases were brought before a professional judge, not a jury. Marx followed Stephan Born's activities in Berlin with natural mistrust — including his report that the League was undiscoverable, dissolved, "everywhere and nowhere."[20] With equally natural mistrust he refused Camphausen's offer to come to Berlin. It was from the most highly developed Prussian province that he wished to push matters on, to promote and help to initiate the "black-red-gold" republic — but to start his real battle only on its soil. He had thought out everything.

Marx proved himself an able politician, a left-wing Metternich, a red Bismarck; he showed caution in his proposals and his actions but singleness of purpose in the aim pursued. As a matter of theory he had turned his back on utopian socialism, love dreams, and the happy brotherhood of mankind, and the change was now put into practice as a matter of pragmatic politics. Marx would not have been averse in principle to the use of weapons, revolt, or terror. His daughter Laura's indignation — years after Marx's death — at Bismarck's insinuation that Cohn-Blind, the assassin, was a pupil of Marx was foolish in the extreme.[21] Admittedly he never either practiced or preached murder, as Laura wrote to Engels in a paroxysm of fury;[22] the use of force in a revolution, however, was to him a matter of course. Weapons, revolt, terror — not *now;* that was the point. Marx's first recommendation of "revolutionary terrorism" as the only method of cutting short the death-throes of the old society appeared in the *Neue Rheinische Zeitung* during the later stages of the 1848 revolution, not during the Paris Commune of 1871.[23]

This is only an apparent contradiction, for this almost ritual chant of radicalism came from Marx only when he had given revolution up for lost — *"après nous le déluge"* carried to its ultimate conclusion.

As a connoisseur of the French scene he realized that even in that country, with its different traditions, the most diverse forces were at work. In the Provisional Government Ledru-Rollin, the left-wing radical Minister of the Interior, sat side by side with Foreign Minister Lamartine, the romantic poet who had saved the tricolor from the assault of the red flag; Louis Blanc, the socialist theorist, whose "National Workshops" — a mixture of kibbutz and nationalized industry — not only ultimately went bankrupt but led to the June revolt and therefore the beginning of the end, sat in cabinet alongside General Cavaignac, the Army Minister who was to crush the June revolt bringing Louis Napoleon to power (5,000 casualties were his entry fee to the office of Minister-President). Somewhat later Marx gave a brilliant analysis of this Hindenburg-like affair in his *Eighteenth Brumaire.* But he had also watched it step by step — and its parallels in Germany. Although, therefore, his hopes and his expectations were pitched no lower, his demands and those of his "Party" were.

The *Neue Rheinische Zeitung* was not alone in finding the German National Assembly, which finally opened in the Paulskirche in Frankfurt on May 18, 1848, to be a mere "talking-shop" and in saying so. Of some 600 deputies, 319 were lawyers or civil servants, 104 were scholars, and 38 were businessmen; there was only one farmer and not a single worker. The President was Freiherr von Gagern, on whose proposal Archduke John of Austria was elected Reich Regent on June 27. Marx was as contemptuous of the Frankfurt Assembly as was the King of Prussia, who maneuvered with remarkable adroitness; he summoned a Prussian National Assembly in Berlin, dispatched it to the provinces, and finally moved in General Wrangel. He, Friedrich Wilhelm IV of Prussia, to whom is attributed the remark that "only soldiers are of use against democrats," ultimately proclaimed — or rather imposed — a constitution and snubbed a delegation from Frankfurt, refusing the offered title of German Kaiser, the crown "of filth and chains."

Marx wrote, made speeches and organized. He went to Berlin and Vienna; for the latter journey, being a "foreigner," he had to obtain the agreement of the "Légation de France à Berlin" before he could get a visa from the Austro-Hungarian Embassy. He held numerous talks in both cities — with leaders of the *democratic* movement. In Berlin he met his old friend Koppen and also

Bakunin. In Vienna, where he stayed a fortnight, he gave lectures on "Wage Labor and Capital," the old subject from the days of the Brussels "Workers Education Association." This was in August. Vienna had been through a period of bloody rioting; the nationality problem was highly explosive. Franz Palacky, the Czech historian, had refused an invitation from the Frankfurt National Assembly which, on Austrian initiative, had had to issue a special declaration for the protection of non-German minorities on May 31. In June Prince Windischgrätz had suppressed the Whitsun revolt by the Czech radicals in Prague. A workers congress assembled in Berlin on August 23, 1848, but Marx did not go to Berlin until August 25. He did little, relying on his ideas gaining ascendancy among the masses and so acquiring material force. The advice that he gave in debate in the "Vienna Democratic Club" was vague; when the question was raised whether a demand for the government's resignation should be forwarded to the Kaiser or the Reichstag, he said that Kaiser or Reichstag were not alternatives; supreme power lay with the people.

Empty phrases once more. "The people" did not know him and he did not know "the people." He visited democratic politicians; he even attended a session of the Prussian National Assembly; he lived in smart hotels; he discussed his politico-economic theories; he took no part in meetings of workers or revolutionary movements — such as those in Berlin, Prague, Vienna, and Dresden. His behavior was impeccable. There could be nothing against him. When street fighting broke out in Frankfurt and there were riots and disturbances in Köln in protest against the armistice of Malmö, the newly installed government of General Pfuël banned the second congress of Rhineland democrats planned for September 25. Seven arrest warrants were issued — against Engels and Wolff, Dronke and Bürgers, Becker, Anneke, and Moll. But none against Karl Marx; he had not spoken at a single public meeting and therefore had made no contribution to the "conspiracy against the established order." The campaign against opposition politicians was in fact no light matter. Ludwig Simon, for instance, the deputy from Trier elected by a large majority to the Frankfurt parliament, was condemned to death by a Prussian military court. When he fled to Switzerland and so escaped execution, a symbolic execution of a dummy was ordered on the market square in Trier; the people of Trier laid wreaths of roses by night on the name board setting out his crimes.

The newspaper had to cease publication until October, the last shareholders having revoked. But not a hair of Marx's head was touched. On his way back from Vienna he made another stay in Berlin in order to collect some 5,000 taler for the *Neue Rheinische Zeitung* and he succeeded in reviving the paper. The board of editors was reinforced by a famous name — Ferdinand Freiligrath. Vladislav Koscielsky, leader of the Polish democratic émigrés, personally contributed 2,000 taler in gratitude to Marx for his and his newspaper's support of the Polish cause.

NOT YET THE DAWN OF DAY FOR THE
SOCIALIST REVOLUTION

Two main threads of the great pattern, two pillars of the entire structure of theory later built up by Marx and Engels, first become clearly visible during this year 1848 — the concept of revolution and the idea of nationality. The two hang closely together.

Marx's revolutionary radicalism, primarily verbal, invariably erupted like a volcano when men were being clubbed down or butchered — a humiliated nation was in his eyes alienated mankind in the plural. The *Neue Rheinische Zeitung* put its faith in terrorism after the suppression of the Vienna rising; Cavaignac was its target after the Paris bloodbath:

> They will ask us whether we have no tears, no sighs, no words of regret for the victims of the people's wrath in the ranks of the National Guard, the Garde Mobile, the Republican Guard and regiments of the Line. The State will look after their widows and orphans, pompous decrees will glorify them, solemn processions will bear their remains to the grave, The official press will declare them immortal, European reaction from east to west will sing their praises.
>
> But the plebeians, tortured by hunger, reviled by the press, abandoned by the doctors, abused as thieves, fire-raisers and galley-slaves by all respectable citizens, their wives and children plunged into limitless misery and the best of their survivors deported overseas — it is the privilege and the right of the democratic press to place a laurel wreath on their lowering brow.[24]

The phraseology of this "*J'accuse*" is hyper-Feuerbach. The political implication is a mustering call — no more but no less either.

This caution, this withdrawal into analysis and reflection, led Marx to apply the brakes to revolutionary fervor rather than incite the masses. This is a thread running through all the articles in the *Neue Rheinische Zeitung;* for instance, he regards it as "the revolutionary right of the masses" by their mere presence to "bring *moral* pressure to bear" on the attitude of constituent assemblies.[25] There is not a single instance of the words "communism" and "communist" being used in the "Organ of Democracy," as the paper was subtitled; it seemed to be obeying a self-imposed ban. Even after his friends had been arrested on September 25, the day before the paper was banned, Marx appeared at the meeting place of the "Kranz" Workers' Association on the Alte Markt and declared that the moment for armed rising had not yet come. He was, in fact, continually having to defend himself against accusations of cowardice, opportunism, or adoption of a rigid and extreme position characteristic of a theorizing "Sun-god," as Gottschalk called him:

For you the misery of the worker, the hunger of the poor has only a scientific doctrinaire interest. . . . You are not affected by what moves the heart of man. . . . Yes, although every day you prune the revolution according to the pattern of accomplished fact, although you have a communist credo, you do not believe in the revolt of the working class . . . you do not even believe in its innate capacity for revolution.[26]

Of course Marx was right when he said that the time was not ripe for revolution; it might well bring to power the opposite of progressive elements among the bourgeoisie. The handful of butchers and carpenters assembled on the Köln marketplace armed with axes was not the advanced guard of a "victorious proletariat." Instead, as Ruge reports, though admittedly bellicose they were entirely democratically minded and in favor of "law and order." One of them said to him: "Suppose revolution's now over, Doctor."[27]

Innumerable and usually deliberate statements by Marx show that he regarded revolution as a process. Moreover Engels, who actually refused even to appear at Party congresses ("Two things which I avoid visiting on principle and only go to on compulsion: congresses and exhibitions . . . the only congress I care for is one with Nim [Helene Demuth] over a bottle of beer from the cool cellar"),[28] even Engels gave an interview to *Le Figaro* two years before his death and evidently thought it sufficiently important to have it published in Lafargue's *Le Socialiste*. In it he says categorically: "But we have no ultimate aim. We are evolutionists; we do not propose to dictate definite laws to mankind. Preconceived notions regarding the detailed organisation of the future society? You won't find a trace of them with us."[29]

Was it as a result of such "defeatist" utterances that the young articled clerk who traveled to Germany, France, and Switzerland in May 1895 to contact Russian émigrés did not go on to London to visit old Engels as might have been expected? His name was Lenin. He and Engels never met. In any case he belonged to a nation hated and despised by Marx and Engels. To Marx, "Russian" was a word of abuse.

In Marx's scheme of things man was the vehicle for all his hopes and the eschatological aspect of the more comprehensive concept "mankind" was a people; it followed, therefore, that nations were potential vehicles for and executors of the "leap forward." Alternatively they were not. Man, family, people, nation formed a logical sequence in Marx's eyes. Consequently a nation could be held responsible like an individual. It could be guilty or innocent, hated or loved. Turks, Irishmen, Frenchmen, Englishmen, Prussians, Russians, or Poles — over the years all were either pungently criticized, condemned, acclaimed, or damned. He dismissed with a contemptuous wave of the hand the "foreign workers" in London such as Kossuth or Mazzini; he burnt incense before the Irish heroes of freedom; he captured and strangled Palmerston in a web of verbal denunciation. Worst of all, however, was invariably — a Russian.

There is no question here of misuse of terms, for instance of the word "Russian" meaning only dignitaries like Czars or Boyars, classes not the people. When Engels returned from Switzerland after inquiring from Marx whether it was safe to do so, saying that he could not stand the no-smoking rule in prison, he wrote in number 194 of the *Neue Rheinische Zeitung,* dated January 13, 1849: "The next world war will sweep away from the earth not only reactionary classes and dynasties but entire reactionary peoples. And that too is progress."[30]

A people as a whole, therefore, could be reactionary and, if such peoples went under, no harm was done. If the word "nation" as used by Marx is understood as a wider synonym for the word "individual," then it becomes clear why, even today, the nationality question remains an unsolved problem in socialist countries. One has only to think of the treatment of Jews in Soviet Russia or the patent imbroglio in present-day Yugoslavia. There is an even more striking example: the sensational breach between Lenin and Stalin. Available evidence, even though only partially published after Khrushchev's speech to the Twentieth Party Congress,[31] shows clearly that it was no mere private disagreement that caused Lenin to include in his will a warning against the uncontrolled power being amassed by Stalin. Admittedly the ostensible reason was the ill-mannered telephone call from Stalin to Lenin's wife Krupskaya, about which she complained to Kamenev, President of the Politburo: ". . . I beg you to protect me from rude interference with my private life and from vile invective and threats."[32] On his deathbed, only four days before his fatal stroke, Lenin dictated a letter to Stalin demanding an apology, failing which he would sever relations with him.

The real reason, however, was a political one — Stalin's nationalities policy which Lenin had helped to initiate but which he now considered totally wrong and dangerous since it jeopardized the autonomy of the Soviet republics in favor of a central Russian authority. Lenin's most important writings during the last years of his life were devoted exclusively to this subject; a section of the dictated notes generally regarded as his political testament opens with the words: "I suppose I have been very remiss with respect to the workers of Russia for not having intervened energetically or decisively enough in the notorious question of autonomisation."[33] Stalin and his friends had brutally suppressed Georgian aspirations toward independence. Lenin's anger with Stalin and his minions was overwhelming; he referred to pan-Russian chauvinism, scoundrels, thugs, a Russian system inherited from

Czarism and covered with only a thin film of Soviet oil. The last article Lenin ever published[34] dealt with this subject; the last notes he dictated to his secretary Lydia Fotieva concerned Stalin's comrades, Georgians condemned to "disappear": "Respected comrades, I am following your case with all my heart. I am shocked by the crudeness of Orjonekidse and the conniving of Stalin and Djerzhinsky."[35]

Copies went to Kamenev and Trotsky whom, in an almost imploring letter written on the previous day, he had asked to bring the matter of the Georgians up in the Central Committee, saying that Stalin could not be trusted. Accordingly, in his famous "political testament" Lenin first recommended Trotsky as the most capable among the political leaders and then urged the removal of Stalin from the post of Secretary-General.

It was all of a piece — brutality and contemptible behavior toward an individual (as it so happened, Lenin's wife) or the intimidation and humiliation of a people. Bad behavior in private affairs is wrong behavior politically.

The two "nationality questions" posed by the authors of the *Neue Rheinische Zeitung* were the Russo-Polish and the Scandinavian. War with Russia and reestablishment of Poland — partitioned between Prussia, Russia, and Austria — was Point 2 in the newspaper's program. Russia, the stronghold of reaction and backbone of the Holy Alliance, would always oppose any revolutionary development in Germany, they maintained, and by revolutionary development they meant progress toward a united nation. $\sqrt{}$ Hegel + Bismarck = Marx? The demand in their program's Point 1 — an indivisible democratic German republic — could not be met without the attainment of Point 2. *Hence* support for Poland. This support was given not so much to Poland as such; it was primarily a call for justice for an oppressed partitioned nation deprived of its identity; it was a means to an end and the end was to weaken Russia. In a series of nine articles published between August 9 and September 7, 1848, the longest ever printed in the *Neue Rheinische Zeitung* (it covers fifty pages in the edition of Marx/Engels works) Engels set out his position on the Polish question. He made no bones about the fact that his viewpoint was a purely pragmatic one, in other words that a democratic Poland was an essential condition for a democratic Germany: "A French historian once said: '*Il y a des peuples nécessaires*' — there exist essential peoples. In the 19th century the Polish people is undoubtedly one of these essential peoples."[36]

Accordingly there are also "nonessential" peoples, possibly in a different century — the Georgians in the twentieth century, perhaps, or the Czechs in 1968?

The newspaper adhered to this concept even more strikingly and unequivocally during the second national conflict of 1848 — the Prusso-Danish war over Schleswig-Holstein. Holstein belonged to the German Confederation but

Schleswig did not. The two duchies were linked in a de facto union, owed allegiance to the Danish crown, but remained independent states. A feeble attempt by the Danish monarchy to turn both territories into integral parts of Denmark was met with energetic resistance; ever since the Zollverein, if not earlier, "sea-girt Schleswig-Holstein stands guard over the customs of Germany" had been almost a national anthem; the peninsula was well placed for maritime traffic and trade. When Prussian troops, quite unjustifiably, invaded, the situation was particularly complicated; the protagonists of the abhorred "Scandinavianism" were the Danish bourgeoisie, the party of the so-called Eider Danes, and in the last analysis they wanted precisely what Marx's prescription called for — increased economic power and national unity in order to initiate a modern constitution and a program of reform. This was opposed by the Duchies that leaned toward Germany in order to retain their feudal privileges and lilliputian dynasties. Surprisingly, however, the *Neue Rheinische Zeitung* was to be found on the side of its fellow-countrymen.

Apparently, therefore, the Danes were not an "essential" nation. The *Neue Rheinische Zeitung*'s remarkable line of argument entirely disregarded something of which historical materialism — and indeed proletarian internationalism — had to take account: that the Danish interest in this matter served a historically progressive purpose. Almost *völkisch* or nationalistic overtones are detectable in the newspaper's views.[37]

As if by a process of osmosis the restorationist trend led to radicalization of the newspaper's attitude. Together with the "Köln Workers Association" and the "Democratic Society," the *Neue Rheinische Zeitung* called a large public meeting on the Frankenplatz in Köln on September 13, 1848. Marx and Engels sat alongside Moll, Schapper, and Wolff in an elected Public Safety Committee. Four days later, on September 17, there took place on a Rhineland meadow in Worringen the mass demonstration at which Marx and Lassalle appeared together. Ten thousand people assembled — farmers and factory workers living in the neighboring villages together with the Düsseldorf Democrats led by Lassalle. Two correspondents of the great American newspaper, the *New York Daily Tribune,* were present — Charles Dana, for whom Marx was later to work, and Albert Brisbane, who described Marx as "a man of some thirty years, solidly built with a fine face and bushy black hair."[38]

This demonstration was a culminating point. The Malmö armistice had been ratified on the previous day. Now the assembly, led by Schapper and with only one dissenting voice, declared itself in favor of the "democratic social republic, the red republic";[39] the red flag flew from the rostrum for the first time. This form of words had not so far been used by the *Neue Rheinische Zeitung*. It had appeared eleven days previously, however, in a correspondent's report from Mucheln; this had said that a public meeting attended by people from Halle, Merseburg, Lützen, and Weissenfels had come out in favor of the "red republic." On September 13 the newspaper had reported that the red flag of the workers was to be seen with increasing frequency alongside the black-red-gold of the democratic movement. Marx's paper now seized upon slogans and demands formulated without its participation and in parallel with it. What such a red republic would look like was not specified. By mid-October the paper had already been in publication again for some days (since issue 114 the editorial staff had been reinforced by Freiligrath, and Wilhelm Wolff was in hiding there, having to creep across a courtyard or a connecting bridge). Marx had suddenly become Chairman of the "Köln Workers Association" and at the end of the month he presided over the general meeting held in Gürzenich. Now the words "revolutionary terror" began to appear; now the paper called for the organization of a volunteers' campaign and collection of weapons to support revolutionary Vienna; now "total revolution" was referred to as the solution. In November, however, Vienna fell; on December 5 the Prussian King dissolved the National Assembly and imposed his own constitution on the country. Marx's words *"La révolution marche"* in a letter to Engels dated November 29[40] sound oddly divorced from reality. Was this the defiance of the utopian concealed beneath radical verbiage?

The tone of Marx's letters to his friend Engels was part political cryptogram from a beleaguered fortress and part a cry for financial assistance from an enterprise facing bankruptcy. Engels meanwhile had spent October amusing himself on a ramble through France, complete with "morally disreputable adventures,"[41] and did not return to Köln till January. The National Assembly had decided to pay no further taxes from November 17 and Marx seized on the decision on the very day it was taken — "from today payment of taxes is high treason; refusal to pay is the first duty of the citizen";[42] during these months the newspaper's most urgent political battle cry was "Pay no taxes." His leading article of November 12, which included this call, eventually led to an order to appear before the Köln court of first instance, which he did on November 14, accompanied by several hundred people. The Köln Public Attorney reported to the Ministry of Justice that the crowd was incensed and, had Marx been arrested, would have been prepared to use force to free him. Marx addressed his sole public speech in Köln to these "helpers" who escorted him to the Eiser Hall on his release. From November 19 the first page of the newspaper invariably carried the title of the article "No more taxes" as a banner headline.

Marx's citizenship position was a complex one and so his encounters with the legal authorities during these months were no longer on the easy footing of the *Rheinische Zeitung* days; at that time he could happily play all sorts of tricks on Dolleschall, the censor. He once heard, for instance, that Dolleschall was anxious to take his daughter, who was of marriageable age, to a particularly grand ball given by the *Oberpräsident;* that evening he failed to produce the obligatory proof copies of the paper. A civil servant must not neglect his duty but neither must he neglect to attend a gala evening given by his superior officer; in increasing agitation the censor accordingly waited until 10 P.M. No proofs. His wife and daughter went on ahead. He sent a message to the printers but no one answered the door. In desperation, therefore, the censor drove to Marx's house some distance away. After much bell-ringing (it was now nearly midnight) Marx's head emerged from a third-floor window: "The proofs," the censor bellowed. "Aren't any," Marx shouted down. "But . . . !" "We're not publishing tomorrow." And with that Marx slammed down the window. Thus fooled, the censor choked with rage but he was more polite thereafter.[43]

Now was neither the time nor place, however, for school-boy political practical joking of this sort. Marx was not a German subject. He had already received a communication dated August 3 and numbered 2678, from the acting Chief of Police addressed to "Herr Dr. Marx, born here"; it was in answer to an application for citizenship made by Marx in April. The Town Clerk of Köln had approved but had forwarded the application for confirmation to the Royal Government. The result was tantamount to a threat of action against him: "Sir, I hereby inform you that, in the light of your circumstances hitherto, the Royal Government has not seen fit to exercise in your favour its authority under para 5 of the law of 31 December 1842 to grant to a foreigner the status of Prussian subject. You will accordingly be regarded as a foreigner as heretofore (paras 15 and 16 of the above-mentioned law)."[44]

Marx protested angrily but fruitlessly to Kühlwetter, the Minister of the Interior, in a document of several pages full of legal niceties. His only identity document was still his French passport made out in obvious haste on March 30, 1848, in the name of Monsieur Charles Marx; it was valid for a year and for a journey "abroad" from Paris to Berlin; the stamp of the "Police Générale du Royaume" was scored through in ink and in manuscript had been added "République française — Liberté, Egalité, Fraternité." Color of eyes and skin were noted but no nationality was given. It was the identity document of a stateless person.

A visit to the Town Clerk by a delegation from the Democratic Association was equally fruitless. The authorities retained their sword of Damocles. As yet they were making no use of it and they tolerated the foreigner within their city walls, but it was clear to all concerned that a time bomb was ticking away.

Had this something to do with Marx's audacity from now on? Did he know that his future did not lie *here?* His two forensic masterpieces, his speeches at the *Neue Rheinische Zeitung* trial on February 7 and 8, 1849,[45] give one to think so. They are straightforward, uncompromisingly honest and so convincing that they earned him applause instead of condemnation and the President of the Court, in the name of the jury, thanked him for his lecture. Marx did not dwell on the details of the case against him and declared haughtily that he was making a sacrifice when he and his friends had on occasions to cross swords in their newspaper with local dignitaries and gendarmes instead of devoting their time to important world events. To the applause of the audience *he* turned into the prosecutor, putting *his* case forward as follows:

Why did the March revolution fail? It reformed only the political summit and left untouched all the foundations of this summit — the old bureaucracy, the old army, the old courts, the old judges born, educated and grown gray in the service of absolutism. The first duty of the press is now to undermine all the foundations of the present political situation.[46]

Friedrich Lessner later recalled how even Marx's opponents were full of admiration as they listened, clearly enjoying the man's intellectual superiority and knowledge.[47] The *Deutsche Londoner Zeitung* reported that on the next day when Marx made an hour-long speech there was an extraordinarily large crowd of people in the courtroom. He emerged from both cases as victor — and a free man. The language he used in public, however, led the fortress commandant of Köln to apply for the expulsion of the man who was "the main source of trouble in the Rhineland."[48] The Minister of the Interior had no objection to expulsion but preferred to leave the timing to the Köln authorities; they wanted if possible to avoid a scandal or perhaps even disturbances.[49]

Developments were now both rapid and contradictory. If studied in detail, moreover, the wildly inflammatory articles or speeches bear the stamp of indecision. An article by Marx dated January 1, 1849, ended with the words "Revolutionary uprising of the French working class, world war — that is the program for the year 1849."[50] Disregarding the prophecy, which was in no way fulfilled, this shows that he was relying on *outside* events to provide the impetus. At the end of his great speech in court he set out with terrifying precision the dual strategy of his revolutionary concept: "Whatever way the new National Assembly may go, the necessary result can only be the complete victory of the counter-revolution or a fresh and successful revolution. Perhaps the victory of the revolution is only possible after a completed counter-revolution."[51]

Marx must have realized that the hypothesis in the last sentence was likely to be the governing factor in his life for the moment. He reacted with even more hectic activity: he negotiated with Moll and Schapper for a reorganization of the League; he rejected the label "communistic"; he resigned from the Democratic Association and approached the Workers Association. Three days earlier the Workers Association had decided to summon a congress of all Workers Associations in the Rhineland and Westphalia; when Marx was suddenly found to have become a member of the six-man committee designated to implement this plan, the organization cracked; many members resigned because the previous leaders had not known what they wanted and seemed to have no prospect of finding out.[52]

Marx split up groups, concluded pacts, maneuvered. His primary purpose, however, was to save his newspaper, which was his property — and not only in the legal sense. It was the sounding board for his ideas and he had built its circulation up to six thousand; even the great *Kölnische Zeitung* only boasted nine thousand subscribers. He printed letters from enraged readers, scornfully labeling them as applause — for instance: "Mr. Editor, Do not rejoice too soon, you off-scouring of all villainy. Our good King will send good-for-nothings back home again. You liar. Our god-blessed King will bear witness against you on the Day of Judgment, you villain mocking at the goodness of God. Do not believe that the majority of people are democrats, for you would be deceiving yourself greatly. . . . A true Prussian."[53]

Marx took no part in the work of the committee to which he had just been elected and which was supposed to organize a nationwide "General Workers Brotherhood." Instead, after thinking of taking the waters for his liver complaint, he traveled to Berlin via Bremen and Hamburg. His purpose was not to organize communist cells; he met only two or three members of the League. He was acting the well-to-do businessman, living in great city mansions and negotiating with potential patrons for his newspaper; they were all without exception democrats. The results were meager, and the paper was ruined. When Marx returned to Köln on May 9, 1849, the final expulsion order soon followed. In March the authorities had been hesitant but now they had no further need to worry about law and order — the King had rejected the constitution, revolts in Baden and the Ruhr area had been suppressed, a week of street fighting had taken place in Dresden (with such diverse "allies" as Richard Wagner and Bakunin now on the run together). In March, when soldiers had aroused Marx one night, he had been able to frighten off the ostensible guardians of the law with a pistol in his dressing-gown pocket[54] and had even been given a ceremonial reception by the Thirty-fourth Infantry Regiment.[55] Now the editorial "fortress," in which weapons were in fact concealed, had to be evacuated.[56] The expulsion order was served on him on May 16. On the same day Jenny Marx once again sold all her furniture. Marx sold the printing press and with the proceeds together with outstanding subscriptions and 300 taler recently collected in Bielefeld settled the most pressing debts and paid the compositors' salaries and the printing bills. He then distributed "travel money" to the other editors, all of whom were also being expelled.

Engels's account of their departure reads as if they were setting off on a beer-drinking evening with the "Rhenania" students association; he describes a withdrawal with arms and baggage, with band playing and flag flying, the flag of the last red issue.[57] Marx's version reads differently. In that famous last red-printed issue of the *Neue Rheinische Zeitung,* which appeared in twenty thousand copies with its first page carrying a poem by Freiligrath, he not only referred to his January prophecy about revolution and world war but nailed to the mast of his sinking flagship the blood-red flag of revolution and terror in all the paper's three hundred issues: "We are ruthless and we ask for no consideration from you. When our turn comes, we shall make no excuses for terrorism."[58]

With Jenny's silver in a borrowed suitcase the family left Köln and went to Frankfurt via Bingen, where Jenny stayed a few days with friends. After an abortive attempt to persuade the left-wing deputies to participate in the revolts in southwest Germany and after the family silver had once more found its way into the pawnshop, Jenny went to her mother with the children. Marx and Engels went on to Karlsruhe and Kaiserslautern. There seemed to be no arena for further activity however. Marx now definitely knew that he could not and would not remain in Germany. He got himself a mandate for Paris from Karl Ludwig Johann d'Ester, member of the Central Committee of the German Democrats, the same political organization on which he had publicly turned his back a month before. During the journey Marx and Engels were arrested by Hessian troops on suspicion of participation in the revolt; they were taken to Darmstadt and then to Frankfurt, where however they were released. The two friends then parted; Engels became adjutant to Willich in the Baden volunteers; Marx obtained a passport in the name of E. Meyen, went back to Bingen for a few days, and on June 3 arrived in Paris where he took lodgings at 45 Rue de Lille Quartier under the name of Ramboz.

The defiant trumpetings of Marx's farewell article sounded credible only to one man — Marx. From Germany came nothing but bad news; refugees such as Weerth, Ewerbeck, Dronke, Seiler, and Wolff were at their wits' end and could see no future; the Hungarian rebellion had been suppressed by Russian troops; Italy was held in check by the French army; in Paris even a peaceful demonstration was dispersed by government troops. "Nevertheless," he wrote to Engels, "a colossal eruption of the revolutionary crater was never more imminent than now in Paris. Details on the subject later. I am in touch with the whole of the revolutionary party and in a few days will have all the revolutionary journals at my disposal."[59]

In fact there was no question of any such thing. When the family rejoined him a month later their first visit was to the pawnshop into which Jenny's last jewelry disappeared. Urgent written requests for money to Freiligrath, Daniels, Engels, Weydemeyer, and Lassalle sound like the last cries of a drowning man. Lassalle lent him 200 taler but was indiscreet enough not to hold his tongue about it, a source of mortal embarrassment to Marx. In spite of this he asked Weydemeyer to approach a lady who had once promised money for his newspaper; could she now make it over to him personally? "Matters are going very well," he wrote to Weydemeyer,[60] adding that the Waterloo of democracy was really a victory. Things were certainly not going well, however, either privately or politically. Efforts to obtain money by reprinting the *Poverty of Philosophy* or an anthology of his articles in the *Neue Rheinische Zeitung* all failed. Revolution simply did not happen — either in France or in Germany; Waterloo *was* Waterloo. What did happen was the next expulsion order."One fine morning," Jenny recalls, "the well-known figure of the police sergeant appeared at our house once more and informed us that 'Karl Marx and his wife had to leave Paris within 24 hours.' "[61] It was proposed to banish Marx to the Department of Morbihan. An open letter in *La Presse* in which he declared that he was in Paris solely for purposes of study obtained him a postponement for an indefinite number of weeks[62] but the order was not canceled. Marx's desperation, disillusionment, fear, and suspicion are clearly visible in the excessive exaggeration with which he lamented to Engels about the place as "the Pontine marshes of Brittany" and the order as "a disguised attempt at murder."[63] In fact this part of Brittany, though admittedly dyed-in-the-wool Catholic backwoods, is scenically beautiful and acceptably healthy.

Two statements are to be found in this same letter — "I am accordingly leaving France" is an angry backward glance sounding like the order to retreat to a beaten army. "So I must go to London and that tomorrow"[64] is the mustering call for fresh reserves — the break, the fresh start, hope for the future.

In late August 1849 Karl Marx arrived in London. Of the numerous friends and foes, associates and opponents whom he met there again the most important was Ferdinand Freiligrath.

CHAPTER FIVE

"NOT AT THE SUMMIT OF THE PARTY"

FERDINAND FREILIGRATH ON THE WAY TO MARX

The astonishing mixture of understanding and contempt for his fellowmen, of *hubris*, disdain, and friendliness which was the hallmark of Marx's character, is particularly well illustrated by his decade-long relationship with Ferdinand Freiligrath.

Freiligrath's debut as a lyric poet was a brilliant one; he was successful and celebrated from the outset. In December 1933, aged twenty-three, he applied to the editor of *Musenalmanach,* the same man who had sent back nineteen-year-old Karl Marx's early poems with "a very insignificant note" which Marx had been forced to swallow with rage and vexation.[1]

Freiligrath had approached this literary pundit, Adelbert von Chamisso, with the utmost respect, offering him "some poetic trivia." More important still, Chamisso turned into a life-long friend of his beloved Freiligrath; *Justizrat* Rauschenbusch, a friend of Freiligrath's, tells of his visits to Chamisso's house when he was invariably greeted by the impatient question "Still nothing from Freiligrath?" — he was a dilatory letter-writer.[2]

Freiligrath had an office job with the cotton and indigo firm of G. P. von Eynern & Sons in Barmen. Here Friedrich Engels, then a seventeen-year-old apprentice, made his acquaintance, or rather saw him but did not meet him. Engels's first published poem, "The Bedouins," clearly shows Freiligrath's influence; nostalgia and antipietism combine to produce a still somewhat indefinite attitude of protest against the mundane Philistine world. Rousseau's antithesis between nature and culture is conceived as a struggle between freedom and servility. Opposition is typified by "Young Germany" and at once Engels is to be found writing: "Freiligrath is turning back to young Germany again, as you must see."[3]

Initially it did not happen. On the contrary, the famous quarrel between Herwegh and Freiligrath drove the latter into the conservative camp instead. The mouthpieces of the young democratic opposition, of "Young Germany," were writers such as Prutz, Dingelstedt, Hoffmann von Fallersleben, and also Herwegh. He had become known through his *Gedichte eines Lebendigen*

(Poems of a Living Soul) published in autumn 1841; their pathos, their resentment of princely power and their as yet indefinite striving toward freedom awoke widespread echoes. In November of that year Freiligrath published in the *Morgenblatt für gebildete Stände* (Morning Paper for Educated Classes) a poem entitled *"Aus Spanien"* (From Spain) in which he stated flatly and unequivocally: "The poet stands upon a higher vantage point than at the summit of the Party."

There was uproar. The sharpest reply came from the *Rheinische Zeitung*, now under the editorship of Karl Marx, in the form of a poem by Herwegh including this: "Party! Party! Who should not take her, for she is still the mother of all victories."[4] In its misconceived confrontation and escalation from trifling disagreement to ideological clash, the quarrel between the two authors is reminiscent of that between Heine and Platen.

Nevertheless, immediately after publication of this poem, Herwegh wrote a letter to Freiligrath:

My dear Freiligrath,
   I should be sorry if you took the poem published in the *Rheinische Zeitung* as a specific attack upon you. . . . I am not and will never be a man of letters or a writer; I simply write what must come out and I have the greatest horror of the art of putting something attractively, no matter what, of the miserable art of writing polite little articles and digging up scandals for criticism. Millions of people can construct verse and write well. That does no good. I want men of one mold, complete men, not men with an eye on the public; I want a direction in which to go and, since our society in general is for ever refusing to take action, I want to take my own direction. If the two of us could pursue a single path linked by a single faith — how glorious, how desirable that would be for me.
   God bless.   YOURS, HERWEGH.[5]

Initially Freiligrath did not answer; in letters to friends[6] he merely expressed surprise at the fanaticism with which Herwegh was trying to win him over to his party, saying that his dictatorial manner amounted almost to a compliment; he referred with respect to Herwegh's energy, saying that any genuine poet must be a man of progress. But, he concluded, was the eternally serene realm of poetry henceforth to be merely an arena for vulgar party clamor? — "I would rather let myself be carved to pieces."[7]

This hardly sounded as if it was mere "comment." No more was the next exchange of civilities. In 1842 Herwegh made a canvassing trip through Prussia as far as Königsberg on behalf of a planned radical newspaper *Deutsche Boten aus der Schweiz* (German News from Switzerland). The journey turned into a triumphal progress and Herwegh received a summons to King Friedrich Wilhelm IV; obviously flattered, he accepted. After his magnificent reception he sent a "private" letter to the King but, through an indiscretion, it was published and appeared in all the newspapers. The King, who was prepared to grant him a private audience but not to be the recipient of public admonitions from some contemporary Marquis Posa, ordered Herwegh out of the country. Freiligrath was not the only one to regard Herwegh's escapade as tomfoolery, as mischievous and injurious to all liberal thought. It was now his turn to send a "letter" to Herwegh, who was downcast anyway; it took the form of a highly polemical poem — a remarkable document. Meanwhile where did Freiligrath stand? Was he turning himself into the advocate of the democracy now betrayed by vanity? Or, as a faithful subject, was he simply taking his revenge on the dead lion? From a letter to his friend Buchner it is clear where he himself thought he stood:

Even his expulsion cannot patch matters up in this case, still less make good the damage. Had it been provoked by his poems or had Herwegh initially been refused entry into Prussia, *eh bien*, that would have been a real commendation for him and could only have increased his popularity. But after this letter, after this miserable display, it is an insult, an insult that can hardly be erased. . . . It is a long time since the good cause has been so compromised by the arrogance and ineptitude of an individual.

In my wrath I have made a poem on the subject. . . .

When one castigates the stupid escapade of a hero of freedom, stupid people can only too easily think that one is aiming at freedom itself.[8]

One of the "stupid people" by whom Freiligrath was anxious not to be misunderstood was Karl Marx. Freiligrath was on the way to Marx.

In polite but unequivocal terms addressed to Minister Eichhorn he refused a state pension granted him by the King from April 1842;[9] he published his *Confession of Faith* which he called "crucial for my life";[10] precisely a year later Schücking, his friend from St. Goar, received another *De Profundis:*

It would overstep the bounds of a letter were I to describe to you now how, since we last saw each other, I have been driven further and further leftwards by study, by reflection and by facts which appear daily before our eyes, how, though not wanting revolution, I have come to realize that reform is essential. . . . I must free myself from this; in the light of my convictions I must adopt the pure unequivocal position for which my honesty yearns. I put that first of everything.[11]

In the preface to his *Confession of Faith* he formally recants:

. . . now at last I have descended from that "higher vantage point" to "the summit of the party." In so doing I must certainly admit that they are right. Firmly and unshakably I align myself with those who brace themselves, brow and breast, against reaction. There is no further life for me without freedom.[12]

The time was now ripe for a personal encounter with Marx. This was no pilgrimage by a convert to his new messiah; instead it was a meeting between two politically committed young authors, both in the throes of a similar phase of development. Freiligrath emphatically refused to admit that any outside influence had led to his conversion; he wished to make clear that only his own irresistible impulses had dictated his graduation to the post of poet of the revolution. His future relationship to Marx, at the time still an unknown émigré in Brussels (on hearing the story a journalist asked Freiligrath: "Excuse me, but who is Marx?"),[13] shows that he did not come to pay homage or expecting to find his messiah. Marx, however, knew only too well who had arrived in Brussels and why he wanted to see him. Heinrich Bürgers tells how the two men came to know each other:

After spending an evening together in Brussels one of the first things Marx said to me in the morning was: "We must go to *Freiligrath* today; he is here and I must make good the injury done him by the *Rheinische Zeitung* at the time when he had not yet come to the summit of the Party; his confession of faith has settled everything." We went that evening and met the young man in the company of his wife and sister-in-law who was on a visit from Weimar; Carl Heinzen, who was also in Brussels, was there too. We soon became good sincere friends.[14]

Freiligrath found Marx "interesting, agreeable and unpretentious"[15] and a friendship began which was destined to pass through numerous peculiar phases. Freiligrath's next effusion — a little book entitled *Ça ira — Sechs Gedichte* (All Will be Well — Six Poems) clearly bore the imprint of Marx's thinking and of Engels's *Condition of the Working Class in England*, which Freiligrath knew about.

Even at this stage, however, there was to be found something which was to be the accompaniment of the two men's friendship and sometimes enmity over the years — Marx's surreptitious derision of Freiligrath, the tone of semi-good-natured, semi-malicious mockery which Marx adopted toward all his contemporaries — behind their backs. Even the word of praise, acceptance of a person or thing has this tinge about it — it is never clear whether he is touching his hat in acknowledgment or tapping his forehead in scorn:

Our friend F [Freiligrath] is the kindest, most unassuming man in private life, who conceals *un esprit très fin et très railleur* [a very subtle and mocking spirit] underneath his genuine simplicity and whose pathos is "genuine" without making him "uncritical" and "superstitious." He is a real revolutionary and an honest man through and through — praise that I would not mete out to so many. Nevertheless a poet, no matter what he may be as a man, requires applause, admiration. I think it lies in the very nature of the species. I am telling you all this merely to call your attention to the fact that, in your correspondence with Freiligrath, you must not forget the difference between a "poet" and a "critic."[16]

They did not see each other in London, where Freiligrath had been since July 1846 as representative of the firm of Huth & Co. A letter of that year to

Karl Buchner, however, leaves no doubt that Freiligrath's subsequent development must be regarded as closely connected with that of Marx and Engels:

I am not a communist, at least not a communist of the ferocious sort, but I am of the opinion that the new doctrine, even if it only introduces a form of transition, is a considerable step forward and that, being rooted in humanity, it will urge, demand and finally bring to a decision more than will a biased political viewpoint. We should free ourselves of illusions about German constitutions and miniconstitutions. Communism will have a future. All its dreams will not be realized but even if, like Columbus, it does not land in India, it will nevertheless discover an America.[17]

On May 1, 1848 Freiligrath left London, with a ceremonial send-off by the émigrés there; he went to Düsseldorf. He had been fired by the revolution and could not stay still. A letter to his ex-fiancée, full of overemotional revolutionary ardor, ends with: "Who knows how soon I shall be shot down, but even that will be beautiful and great." An earlier passage in the letter reads:

The people must be kept on their guard lest their dearly bought rights be curtailed or totally removed from them again by unscrupulous oppressors. This is initially my battle station: using the weapons of the mind, to warn and to rouse over and over again. If, however, through the villainy of our princes, something else should happen, then I can play the man just as well behind a barricade as in a battle against the Russians. The future is pregnant with something serious and great.[18]

Freiligrath took part in innumerable meetings and committees. By June 4 he had become an honorary member of the Köln Workers Association. His first poem published in Marx's Neue Rheinische Zeitung (on June 6, 1848), entitled "Trotzalledem" (Despite All), carries a note "Early June."

A period of very close collaboration now began. Marx published Freiligrath's poems as often as he could — his influence was clearly to be seen in them. The main theme, for instance, of the poem "Die Toten an die Lebendigen" (The Dead to the Living), which appeared in July, about the time that the counterrevolution was taking shape, was the same as that with which Marx had introduced his article "The June Revolution": "The Paris workers have been suppressed by superior force but they have not succumbed to it. They have been defeated but their opponents have been vanquished."[19] The result was explosive. Nine thousand leaflets of it were printed; copies circulated throughout the country; it was recited at meetings. Freiligrath was arrested. He was released five weeks later — and carried home shoulder-high by a jubilant crowd. While he was under arrest the Neue Rheinische Zeitung had also been banned. When it was permitted to reappear a week after Freiligrath's release it carried an editorial notice signed by Karl Marx: "The board of editors remains unchanged. Ferdinand Freiligrath has joined it."[20]

As long as it still existed the newspaper published all Freiligrath's poems. The famous final red-printed number opened with his "Farewell Message from the *Neue Rheinische Zeitung*," a poem the genesis of which is recounted by an eyewitness:

Freiligrath was asked to write a farewell poem by one of his co-editors who visited him at home that evening. At first he did not feel in the mood but his friend continued to press him. They were together all night until at last, about 5 A.M. the poet sat down at his desk and wrote the poem straight down.[21]

REUNION IN THE "DUNG AND GUANO" OF
EXILE IN LONDON

The members of the editorial board scattered all over the place. Marx and Engels went initially to Baden; Wilhelm Wolff went to Switzerland; and Georg Weerth to Belgium. After an abortive trip to Amsterdam in the hope of salvaging 1,000 taler which an unknown lady had made available for the *Neue Rheinische Zeitung* but was now demanding back, Freiligrath remained in Köln for the time being.

He and Marx did not meet again until the London period. Much had changed, however. The refugees of revolution had been chasing over Europe in all directions; no one knew exactly where the others were. Freiligrath thought that Marx was on his way to Texas. Their locations were as uncertain as their means of livelihood. In fact Marx had been deported and pushed over the frontier on May 16, 1849. He fled to Paris. From Paris he was expelled to Morbihan, where on August 23 he wrote to Engels that curious letter which reads like a mixture of SOS, an order, and a business memorandum:

I have a positive prospect of founding a German newspaper in London. Part of the money is already assured. . . . So you must go to London at once . . . and what would you be about in Switzerland where you can do nothing? . . . I am definitely counting on this. You cannot remain in Switzerland. In London we will do business. . . .[22]

Simultaneously Marx wrote, among others, to Freiligrath asking primarily for money — could he discreetly raise 200–300 taler? Similar letters went to Lassalle. Like all émigrés and exiles at all times and places Marx was dreaming of continuing to do what he had just been forced to abandon — to publish a newspaper, the *Neue Rheinische Zeitung–Politisch-ökonomische Revue* (New Rhineland Newspaper–Political and Economic Review). His purpose was to salvage at least the ideas even if material power, the revolution, had already been lost; after the failure of the *Rheinische Zeitung* and the ban on the *Neue Rheinische Zeitung* his object was to create at least some forum of his own, some political and financial platform. And he was also determined to assemble the faithful around him, above all Engels. After his postrevolutionary military adventures as one of Willich's volunteers, Engels had embarked on a peculiarly gay and bucolic expedition on foot up the Rhine valley to Switzerland, taking his fill of the good things and the girls of the Rhineland. Not until October 6 did he take ship from Genoa for London, where he arrived on November 10. The two men plunged into innumerable activities, continually bombarding their only contact in Köln at the time; on occasions Freiligrath answered ill-humoredly: "You send me too many 'jobs' all at once — extracting money, canvassing publishers, translating twenty-six four-line stanzas '*dans les vingt-quatre heures*' — *pas possible*."[23]

In fact the overlapping and competing interests begin to be difficult to disentangle. Politically Marx and Engels by no means always took seriously what they recognized as politically correct — in other words what they primarily wanted to publish. In a mood reminiscent of Engels's gay months from May to November 1849, Marx referred to the revolution in Baden and the Palatinate as a "nonsense."[24]

This "nonsense," however, was precisely what he urged Engels to write about in the planned newspaper: ". . . I am convinced that the thing will go and will bring you in money."[25]

Canvassing booksellers, founding newspapers, placing articles, hunting publishers — these were now the activities pursued by Marx with almost obsessional pertinacity; as we shall see, they were not invariably or exclusively devoted to any great cause. Nevertheless — the *Neue Rheinische Zeitung–Politisch-ökonomische Revue* appeared; six issues were published between March and November 1850 subtitled "Organ of the League of German Communists"; they were edited in London and printed in Hamburg; New York, the third place mentioned on the title page, was an aspiration rather than a reality. London was seething with émigrés. Alexander Herzen, the Russian émigré millionaire, editor of the *Glocke,* friend and patron of Bakunin and Turgenev, whose bizarre way of life has been so vividly described by Malvida von Meysenbug with whom he cohabited, gives in his memoirs *Mein Leben* a picture of the decadence of émigré society, particularly the Germans. There was no common plan, he says; they were united only through hatred and malicious mutual persecution. The atmosphere was poisoned by backbiting, spite, sarcastic gossip about family details, and accusations of criminality. For his part Marx refers in disgust to the "émigré dung and guano of these pretty birds" when writing to Engels from London;[26] he ridicules the "full-scale democracy searching for agreement, which has dissolved into three cliques — the Ruge clique, the Kinkel clique and the indescribable Willich clique."[27] Nevertheless with his jealous mistrust of *all* men around him and with an obvious pleasure in gossip, intrigue, and malice, he played an active part even in the most puerile affairs. Alexander Herzen lamented that "German émigré society differs from the rest in that it is long-winded, boring and quarrelsome. It had no enthusiasts as had the Italians, no hotheads or glib tongues as had the French";[28] this was understandable in the light of the "who-knows-what-about-whom" gossip that was so often the rule — who had V.D., who had refused to shake hands with whom, who was pursuing what lady. Marx's interminable and chaotic letters are full of such spicy, unsavory gossip.[29] Franz Mehring notes sadly: "For the sake of their great purpose they were forced to argue with very small people about very small matters. These small people and small matters cannot be meaningfully described to present-day readers without an inordinate expenditure of time and space."[30]

Everyone realized the danger that such goings-on could be the death of any real work, any genuine activity, that such movement as was taking place would not advance matters by one iota, and that the clock, like that in the Chateau of Versailles, might continue to point to the hour at which the King died; the clock was not being wound up. Herzen continues:

They devote their attention solely to a single event, to the conclusion of a single defined occurrence. They talk about it, think about it and are continually reverting to it. Anyone meeting these same people and these same groups after five or six months or two to three years is horrified; the same quarrels are still going on with the same people involved and the same recriminations; only the wrinkles on their faces, carved by poverty and privation, have increased; coats and dresses are shabbier; there is more grey hair; all of them are older, skinnier and more dismal. . . . But their speeches are still just the same.[31]

The quarreling was not merely concerned with political programs, trends, or aims. The target was "the other fellow" and his "clique."[32]

When Freiligrath reached London in the spring of 1851 (he left Köln fearing that proceedings might be taken against him for the second volume of his *Neuere politische und soziale Gedichte* [Recent Political and Social Poems]), he tumbled straight into these cliques, each of which was regarded by its leader as his property. Marx's first report to Engels was triumphant:

He had hardly arrived when the hooks were out from all the émigré cliques to capture him for some coterie or other — Kinkel's philanthropist friends, Howitt's aesthetes and so forth. To all these efforts he replied bluntly that he belonged to the *Rheinische Zeitung*, had nothing to do with the cosmopolitan cauldron and would only associate with "Dr. Marx and his closest friends."[33]

Kinkel — the first mention of a mortal enemy's name, and in this case that of a somewhat tragicomic figure. He had originally been an orthodox theologian but had turned into an "apostate" by marrying a Catholic divorcée; his "damned speechifying" (as Freiligrath once called it) had drawn him into the extreme left for a time but he had then swung back to the conservative camp. During the campaign over the Reich constitution he had joined Willich's volunteers, the same unit in which Engels and Moll had also fought. At the battle on the Murg he was wounded, taken prisoner, and sentenced to fortress imprisonment for life by court-martial. His sentence and his speech for the defense in Rastatt, extolling the "Hohenzollern Empire" at the time twenty-six of his fellow prisoners were executed, caused further uproar. Issue number 4 of the *Neue Rheinische Zeitung–Politisch-ökonomische Revue* carried a sharp attack on this time-serving speech. On the other hand public opinion was incensed over the King's decision to send Kinkel to hard labor, though in this case he was the victim of a momentous misunderstanding; hard labor would have been better than fortress *imprisonment* which people confused with fortress *arrest*. Fortress imprisonment was about the worst thing that could happen to a prisoner; ten to twenty men were herded together in tiny cells with only a single plank bed, the slightest offense brought a beating, the work was degrading, and the food was bad. The result of the public protest, therefore, was that Kinkel was "saved" from the far easier "hard labor"; ministerial authorities could hardly forbid corporal punishment, still less forced labor. All Germany was again aroused by the "Song of the Spools," which clearly referred to Kinkel, who was working on a spooling-wheel. Kinkel himself wrote to his wife in his own brand of sentimentality and self-conceit: "The factional struggles and the play of fate are approaching madness when the hand which gave the German nation 'Otto der Schutz' now turns the spooling wheel."[34]

Kinkel's fate, a cause célèbre of the postrevolutionary period, was also regarded as an illustration of Friedrich Wilhelm IV's vindictiveness, particularly when it became known that the "All Highest" had decided against appeals from the minister and the prison governor that the "prisoner Kinkel" be permitted to emigrate to America (as he had requested) after the lapse of a year.

A cult formed round Kinkel. Money collections were made among wide circles of the democratic bourgeoisie. Finally, in collusion with Kinkel's wife, Carl Schurz (who later fought in the American Civil War and ended as a Senator and Minister of the Interior of the United States) succeeded in organizing a bold prison break and escape. After months of preparation and the bribing of a warder, Kinkel escaped by night from his cell in Spandau and, via Rostock, reached England where a triumphal reception awaited him.

Kinkel was now one of the most prominent German émigrés in London; everyone knew him. His fame was equal to that of — not Karl Marx, whom no one had received or knew, but of Ferdinand Freiligrath, who had once been carried shoulder-high through the streets of Köln. It was inevitable that the two should meet — that Marx should take great pains to keep Freiligrath away from Kinkel and attach him to his own group, also that he should vilify Kinkel, whose way of life was in fact honest, unobtrusive, and prosaic. Life in Kinkel's house was a model of propriety; Frau Kinkel followed her husband about with never-failing solicitude, giving him a specially woven belt with a revolver when there was fog, adjuring him to take precautions against the wind and even more against a pretty face, and recompensing him for his obedience with a firm belief in his genius. When a friend told her of Heine's death she was merely relieved: she had always been afraid that he would produce some acid epigram about her Gottfried. Some minutes passed before she added: "What a loss for Germany!"[35] Conversation in the Kinkel home might have come straight from a comedy or sentimental novel of the time:

"Best beloved Johanna," he would say in booming unhurried tones, "be so good, my angel, as to pour me another cup of that excellent tea which you make so well."

"It is too heavenly, dearest Gottfried, that it is to your taste. Put a few drops of cream into it for me, my best beloved."[36]

Marx, always on the lookout for a laughingstock, was amused that at the same time London should be buzzing with rumors about infidelities on the part of both the partners in this model ménage. He was less amused by Freiligrath's reconciliation with Kinkel. As early as 1852 Weydemeyer's New York periodical, *Die Revolution,* had published a poem by Freiligrath criticizing Kinkel, or rather a loan he had raised in America. The introduction to the German version in Cotta's *Morgenblatt* probably originated from Marx.[37]

During this initial period of London exile the two friends saw each other frequently; numerous letters are invitations from one or the other to dinner or some other assignation: "Till tomorrow evening then. Because of putting the children to bed, however, my wife will not be ready to leave before 6:30, so don't let yours be impatient if we don't arrive until an hour or an hour and a quarter after that."[38]

"Just Freiligrath" was his nickname in the Marx house — he had been highly amused at being thus referred to by their small son. He would often pay a visit early in the morning and on one occasion caught Frau Marx still dressing; thinking it was a stranger she fled to the next room in her dressing gown but her five-year-old son and heir shouted: "It's just Freiligrath."

Freiligrath was always ready to help, even in domestic matters; when Marx's daughter Laura was ill, for instance, he would arrive with acorn coffee from the German-Christian hostel or with sweets.

He was indefatigable too in caring for refugees and supporting those sentenced at the Köln communist trial.[39] He was a member of various aid committees and signed or drafted appeals or declarations; he was one of the most active members of the League of Communists.

To put his personal finances in order, at the end of July 1852 he joined a firm dealing in Indian silkwear as a salesman at a salary of £200 a year, but in February 1855 he was dismissed for indolence. In June 1856, however, he became manager of the London branch of the Banque Générale Suisse at the respectable annual salary of £300, later increased to £350.

For Marx this was a black period; he was in dire straits, searching for every pound, doing journalistic bread-and-butter work that he despised. His health was giving way due to night work, oversmoking, overindulgence in heavy wines and overseasoned food, leading to loss of appetite; he was immersed in the exiles' quarrels, and his continual attempts to come to grips with his "main business," the book on economics, failed. Finally came the death of his beloved son Edgar, which almost led to a breakdown.

His friend Freiligrath did not leave him in the lurch. He helped primarily on the financial side, in particular by arranging overdrafts or advances for Marx in foreign currency from America. He negotiated with Lassalle on Marx's behalf about publication of the (still nonexistent) book on economics. At times these plans sounded as illusory as Marx's continual promises to complete the book.[40]

FROM SUSPICIOUS SUPERFICIAL RELATIONSHIP TO POLITICAL ANTAGONISM

But Freiligrath was becoming estranged from Marx politically. He had no intention of placing himself under the aegis of some clique or accepting rules of behavior prescribing who he should go about with or what he should write poetry about. *Horribile dictu* — he renewed his acquaintance with the outlawed Kinkel.

Freiligrath was now in his midforties. He had been a revolutionary but was one no longer. Already, in Marx's eyes, he had become "Mr. Philistine Freiligrath," "the snuffling Westphalian big-mouth," "the swine," "a shit."[41] What had happened was this: on November 15, 1858, Johanna Kinkel died as a result of a fall from a window; it was not clear whether it was suicide owing to the collapse of her marriage or an accident. In connection with the somewhat embarrassing overly ceremonial funeral, Freiligrath had published a poem entitled "Nach Johanna Kinkels Begräbnis" (After Johanna Kinkel's Funeral) and in a later collection of his poems had dropped the earlier one *against* Kinkel and retained this one.[42] Marx was furious.

In his perennial suspicion he even went so far as to throw doubt on Freiligrath's currency transactions and to question his loyalty, which was above all suspicion. But he did not break with Freiligrath — because he needed him. As early as 1852 Jenny Marx had admitted to a friend: "Politics and diplomacy demand that there should be no open breach with him; a superficial relationship will be maintained."[43]

Marx now not only besought Engels to take urgent action to detach Freiligrath from "these swine" but he also continued to make use of the "Philistine who has become extraordinarily vulgar in his views";[44] moreover the use made of him was by no means in the interests of the "great cause," as Marxist gospel would have us believe: "Have not yet seen Freiligrath. It is 'distasteful' to me to meet the fellow but I must take a bite at the cherry. This is politic after our mutual assurances of friendship."[45]

For Freiligrath had been guilty of another crime. Without Marx's authorization a great Schiller Festival had been organized and had taken place in London to commemorate Friedrich Schiller's 100th birthday — and this had been done by the friends and dependents of Kinkel! Freiligrath had been specifically warned by Marx not to participate but he had disregarded this advice. Marx intervened with Lassalle who replied somewhat casually: "Perhaps it would have been better had he kept away from the meeting itself but in any case he did well to compose the cantata. It was by far the finest thing that appeared in connection with the celebrations."[46]

Marx — quite wrongly — looked upon the whole ceremony as nothing but humbug. It was not the customary commemorative revel but a left-wing rally that had wide repercussions among the left in general; among the participants in London was the Workers' Educational Association, which Wilhelm Liebknecht had addressed on the previous day at a Robert Blum festival. Parallel demonstrations took place in Paris and Zurich with Schily and Herwegh respectively as guest speakers. Even in Manchester there was a memorial evening at which an address was given by Carl Siebel, a distant relative of Engels who described him as "a thoroughly bad poet."[47] Engels himself later became President of the Schiller Institute in Manchester, which was endowed by Wilhelm Wolff. For Marx, who had nothing to do with it, all this was treachery, and commercialism.

The latter was a curious indictment of a man about whom he was writing at the same time:

Nevertheless I cannot and must not let it come to an *éclat* with the fellow. He procures currency via the *Tribune* and I must always recognize that that is a service he renders (although he has gained credit for *himself* rather than *me* with Bischoffsheim thereby). Otherwise I should be back in the old trouble as far as money from the *Tribune* is concerned.[48]

Freiligrath added yet one more to his spiritual sins, however, as a result of which he became anathema and was consigned to the devil. Not only did he himself choose the company he wished to frequent, not only did he write on occasions and for publications for which *he* wished to write (and refuse others, such as the weekly *Das Volk* with which Marx was connected), but he refused to participate in the savage and to him meaningless émigré intrigues; he remained unconcerned and uninterested in the "Vogt affair" which was of such importance to Marx.

Marx had regaled certain gossip gathered from Karl Blind, a refugee from Baden, to Elard Biscamp, the proprietor of *Das Volk*. The story was that Karl Vogt, now a professor in Geneva, formerly leader of the left in the Frankfurt National Assembly along with Robert Blum and one of the five Reich Regents, had been bribed and was a Bonapartist agent; 30,000 guilders were mentioned, also a secret meeting between Prince Jérôme Napoleon and Jean Jacques Fazy, head of the Geneva cantonal government. Marx loved such tales. Biscamp wrote in *Das Volk* about "Reich Regent turned Reich traitor." Vogt, who was in fact innocent but whose materialist erudition was confined to flashes of intellect such as "the relationship between thoughts and the brain is the same as that between gall and the liver or urine and the kidneys," replied indignantly. His statement about Marx's "band of rascals" whose conspiracies plunged the workers into misery has since become a household word, although Marx had nothing to do with the "band of rascals," which was actually a group of young German émigrés who had both entertained and terrified the citizens of Geneva in 1849 and 1850 by drunkenness and wild escapades. Wilhelm Liebknecht then found in the compositors' room of *Das Volk* galleys of an anonymous leaflet attacking Vogt — they carried Blind's handwriting. He sent the galleys to the *Augsburger Allgemeine Zeitung,* of which he was a correspondent, saying that these came from a respectable German émigré and everything could be proved.

Nothing could be proved, of course. Vogt filed a lawsuit, and Blind contested it. Liebknecht, and therefore indirectly Marx as retailer of the story, were made to look ridiculous. Statements went back and forth; plaintiffs, witnesses, false witnesses, defendants assembled before the Augsburg District Court. Gustav Eduard Kolb, one of the editors of the *Augsburger Allgemeine* even named Freiligrath as a staff member of *Volk* and accuser of Vogt. Both statements were untrue and in deference to the truth Freiligrath issued a short statement denying them. Marx scented defection, betrayal, and, what is more, corruption; Vogt and Fazy did in fact know each other well (both lived in

Geneva) and Freiligrath was dependent on Fazy for his position with the Swiss Bank. A pamphlet by Vogt entitled "My Action against the *Augsburger Allgemeine Zeitung*" now appeared. Marx was wild.

The whole affair was indescribably silly — a totally unjustified mountain out of a molehill. Why should Freiligrath issue a statement attacking Vogt? He did not know the man, he had nothing whatsoever to do with the quarrel, his name had been dragged into it for no good reason. Even Marx himself was not directly involved; he had turned the dispute into his own when, in the last analysis, he too had nothing to do with it. Despite all this, for the sake of the Party — but there was in fact no Party — he wanted on the one hand to suppress the Schiller festivities and Freiligrath's cantata and on the other to extract declarations of solidarity.

Freiligrath refused. A flood of letters poured out of Marx's study, and an intricate machine of intrigue and counterintrigue was set in motion. Representations and counterrepresentations were made; visits and return visits took place; the whole thing was farcical. Engels now plunged into the fray, attacking Freiligrath. He was no better able than Marx to forgive Freiligrath for the fact that just at this moment an adulatory article in praise of Freiligrath had appeared in the *Gartenlaube;* it was written by Heinrich Beta-Bettziech, a friend of Kinkel's, and ended with an attack on Marx, who was said to have muzzled Freiligrath and taken away his character with his poison pen and hatred — a whisper from Marx and the poet should keep silence.

Marx and Engels, who themselves were continually manipulating the press, to draw attention to themselves,[49] wrote articles for and against each other using pseudonyms, spied hack work, machinations, incense, narrow-mindedness, and romantic mendacity:

. . . and it is proof of even greater narrow-mindedness when he more or less throws himself into the arms of a circle where Kinkel's competition awaits him from the outset. *Mais que voulez-vous?* The poet must have incense if he is to live, a great deal of incense, and Mrs. Poet laps up even more. . . . What a petty, dirty, wretched business it is with these poets.[50]

The use of the plural here should be noted — poets. All the feeling of suspicion on the part of the politicals is suddenly aroused against the unreliability of the men of letters; it is indicative of the mental reserve which invariably characterized both Marx and Engels at heart whether applied to Heine or Börne, Freiligrath or Herwegh. Men of letters were born traitors; even Franz Mehring, who was at one time co-founder of the German Communist Party together with Karl Liebknecht and Rosa Luxemburg, was "a liar."[51] There is here a foretaste of Lenin's attitude to Mayakovsky and Gorki, of Stalin's frightful characterization of authors as "engineers of the human soul"; what is in fact independence is stigmatized as irrationalism.

Marx even threatened to make use of old letters from Freiligrath that he had kept. Freiligrath's answer was remarkably dignified — an imperishable document:

Now let me also say something to you quite frankly and honestly. However great my personal friendship for you, however firmly I adhere to the principles we hold in common, I must definitely refuse to turn your quarrel with Vogt, Blind, the *National Zeitung* and the *Daily Telegraph* into my own. It is distasteful to me, something which you too may say about its repercussions; I did not in any way help you to initiate it; I regard myself as in no way obligated to follow you through this labyrinth.

The fact that you have had me cited as a witness for the forthcoming action in London and that you provide the Berliner with old letters from me *ad acta* is another matter and if you wish to proceed in this fashion against my will, I can of course do nothing to stop it. . . . . Nevertheless, although I have always remained faithful to the banner of "la classe la plus laborieuse et la plus misérable" and shall so remain, you know as well as I do that my relationship to the Party as it was and my relationship to the Party as it is are two different things. When towards the end of 1852 the League was declared dissolved following the Köln trial, I regarded myself as released from all ties binding me to the Party as such and I retained only a personal relationship to you, my friend and *like-minded comrade*. For the last seven years I have been divorced from the *Party*; I have not attended its meetings; its actions and decisions have been unknown to me. In practice, therefore, I have long since severed my connection with the Party; we have neither of us ever dissembled about this; there was a sort of tacit agreement between us. And I can only say that I felt happy with this arrangement. My nature, like that of any poet, needs freedom. The Party is also a cage and it is easier to sing outside it, even *for* the Party than inside it. I was a poet of the proletariat and the revolution long before I was a member of the League and one of the editors of the *Neue Rheinische Zeitung*. In future, therefore, I wish to stand on my own feet, to owe allegiance only to myself and arrange my own affairs.[52]

·CHAPTER SIX·

HELL IN LONDON

THE PETIT-BOURGEOIS FAMILY DICTATOR

For decades Marx's life in England was destined to be governed by quarrels. Although he remained "resident" in London for the rest of his life, these years were marked by restlessness, even instability. This continuous high-tension existence, his typhoonlike hithering and thithering, becomes more comprehensible when the fate of his family is taken into account.

He arrived in London at the end of August 1849 completely penniless. In the spring he had been to Hamburg to collect money for the *Neue Rheinische Zeitung*, living in typical Marx fashion — "I had just enough in my pocket to get to Hamburg. I spent a fortnight in a first-rate hotel, however."[1]

He was forced to leave behind him in Paris his wife, seven months pregnant once more, his two daughters, Jenny and Laura, and his son, Edgar; only with great difficulty had he been able to obtain them a residence permit for a further fourteen days — there was no money for the journey. Shortly after their arrival his second son, Guido, was born. He was nicknamed "Little Fawkes," since his birthday was November 5 when, as Jenny Marx recalls, a crowd complete with grotesque masks and model donkeys was celebrating Guy Fawkes Day. So each of the Marx children had been born in a different country.

The family first lived in Chelsea whence they were evicted and their belongings seized for arrears of rent; they moved to the "German Hotel," 1 Leicester Square. It was no "normal move." Jenny Marx gives a vivid description of it in a piteous letter to Joseph Weydemeyer:

I shall describe to you just *one* day of that life exactly as it was and you will realize that few refugees have probably gone through anything like it. As wet-nurses here are too expensive I decided to feed my child myself in spite of continual terrible pains in my breast and back. But the poor little angel drank in so much worry and secret anxiety that he was always poorly and in great pain both day and night. He has not slept a single night since he came into the world, two or three hours at most. Recently he has had violent convulsions too and has always hovered between death and this miserable life. In his pain he sucked so hard that my breast became sore, the skin cracked and blood often poured into his trembling little mouth. I was sitting like that with him one day when our landlady suddenly appeared. We had paid her 250 taler during the winter and had an agreement to give the money in future not to her but to her own landlord who had a bailiff's warrant out against her. She denied the agreement and demanded five pounds that we still owed her. As we did not have the money at the time (Naut's letter did not arrive till later) two bailiffs came and confiscated all my few possessions — linen, beds, clothes — everything, even my poor child's cradle and my daughters' best toys; they stood there weeping bitterly. They threatened to take it all away in two hours' time and I would then have to lie on the floor with my freezing children and sore breast. Our friend Schramm hurried into town to get help for us. He got into a cab but the horses bolted; he jumped out and was brought back covered in blood to the house where I was wailing with my poor shivering children.

We had to leave the house next day. It was cold, rainy and overcast. My husband looked for accommodation for us; when he mentioned the four children no one would take us in. Finally a friend helped us; we paid our rent and I hastily sold all my beds to pay the chemist, the baker, the butcher and the milkman who, alarmed at the scandal over the confiscation, suddenly besieged me with their bills. The beds which we had sold were taken out and put on a cart — but what then happened? It was well after sunset and so it was contrary to English law. The landlord rushed up to us with two constables, maintaining that there might be some of his belongings among the things and that we were trying to get away abroad. In less than five minutes there were two or three hundred people gawking in front of our door — the whole Chelsea mob. The beds were brought in again and we were only allowed to hand them over to the purchaser after sunrise next day. When we had sold all our possessions we were in a position to pay our debts to the last farthing. I went with my little darlings to the two small rooms we are now occupying in the German Hotel, 1 Leicester Square, where for £5½ per week we were received like human beings.[2]

The family's first house, where they lived for six months, was in Soho — 64 Dean Street; finally, for the following six years, they occupied a two-room apartment in the same street (number 28). It became the meeting point for refugees from Poland, France, Germany, or Italy; in it Marx gave lectures, wrote articles, planned newspapers, corresponded with socialists and revolutionaries all over the world. It was a little private hell from which there was no escape (the circular reading room of the British Museum was not opened until 1857); it destroyed both the nerves and the health of his wife and is described as follows in a police informer's report:

He lives in one of the worst and therefore one of the cheapest quarters in London. He occupies two rooms . . . there is not a single clean or solid piece of furniture to be seen in the whole place; everything is broken, battered, torn and thickly covered in dust. Manuscripts, books and newspapers lie about higgledy-piggledy along with children's toys, bits of his wife's sewing things, a few teacups with chipped rims, dirty spoons, knives, forks, candlesticks, an inkpot, beer mugs, clay pipes, tobacco ash — everything jumbled together on the same table. On entering the room your eyes smart so much from smoke and tobacco fumes that you have to feel your way forward as if in a cave until you have got used to it and can distinguish this or that object through the murk. Sitting down is quite a dangerous affair. Here is a chair with only three legs, there another which seems to be intact but on which the children are playing at cookery. This is offered to the guest but the children's cooking is not removed and you sit down at the risk of ruining your trousers. None of this occasions Marx or his wife the slightest embarrassment. You are received in the most friendly manner, cordially offered pipes, tobacco or whatever else is available. In any case the clever agreeable talk compensates to some extent for the domestic shortcomings and makes the discomfort endurable.[3]

Nevertheless Marx was by no means a bohemian. The reason was simply that recklessness regarding himself and his family was allied to a total disregard for money amounting almost to contempt. This flaw in his makeup can hardly be summarized by his mother's somewhat jejeune comment that he had much better bother about capital than write about it. It was an attitude in which pride and generosity were inextricably intermingled with lamentable pettiness. He was entirely indifferent to the source from which the money came; if it was there, it was spent. When he received the considerable sum of 6,000 francs from his mother as a share of his inheritance in February 1848 (with in addition a 1,200-taler rebate on a sum previously spent on account) he immediately gave away even larger amounts to arm the Brussels workers and shortly thereafter for the *Neue Rheinische Zeitung*.[4]

A bare year later his wife had to pawn all their furniture and a month after that her silver. A little later she was wanting to sell it all and the remains of Marx's library in Köln as well; when Weydemeyer heard that the proceeds would hardly be more than the sum she had borrowed, however, he stopped the sale. Marx reacted to Weydemeyer's offer of help and a whip-round for money as if it were an insult and the affair ended in a quarrel. On other occasions, however, he was quite happy for Lassalle to collect money, to receive tiny contributions (£5) from Weerth or "loans" of 30 taler from an unknown bookseller. He would draw bills on his friends without their knowledge. He carried on a bitter war with his mother about money — "There is nothing to be done with my old woman as was proved once again in Trier";[5] he even threatened to draw bills on her without permission and, if she did not honor them, to go to Prussia and allow himself to be locked up.[6]

Obviously no one in the family had the least idea about saving or even being vaguely practical in money matters. Jenny, the daughter, later told a story about her mother's honeymoon:[7] shortly after her marriage she had received a small legacy; the young couple had the money paid over in cash, put it into a two-handled box, and carted it into the cab, across the railway station and into various hotels. When visited by impecunious friends the box was lying open on the table and anyone could help himself as he liked;

naturally it was soon empty. Years later Marx even pawned his wife's "last unpledged dress"[8] in order to help his sick friend Eccarius. Karl and Jenny Marx took turns in making "forays to Holland, the land of our fathers, of tobacco and cheese,"[9] in other words to Karl's uncle (his mother's brother) who was well off and always gave them a friendly reception.

Immediately after Jenny's mother died in July 1856 and a small legacy was consequently in the offing (as well as £150 from one of Jenny's Scottish relatives), the family moved that September into a smart town house, 9 Grafton Terrace: it was large enough to accommodate several families today. For a whole three weeks no word of this was passed to Engels. Though the rent was comparatively low, £24 a year, the Marx family — Eleanor, the youngest daughter known as Tussy, was eighteen months old at the time — was already in debt when they moved in. Jenny Marx called it a "really princely" dwelling and with much relief redeemed her linen and silver from "Uncle," as the pawnbroker was called; she "counted with great pleasure the damask napkins of ancient Scottish origin."[10] This pleasant life of bourgeois comfort and ease did not last long, however; everything soon began to find its way back to the "pop-shop" (as the children had christened the mysterious emporium) and fresh debts were pressing. Engels, in addition to being a stalwart friend in need and acting as "fire brigade," produced a monthly contribution of £5 from January 1857, contributions, loans, and gifts, sometimes of considerable size, flowed in from all sides and were accepted by Marx with lordly equanimity — 50 taler from Hermann Becker in Köln, for instance, £50 from friends in Köln, £5 from Weerth, £10 from Freiligrath. Yet despite all this *The Eighteenth Brumaire* could only be printed with the help of an anonymous Frankfurt tailor who had forty dollars savings in America;[11] the *New York Daily Tribune* paid £2 per article (Engels had to translate, or even write, almost all of them; Charles Dana, Marx's American editor, called him one of the newspaper's "best paid members of staff").[12] Yet the Marx domestic balance sheet was never in order. When Marx received the princely sum of £825, a generous legacy from his friend Wilhelm Wolff, and simultaneously the rest of his inheritance from his mother, who died leaving barely 50,000 taler in all (Engels had to lend him money for the journey to the funeral), a magnificent house was rented forthwith, a sort of town mansion — Modena Villas, christened "Emigration Medina" by Engels (from May the address was 1 Maitland Park Road). The house no longer exists but contemporaries describe it as ostentatiously large — Marx's daughters could easily give dances for over fifty people in it. When Engels, who was well off but childless, moved to London and was looking for a house, he wrote that two living rooms, a study, and four to five bedrooms would be enough for him, adding: "It does not have to be as big a house as yours and smaller rooms would do for me." After he had moved into his four-story house —

a far more modest one than the Marxes' — Jenny remarked: "After all we live in a veritable palace and, to my mind far too large and expensive a house."[13] Marx's income and general financial arrangements are totally obscure; Engels was by no means the only "source"; from November 1855, for instance, he received 20 U.S. dollars per week[14] and in the same year Engels refers to a sum of £200.[15] During the period April 1860 to May 1861 alone it can be reckoned that a total of £369 was received from various donors — Engels, Lassalle, and the Amsterdam uncle.

In his comprehensive treatise on the Marx-Engels correspondence, written in 1932, Willy Haas says:

The situation is so often presented as if Marx in London was permanently on the verge of starvation. I have tried, working from Marx's innumerable begging letters to Engels with their detailed reckonings — such letters account for nearly half of the two volumes — to deduce, even if only roughly, what Marx may have spent per month on his small establishment in London. It can hardly have been less than £35 on average, in other words about 1,000 marks at present-day values. This is, after all, quite a decent sum for a radical revolutionary and proletarian leader with a small family, though it must be admitted that a Marxist Minister in Prussia today draws more. Marx never seriously considered his daughters going out to work. In one begging letter to Engels he did in fact say that he had made up his mind to break up the establishment, let the girls take jobs as governesses somewhere and himself retire to come cheap lodging with his wife. . . . That, however, sounds like a man writing to his friend: "You need not worry about me anymore; I have already bought myself a loaded revolver" — and the effect on Engels was what one might expect.[16]

Marx took so little stock of where the money came from or how much he had that he did not even note the size of bills which he drew — and then wrote almost complainingly to Engels about his "adventures";[17] Engels, who was accustomed to balancing the debit and credit sides of an account and was an honest, experienced businessman, must have found it fairly onerous keeping track of his friend's semi-naïve, semi-slick financial maneuvers, particularly, for instance, when he was wanting to take up a life assurance loan, the size of which he either did not know or was not prepared to say:

Apropos of this business you must let me know what happened as regards the loan. How much have you assured your life for, at what premium and is the policy still valid? It would, for instance, be possible either to extract some more through this same company or obtain an advance on the policy itself. But how am I to put up money for you when you leave me totally in the dark on all these matters?[18]

The first official cost-of-living index and record of consumer goods prices refer to the year 1903. The index reckons rent as normally one-sixth or one-seventh of total income; life in Modena Villas, therefore, can hardly have cost less than £430 per year.[19] Marx himself, in a letter of 1868 to Ludwig Kugelmann, mentions a sum of £400 to £500 as his annual living expenses.[20] At this period the weekly wage of a Scottish miner with an average family of six children was 24 shillings, that of a Manchester cotton worker 28 shillings, and a craftsman in the London building trade 32 shillings.[21]

Apart from a short interlude, the Marx family lived in roomy, even luxurious, houses, sometimes with two maids in attendance. Family life resembled a solar system; it revolved entirely round "Mohr" (Moor) — so called because of his jet-black hair and dark complexion. It was a curious existence alternating between ostentation and middle-class convention, between German bourgeois authoritarianism and maintenance of an international open house.

Marx had a horror of a "purely proletarian set-up"[22] and Frau Marx was not alone in her ambition to maintain some show of bourgeois prosperity; even so it was little short of grotesque — and proof of the extent to which the customs of his adopted country were still foreign to Marx even after nearly twenty years in London — that he should make his wife send out visiting cards showing her as "née Baronesse Westphalen";[23] nothing impresses the English less than a foreign title, usually thought to be bogus, particularly when claimed by a woman. Marx never lost this extraordinary unfamiliarity with the ways of his adopted country. Even in 1867, when his daughter Laura wished to marry, he had to ask Engels for advice as to how one went about it in England, saying that he had no notion of the laws and formalities.[24] After almost ten years in England he was forced to admit to Engels that he had "totally failed" in an attempt to find two respectable citizens to guarantee a proposed loan.[25]

Marx did not like to admit to anyone, whether comrades-in-arms like Liebknecht, suspected rivals like Lassalle, or English acquaintances like Henry Hyndman, that it was sometimes difficult to provide an adequate dinner. Instead, the family discussed and bemoaned their guests' appetites afterwards. The penury of the household had to be concealed even from his own son-in-law. The words "respectable" or "*il faut cacher*" appear over and over again — regarding redemption of the ladies' watches and jewelry from the pawnshop so that they might appear "respectable at the sea-side" in Ramsgate,[26] for instance, or entertaining Weerth, his old comrade-in-arms:

You know that I like Weerth very much but it is painful when one sits in muck up to the neck to have so fine a gentleman opposite one *auquel il faut cacher les parties trop honteuses* [from whom one must conceal the more embarrassing things]. Such a situation produces mutual *gene* and I hope that he will leave for Manchester tomorrow and that when he returns he will find me in circumstances such that I can once more converse with him *franchement*.[27]

They were certainly in no position to be generous parents — they had their eye firmly on the "dowry" which Paul Lafargue was to bring with him on marriage to daughter Laura. Their future son-in-law's grandmother had been a mulatto girl and his grandfather a rich farmer in Cuba, but Frau Jenny was more than ready to make excuses for his resulting unfortunate "dark olive complexion and extraordinary eyes"; in a fit of *non-olet* enthusiasm she wrote to her friend Ernestine Liebknecht that his parents were very well off, owning considerable estates in Cuba and houses in Santiago and Bordeaux, where his father had established a flourishing wine-merchant's business;[28] fortunately, she went on, Laura's betrothed was the only son so all this would belong to him one day and he would never be dependent on earning his living. Moreover, 100,000 francs were due to arrive on the wedding day. These expectations of bourgeois bliss were even more bluntly set out in a pompous letter written in stilted French by the *pater familias* to his prospective son-in-law — a document of yeomanlike morality:

My dear Lafargue,
Allow me to make the following observations:
1. If you wish to continue your relations with my daughter, you will have to discard your manner of "paying court" to her. You are well aware that no engagement has been entered into, that as yet everything is provisional. And even if she were formally your betrothed, you should not forget that this concerns a long-term affair. An all too intimate deportment is the more unbecoming in so far as the two lovers will be living in the same place for a necessarily prolonged period of severe test and purgatory. I have observed with dismay your change of conduct from day to day over a period of a single week. To my mind true love expresses itself in the lover's restraint, modest bearing, even diffidence regarding the adored one, and certainly not in unconstrained passion and manifestations of premature familiarity. Should you plead your Creole temperament, it becomes my duty to interpose my sound sense between your temperament and my daughter. If in her presence you are unable to love her in a manner that conforms with the latitude of London, you will have to resign yourself to loving her from a distance. I am sure you take my meaning.
2. Before definitely settling your relations with Laura I require a clear explanation of your economic position. My daughter believes that I am conversant with your affairs. She is mistaken. I have not raised this matter because, in my view, it was for you to take the initiative. You know that I have sacrificed my whole fortune to the revolutionary struggle. I do not regret it. On the contrary. Had I my career to start again, I should do the same. Only I would not marry. As far as lies in my power I intend to save my daughter from the reefs on which her mother's life has been wrecked. . . . As regards your present circumstances the information which I have not sought but which has reached me by chance, is by no means reassuring. . . . As regards your family I know nothing. If they live in well-to-do circumstances, that is no proof that they are willing to make sacrifices for you. I do not even know how they view your plans for marriage. I repeat, I must have definite elucidation on all these matters. Moreover you, as an avowed realist, will hardly expect that I should treat my daughter's future as an idealist. You, a man

so practical that you would abolish poetry altogether, cannot wish to wax poetical at the expense of my child.

3. To forestall any misinterpretation of this letter, I can assure you that, were you in a position to contract marriage as from today, it would not happen. My daughter would refuse. I myself should object. You must have done something in life before thinking of marriage and it will mean a long testing time for you and for Laura.[29]

For Marx such involvement in family affairs was a pseudo-activity, a "business" action unconnected with any real, all-embracing system. The impression left by his "honest John" approach is similar to the family's ostensible petit-bourgeois way of life. The mixture of propriety and prudery referred to by contemporaries is all of the same pattern. Stag parties with red wine, risqué jokes and uproarious singing about "Young, young roommate" could be brought to an abrupt end if Marx heard sounds in the adjoining room; red in the face he would hiss: "Quiet, quiet! The girls!"[30]

Marx also practiced fencing with the French émigrés in an "armory" near Oxford Street, his impetuosity compensating for his lack of skill. He also enjoyed "pub crawls" from bar to bar between Oxford Street and Hampstead Road; since there were innumerable bars on this route, each of which had to be visited under the rules, it is not surprising that these expeditions sometimes ended riotously. On one occasion Marx and his fellow-tipplers stormed through the streets early in the morning, smashing gaslights, and only escaped the police after a wild chase through alleyways and backyards.[31]

Superficially, therefore, Marx was always ready for a game, for a talk, or for company, but in fact he was a completely introverted, lonely, isolated being — as if he felt that he must shield the recesses of his mind from the outside world in order to devote them to the colossal effort involved in his vast work of genius; for it he reserved and expended all the emotional energy he possessed; *that* was his child. This man experienced love in the process of thinking; his libido was devoted to a human being who had yet to appear; human beings as they existed he found disturbing and crept away from them into a complex shell, from the interstices of which anger would flare out at one moment, uproarious friendliness and apparent joviality at another:

> *. . . the elements*
> *So mix'd in him that Nature might stand up*
> *And say to all the world: This was a man!* [32]

This was the phrase with which Eleanor, certainly the closest to him, ended her appreciation of her father's life.

"Children must educate their parents"[33] has been handed down as one of Marx's paternal sayings — when still under thirty he had been dubbed "Father

Marx" by members of the Communist League, and his daughters called him Mohr. Every Sunday an educational ritual took place: Marx organized naval battles with whole fleets of paper ships of his own construction; they were eventually set on fire and sunk or doused in basins of water to the accompaniment of much cheering. Alternatively the family went for long country walks, Marx telling the children fairy stories invented as he went along and spun out to fit the length of the walk. He had even promised to write them a play, "The Gracchi."

There was always an established order of march.[34] The vanguard, for instance, consisted of the girls, Wilhelm Liebknecht, and a couple of friends, the girls running and jumping or picking flowers. Behind came a connecting file and then the main body of the army — Marx, his wife, and any visitor meriting special attention. Helene Demuth followed at a discreet distance carrying the basket full of bread, sausage, cheese, and drinks and helped by the "lower-level" guests. They camped out on the grass, picnicked, read the Sunday newspapers, and talked politics. The children played among the gorse bushes on Hampstead Heath, romped or ran races, picked chestnuts or tried a donkey ride. Although a remarkably bad rider, Marx had certain pretensions even in this field, maintaining that he was a virtuoso in the art (which he clearly was not) and had learned to ride as a student — Engels asserted that he had never taken more than three riding lessons. Liebknecht describes one of these days in the country:

The order of march on the way back was different from that on the way out. The children had tired themselves out running about and formed the rearguard with Lenchen who was lighter of foot with an empty basket and no load to carry and so could take charge of them. Usually we struck up a song, only rarely political songs, mainly folk songs, especially sentimental songs and — this is no tall story — "patriotic" songs from the "Fatherland" such as *O Strassburg, O Strassburg, du wunderschöne Stadt*," which was a great favourite. Alternatively the children would sing Negro songs to us and even dance as well — if their legs had recovered somewhat. During the march talk of politics or refugee sorrows was not permitted. On the other hand we spoke much of literature and art when Marx had an opportunity to display his tremendous memory; he would recite long passages from the "Divine Comedy", almost all of which he knew by heart, and scenes from Shakespeare, in which case his wife, who had an excellent knowledge of Shakespeare, would often take over from him. If he was in particularly high spirits he would give us Seidelmann playing Mephistopheles. He had a passion for Seidelmann whom he had seen and heard when a student in Berlin, and Faust was his favourite German poetry. I would not say that Marx recited well — he overemphasized grossly — but he never missed the point and invariably expressed the sense correctly; in short he was effective and the comic impression made by the first words which he spat out so emphatically passed when one saw that he was totally immersed in the spirit of the part he was playing, had grasped it completely and was entirely master of the part.[35]

Were these daughters — Marx's only children to survive — strictly brought up or left to go their own way? One thing seems certain: peace and quiet, thorough schooling, and parental authority were not their lot. Even at the age of fourteen Eleanor was still not really at home in any language — she spoke German but could hardly write it, her French was defective, her English incorrect and adequate only for home use.[36] She became naturalized later; a passport issued by the Foreign Office on April 22, 1871, describes her as "British Subject." All their lives the sisters corresponded with each other in English. On the one hand there was continual talk of the daughters' education, their progress, and their political interests; on the other hand no consideration was ever given to any form of professional training. Instead, a piano was obtained or dances were given in the house;[37] alternatively, to Frau Marx's intense delight, invitations from the British aristocracy were accepted — high society for the daughters.[38] Jenny's marriage to the French socialist Charles Longuet and Laura's to Paul Lafargue were clearly all that the parents had visualized as their daughters' future life. Here again are to be seen those two strands in Marx's character, closely parelleling each other, yet not overlapping or complementing each other, this mixture of affection and genuine concern (particularly in the case of the grandchildren) on the one hand and coldest indifference on the other. Marx, the man devoted to a system, cannot have been unaware of the kaleidoscopic inconsistency, reaching hectic heights of enthusiasm, which characterized all his daughters' political activities. At one moment they were ardent in their worship of the Paris Commune and its heroes, at another they were involved in a gala memorial evening for the fallen of the communards, at which his favorite daughter Eleanor recited the ballad of the Pied Piper of Hamelin in English. The gathering took place in the fairly large, though badly lit and half-empty hall of a church school; Marx, Engels, and Bebel were in the audience and also Leo Hartmann, the Czar's would-be assassin, whom Tussy worshipped. On the back of the program was an appeal for a collection in aid of surviving dependents, starting with the words: "Her Majesty the Queen has headed the list with £ 10."[39]

Marx was with them in such matters. He was also present for Tussy's first appearance on the stage, backed by G. B. Shaw; Jenny was beside him, her former beauty marred by her waxy complexion and red swellings under the eyes. He tolerated Eleanor's adherence to his mortal enemy Hyndman's "Democratic Federation." Even Tussy's enthusiasm for the Irish freedom fighters — inspired by her friendship with Engels's Irish mistress — earned her no more than the nickname "This grrreat unhappy nation." Although Marx always emphasized how intolerable to him was the thought that Eleanor, who was unmarried, might be sacrificed on the "altar of the family" and ultimately waste her life looking after a sick and aging man, that was precisely what happened.

Eleanor Marx's biography reads like a tragedy — as do those of the other two daughters. In the end Marx poured scorn on both his sons-in-law: "Longuet as the last Proudhonist and Lafargue as the last Bakunist! The devil take them both."[40] The oft-quoted (and generally misquoted) remark by Marx, "I am no Marxist," was also made in this connection.[41] It is comprehensible only in context; at times he was so despairing over Lafargue's theoretical gibberish, allegedly based on Marx, that he once said: "If that is Marxism, I am no Marxist." It is certainly not to be taken as a recantation or deviation from his own doctrine but, on the contrary, as a defense of that doctrine against those who would distort it. This did not prevent him, however, from taking an interest in the affairs, sometimes thoroughly unsavory ones, of these two young men who treated him with friendly detachment. He intervened, for instance, on Lafargue's behalf when he resigned from a photo-lithography and engraving firm that he had formed.[42] His own visits and other people's letters and accounts, however, forced Marx to realize that Longuet was a bohemian lazybones; he seldom rose before midday and in the afternoon went to Paris from Argenteuil where, "as befitted his station," he was living in a rich man's former summer residence. With his violent domestic scenes, rages, and fecklessness, he slowly but surely wrecked the life of his wife Jenny, Marx's firstborn.[43]

There is no need to look further than Jenny's letters to her sister Tussy in London envying and congratulating her on her plans for a stage career and commenting that at least she would not be condemned to spend her life watching a *pot au feu*.[44]

There is no evidence that Marx intervened. When Charles Longuet intruded into Marx's *own* affairs, however, that was a very different matter; a few days after Jenny Marx's death an insignificant article appeared in Clemenceau's periodical *La Justice,* of which Longuet was one of the editors, telling of the difficulties encountered by young Marx with the von Westphalen family because of his Jewish origin; the result was an angry peremptory letter: "I should be much obliged to Longuet if he would not mention my name in his writings in future."[45]

Marx equally disregarded the fact that Paul Lafargue, who to everyone's surprise ultimately turned out to be by no means rich (his best-known book was entitled *In Praise of Idleness*), was continually calling upon Friedrich Engels for assistance, and also the increasing frigidity of the relationship between Laura and Eleanor; this led to so total an estrangement that Laura did not even come to her father's funeral and sent testy letters attempting to dispute old Engels's and her sister Eleanor's right to dispose of his estate.

The egoism of the man, sucking in human beings but never allowing his environment — in other words, society — to impinge except through a fine-mesh filter system, was illustrated again in his relationship to his favorite but unhappy daughter Tussy. The key to the riddle perhaps lies in the sentence: "Father was talking of my eldest sister and of me and said: 'Jenny is most like me but Tussy *is* me.' "[46]

In a macabre way this remark is reminiscent of the quotation from Hegel's lectures on the philosophy of history with which Marx opened his *Eighteenth Brumaire*, his most important work of the early London years: "Hegel remarks somewhere that all facts and personages of great importance in world history occur, as it were, twice. He forgot to add: the first time as tragedy, the second as farce."[47]

Eleanor was undoubtedly an unusual woman; she was not a beauty in the true sense of the word but with her great dark eyes and her father's jet-black curly hair she exerted a profound influence on people. As a young girl she traveled almost uninterruptedly, sometimes spending months with Engels in Manchester, accompanying him and his mistress to the sea and to all sorts of entertainments such as fireworks, weekend parties, picnics, or even welcoming ceremonies for the Prince and Princess of Wales when they came to open an agricultural exhibition. Alternatively she acted as secretary to her father on his travels. She seems to have been entirely carefree during a two-month stay in Paris in the spring of 1869, strolling through the Second Empire's capital of two million inhabitants and along the newly constructed boulevards and avenues on which Haussmann had spent millions of francs between 1853 and 1865; she went on sight-seeing tours, enjoyed the opening of the great department stores, open-air puppet shows, or Sardou's *Seraphine* in the theater. All this, however, was also escapism, partly from the permanent nagging and nervous irritability of her mother, with whom the daughters' relations were often strained, and partly from herself. Eleanor was full of energy and ambition to live her own life — but how, where, and with what? Her passion was the theater (her sister Jenny had once played Lady Macbeth on a London stage);[48] she translated articles by an English expert on Shakespeare and made much use of the Reading Room in the British Museum; she was even granted a privilege denied to her father and one on which no one since Gladstone could pride himself: she was allowed to work there even on days when the Reading Room was closed to the public. Her life was a hectic hither and thither, alternating between visits to her sisters in France, worries about Jenny's little son, and severe attacks of hysterics, insomnia, depression, and weeping fits. When aged twenty-seven she wrote to her sister Jenny: "It drives me half mad to sit here when perhaps my last chance of doing something is going."[49]

Eleanor Marx's struggle to reach some professional position was a fairly desperate struggle for self-justification. While Marx made an occasional, though mild, complaint that she did not help him enough, she tried to extract money from him for her theatrical training, even using a sort of "political economy" phraseology: "I feel sorry to cost Papa so much, but after all very small sums were expended on my education . . . and I think that, if I do succeed, it will have been a good investment."[50]

There was a quite specific, concrete reason for her slight irritation with her father, her lamentations about her hopeless situation and her ruined life, her mental and spiritual blackouts, incomprehensible to her father and incurable by doctors: Karl Marx had forbidden his favorite daughter to associate with the man she loved, the French Communard Prosper-Olivier Lissagaray. There were no rational grounds on which Eleanor was forbidden to see the man to whom she had long been engaged — gossip even had it that they were secretly married. Lissagaray, the socialist, had been living in England ever since the suppression of the Paris Commune, and Marx had a high opinion of his book on the subject; he even used the book himself and tried to arrange its translation into German. Had he had enough of two French sons-in-law? This can hardly have been the only reason. With his two elder daughters far away and unsatisfactorily married, with his wife frequently driving him out of the house with her shrewish irritability, and with her submissive domestic alter ego Helene weighing on his conscience, did he want to fetter *one* female totally to himself, shared with no one?

Eleanor's fits of insomnia, her hunger strikes, her swoons, her aimless journeyings, or her incongruous political and professional engagements do not betray an unstable character but should rather be interpreted as frenzied tugging at the chains. This was a cloud that threatened to destroy her relationship with her father — "How I love him no one can know and yet we must each of us, after all, live our own life."[51] After Jenny's death Tussy lamented that her mother had died thinking her hard and egoistic, never realizing that she had sacrificed the best years of her life to her father and mother.[52] One of her most touching letters, imploring but helpless, is also clear evidence of the dominating attitude of its addressee:

My dearest Mohr,
I am going to ask you something but first I want you to promise me that you will not be very angry. I want to know, dear Mohr, when I may see L. again. It is so *very* hard *never* to see him. I have been doing my best to be patient but it is so difficult and I don't feel that I can be much longer. I do not expect you to say that he can come here. I should not even wish it but could I not, now and then, go for a little walk with him? . . . No one, moreover, will be astonished to see us together as everybody knows we are engaged. . . . It is *so* long since I saw him and I am beginning to feel so very miserable notwithstanding all my efforts to keep up, for I have tried hard to be merry and cheerful. I cannot much longer. Believe

me, dear Mohr, if I could see him now and then, it would do me more good than all Dr. Anderson's prescriptions put together — I know that by experience. . . . My dearest Mohr, please don't be angry with me for writing this and forgive me for being selfish enough to worry you again.

Your Tussy.[53]

Eleanor Marx's life never found its balance, however. She appeared once or twice in small theater pieces; she associated with socialists, scientists, and members of Oscar Wilde's mother's circle; finally she committed herself to an impostor. This was Edward Aveling, her elder by six years, of whom the story is told that, as a youngster, when asked "Will you take peas or potatoes?" he would reply "Both, please" with delightful self-assurance. He had married young and soon fulfilled his brother's prophecy: "He married Bell Frank for her money. She could only get half of it. He soon made her do that. When unable to get any more out of her, he left her."[54]

Eleanor lived with him, out of wedlock, for the last fifteen years of her life and introduced him into London's radical democratic circles. He pretended to possess intellectual and political affiliations to socialist movements, even maintaining in an article that he had stood mourning beside Karl Marx's grave — in which there is not a word of truth.[55] He was a medical student and natural scientist but never pursued these subjects as a profession; allegedly he had been to Harrow and was Professor of Chemistry and Physics at New College, Oxford — which equally was not true. Bernard Shaw, who was a friend of Eleanor's, pictured this unhappy nonmarriage in his play *The Doctor's Dilemma*, Aveling being portrayed in the painter Dubedat and Eleanor Marx in Jennifer — her lyrically aesthetic beauty, his capacity to delude naïve women and his unaffected cynicism in matters of money and the good things of life. Even in his later years Shaw described him as "totally unscrupulous in financial or sexual matters."[56]

Eleanor Marx's life was spent. Her parents, Engels, and Helene Demuth were all dead. She had lost touch with Laura Lafargue, her only sister. Even at the outset of her liaison with Aveling an acquaintance, meeting her in the British Museum, had been taken aback by the slovenly appearance of this once elegant woman, and her unhealthy complexion, as if dependent on drugs and stimulants — "I should fear that the chances were against her remaining long within the pale of respectable society."[57]

This word "respectable," the word that had hung over the Marx household and family like the sword of justice, here it is again — a dead, empty word!

Her last letter, dated March 1, 1898, was characterized mainly by anxiety for her supposedly sick lover, but it foreshadowed the end: "This is a bad time for me. I fear there is little hope; pain and suffering are great. Why we go on this way is incomprehensible to me. I am ready to go and would be glad to do so. But I am obliged to remain so long as he needs help."[58]

Aveling did not need any help. Behind the back of the woman who had clung to him for fifteen years he had married a young actress. When Eleanor Marx heard of it, she committed suicide, just four weeks after dispatch of that letter to the last man in whom she confided — and he was her half brother, Frederick Demuth.

THE ILLEGITIMATE SON

Karl Marx had a son by Helene Demuth, his housekeeper; as a result of the most recent Karl Marx research this is now accepted as proven fact.[59] For disciples and idol-worshippers the thought is not a pleasing one and there is no consolation to be had from emotional references to the prerogative of genius, to Beethoven's illegitimate daughters or the double love-life of the respectable bourgeois Dickens. If Henry Frederick Demuth was Karl Marx's son, the new mankind's Preacher lived an almost lifelong lie, scorned, humiliated, and disowned his only surviving son. The spectacle of the Sunday order of march over Hampstead Heath with Helene Demuth trailing behind carrying the provisions basket is not merely humiliating but disgraceful.

In fact, Helene Demuth gave birth to a son on June 23, 1851. His name is given as Henry Frederick Demuth in the register of births — in which the event was not recorded until August 1, though that is not contrary to English law. This was precisely the time at which Jenny Marx wrote in her memoirs: "In the early summer of 1851 an event occurred that I do not wish to relate here in detail, although it greatly contributed to an increase in our worries, both personal and others."[60]

Immediately on birth Frederick Demuth was handed over to foster parents, an impoverished driver and his wife, named Lewis. There is no evidence for the supposition that he was known by his foster parents' name until his mother's death;[61] when Helene Demuth died in 1890 after seven years as housekeeper to Friedrich Engels, she left a will in favor of "Frederick Lewis Demuth of 25 Gransden Avenue, London Lane, Hackney"; her "monies, effects and other property," the reward of a hardworking life, amounted to £95 in all.[62] By this time Frederick Demuth, who had originally trained as a gunsmith, was a married man; he gave his profession as "driver" and was well respected in the working-class quarter of Hackney. He wore a bowler hat instead of a cap and had dyed his hair and mustache in order to appear younger than he was; when going to work he carried his lunch in a briefcase. At this time he paid regular visits to his mother in Engels's house — but was confined to the kitchen. Through all the years when Helene Demuth was working in the Marx household there is no indication of the existence of her son. Equally we do not know when the daughters, Eleanor and Laura, came to know of "Nim's" son (Nim, Nym, or Nimmy was the Marx grandchildren's nickname for Helene Demuth). In any case they knew him, and Eleanor loved him dearly; only eight weeks before her suicide she wrote: "You are the only friend with whom I can be quite frank. . . . I tell you what I would tell to no other person."[63] At this point Eleanor knew the truth — if truth it was. When Frederick Demuth's wife left him for a soldier two years after his mother's death, taking with her £29 which he was holding for a workers' welfare fund, Eleanor wrote to her sister Laura and her widower brother-in-law Longuet for assistance. Her melancholy lament, however, still clearly referred to Friedrich Engels: "Is it not wonderful, when you come to look things squarely in the face, how rarely we seem to practise all the fine things we preach — to others."[64]

Until a few days before his death Engels was always regarded as the boy's father. This is the purport of the document that brought the whole affair to light, Louise Kautsky-Freyberger's letter to August Bebel of September 2/4, 1898:

I have it from General himself that Freddy Demuth is Marx's son. Tussy pressed me so hard that I asked the old man direct. General was most surprised that Tussy should cling so persistently to her belief and authorized me then and there to deny the gossip that Freddy was his son should this be necessary. You will remember that I told you this long before General's death.

In addition, a few days before his death General confirmed to Mr. Moore that Frederick Demuth was the son of Karl Marx and Helene Demuth; Moore thereupon went to Tussy in Orpington and told her. Tussy maintained that General was lying and that he himself had always said that he was the father. Moore returned from Orpington and urgently questioned General once more but the old man stuck to his assertion that Freddy was Marx's son and said to Moore: "Tussy wants to make an idol of her father".

On Sunday, the day before his death, General himself wrote it down for Tussy on a slate and Tussy came out so shattered that she forgot all her hatred for me and wept bitterly with her arms round my neck.

General authorized us (Mr. Moore, Ludwig and myself) to make use of this information only if he should be accused of having treated Freddy shabbily; he said that he did not wish his name to be besmirched, particularly when it would do no one any good. He had stood in for Marx in order to save him from a serious domestic quarrel. Apart from us and Mr. Moore I think that of the Marx children only Laura suspected the story, though she may not have had direct knowledge of it; Lessner and the pawnbroker also knew that a Marx son existed. After Freddy's letters came to light Lessner said to me: "Freddy is in fact Tussy's brother; we were sure of it but could never find out where the boy had been brought up."

Freddy looks like Marx and it is mere blind prejudice to try and see some similarity to General in that typically Jewish face with its long blue-black hair. I have seen the letter which Marx wrote to General in Manchester at the time; General was then not yet living in London but I believe that he had this letter but, like so much of their correspondence, has destroyed it.

That is all I know about the affair; Freddy has never learnt who his father was, either from his mother or from General. . . .

For Marx separation from his wife, who was terribly jealous, was always before his eyes; he did not love the boy; he did not dare do anything for him — the scandal would have been too great. He was sent as a paying guest to a Mrs. Louis (I think that is how she writes her name) and he took his name too from his foster mother and adopted the name Demuth only after Nimm's death. Tussy knew perfectly well that Frau Marx once ran away from her husband in London and went to Germany and that Marx and his wife did not sleep together for years; it did not suit her, however, to give the real reason; she idolized her father and would concoct the most beautiful myths.[65]

At first sight this letter is clear and unequivocal. Yet it leaves almost every sort of question unanswered. Louise Kautsky-Freyberger — her second husband was Dr. Freyberger, Engels's physician — became Engels's secretary and housekeeper after Helene Demuth's death; she was clearly on especially intimate terms with him and undoubtedly held a position of confidence.[66] But — no original of this letter exists. Blumenberg and other biographers have been able to cite only a typed copy of unknown origin. Nevertheless the letter preserved in the Internationaal Instituut Voor Sociale Geschiedenes in Amsterdam shows certain specific features to be found in other — handwritten — letters from Louise Kautsky-Freyberger. There are the opening words "dearest August," for instance, situated under the address in the top right-hand corner, "41 Regents Park Road, N.W." This was how she usually addressed Bebel, who was a close friend. The three yellowed pages of typing also contain typical abbreviations such as "u" for *und* and certain orthographical quirks such as "nöthig" instead of "nötig" and "thun" instead of "tun" as are to be found in indisputable originals. Equally there is the abbreviation "G" for "General" (meaning Engels) and the typical, slightly ungrammatical, phraseology such as "General said" or "Moore asked General." To judge from the date, the letter was written three years after Engels's death, but meanwhile there had been no accusations of "shabbiness toward Freddy" or "gossip" which the authorization to impart this information had been given to refute. Why, therefore, was the letter written? Werner Blumenberg even says that "about 1900 all socialist leaders knew that Marx was Frederick Demuth's father"[67] but he produces not a shred of evidence for this statement; in fact there is none. Even Sam Moore, the lawyer mentioned in the letter, one of Marx's and Engels's oldest cronies, translator of the *Communist Manifesto* and one of the translators of volume 1 of *Das Kapital,* gives no indication. The story of the circumspect Engels, who had destroyed mountains of "incriminating" correspondence with Marx, being so prudent as to write the information for Tussy on a slate instead of on paper, may perhaps be accepted but the fact that a man generally so generous did not leave Frederick Demuth even a shilling in his will looks like confirmation of the tale of "unwilling paternity." Is it conceivable, however, in view of the innumerable, almost deliberately engineered, enmities, bitter feuds, intrigues, and quarrels in which Marx was involved, that never a mention of this from one of Marx's opponents is to be found, if it was in fact "known to all"? Nothing in publications, nothing in letters, nothing in memoirs? There is no need to go so far in reverential whitewashing of Marx as to imply that Helene Demuth was a sort of "common-property whore" in the Marx house[68] — Louise Kautsky's letter is full of inconsistencies. When did Jenny Marx "run away," for instance? There is not a single indication of this in all the literature on the subject; her trips to Germany are known with their dates. And what is the basis of the remark that Marx and his wife "had not slept together for years"? — Tussy must have known about that. Tussy was born in 1855, in other words four years *after* Frederick Demuth; at that time, therefore, the couple was following normal custom. A year later Jenny had a miscarriage. Moreover in the two-room apartment in Dean Street there was hardly room for separate bedrooms with six people living there. From what time, therefore, could Tussy have "known this very well"? After Frau Marx's last pregnancy — when she was aged forty-three? Or at the time when Frederick Demuth was conceived or born, when she was not born herself? And why should Marx have written Engels a letter — which Louise Kautsky purports to have seen — when Engels was frequently in London at the time in question? He was there in 1850 until November 7 and — at Marx's request — spent the early part of March 1851 and the period from June 8 to June 14 in London. At that time Helene Demuth was in the sixth or possibly ninth month of her pregnancy, a fact that could hardly have passed without notice. If there had been anything to settle between the two men, it could have been talked over quietly.

On the other hand — and irrespective of who the child's father was — how is it that never on a single occasion is he referred to over a period of decades? If both the intimate and less intimate members of the Marx family believed that Frederick was the result of a lapse by Friedrich, that would have been no reason to preserve conspiratorial silence on the subject. The daughters who had grown up meanwhile and who allegedly looked upon Helene Demuth as a second mother — did they never cudgel their brains about her as a real mother? From the sons-in-law and grandchildren, never a word. Never a question about the whereabouts of the child, never a word about a visit to the Marx house or any anxiety about the child on the part of its mother. This conspiracy of silence is remarkable and would be senseless if Engels had actually been accepted as the father — Friedrich Engels's life outside the current rules of morality was well known. He lived in sin for years with his Irish "workmaid" Mary Burns but in secret, in a house in the suburbs; she never appeared in his official residence where he was regarded as a respectable member of Manchester society. Later Mary's sister Lizzy joined the household; Engels loved both women. This curious triangular relationship, and the fact that he "lived with" Lizzy after her sister's death, was both known and a favorite subject of gossip in the Marx house.

The motives and reactions of the two men are therefore nebulous, but the behavior of the women involved is incomprehensible. Equally obscure is the life of this supposed son of Marx. In 1972 a British journalist tracked down Demuth's son Harry, then in his nineties,[69] but little more emerged than was already known: Frederick Demuth lived a modest existence, occasionally supported by the Marx offspring; to the end of his days he was an "engineering worker" drawing nine shillings per week. His occasional letters to Marx's eldest surviving daughter, Laura Lafargue, deal primarily with his concern about the professional advancement of his son Harry, who had meanwhile married and fathered several children. Laura Lafargue is said to have introduced him to Clara Zetkin on one occasion in Paris as "my half brother."[70] For the last years of his life he lived with Miss Laura Payne; he had meanwhile obviously read Marx's and Engels's writings but there is nothing to show that he knew *whose* books he was reading. He became treasurer of Branch 194 of the English Metalworkers Trade Union and co-founder of the Labour Party in the Hackney constituency. When he died on January 28, 1929, he took his secret with him to the grave — when confronted with the rumors, not even his son could say whether he "knew." No one can conclusively prove today whether Frederick Demuth was the son of Karl Marx — who longed for sons all his life, who never saw one of his own sons grow up, and who, if the story is true, then cast off his sole male heir as a foundling. Frederick Demuth too left behind him his own secret: his will revealed that the beloved son Harry was not his son but an adopted child; the astonishing sum of £2,000 was left to "Mr Harry Demuth my nephew known as my son."[71]

FRIEDRICH ENGELS — LIFELONG FRIENDSHIP
NOT WITHOUT ITS VICISSITUDES

One human being, one man, remained loyal to Karl Marx beyond the grave, even beyond his own death — Friedrich Engels. With rare devotion and humility he "played second fiddle" for decades.[72] At the age of twenty he wrote a poem in praise of Marx, whom he did not yet know; from that time, until his ultimate sacrifice to protect his friend's honor in the matter of Frederick Demuth, the dignity he preserved and the regard he showed lent a special significance to the word friendship. He was two and a half years younger than Marx, son of a well-to-do textile manufacturer in Barmen. In his house surrounded by its parklike garden he would give chamber music evenings (he could himself play the bassoon and the cello); in a sense he was the complement and the antithesis to Marx. His was the political brain[73] — even in later years there were to be heard warning voices about the "risk of affinity with Engels"[74] and rumors about "the wicked Engels who has led the good Marx astray."[75] The tale of Engels, the witty, the artistic, and the scholarly, has been a persistent one — but it is based on a misconception. Stephan Born recalls, for instance, that when in Paris[76] it never entered Engels's head to show him anything of the city's artistic treasures, still less go to the Louvre with him; he preferred a Palais Royal comedy to *Phaedra* in the Théâtre Français; the drum was the only musical instrument he understood or which gave him any pleasure, he would say. As a fourth-form boy in a church school he had once asked "Who was Goethe?" and had been given the answer "A godless man." When he was an old man a phrenologist from Yarmouth once examined his skull and pronounced, to the vast amusement of all his friends, that here was "a good businessman with no talent for languages"[77] (meaning no doubt for anything musical). His reading at the age of fifteen was definitely not Heine's *Travel Pictures,* which had just appeared or other contemporary literary works by such as Chamisso, Eichendorf or Brentano; nor did he read Mörike's recently published *Maler Nolten* or Balzac or Hugo, normal reading for boys of his age. Instead, his father lamented when he once more found in his son's desk "a smutty book from the public library, some story of 13th-century knights."

At that time Engels was still at Elberfeld High School. His time at school and his apprenticeship in his father's firm showed that here was a young man with a remarkably early sense of realism. As a result primarily of a practical rather than "philosophical" education followed by short trips to Italy, Switzerland, and England, he quickly turned his back on the lyric muse and poetic dreams, though in Barmen he admired and tried to imitate Freiligrath.

In a letter from Bremen signed "Friedrich Engels, a young German" (the "young" with a small *y*) he was ready to concede divinity only to a doctrine that was proof against reason.[78] Even at this stage, however, he was producing his own version of literary sedition; critical reports on conditions in society and the schools headed "Letters from Wuppertal" and signed "Friedrich Oswald" appeared in Gutzkow's *Telegraph für Deutschland.* These "letters" heralded a new form of writing — sociological journalism. He came of a family in which the father was regarded as one of the Maecenases of his city and, from a sense of religious responsibility, was still the moving force behind the construction of a poorhouse and an orphanage years after publication of the *Communist Manifesto,* in which the mother donated 2,000 taler for the care of orphans and 15,000 taler to her parish church. He clearly thought it his mission to carry on this tradition in the secular field; the "grace of God" was to him still a possible phrase but the gracelessness of the world produced an impossible form of existence. His confirmation text read: "Forgetting those things which are behind and reaching forth unto those things which are before, I press toward the mark for the prize of the high calling of God through Christ Jesus."[79] Friedrich Engels took the mission contained in Philippians 3: 13–14 in its literal, in other words worldly, sense — he pressed toward the mark that he had set for himself.

Around 1840 Engels took part in a small literary circle laboriously assembled by the assiduous Elberfeld writer Carl de Haas; among other indications a detailed letter from Engels makes its total mediocrity clear.[80] Members met towards evening, read plays by German poets or Shakespeare, drank tea, held heated discussions, and — "to take the heat out of it" — played their own compositions or sang songs. Then the newssheet of the circle was read with its rules, requirements, and proposals. "Material received spontaneously" was also read and criticized.

Engels's half-finished play, "Cola di Rienzi,"[81] originates from this period; it was only recently found in a dusty folio among Adolf Schults's papers. Typical of its phraseology are "Never more," "Away with your impudence," "Think of the retribution," "Have mercy," and "Ha, Traitor" — remarkably teenage rhetoric for a young man who already had an unhappy love affair behind him. Worse still, the general motif was a political one; Engels was trying to present the alternatives of despot or popular tyrant. Cola di Rienzi, appointed notary of the Rome City Chamber by Pope Clement VI on the recommendation of Petrarcas, announced the establishment of a people's state after his putsch, made when aged only thirty. The plot revolved around the question of political fantasy, possible tactics, pacts with the nobility and the Church — the theme in fact of Lassalle's *Sickingen,* subsequently so cogently criticized by Engels. What he wrote down, however, amounted not only to the anticipated abortive attempt to come to grips with the dialectic of history but simply heroic nonsense — five years after the twenty-two-year-old Büchner had written his *Danton's Death.* A search for any genuine political idea nevertheless shows that one factor recurs in various expressions: the people do deserve the self-sacrifice of a man like Rienzi; so thinks the "People's Tribune" himself.

This hint at this stage of a theory of the "Plenipotentiary" gives food for thought; it is an idea that runs through all Engels's writings over decades; toward the end of his life he gave so forceful expression to it in a letter to Paul Lafargue that in the present day it could hardly serve as a theme for a trade union congress on co-determination:

Go and run one of the big Barcelona factories without direction, that is without authority! Or administer a railway without the certainty that every engine-driver, fireman, etc., will be at his post at precisely the time when he should be there! I should very much like to know whether the gallant Bakunin would entrust his large person to a railway carriage if that railway were administered according to principles by which nobody would be at his post if he did not please to submit to the authority of regulations far more authoritarian in any possible state of society than those of the Basel Congress! All these fine ultra-radical and revolutionary phrases merely serve to conceal the utter poverty of ideas and the most complete ignorance of the conditions in which the daily life of society is carried on. Go and abolish "all authority even with consent" amongst the sailors on a ship.[82]

With his reports from Wuppertal Engels was far ahead of the "dark fellow from Trier." Undoubtedly Marx was attracted to his lifelong subject by Engels's *Outlines of a Critique of Political Economy* published in the *Deutsch-Französische Jahrbücher;* it may also be taken as certain that Marx's articles in the *Rheinische Zeitung* — about the Moselle farmers, for instance — were inspired by Engels's form of journalism; there is a clear connection between (for instance) Engels's article in the *Rheinische Zeitung* entitled "In place of criticism of the Prussian press laws," one of the most important journalistic and political subjects of the time, and Marx's fundamental research on the matter.

The two men first met in late November 1842 in the editorial office of this paper, Marx's first venture. Their encounter was a frosty, noncommittal one. Engels had come from Berlin where, shortly after Marx's period there, he had joined the Guard Foot Artillery Regiment as a volunteer; not having matriculated, he had attended the lectures in the university, which was near his barracks and his lodgings in the Dorotheenstrasse, as an external student. Not only did he forthwith become the most humorous caricaturist of the Doctors' Club, but he was soon its most radical member.

After Barmen and Bremen, Engels enjoyed the plethora of information available in Berlin; he listened with curiosity to Schelling's famous inaugural speech and was a regular attendant in Auditorium 6, where Schelling gave his anti-Hegel lectures on the philosophy of the Revelation. Engels considered them an insult to the memory of Hegel and scandalous attacks on all the more recent philosophy — Feuerbach, Strauss, Bauer, Ruge, precisely the thinkers whose disciple he was. Though only a business apprentice aged twenty-one, Engels set forth with characteristic impudence to defend Hegel, of whom he knew little; though carrying so few guns, he charged into battle with his fledgling monograph, printed anonymously in Switzerland: *Schelling and Revelation. Critique of the recent reactionary attack on free philosophy*. Ruge thought Bakunin to be the author and said: "This nice young man is outstripping all the old donkeys in Berlin."[83]

At this time, however, Marx's political ideas were diametrically opposed to this sort of thing; he was steering his newspaper on quite another course. He considered the introduction of communist or socialist dogma to be nothing less than immoral, as he said in a letter to Ruge of November 30, 1842. The gropings of the Doctors' Club were now behind him; he was in process of developing a political theory with very definite strategic aims. He must have found this well-dressed journalist with his radical gestures a very strange person — and the journalist must have found himself meeting an unkempt monster. The conversation that set Engels off down the new road took place with Moses Hess, author of *European Triarchy,* whom Engels regarded as the first communist and who later recalled: "We talked about the problems of the day and he, a dyed-in-the-wool revolutionary, left as an enthusiastic communist."[84]

Not long afterward, however, Engels was writing to Marx poking fun at Hess, at his liaison with his beloved Sybille Pesch and his "cuckolding": "I dealt with him so coldly and contemptuously that he will have no wish to come back. All I did for him was to give him some good advice about the V.D. which he had contracted in Germany."[85]

Between these two incidents came Engels's first more businesslike visits to England, the beginning of his correspondence with Marx, and his first longer visit to Marx in Paris in autumn 1844. This was the point at which the two men's friendship began, when they found that they agreed on almost all philosophical and political questions.

It was in Paris that Engels wrote the first pages of *The Holy Family,* the philippic against Bauer and the Berliners, whom, however, he still respected. His reports to Marx in Paris were almost hectic — "as far as coming over to you is concerned, there is no doubt that I shall be there in, say, two years."[86] His description of the state of affairs in Elberfeld, striking a hopeful note, betrayed his anxiety to become the complete Philistine, to assure his reputation, to be thought as sound as a German: "Yesterday we held our third communist meeting in the biggest hall and the best hotel in town. . . . The stupidest, idlest and most Philistine people, who have never shown interest in anything at all, are beginning to become almost enthusiastic about communism."[87]

One of the characteristics both of Friedrich Engels himself and his historical and political program is that, in a tone of complete self-assurance, he would state convictions rather than facts. Obviously "the whole of Elberfeld" did not assemble at communist meetings; similarly his *Condition of the Working Class in England* was not based on accurate fact. It was an appeal to conscience, full of righteous indignation — but it was not a work of scholarship. He had pieced it together in a matter of a few weeks from English newspapers and books.[88]

He worked at a furious journalistic tempo to the detriment of reasoned argumentation. He frequently relied on unproven sources and accepted suppositions, such as that the entrepreneurs provoked strikes, or conclusions which were not true — as, for instance, that child labor was an indispensable component of industrialized society. Old or antiquated details appear as something new; nowhere is it stated whether he is relying on his own observation or other sources; suppositions often appear in place of information. The *Working Class in England* is a splendid pamphlet, nothing less but nothing more either.[89]

Victor Aimé Huber, who visited the English industrial districts in 1844, described Engels's book as something written in bitterness and passion, painting a picture of blood, murder and fire; and he was right. But its purpose was not what he thought. It was to horrify, to rouse people — these fellows should think about him. Engels's writings have a sort of built-in impulse to action; they reach out beyond the material he sets out, the situation he examines. In fact he is "pressing toward the mark" but, as happens with remarkable frequency with the pundits of historical materialism, the process almost invariably leads to erroneous historical analyses.

"Revolutionary uprising of the French working class, world war — that is the program for the year 1849"[90] — but it was a year of complete peace. "In August 1850 at latest," then in 1851, then in 1852, economic crisis and revolution were to come — but the reality was disillusioning: ". . . simply so that they [the proletariat] have an excuse not to fight."[91] Marx asked Engels what had become of the crisis, saying that he could not make head or tail of this commercial business, but Engels had the answer pat: "Between November 1852 and February 1853 . . . and we could just as well have it as early as September. But it will be a good one."[92] But it did not happen, neither a good one nor a less good one. In 1854 the Crimean War brought hope; Engels wrote in the *New York Daily Tribune* that the revolution would erupt "in shining armour, sword in hand, like Minerva from the head of Zeus. The threatened European war will give the signal. . . ."[93] But there was no signal, no revolution. So the years 1855 and 1856 passed. Engels raved: "Now the last phase of the swindle is beginning. . . . This time the crash will beat anything known before."[94] Marx referred to "things on a European scale never reached before." But nothing happened. They went on waiting for the revolution, a socialist revolution; in 1858 it was to come through and from Russia, in 1859 as a result of the Franco-Austrian War in Italy.

Here was an error, in fact, by Engels, the military expert who was so pleased with his nickname "General."[95] Between June 20 and July 6 he wrote a series of five articles for the *Manchester Guardian* commenting as a military authority on the war of 1866. The fourth article, in which he violently criticized the Prussian plan of campaign and accused Moltke of elementary violations of the "supreme laws of the art of war," appeared on the very day of the Prussian victory of Sadowa. "So decisive a battle won in eight hours — such a thing has ever been seen before," he admitted dejectedly.[96] Nevertheless he still knew precisely how humiliating the peace treaty would be and what territories Berlin, Paris, and St. Petersburg would carve out of the corpse of Austria. In fact not an inch of Austrian territory went to one of the signatory powers.

"Mohr and General" issued bulletins as if they were world powers — prognoses, judgments, condemnations. Yet it remains a remarkable fact that they always moved in the gray area between utopia and illusion. Their politico-historical misjudgments are legion — in 1877 "the good Turks" were to be victorious over the Russians but were in fact defeated; 1882 produced "as splendid a revolutionary situation as has never been seen,"[97] and in 1884 Engels could "calculate mathematically the time of final victory."[98] These never-fulfilled prophecies instead of concrete scientific proposals undoubtedly contributed to the personal and political isolation in which Marx and Engels lived and from which they suffered. Only on one single occasion, in a great self-criticizing disquisition written toward the end of his life, did Engels use the word "illusion" in connection with his own and Marx's concept of historical materialism:

But history has shown us too to have been wrong, has revealed our point of view of that time to have been an illusion. It has done even more; it has not merely dispelled the erroneous notions we then held; it has also completely transformed the conditions under which the proletariat has to fight. The mode of struggle of 1848 is today obsolete in every respect and this is a point which deserves closer examination on the present occasion. . . . History has proved us, and all who thought like us, wrong.[99]

As far as Marx was concerned too this motif of anticipated salvation, of prophecy, is to be found over and over again; he pronounced what mankind should be, not what it was. There is undoubtedly a connection here with the gross misjudgments made in critical political situations even in the recent past and the present. An example is the mistaken policy of the German Communist Party under the Weimar Republic in face of advancing fascism when, by sheer falsehood, it deceived both itself, its members, and the electorate.

The question remains whether, in the process of analyzing the perilous march of history, an "element of the ultimate state" can be distilled or at least dimly perceived, as Ernst Bloch puts it, or whether he is not to some extent justified in characterizing all this as the "formless bluster of eternal, and therefore hopeless, striving,"[100] which he rejects. The abstraction of utopian thinking leads to intolerance of its critics. Engels once made the apodictic remark to the bourgeois republican Karl Heinzen that communism was not a doctrine but a movement; not illogically Heinzen replied: "If communism is a movement, a movement toward a goal, then when the goal is reached movement naturally ceases or must be converted into fresh movement. Communism is therefore at an end as soon as it has been realised."[101] To this Engels reacted indignantly, saying that he considered it "an avalanche of muck" to which the only reply was a box on the ear.

When Engels moved to England in 1850 he was aged thirty. A police dossier describes what he looked like:

Aged 26–28, height 5′6″, blonde hair, wide forehead, blonde eyebrows, blue eyes, well-proportioned nose and mouth, reddish beard, oval chin, oval face, healthy complexion, slim build. Special characteristics: talks very fast and is short-sighted.[102]

At this point he had clearly abandoned any idea of taking up a profession of his own. He joined his father's firm, Ermen & Engels, in Manchester, with which he remained connected all his life despite various vicissitudes, disputes about his inheritance, changes of partnership, and alterations in the method of drawing his salary.[103] He disliked commerce and was continually bemoaning its pressures and constraints — "I must be in the office by 10:00 A.M. at the very latest tomorrow";[104] nevertheless it enabled him to live the life of an opulent man of the world. Engels was a well-respected gentleman in Manchester society; he was member of the exclusive Albert Club, of the Manchester Foreign Library, and of the Stock Exchange.[105] He owned a smart house in town in which he entertained his business friends, industrialists, and the nobility and gentry of Manchester with choice wines and champagne, and which was also sufficiently "presentable" when his father visited to England. In addition, however, he occupied a house in the suburbs where he lived his "real life" with his mistress Mary Burns and her sister, Lizzy.[106] This dual existence, contravening all conventional morality, did not prevent him partaking of the pleasures of high society, in particular fox-hunting, which he loved and for which he kept his own hunter.

Even Marx was persuaded to take part in these amusements when he came on a visit, and Engels was able to report enthusiastically to Jenny that they had been on horseback for two hours and that Marx was showing increasing "enthusiasm for the thing."[107] Standard features of the Engels household were convivial evenings with the wine flowing when he would sing his favorite song, which he had translated, the "Vicar of Bray," or students' drinking songs or even "Die Wacht am Rhein." Preparations for Christmas were colossal.

The dispatch of cases of champagne, Bordeaux, sherry, port, and mature Rhine wine to his London friend plays a not inconsiderable part in Engels's correspondence with Marx — sherry and port were regarded as medicinal.

The society in which the two friends moved was by no means confined to refugees, communards, and comrades — rather the reverse; the more senior the position he occupied and the more numerous his orders and decorations, the more important a man was considered to be. Doctors, professors, and lawyers frequented the house. When Sam Moore, his long-standing friend and collaborator, was appointed Chief Justice of the Territories of the Royal Niger Company, Chartered and Limited, Engels was in no way put out that a man who had helped to translate *Capital* should occupy the position of a colonial governor. Instead he congratulated the new overseer of "the very cream of Nigritian Niger Niggerdom"[108] and was delighted that he should have good pay, a pension, and easy work in a pleasant climate, as was only fitting for an ex-volunteer officer.

Hellmuth von Gerlach, the German writer who years later became author of *Weltbühnen* and a friend of Ossietsky and Tucholsky, was astounded when Major Wachs of the Great General Staff, regarded as a strategic authority by the entire German right-wing press, gave him a recommendation to "my friend Engels"[109] during a conversation in the Social-Conservative Club in Berlin.

Engels's house became a focal point for all sorts of flirtations and match-making; passing émigrés would curry favor with "Pumps," Engels's consort's unattractive niece, or try to oust each other in the ladies' good books. Primarily, however, from the very first letter with its request for money, this house constituted a wailing wall for Marx. The tone of the letters varied between the imperious, the imploring, the calculating, and the SOS call.

Engels loaned, in other words gave, money continuously — sometimes £1, sometimes £100. From 1857 he made regular payments and from 1868 provided a generous annual pension — some £2,000 at present-day values.[110] Yet Marx's requests for money were unending. For his friend's sake Engels embarked on risky exchange transactions and raided his firm's till;[111] in one letter, while lamenting about "vile commerce," he suddenly evoked a most unpleasing spectre — "unless the revolution intervenes and puts an end to all financial plans."[112] Marx was naturally well aware of what he owed Engels — rescue from genuine want, a double room with sitting room at a seaside resort,[113] or, as he wrote to Kugelmann, freedom from the necessity to "take up business."[114] He did not fail to acknowledge his debt or express his gratitude: "Your self-sacrificing concern for me is incredible and I am often ashamed at heart — but I do not wish to pursue this subject now."[115]

The two men were in fact complements of each other and were linked by an intellectual friendship of rare depth. In later years the stage for this relationship was primarily the now historic study on the first floor of Marx's house in Maitland Park Road, with its view over the park from its broad window.[116] On either side of the fireplace opposite the window were bookshelves stacked with packets of newspapers and piles of manuscripts. Opposite the fireplace stood two tables, equally loaded with newspapers, papers, and books. In the middle of the room was a plain, comparatively small writing desk and a wooden armchair, facing the window was a leather-covered sofa. The room must have given any visitor an impression of the greatest disorder — photographs of his family, of his friend Engels, of his patron Wilhelm Wolff, paperweights, ashtrays, cigars and matches (of which Marx used a great many because his pipes and cigars were always going out). But things were arranged *his* way; in no time he himself could find quotations or figures in the jumble of papers, extracts, and notes. "Books are my slaves and must serve my will," he would say;[117] he rummaged around in them, turned down corners and scribbled in margins. "I am a machine condemned to devour books and then throw them up in different form on to the dungheap of history"[118] was his description of himself. His system of making extracts is highly indicative of his mental makeup. Recent detailed research[119] has brought to light the fact that Marx did not copy out or translate correctly passages which he extracted — from Adam Smith for instance — by a sort of polemical method of collation he created an atmosphere of antipathy; by this method he infused into these extracts precisely what he needed later for an aggressive system of argumentation — based on these "sources." Maximilien Rubel, the French expert on Marx, describes this procedure as "passionate, impulsive, full of self-justificatory anger."[120]

J. P. Mayer, editor of Marx's *Early Writings,* has shown that, in his extracts from Montesquieu's *Esprit des Lois,* Marx simply pushed under the rug such passages as did not fit his line of argument.[121]

On the carpet in Marx's study was a well-worn path showing how he tramped back and forth ruminating; in two opposite corners were also two holes where, after hours of "walking," Marx and Engels would stand arguing or even saying nothing and then suddenly each turning abruptly around on the spot. Frequently they would talk endlessly to themselves until, after a time, they would burst out laughing on realizing that they had each been discussing *their own* plans *with themselves* without listening at all to what the other was saying.[122]

There was a different note, a different ingredient in this relationship, however — frigidity, aloofness, even suspicion. Again and again there are indications that, on Marx's side, the friendship was not an unbroken one; not even this friendship was proof against his propensity for mockery and disdain. Only fragmentary indications can be extracted from the few still extant documents — with few exceptions Marx's daughters Laura and Eleanor destroyed all their parents' correspondence precisely because it contained offensive remarks about Engels.[123] For his part, Engels, who had advised Marx as early as 1858 not to keep certain letters,[124] destroyed many important letters from Marx in order to conceal indiscretions and personal intrigues.[125] One thing is certain: Marx definitely misused Engels on work that did not interest him and for which he (Marx) pocketed the money. He did not merely request, he simply demanded from Engels innumerable articles for Dana's *New York Daily Tribune,* at that time the largest newspaper in the world, with a circulation of 300,000; frequently he actually issued orders.[126]

Even in face of this friendship Marx would withdraw into his shell of solitude. Marx regarded the most trifling personal affairs (the fact that Engels was seeing more of Wilhelm Wolff, for instance) as cause for suspicion:

. . . it occurred to me that the most likely outcome would be that I should receive no personal letter from you for a time (say 1–2 weeks), after which it could be assumed that some grass had grown over the affair. At least, since the arrival of Mr Lupus in Manchester, that is the method that you have observed with curious consistency in all matters concerning me and the two gentlemen [Wolff and Dronke]. It is therefore better, so as not to reduce our correspondence to a purely telegraphic one, for us both to omit all references to your friends and protégés there.[127]

This propensity for taking quick jealous offense, together with fear lest someone be building up an area of independence for themselves inside a system in which dependence was the rule, was paralleled by every conceivable form of maliciousness. Various sources testify to the fact that Frau Marx could not stand Engels; if from nothing else this is clear from the fact that all her life she addressed him as "Herr Engels." She never accepted the immorality of his private life. During twenty-five years of friendship — during which she largely lived off Engels and occasionally herself wrote asking for money — she never once visited him in Manchester despite numerous invitations. Only once did she accompany her husband there — in the spring of 1855, shortly after the death of her son Edgar. When in Manchester on another occasion she preferred to stay with Sam Moore, on whose notepaper she wrote a spiteful, censorious "Court Circular" and whose house she described as her "pleasant warm home" in contrast to that of Engels:

. . . as a result of living permanently among Philistines there has been introduced into G's [General's] house a sort of formal rigidity and conventional English behavior; particularly at the dinner table this creates an unpleasant atmosphere and means that one cannot breathe freely. The children were being watched and corrected all the time; one must eat properly and speak properly; only the drinking is not according to rule. To my great astonishment there was neither beer nor wine on the table . . . he only drinks a little wine in the evening when playing whist. As a concession I was allowed a spoonful of cognac in my water. The food is simple in the extreme . . . on the other hand the table is royally decked and two maids wait on either side.[128]

Writing to her daughter Tussy who was visiting Engels in Manchester, Frau Marx even amended her letter, making it spiteful rather than merely hostile. She originally wrote "Give greetings from me to Engels and his wife," but altered it to read: "Give greetings from me to 'my wife,'" a scurrilous allusion to the fact that Engels's mistress was longing to be introduced one day as "my wife" and was continually making scenes about their common-law marriage.[129]

One of the few extant letters from Marx to his wife refers in most ungracious terms to "Mr. Chitty," the current nickname for their generous friend, and betrays an attitude both malicious and indecorous. Mary Burns's sister Lizzy, with whom Engels had lived, had recently died and on her deathbed he had granted her what she had badly wanted for years and had married her.[130] Prying mercilessly into his friend's private affairs, Marx made fun of him, his love life, and his wife's illiteracy:

I cannot resist telling you of something so peculiar that it is reminiscent both of Balzac and Paul de Kock. When Tussy, Mrs. Renshaw and Pumps (she has been knighted — Engels now calls her Pumpsia) were going through the deceased's possessions, Mrs. Renshaw found, among other things, a small bundle of letters (about 8, of which 6 were from members of the Marx family and 2 from Williams [Ramsgate]). She was about to hand them to Mr. Chitty, who was there, but he said: "No, burn them. I don't need to see her letters. I know that she could never have deceived me." Would Figaro (I mean the genuine Beaumarchais one) have felt that way? Mrs. Renshaw later said to Tussy: "Of course, since he had to write her letters and read out to her any she received, he could be reasonably sure that they held no secrets for him — but perhaps they did for her."[131]

This venomous Philistine attitude is all the more perplexing in that a similar situation had arisen before and had nearly led to a breach between the two friends. When Mary Burns, Engels's first mistress, died, he wrote in despair to Marx announcing the news; next day, January 8, 1863, however, Marx replied with an incredibly cold and indifferent letter. He expressed surprise and regret only in a single sentence — "she was very good-natured and witty"[132] — the rest of the one-and-a-half-page letter was entirely full of laments about his appalling financial situation, even including the remarkable comment that it would have been better had his mother died (he was waiting for her money). Engels was totally shattered:

Dear Marx,
You will of course realise that in this case my own misfortune and the frigid way you took it have made it absolutely impossible for me to answer you earlier.

All my friends, even my philistine acquaintances, have shown me on this occasion, which Heaven knows has hit me pretty hard, more sympathy and friendship than I could expect. You found it a suitable time to drive home your cool philosophical attitude. So be it!

You know how my finances stand; you know also that I am doing everything to save you from ruin. But I cannot now raise the larger sum of which you speak, as you must also know.[133]

This was the only occasion on which Marx apologized to anyone. Engels accepted the apology but his comment showed that the friendship was in danger of breaking up — "I tell you, your letter stuck in my head for a whole week; I could not forget it. Never mind; your last letter made it quits and I am glad that when I lost Mary, I did not lose my oldest and best friend."[134] Marx had presumed too much on the friendship's ability to carry strain. Although the crack was papered over, Engels never entirely forgot the incident. A letter to his brother-in-law, written years later condoling on the death of his favorite sister Maria, shows how hurt he must have been at the time.[135]

The background to this incident, however, is not merely tactless hamfistedness on the part of an egomaniac, coldly disinterested in the fortunes even of his closest friend, instead it is evidence of a highly important psychological and ideological fact: Karl Marx's attitude to death was a defensive one. With the cynicism to which he admitted in his letter of apology to Engels and in which he almost invariably took refuge in face of the phenomenon of death, he dismissed all thought of the fate of the individual — not *the* man but *men;* the individual was only part of a whole. Even when aged only twenty-six he pronounced that man never died completely: "Death appears as a hard-won victory of the species over the individual and to be a factor running counter to the unity of the species; but the specific individual is only a *specific species-being* and as such mortal."[136]

Marx's utterances on the phenomenon of death are very rare and somewhat disconnected; again and again, however, and in various places, the notion is detectable that he who lives no life other than his own constricted one, he who has no part in the life of others, in communal life, must inevitably be threatened with the extinction of life, in fact with *his own* death.[137] In his study on Plutarch, written as a student, Marx expressed it thus: "Only it is not life that passes away, but merely this individual being."[138]

There are two ingredients in this concept of mankind so characteristic of Marxist thinking and culminating in the communist writer Louis Aragon's creed "one does not die since there are others" — action as a postulate and a low opinion of mankind. Concentration on action as the ultimate purpose of the advance of wisdom is one of the commandments in the Talmud[139] — "ultimately this, and this only, matters — action." It is an integral part of the theme of the prophets. The feeling of being the child of a father and ancestor of grandchildren[140] both raises and lowers the stature of the individual; he is one of the relays bearing the torch and an essential link in a chain. The subordination of the individual is reflected in the vagueness of prophecy. Here again Marx is firmly rooted in the categoric system of Jewish thinking. For the prophet the day of fulfillment is not established; it is a general future like the future of the generality — and in the light of it both the present and the past are judged analytically. Even though the precise state of affairs in this promised future is not definable, day-to-day life, *active communal* life, is directed toward it. This is the central core of Marx's concept of death; it is not, as trite, so-called modern theology would sometimes have it, the notion that death is a sentence of judgment and a logical conclusion to exploitation.[141] In one of his articles Marx did in fact refer to suicide,[142] saying that their increasing misery was driving a greater and greater number of proletarians to suicide. But this was not an original work by him; the article was primarily a translation of passages from the memoirs of Peuchet, who was archivist in the Prefecture of Police in Paris for years; it was more a statistical report than a fundamental examination of the subject. In one letter to Engels in 1873 Marx refers to the possibility of suicide as "the most proper . . . manner . . . whereby a man can remove himself from the world";[143] this should be interpreted, however, in the light of his conviction that the individual whose activity and whose work was behind him was superfluous. Man's life, he maintained, ran out *here;* the rule for him was to struggle in this present world, not to await the hereafter.

This is the reason for one of the horrifying blind spots in socialist literature. There is no such thing as death, the overwhelming final end, or existence as life until death. Death as killing, dying as the meeting with death, the end as a sacrifice — all those, yes. Death as a threat and a futility — no. Think of Maxim Gorky's drama *The Foes,* written in 1903, in which a comrade who shoots a factory owner is declared "more important and more valuable" than a younger — and therefore "less important and less valuable" — comrade who is designated to present himself as the culprit; think of Bertolt Brecht's play *Die Massnahme,* which deals with the same subject of death "by order": the individual does not count. Love is reduced to the process of reproduction, death to the end of a man's scope for action.

Marx was, so to speak, totally unmoved by the ending of a full life. He attended the funerals neither of his father nor his mother nor his wife. The death of the two women with whom Friedrich Engels had lived clearly affected him not at all. Only on one single occasion did he let out a cry of anguish — when his son Edgar died. He wrote to Lassalle: "Bacon says that really important men have so many relations with nature and the world that they recover easily from every loss. I do not belong to these important men. The death of my child has deeply shaken my heart and mind and to me the loss is still as raw as on the first day.[144]

The death of the eight-year-old boy was an unfulfilled promise; on this one occasion Marx broke down.[145]

The counterpart to Marx's insulation of himself from other men was his isolation in society. Marx never became an "Englishman" — even less so than Engels. He did not even speak or write good English — and that in a country where language is a mark of class or at least of caste. This was a complete prescription for nonintegration. Both he and Engels were admittedly enthusiastic philologists — Engels corresponded in Spanish, Portuguese, Italian, Polish, and Russian; he had a slight impediment and it was said of him that he stuttered in twenty languages. In his later years Marx learned Russian, to the annoyance of Engels who, when reproached for studying all sorts of things merely for fun, replied: "I would gladly burn the Russian publications on the state of their agriculture which have been keeping you from completing *Capital* for years."[146]

The two remained almost without contacts in English society; they had practically no touch with English politicians. Engels was most offended that his house, which Continental admirers had christened "the Mecca of socialism," exercised practically no attraction for the English leaders of the working-class movement.[147]

As a country of exile England offered the great advantage that foreign revolutionaries were left unmolested, but the background to this was a punctilious, polite, calm indifference that had its disadvantages. Mid-nineteenth-century London was a city of two million people in a country of barely twenty million inhabitants; it was the focal point of a gigantic industrial upsurge, during which the radical goings-on beyond the Channel were observed with amused detachment. Famous popular leaders like Garibaldi or Kossuth were publicly acclaimed but were looked upon rather as romantic, exotic heroes whose heroic phrases people enjoyed as they enjoyed the theater — and then forgot them again. Marx, however, was in no way famous. The attitude to émigrés like him was one of polite disinterest. Provided they did not make themselves "conspicuous" they could do as they pleased — in a vacuum.

In the early days Engels did make friends with Julian Harney, the Chartist leader, but like many Continental Europeans he had overestimated the Chartist movement. It was not an organized workers' movement but a conglomeration of romantic Tories, expropriated farmers, Protestant reformists, and extremists, along with some radical philosophers. From the viewpoint of the pre-revolutionary period this overestimation was understandable. The "People's Charter" had been drafted in 1837, by which time trade union organizations already existed; it demanded constituencies of equal size, universal secret suffrage, and salaries for members of parliament; it was therefore a step forward. Petitions supporting it were immensely successful; the words "mass movement" could justifiably be used. Though the Charter carried 1,280,000 signatures (the total electorate at the time was 839,000), Parliament rejected it on July 12, 1839, and two of the Chartist leaders, O'Brien and O'Connor, were arrested. The reaction to this was an increase in the membership of the Chartist party to 40,000 by 1841; its newspaper, the *Northern Star,* reached a circulation of 50,000. When a new charter was submitted to Parliament in 1842 — and again rejected — it carried 3,315,000 signatures, over half the male population of Great Britain. The Chartists now allied themselves more closely to the trade unions, whose strikes they supported — at the price of similar harassment. By 1846 the movement had been broken. When Engels made the acquaintance of Julian Harney, one of the two leaders of the tiny left wing, he was already a man of the past, without authority or influence. Marx attended the "Fraternal Democrats' " New Year banquet in 1849 when Harney was in the chair, but he did so out of politeness rather than as a matter of policy; he was soon making fun of this "very impressionable plebeian"[148] who, nevertheless, published the first English version of the *Communist Manifesto* in his newspaper *Red Republican* in 1851.

Marx's and Engels's attempts to rescue the English working class from its state of political castration[149] failed — "the reform movement in England, which we had created, nearly killed us."[150]

Years later Engels himself admitted that there was no question of a workers' movement in the Continental sense — in other words that he and Marx had had not the smallest influence on developments in England.[151] Marx's last remark on the country that had harbored him for the longest period of his life was "to the devil with the British."[152] Even in 1892 Engels was still lamenting that the English working class was so deeply infected with the parliamentary spirit that it could not take one step forward without at the same time taking three-quarters or seven-eighths of a step backward.[153]

The "Hyndman Affair" also fits into this picture. Henry Myers Hyndman was the leading English socialist and had founded the "Democratic Federation," rechristened the "Social Democratic Federation" in 1884. He played an outstanding role in English society and politics, not least because of his considerable private means. He called himself a Marxist even before getting to know Marx personally. The two were introduced by Carl Hirsch, cofounder of the Social-Democratic Workers' Party, and a lively friendship soon developed. This is clear from his frequent visits and the prolonged discussions that took place during "walks" in Marx's study — despite the fact that Marx later described the visits as "tiresome," as "invasions with too much staying power,"[154] and as "intrusions."[155] There is a well-known story that, Marx being of a friendly disposition, his time was often taken up

by highly boring visitors and that on one occasion when he observed, with a
glance at the door, that time was pressing and that he had much to do, his
visitor replied condescendingly: "But, my dear Marx, that doesn't matter."[156] It seems improbable, however, that he would have been prepared,
over a considerable period, to hold discussions and go out to dinner with the
only leading British politician whom he knew personally unless he had taken
some interest in the man. Hyndman describes their meetings as extremely
friendly, even intimate;[157] it is he, for instance, who has given an account of
the derogatory way in which Frau Marx talked to his wife about Engels:

Marx was "considerably indebted to Engels financially" to put it bluntly. The
thought of this was intolerable to Frau Marx. She did not fail to recognise
Engels's services to her husband but she disliked the situation and bemoaned his
influence over his great friend. Talking to my wife she more than once referred to
him as Marx's "evil spirit" and wanted to be able to liberate her husband from the
necessity to rely on this efficient, devoted but not very congenial amanuensis.[158]

This may perhaps be written off as gossip between two ladies talking about
their domestic worries over tea or coffee[159] but Jenny did not have an
opportunity of doing this very often. Moreover Hyndman was not the only
one to remark on Engels's wild jealousy of anybody who became friendly
with Marx; it is also mentioned by completely disinterested observers who are
therefore above suspicion, such as Ernest Belfort Bax, who by the way, was
the English author to whom Marx ascribed authorship of "the first English
publication . . . which is pervaded by a real enthusiasm for the new ideas."[160]
    It is perfectly possible that Engels's "literally feminine prejudice against
people with whom he had fallen out"[161] had something to do with the
suspicion that Marx might now be receiving financial support from Hyndman;
Frau Marx's frank statements to Mrs. Hyndman may also be taken to imply
as much — in any case she never took tea with one of Engels's ladies.
    The fact remains that the breach with Marx, totally unexpected by
Hyndman, took place as a result of an intervention by Engels that aroused
Marx's suspicions. Hyndman's book, *England for All,* was largely a popular
version of Marxist ideas — but he did not quote his source. Now this was
precisely the procedure which Marx and Engels had followed in all their
writings. In a postscript, moreover, Hyndman had explicitly referred to the
fact that he was indebted to the work of a great thinker and original writer.
Hyndman said later that he had not given Marx's name since he was an
abomination to the few who knew him and this would be a reason to reject
his ideas, also because, for the many Englishmen who did not know him,
ideas originating from a German and a Jew would make the book an object
of suspicion. This is admittedly a rather weak argument, but it is certainly not
that of a thief and plagiarist. Precisely this, however, was now given as the

reason for Hyndman's dismissal from "court" and imputed to him in letters to third parties; he himself was snubbed in a long contemptuous letter.[162] Engels proved almost more irreconcilable than Marx; in letters to Bernstein as late as 1882 he described Hyndman as "an ambitious parliamentary candidate . . . entirely without significance" and categorically denied any personal acquaintanceship with him.[163] Karl Kautsky remarked in some puzzlement:

Many people have complained about Engels's attitude to the social-democratic movement in England, the advance of which I have been able to observe personally since 1881. After Marx's death Engels, living in London, was recognized and respected as their leading theorist by all the social-democratic parties of the world; yet after 1881 he never established any closer relationship with the socialists of England, not even with the Marxists among them, not even with their leader, H. M. Hyndman. Hyndman, the founder of Marxist social-democracy in England, and Engels both lived in the same city and regarded advocacy of the same cause as their mission in life. Yet they never managed to meet.[164]

Secretiveness, aloofness, suspicion, even dishonesty therefore played their part in this involved, kaleidoscopic friendship. To Engels's complete horror, for instance, Marx had left him totally in the dark as to the progress of his work on economics. Only after Marx's death did Engels realize what a jumble of extracts, note-sheets, and outline plans he had "inherited." Marx had always evaded his pressing questions simply by not answering them, and Engels subsequently reproached himself for failure to drive him harder and more persistently or at least to issue warnings against being diverted to side-issues. "You ask," he wrote to August Bebel, "how it came about that the progress of the thing was concealed even from me. It is quite simple: had I known, I would have given him no peace day or night until it was completely ready and printed. And Marx knew that better than anybody."[165]

The history of Marx's (and later Engels's) papers reads like a detective story with all the usual features[166] — undercover sales, theft, embezzlement, manuscripts spirited away by night in herring boats, offers up to a quarter-million dollars, interventions by foreign embassies, luxurious villas with swimming pools, hunts by Interpol. Even today the whereabouts of numerous sections are still obscure, and original manuscripts appear at public auctions; in 1966, for instance, two small folios of extracts from the early 1850s sold for 33,000 Deutschmarks at an auction in Marburg.

In any case disputes began even while Engels was still alive; he destroyed piles of Marx's letters dealing with personal matters;[167] Eleanor Marx took the utmost care to destroy all letters which might hurt Engels.[168] Immediately on her father's death Laura wrote to Engels in terms normally only to be expected from a solicitor — "she would be most obliged"; "he must understand"; *she* knew what her father's *real* intentions were with regard to his papers.[169] Not only did she make difficulties about the furniture (the famous armchair in which Marx died, for instance, and which is now in Moscow, a present from the Lafargue family), but she complained that she had been informed of her father's death too late, an insinuation clearly connected with the inheritance quarrel; moreover, Laura's *husband* was at the funeral as a result of a telegram from Engels.[170] The dispute was primarily concerned with the right of possession of Marx's papers. Laura (she was on such bad terms with her sister that a letter of condolences inadvertently opened by Tussy had to be relayed to her in Paris "diplomatically" via Lenchen Demuth and Engels,[171] and in June 1885 she was asking Engels whether Tussy was still in the land of the living[172]) disputed Marx's intention to appoint Engels and Tussy as literary executors (Marx had died intestate). "I requested you the other day," she wrote to Engels, "to inform me . . . whether Mohr had told *you personally* that he wished Tussy to be his literary executrix. You have not answered me. Had you answered in the affirmative I should have simply concluded that long illness had changed my dear father."[173]

Engels's reply to this, written in stilted English, reads like a dignified rebuke, but his irritation shows through clearly:

If you wish to have Mohr's exact words, Tussy will no doubt give them to you if you ask her to do so.

We spoke about these matters when Paul was here and he will no doubt remember. As to the expression "literary executors," I am alone responsible for it. I could not find another at the time and if by it I have in any way offended you, I humbly ask your pardon.

How the disposition *itself* can wound you I cannot see. The work must be done *here on the spot*. The real work, that you know as well as Tussy does, will mostly have to be done by me. But as Mohr had one daughter living in London, I find it but natural that he should associate her with me in such work as she could do. Had you been living here instead of in Paris, all the three of us would have been jointly appointed, no doubt about that.

But there is another view of the case. According to English law (Sam Moore has explained this to us) the only person living who is the legal representative of Mohr in England is Tussy. Or rather the only person who can become his legal representative by taking out *letters of administration*. This must be done by the next of kin living in England — Tussy, unless she refuses and proposes some other person who, however, must equally be resident in the United Kingdom. I am therefore legally excluded. For various reasons letters of administration must be taken out.

Of the projects Mohr discussed with you at Vevey I was of course utterly ignorant and only regret you did not come over since 14th March when we should have known and complied with them as much as possible. . . .

I have said nothing to Tussy about your letter since I do not wish to come between two sisters in any way. If, therefore, you would wish to have any further explanations from her, please write to her direct . . . nothing would render the work more difficult than fresh misunderstandings between you and Tussy. All that we are trying to do is to perpetuate the memory of Mohr in worthy fashion and first will and must come the publication of his papers.[174]

The entire correspondence between Laura Lafargue and Friedrich Engels makes unpleasant reading. The general tone, even years after Marx's death, is seldom cordial. The endings are formal, if not frigid — "*bien à vous*," "*tout à vous*," "Yours." Engels is the better at observing the proprieties, continually inviting, if not urging, the Lafargues to pay a visit, pressing for replies or reports that had been promised but were not forthcoming. The answers from Paris fall into two categories: the evasive, excuses why things could not be done "just now" (they were moving, it was too hot, it was too cold, they had just engaged new staff), and second, requests for money. Quite unabashed the Lafargues allowed themselves to be supported continuously by Engels for the rest of his life to a truly embarrassing extent — as if this had been a legitimate "legacy." Money, money, money was requested, almost demanded. Though Engels found it perfectly possible to travel to Norway or America, he did not visit Paris. Nevertheless, in a touching combination of helplessness and readiness to help, he contributed generously. Frequently the only reaction was "*Merci* cheque"[175] — or a demand for more. Only once, only on one single occasion, did Laura express genuine gratitude:

My dear General,
I received your letter and cheque on the 14th. I don't know how to thank you for all your goodness to us, but I have come to connect the thought of you with everything that is pleasant, and whenever I sit down to an exceptionally good dinner or an extra "bock" or enjoy a day in the country or a new book, I say: "Well, that we owe to the General."[176]

In a ridiculous way this correspondence, extending over years, is sometimes reminiscent of that between Marx and Engels, for instance Engels's ejaculation: "How can I advise you on business if you give me all the information *afterwards?*"[177] Only on rare occasions are Engels's letters written in a lighter, more intimate vein — minor comments on Tussy's and Aveling's theatrical successes, gossip about one of Kautsky's disreputable love affairs, lamentations that the "Chateaux bottlings such as Lafite, Lagrange and other grands crus" were being bought up by Jews, parvenus, and others who did not appreciate them and "not by us who know how to appreciate them."[178] In general one senses that relations were strained and the slightest misunderstanding produces a tone of asperity, which Engels's annual Christmas parcel did little to alleviate. An angry letter of protest from London because Lafargue had published a private letter in the *Socialiste*[179] immediately led

Laura to assume that certain criticisms by Engels of her translation of the *Manifesto* resulted from his vexation over the affair.[180] When Engels complained that she did not answer letters, she merely replied with a sarcastic: "I stuck to the *silence qui est d'or*."[181]

On the other side Lafargue dispensed unsolicited advice on political maneuvers or condescending eulogies, for instance on Engels's publication of Marx's *Critique of the Gotha Programme*.[182] Moreover, Engels's detailed accounts of his labors on Marx's important papers, of their devastating state of disorganization, with disorderly collections of quotations and erroneous source references, definitely sound as if they were written for effect.

FICTION AS HISTORY, INTRIGUE AS POLEMICS —
A THREAT OF EXPULSION

In his lifetime, however, Marx's attention was concentrated mainly on his book, the mammoth unfinished symphony, the product of three and a half decades of exile in London, its growth governed by curious twists and turns so that one is often left wondering: is he gingerly moving toward it or slinking away from it? The whole of Marx's first ten years in London was a phase of indecision both politically and scientifically. The "World Society of Revolutionary Communists" was formed; Article 1 of its statutes read: "The aim of the Association is the overthrow of all privileged classes and their subjection to the dictatorship of the proletariat by maintaining the revolution permanently in being until the realization of communism, which will be the ultimate form of organization of the human family."[183]

It was designed to be an organization bringing the League of Communists together with the French Blanquist émigrés and the revolutionary Chartists. Yet in November that year (1850) Marx and Engels resigned from it again. In fact the League of Communists split into various factions after the spectacular argument when Marx accused Willich and Schapper of using revolutionary language; on a proposal from Marx the central authority was transferred to Köln, a masterstroke the results of which became obvious years later in the disagreements within the First International. The move to Köln of all places, where the anti-communist trial was to take place shortly thereafter, was in fact an interment, not a move. So on November 17, 1852, again on a proposal from Marx, the League dissolved itself. Here is another illustration of Marx's political tactics; men were ruthlessly expendable; in 1849 Engels was writing, "Willich was the only officer who was any good and so I went to him and became his adjutant"[184] but now the cry was "Willich has completely gone to the dogs."[185]

Willich — and Schapper with him — was becoming increasingly opposed to Marx's political and economic theory and to his idea of revolution born of crisis; Willich's thinking was closer to that of Weitling who had founded a newspaper in New York entitled *Republik der Arbeiter* (Workers' Republic) and was publishing a series of articles critical of Marx or rather of "the trend of economic criticism represented in Germany primarily by Karl Marx and his blind followers. They count on the emergence of class conflict and on crises just as the Neptunists insist that the earth was formed by water precipitation; they predict the moment of revolution as if they were calculating the formation of geological strata."[186]

Differences of theory, however, were not the only reason for the quarrel with Willich. He was a professional soldier of aristocratic background and was by no means averse to the rumor that he was descended from the Hohenzollerns. Marx disliked him socially; his glib tongue and the ill-mannered bravado with which, for instance, he once barged into the Marxes' bedroom early in the morning "with a Prussian neigh" got on Marx's nerves. He even tried to start a flirtation with Jenny Marx, who thought that he wanted "to pursue the worm that lives in every marriage and lure it out."[187] Willich posed not only as the man of action but also partly as the carefree playboy and partly as boon companion of the workers among whom he lived and who worshipped him; Marx, the thinker, they merely respected and this was what Marx found repugnant. The culmination of the dispute, once more not without its farcical aspects, came at a meeting of the Central Authority on September 1, 1850, when the quarreling reached such a pitch that Willich challenged Marx to a duel.

The leader of the international workers movement capering around in a duel! Marx declined but allowed someone else to fight for him — Konrad Schramm, now also hurling insults at Willich, stood in for him. A special journey was made to Belgium (dueling in England being forbidden) and pistols were drawn. In his memoirs Liebknecht tells how, next day, people in London anxiously awaited the outcome, for Willich was an excellent shot and Schramm had never handled a pistol in his life; the door of Marx's house opened and Barthélemy, Willich's second, entered, announcing in sepulchral tones: "*Schramm a une balle dans la tête*" (Schramm has a bullet in the head).[188] Then, bowing low, he left the house. Next day, however, Schramm appeared laughing gaily and with a horrific bandage around his head; he had only been struck a glancing blow.

This ended the bitterest phase of the quarrel. Engels wrote that, when in London for Christmas 1852, he had visited bars into which he would not have dared go six months earlier for fear of being beaten up by the Kinkel-Willich-Ruge gang.[189] Verbal blows were admittedly exchanged over the Köln communist trial, but then Willich became a Major General fighting on the northern side in the American Civil War alongside General Sherman; his courage and chivalry were such that on his death in Ohio no fewer than 2,500 people followed his coffin; by this time he was a much-bemedaled United States citizen. In face of this even Karl Marx in far-off London lowered his sword; in a postscript written in 1875 to a new edition of his *Revelations on the Communist Trial in Köln*, which Willich had savagely attacked, he wrote that Willich had proved himself to be something more than a dreamer.[190]

Years of irresolution. In 1850 a fresh *Neue Rheinische Zeitung–Politisch-ökonomische Revue* was formed as a limited liability company; the intention was to "transform this weekly periodical into a daily newspaper forthwith as soon as circumstances allow its return to Germany."[191]

It was soon abandoned; in other words it was a failure for both internal and external reasons. Perpetual revolutionary ardor was out of tune with the paper's intellectual line, and Marx was clearly beginning to realize that the economic situation was not yet ripe for his political purposes. From the "technical" point of view the paper was short of money from the outset; Julius Schuberth, the publisher in Hamburg, had restricted his agreement to *production,* demanding fifty percent of the retail price to defray cost of publication; Marx had to bear the cost of everything else — distribution, recruiting of agents, and so forth. This he undertook to do in the hope of getting money from "somewhere" — Holland, America, Germany. The money did not come in nor could the newspaper appear; Marx sent in no manuscripts. When they eventually arrived no one could decipher his illegible handwriting, so delay after delay. Moreover, the tone of Marx's articles was too direct for the publisher, who asked him to water them down since "he could handle language like no one else on earth."[192] Whether as a result of passive resistance against undesirable contents or — as Marx suspected — the publisher's commercial incompetence, the outcome was disastrous. The last number, a double issue, appeared in September 1850.

For Marx the year 1851 was occupied in study; he devoured whole libraries on currency problems; he filled fourteen notebooks with extracts; visitors remarked that instead of words of welcome they were received with lists of questions on economics.[193] By April 2, however, he was writing to Engels: "This is beginning to bore me. Fundamentally this science has made no more progress since A. Smith and D. Ricardo."[194]

Two years later he was talking about boredom in relation to writing for newspapers and longing to return to the scientific work of which he had just been complaining.[195] In fact Marx did not work at his real task for years; for four years he never entered the British Museum. Instead he wrote articles on secret diplomacy between England and Russia or the partition of Turkey;

he read J. Hamer-Purpstall's *History of the Ottoman Empire;* he learned Spanish by reading Calderon and Cervantes; he studied L. Mieroslavsky's *History of the Polish Commune in the XVIII Century;* he wrote nearly a dozen articles on the Indian Mutiny of 1857; he wrote articles about China, India, the Anglo-Persian Peace Treaty, the role of the East India Company, the problem of the Danube princelings. Marx's articles written for the *New York Daily Tribune* in the first quarter of 1858 deal with the French crisis, British trade, the East India Company's loans, the assassination of Orsini, introduction of the prefectoral system in France, and Pélissier's mission to England. On the recommendation of Lassalle, who was a correspondent, he wrote similar articles for the *Neue Oder-Zeitung* of Breslau (in general he used as a basis his English articles for the *New York Daily Tribune* — there were some one hundred of them in 1855 alone). Brockhaus (the German encyclopedia) turned down an article on contemporary economic literature in England. A brochure on Bruno Bauer's Russophile writings was left unfinished. Charles Anderson Dana, who in 1841 joined the New England Brook Farm formed on the lines of Fourier's "Phalanstères" and whose *New York Daily Tribune* regularly printed Marx's articles from 1851 onward, proposed that he write an article on aesthetics for the *New American Cyclopaedia,* but he did not follow up the suggestion; he did read Friedrich Theodor Vischer's *Asthetik* but never wrote the single page requested. At the same time Marx took part in the various activities of the Workers' Education Association — excursions to the country, fencing tournaments, or chess evenings. He even expanded the private course on political economy initially held in his house for a few functionaries of the League, and from November 1850 to summer 1851 gave a series of lectures on "bourgeois property" to a packed hall in Great Windmill Street; as a result of his adroit question-and-answer technique they sometimes took on the character of a seminar. It is an extraordinary, almost ominous, thought that here was this man with an outstanding brain, often without a penny in his pocket to buy a newspaper, lecturing to a handful of divided, impotent, unemployed émigrés in a down-at-the-heels meetinghall on the first floor of 20 Great Windmill Street and chalking up on a blackboard the sentences with which *Das Kapital* eventually opened — while in Germany all sorts of dunderheads were calling themselves professors. The picture is no less sinister when one reads an informer's report about these evenings when there was talk of axes and guillotines, of regicide and assassination of the "English Moon Calf,"[196] the Queen of England, living only a few hundred yards away in Buckingham Palace. Again the Bull's Head Tavern near New Oxford Street, where Marx formed an anti-Willich splinter group known as the "Society of Dr. Marx" (it disappeared again in autumn 1851, together with its president, Gottlieb Ludwig Stechan, a cabinetmaker), was not so much a meeting place for sinister cutthroats and conspirators as a sort of popular high school where the émigrés learned English or listened to Liebknecht's lectures on the theory of pauperization.

The semi-comic figures of the London émigrés on the platform amused and irritated Marx to such an extent that he was only too easily persuaded to write a pamphlet about them — another superfluous piece of work diverting him from his real subject. "We are crying with laughter at the pickling of these blockheads,"[197] he wrote enthusiastically to Jenny from Manchester where he was staying with Engels and preparing a manuscript on the "Great Men in Exile." It is a real compendium of scurrilous comment, full of inaccuracies and spiteful remarks; the distorted picture of the honest German revolutionary Harro Harring is only one example out of many of Marx's thirst for denunciation. The fact that this diatribe was, so to speak, a product of precisely that on which he wished to pour scorn clearly escaped Marx. The idea of writing this pamphlet was given him by a Hungarian refugee, Colonel Janos Bangya, an inscrutable character who floated around in all sorts of émigré committees, promising money and boasting about contacts; he promised Marx £25 for a "character sketch." Overjoyed at the prospect of taking a swipe at all these people simultaneously, Marx, normally so susceptible to suspicion, allowed himself to be taken in by a swindler — the publisher did not exist but a recipient was available, the man who had commissioned the book; Colonel Bangya sold the manuscript, of which no precise copy existed, to the German police.[198] The vendetta never took place.

Running away and running round in circles — during these years Karl Marx alternately advanced toward and then retreated from his "main business" in a curious ritual of fear. This much is clear: he found it easier to formulate his great assault on history and society if he could approach it via a minor assault on specific people. He was not merely being diverted into pamphlet-writing; here was the throb of a specific talent for lucid, vivid, comprehensible argumentation inspired by attack on some tangible target.

When Ernest Jones, second of the two left-wing Chartist leaders, born and brought up in Germany and of all Englishmen the nearest to the Marx-type Continental socialist, gave him all sorts of details about conditions in England and Scotland, all this information was "logged in." It was from Jones, for instance, that Marx learned that common land in Scotland was being taken into private ownership and farmers and smallholders were being driven out to make room for nature reserves or grouse moors. Jones was also the source of material for his savage and sensational article in the *New York Daily Tribune:* the Duchess of Sutherland had made philanthropic pronouncements in favor of the Negro cause in America. In a brilliant piece of acid polemics Marx now drew a picture of a hardhearted, haughty, capricious old woman, vindictive, cold, and crazy, who not only humiliated entire peoples but drove them out of house and home. But — Marx was not merely describing an evil, blue-blooded old hag; his target was a system. The article is a rough draft of the corresponding — and more detailed — passage in *Capital*.

Karl Marx's "journalism" was more than journalism. He possessed emotional appeal, but his penetrating, sarcastic articles invariably aimed beyond his immediate subject; his analyses of a "case" were not the jeremiads of a humanitarian, noble-minded idealist but pragmatic, mistrustful questionings into history. Here was the "well-tuned piano"; the "art of the fugue" was to follow later.

In May 1851 numerous arrests were made in Köln. The Prussian government produced a dossier of forgeries, based on informers' reports, about clandestine plots and thefts of genuine records and announced that it had "uncovered" an international conspiracy. The Bonapartist police, on the eve of the coup d'état analyzed so brilliantly by Marx, were ready to assist in the fabrication of a "Franco-German" plot. The main document for the prosecution was a collection of forgeries made by various police officers, informers, and political mountebanks; it took no account of the internal dissensions among the various political groupings — the "Willich/Schapper Party" and the "Marx Party," for instance, which had always rejected putschs and revolutionary activity. Marx expended vast energy in exposing the case for the prosecution in the Köln communist trial for what it was — a figment of the imagination. His desire to help his hard-pressed comrades in Köln was equaled by his thirst for battle. A voluminous correspondence started, all of which had to be forwarded to Germany by devious means, since all direct mail was opened and censored; Engels and Weerth dispatched it in commercial wrappings, with fake delivery notes or under forged adhesive labels; Frau Marx and various assistants did the writing while other people trotted off to various post offices; meanwhile the children whined because Marx was continuously scolding them.

All these activities were by no means without their danger. Reports were continually arriving from Prussia that the British authorities suspected Marx of being leader of an intrepid gang that would not shrink even from regicide; not only was the assassination attempt of May 22, 1850, laid at his door, but he was said to be planning an attack on Queen Victoria and her consort, Prince Albert. Von Manteuffel, the Prussian Minister-President, passed this "information" on officially to the Foreign Office; Marx was threatened with deportation. The extent to which all this was purely the product of astute fabrication is shown by a secret memorandum from Friedrich Wilhelm IV to Otto von Manteuffel, who wanted to retaliate for Kinkel's successful escape:

My dear Manteuffel,

. . . this has given me an idea which I would not classify as entirely straightforward. Would not Stieber be the most valuable person to publicize the machinations of the escape conspiracy and give the Prussian public the spectacle, for which it has rightly yearned for so long, of a plot which has been detected and received due punishment?

Make haste, therefore, to appoint Stieber and have him show what he can do. . . .

Burn this note.

There is not a moment to lose.

Vale.

Friedrich Wilhelm.[199]

Manteuffel did not burn the note. Stieber was one of the principal agents and forgers pilloried by Marx in his vitriolic *Revelations;* in these he made clear that he had certainly not been the intermediary between the ostensibly disunited comrades in Köln and the incendiarists in London. The Public Prosecutor was compelled to drop Stieber's "unfortunate" book from the case. Nevertheless, seven of the eleven accused were sentenced.[200]

Marx was not deported. Nevertheless his *Revelations on the Köln Communist Trial* did not reach Germany. The two thousand copies at ten silver groschen apiece were confiscated on crossing the Baden frontier. In America, where the whole affair was of interest only to a few of the refugees of 1848, the *New England Zeitung* of Boston did print the *Revelations;* Engels had 440 special copies printed at his own expense but it is not known whether, as intended, they were ever distributed in the Rhineland — with the help of Lassalle.

This polemic presented stories as history, intrigues as sociological happenings. It was a finger-exercise in pugnacity, testimony, and judgment with drawn sword all at the same time. It was followed by Marx's analysis of the Bonapartists' coup d'état, *The Eighteenth Brumaire of Louis Bonaparte*, which was a stroke of genius.

In 1895, when Engels published Marx's series of articles "1848–1849" written for the ephemeral *Neue Rheinische Zeitung,* he headed them "The Class Struggles in France 1848–1850" describing them as "Marx's first attempt to explain a section of contemporary history by means of his materialist conception on the basis of the given economic situation."[201] This could be said even more aptly of the splendid piece of prose that Marx wrote during the winter of 1851 and the spring of 1852 and which first appeared in a series of "informal issues" in Weydemeyer's luckless American periodical *Die Revolution.*[202]

The coup d'état carried out by Louis Napoleon, Bonaparte's nephew, on December 2, 1851, the arrest of leading members of the Convention, the bloody suppression of attempted revolt in Paris, and finally his coronation as

Napoleon III, Emperor of the French, caused shock, protest, and horror on all sides. Though he was officially recognized by all the Powers, the Czar Nicholas I refused to address him as *"frère."* Comparison of Victor Hugo's famous monograph *Napoleon the Little,* however, and that of Marx demonstrates that the words shock, protest, and horror can have very different meanings.

Napoleon the Little, published in ten editions in rapid succession, is a pasquinade, a romantic, sentimental, whining lament on the level of "others filch handkerchiefs, he steals an Empire."[203] He wails "Ah, these rulers of the day,"[204] "and this man is the Emperor's nephew . . . and this knave tells France that he has saved her."[205]

The attitude of Victor Hugo, the honest protesting émigré, his almost culinary revulsion, demonstrates horror at the visible apparition and total lack of comprehension of the reasons for it. The bourgeois liberal, hiding his eyes in defensive shame, condemns himself to blindness and inarticulateness. The entire book is a mere torrent of words, meaningless posturing.

Karl Marx's book opens, not with some clever aphorism, but with a passion reminiscent of his school-leaving essay:

Men make their own history but they do not make it just as they please; they do not make it under circumstances chosen by themselves, but under circumstances directly encountered, given and transmitted from the past. The tradition of all the dead generations weighs like a nightmare on the brain of the living.[206]

Whereas Victor Hugo, "faced with this unutterable crime," explicitly declares that he is "only a historiographer" registering the crime, a minute-writer in other words, Marx gives an analysis showing *how* the coup d'état came about, what the political and economic causes were, and what the inevitable political results must be. Even where the two books correspond almost word for word, the difference between the lachrymose and the dialectical approach is obvious.

Marx declares that failure to differentiate between the lily and the tricolor, between the Houses of Bourbon and Orleans, is equivalent to failure to differentiate between large landed property and capital; he maintains that the pre–Second Empire form of state was inherently contradictory; it bore the name neither of Bourbon nor of Orleans but of capital and, even while thinking that it was girding its loins for a fresh upsurge, it carried within it the germ of its doom.

This is one of Marx's very great books, full of cold fanaticism, sparkling mastery of language, and explosive intellectual force. Marx calls the demands of the Paris proletariat "utopian nonsense."[207] He rejects the old, oft-repeated notion of the violation of a people: "A nation and a woman are not forgiven the unguarded hour in which the first adventurer that came along could violate them."[208] This is no playing with words; in complete detail it is historical materialism.

The book remained unknown in Europe. Not a single bourgeois newspaper mentioned it. It was not published in Germany until twenty years later.

CHAPTER SEVEN

LASSALLE–
"JEWISH NIGGER"

"I CANNOT STAND TIDY BUT SHABBY CLOTHES"

An increasingly powerful workers' movement had been formed in Germany, parallel to but separate from that of Karl Marx. Its momentum and its impetus came from someone quite different — Ferdinand Lassalle. The relationship between Karl Marx and Ferdinand Lassalle was a highly special one, a pocket drama composed of tragedy and comedy, hatred, envy, and admiration, mendacity, malice, and perjury. Franz Mehring describes it as "the most difficult psychological problem of [Marx's] life."[1]

Lassalle, seven years younger than Marx, grew up in Breslau in a home characterized by upper-class Jewish liberalism; his father was a City Councillor, a member of the most important parliamentary conclave of the pre-March era; his mother came from Franconia and had little affinity with the city, clearly preferring to cling to her Jewish rites, such as the Seder and the eating of kosher meat. The rules were not strictly kept, however; card games were allowed on the Sabbath; the father was quite prepared to eat ham paté and, when his son was taking a trip to the East in 1856, he was asked to bring back not only earth from the Temple compound, but holy water from the Jordan for the Cardinal — all evidence of a degree of "emancipation." "As if one could eat gentile meat and still be a good Jew,"[2] Ferdinand Lassalle wrote in his diary at the age of fifteen. He adopted a somewhat haughty attitude in conversation with his father, who was horrified at his son's intention to become a poet. The general tone in which he wrote was reminiscent of young Marx's starry-eyed letters to his father. Prometheus with Jewish ringlets.

Lassalle's letters to his father are only superficially concerned with this problem; they are in fact part of his self-questioning process, almost literary studies designed for an audience. On one occasion, mortified by a box on the ear from his father, he tried to drown himself but, when discovered, merely replied quite calmly: "I was looking at the river." In a similarly relaxed tone he wrote: "Philosophy drew near to me." When only fifteen, with complete self-assurance he called himself an egoist; similarly, after due deliberation, he could write: "Had I been born a prince or a duke, I would be heart and soul an aristocrat, but since I am merely the son of a simple bourgeois, I shall be a democrat in time."[3]

Marx, the lawyer's son from Trier, had written: "If we have considered all this, and if the conditions of our life permit us to choose any profession we like, we may adopt the one that assures us the greatest worth, one which is based on ideas of whose truth we are thoroughly convinced."[4]

Even when still a schoolboy, Lassalle, with the almost grotesque capacity of the scholar for looking at himself from a distance, called his own day-dreams puerile (his favorite picture was of himself, sword in hand, leading the Jews to independence). He too was the angel from heaven, the messenger of salvation, the chosen one, whose craven, broken-backed people was not worthy of him. He too had the Jew's self-hate that lay at the root of the search for a "substitute people" — the workers, more free, more proud, more diligent.

He doctored his school reports, concealing his marks from his father and remarking nonchalantly: "My mother has power of attorney."[5] His family asked his advice about his sister's marriage contract; he "safeguarded" his sister's compromising letters. Here was a young man who saw his way ahead clearly. Obstacles existed only to be overcome. School was an institution which he despised — as his masters understood only to well: "Gentlemen, you must realize that Lassalle looks at everything with the eye of the philosopher. We are not his superiors. He does not accept the notion of a superior. We are his subordinates since, after all, we are paid. . . ."[6]

When these subordinates had the temerity to make difficulties for him over his matriculation, he turned to the Minister of Culture, Eichhorn — at the age of seventeen! — "This is no insignificant matter; it concerns the oppression of an individual who can be of service to his country and will devote his energies thereto."[7]

One is entitled to ask what philosophy was drawing near to him.

In 1843 he went to Berlin, where Hegel's ideas were in ferment at the time. Karl Marx had moved from Trier just a year before and had been running the *Rheinische Zeitung* in Köln since October 1842. Berlin was Lassalle's training ground; he lived an ascetic existence but at the same time tested the prospects of becoming a social success. He could afford neither coffee nor butter; he studied Hegel from 4:00 A.M. to 9:00; yet:

I often ask mother to send me some shirts, both day shirts and nightshirts; I do not make out very well with mine since I need three shirts a week in summer. However they should be finer than those which Papa bought for me; those are very ordinary and a good shirt is one of the first essentials for a proper person. . . . I cannot stand the compromise of "tidy but shabby clothing."[8]

He had affairs with women but he did not fall in love; he noted "the first quiverings of communism" in connection with the weavers' revolt but he did not become involved. Even as early as this "the proletariat" was a class in his eyes — but not a reality. It never entered the head of this revolutionary son of a bourgeois Jew to earn money by taking up a profession. He became involved in all sorts of money transactions, gambled, lost, invested, won — appealing for money was his profession; money there had to be, somehow, from somewhere and as much as possible: from his father, his brother-in-law, every conceivable acquaintance. All were harnessed to the procurement of it. It was *their* business to take care of it; he had greater things in mind. A single letter to his mother shows the range of his preoccupations: assassination attempt on the King, relationship with nature, historical position of the Jewish people, riding lessons. The habit of rehearsing his speeches in court before a mirror was not confined to his later years; even at this early stage the studied negligence of the folds in his cravat was a matter for contemplation. Money transactions gained him his first contact with a nationally famous figure, Heinrich Heine. The first article which the Breslau schoolboy ever published was devoted to Heine, to his feud with Börne. Now Lassalle visited Heine in Paris and tried to introduce some method into his bizarre negotiations with his uncle Karl in Hamburg. A letter from Heine to Varnhagen of 1846 was enough to guarantee an entrée to anyone wishing to draw attention to himself:

My Friend,
Herr Lassalle, who brings you this letter, is a young man of the most remarkable intellectual ability, of the most fundamental erudition, the widest knowledge and the greatest sagacity that I have ever met; he combines the richest talent for exposition with such determination and agility in action that I am left astounded; if he retains his goodwill towards me, I anticipate the most effective assistance from him. In any case this combination of knowledge and ability, of talent and character was for me a most pleasant phenomenon and, with your versatility in appreciating merit, you will assuredly vouch for my accuracy. Herr Lassalle is a distinctive offspring of the new generation which rejects the resignation and moderation with which we have idled and drivelled our way through *our* time with a greater or lesser degree of hypocrisy. This new generation wishes to take its fill of life and leave its visible mark; we, the older generation, bowed humbly before the invisible, snatched at shadows and scents of flowers, resigned ourselves and moaned and were perhaps happier than these tough gladiators who face death in battle so proudly. The Thousand Year Reich of romanticism is at an end and I myself was its last, deposed, mythical monarch.[9]

Nevertheless the charm and appeal of this letter had its counterpart in melancholy and bitterness, and in perspicacity too. Lassalle displayed this letter over and over again as proof that he was "an offspring of the new generation" and it seems doubtful whether he did so in ignorance of the reserve and distaste implied in Heine's estimate of him. When the letter was published in the *Neue Rheinische Zeitung* a disillusioned Heine enquired of Georg Weerth, one of the editors, who had released the letter for publication. In letters to his brother Gustav he refers to the young man's malevolence and to his own anxiety lest, after his death, anyone might claim to have been his friend; he even uses the words murder, forgery, and theft. A month later Heine prudently withdrew from the affair.

Lassalle, however, had now become involved in a much more absorbing cause célèbre, the "case" of his life — Countess Hatzfeldt's divorce. In this affair he asked Heine of all people to undertake discreet investigations into the affairs of Count Edmund von Hatzfeldt's mistress (in interminable legal maneuvers the Count was disputing his wife's right to her house, her chateau, and her property). Heine was circumspect but definite in dealing with the "tough gladiator":

I have indeed received your two letters both dated 27 February. Their principal subject caused me some astonishment, in fact I raised my eyebrows at your inexperience; however I have understood and considered the core of the matter. How little I am suited to do this — it is more suitable for a character in a Sue detective story than for a person in my circumstances — is clear to me from the fact that so far I have been unable even to reconnoitre the ground, a contributory factor admittedly being my shocking state of health at the moment. . . .[10]

What was it all about?

BATTLE FOR COUNTESS HATZFELDT'S MILLIONS — START OF A POLITICAL CAREER

The Hatzfeldt battle — more breathtaking, more decisive, and more bitter than Heine's Hamburg war over his legacy (which ended in a deplorable compromise) — possessed all the features of a cloak-and-dagger tragedy: an interminable series of lawsuits, statements on oath, perjuries, accusations, counteraccusations, briberies; an army of witnesses, genuine or false, spies, and informers concentrated round the affair. The problem was this: Count Hatzfeldt, who was both rich and powerful, would not agree to a divorce and had no wish to reach a settlement with his wife and their son; he had, however, made over large sums of money and given assurances for the future to his mistress. This had to be proved. A deed-box was stolen and letters intercepted. Lassalle could now prove everything, but in the process gained an unenviable reputation as a housebreaker and thief, a man who would shrink from nothing.

Like Countess Hatzfeldt, he was interested less in the money than in the attempt to conduct a great historic and indeed political lawsuit. It was *the* emancipation case par excellence — a woman was to demonstrate her independence of her lord and master's arbitrary and unreasonable right to dispose of everything. In fact "the entire Rhineland" took the liveliest interest in the progress of the affair. The count's omnipotence was almost medieval; he had already taken two children away from their mother and the battle now raged round the son Paul, later a diplomat under the Empire. He forbade his wife to leave the chateau; he compelled her to associate with him, but only by letter passed from one room to another; then again he forbade her to enter the chateau and ordered the staff not to let her in. The Countess forced her way in with a squad of peasants. The King himself intervened in this marital scandal.

Lassalle, who had returned to Berlin in 1846, had found his platform. He was not a divorce-court lawyer; he was a politician. He showed a masterly capacity for brushing all legalities aside in his major speeches and interventions — for him the moral chaos of a private affair was the prototype of the chaos in the state, the villainy of a powerful man mirrored the depravity of authority. His deed-box speech of 1848 was a denunciation frequently interrupted by applause from the democratically minded audience.

Lassalle's victories were triumphs and even his defeats were victories. He had become famous. When he was arrested in February 1848, people demonstrated; when he was released on August 11, he was cheered in the street. No one had hitherto launched public attacks on the state and the existing order with such logic. Where did he stand politically? Did he know Marx?

Arnold Mendelssohn, one of his closest associates (and heavily involved in the deed-box affair) had read *The Condition of the Working Class in England* and *The Holy Family*. He talked of the Chartist movement and of organized struggle by workers grouped in associations, but did not use the expression "class warfare." It seems improbable that Lassalle was unaware of these books, names, and notions. He seems not to have known of the *Communist Manifesto*,[11] however, and knew nothing of the League of Communists; the expression "Marxism," which probably originated from Bakunin, was unknown to Lassalle;[12] he is not to be found using these phrases on any single occasion (any more than they were to be found in the *Neue Rheinische Zeitung,* by the way). Revolutionary popular upheavals were something foreign to him — the mass of the people were the source of a mandate whether it was issued outside the Countess's house or on Worringen Heath in 1848, when Ferdinand Lassalle from Düsseldorf and Karl Marx from Köln met.

At that time Marx had also made the acquaintance of Countess Hatzfeldt and had come to appreciate her; in a short letter of introduction to Herwegh he had written: "For a *German* this woman has displayed great energy in her duel with her husband."[13]

When Marx went to Köln Lassalle was in prison. The Countess was penniless and in great agitation about her son. Marx took charge of her, lent her money, was often in her house in Düsseldorf, and joined with her in public demonstrations in support of the imprisoned Lassalle — one of the extremely rare instances of this type of activity throughout Marx's life.

The real root of the Marx-Lassalle alliance certainly did not lie in their sympathy for a depraved aristocratic lady or anxiety about her son, whom Georg Weerth kept in hiding for a while. They were at one in their political ideas — and these were set out in the *Neue Rheinische Zeitung;* the fact that Marx made available the columns of his most important journalistic instrument for Lassalle's voluminous reporting of the deed-box affair (which Engels later attempted to deny in order to present a picture of antipathy between the two from the outset)[14] is only an outward sign. The two men's views coincided on what was right and practicable in politics.

Lassalle's concept is set out by his biographer, Shlomo Na'aman: "There are men who partake in an idea and there are men without substance. Those without substance are a means to an end; participation in the idea is an end in itself."[15] Following this line of thought, the workers were a means to an end in the 1848 revolution; they were to exert leverage — on the bourgeoisie. It was not the workers whose demands were to be met but the bourgeoisie who would set up a form of bourgeois democracy as an expression of the predominance of their class; the workers were to organize themselves but only in a sort of low-pressure agency. Marx considered this pressure from below to be far more effective than, for instance, workers' representation in Parliament. He had no wish to see worker candidates; for instance, he hailed the withdrawal of Weber, who had stood for Elberfeld. Engels supported precisely this viewpoint in a warning note to Marx in April 1848: "The workers are beginning to stir somewhat, still very crudely but on a large scale. They have at once formed coalitions. This is, however, an obstacle to *us*."[16]

All this can be traced back to the dialectical concept of long-term strategy and short-term pragmatic tactics — revolution is the ultimate aim, but not now and not in this way. Only from within a victorious bourgeoisie, which will necessarily develop mechanisms of oppression as must any ruling class, can the proletariat develop as a "class of its own," in other words a class with its own concept of itself, consciousness of itself, and clear ideas of its aims. Bourgeois democracy and capitalism were the seedbeds, the essential prerequisites, positive from the point of view of history, desirable.

At the same time there existed a small stratum of society that knew all this, that could perceive, indicate, and provoke the threatening doom; this was the "management" or directorate. It laid down the moment of upheaval; it directed the spontaneous reactions. This combination of historically correct diagnosis and a concept of political practice which was the preserve of a few initiates produced a pontifical remark from Marx later in his London exile: "We have received our appointment as representatives of the proletarian party from nobody *but ourselves*."[17] It was only logical that he should sometimes receive mail in London addressed to "Charles Marx, the future Dictator of Germany."[18]

At this point, 1848, the Frankfurt National Assembly was simply an object of contempt, and even the Berlin National Assembly was treated with greater respect. The historical analysis was right: there *was* no proletariat. Neither Köln nor Düsseldorf was an industrial city. In the Ruhr area Marx at any rate was totally unknown; no one had ever heard of the *Communist Manifesto;* Bebel wrote that it was "totally unknown"[19] to him. Even in Essen there were hardly any organized workers. In the mining areas people appeared with black-and-white cockades and in 1849 refused all assistance to the fugitive fighters from Elberfeld. This chaos was no doubt the reason why Marx always referred to the workers as "*Knoten*" and tramps.

Marx's and Lassalle's ideas on political organization were very similar: a cadre party and *dirigiste* leadership. Their ideas on political aims and methods of attaining them diverged. Marx thought solely in historical, in other words variable, terms. "Democracy," "people," "freedom" were not entities per se. In his speech on February 8, 1849, at the trial of the Köln Democratic Committee (the case arose from the call to refuse to pay taxes, the *Neue Rheinische Zeitung's* final apotheosis and trumpet-call), he deliberately refrained from taking his stand on current law; he did not recognize current law as valid law; the legislature and executive were no longer his own:

The National Assembly has no rights of its own; the people have transferred to it the affirmation of their own rights. If it does not fulfill this mandate, it is extinct. The people themselves then enter the stage and act by virtue of their own plenipotentiary powers.[20]

Since democracy was regarded as a phase, Marx could perfectly well call his newspaper the "Organ of Democracy" — it was an indefinite term, variable.

Things were quite different with Lassalle. The similarities in his speech of May 3, 1849, in his own defense when he was accused of "incitement to take up arms against the ruling authorities of the country," are only superficial; the difference is striking. (As is known, the speech was never made but was printed and distributed by Lassalle beforehand.) Lassalle in fact *defended* the law; *he* took his stand on legality; it was *the government* that had infringed the law.

Ideas which for Marx were historical, for Lassalle were ideas of the law of nature; and this meant that, in complete contrast to those of Marx, they were immutable — not proletariat but "people." Lassalle would never have manned the barricades wearing a black-red-gold sash, as Engels did in Elberfeld; he would never have made a speech or issued an appeal infringing the existing legal code. For this reason he was later able to invoke it with righteous indignation. In any case, to him the proletariat was an idea, not a reality nor a truth nor an experience. In a half-finished manuscript written a year after the speech in his own defense the concluding sentence reads: "How the proletariat develops from large-scale industry we will see later."[21]

From now on this time-fuse was ticking away, and it was destined to produce innumerable small explosions in the Marx-Lassalle relationship. For Lassalle the proletariat was a democratic, petit-bourgeois concept. Marx's concept was more revolutionary; his tactics can be described as veer and haul, sometimes running counter to his long-term strategic aim; he could enter into temporary alliance with partners whom he despised. Here was the antithesis between reform and revolution, between democratic socialism and people's democracy.

TWO DIFFERING CONCEPTS OF POLITICS

In the 1850s Marx inevitably stood aloof from Lassalle's training courses and educational associations, as aloof as he did from all similar clubs and circles in Brussels, Paris, or London. If he did attend such gatherings or even address them himself, he did so only because they served in two ways as rehearsals, either for the elaboration of some point of theory or for working out a form of organization. His appearances were select private affairs and, as Liebknecht records, he generally only agreed to them unwillingly.[22] Liebknecht is also the source of the incidental story[23] that at these meetings Marx spoke very indistinctly; a member of his audience in the Workers' Education Association was very pleased that he had understood everything with the exception of the word "*Achtblättler*" (eight-leafed), which Marx was always using. He knew about "four-leafed," he said, but what was "eight-leafed"? The culprit was Marx's Rhineland accent; he was referring to "*Arbeiter*" (workers).

In an allusion to this, the Kugelmanns later presented Marx with a notebook, on the silken cover of which a friend's wife had stuck a picture of an oak tree surrounded by eight ivy leaves; the tree was intended to represent

Marx and the green leaves the "Eight-leafers"; underneath was the word "Unite."[24]

On another occasion Marx's Rhineland dialect left his audience in some puzzlement — when he apparently referred to a society of "Timocrats" (in other words, people of property) when he meant "democrats."[25]

So there, on the one hand, was Marx, living in the most depressing circumstances in London, shy of appearing in public, shy even in front of his "tramps," laboring uninterruptedly at a literally overwhelming work of theory. On the other hand was Lassalle in Düsseldorf, living a life of splendor and frivolity, a publicly recognized, indeed increasingly famous, figure, politically effective and highly productive. With a sort of desperate defiance Marx refers to the "authentic isolation" in which he and Engels now found themselves and which was entirely fitting to their position and their principles[26] — "and the democratic, red or even communist mob will never *love* us."[27] Marx set no store by these popular movements, which he consigned to the devil,[28] and Engels only confirmed him in his leaning toward aristocratic ways:

At last we have another opportunity — the first for a long time — to show that we have no need of popularity or of support from any party in any country, that our position is totally independent of such trifles. From now on we are responsible only for ourselves and when the moment arrives for these gentlemen to require us, we are in a position to dictate our own terms. Until then at least we have some peace. Admittedly we are to a degree lonely as well . . . have we not acted for a number of years as if any Tom, Dick and Harry was a member of our party when in fact we had no party and when people whom we reckoned, at least officially, as belonging to our party (with the proviso that between ourselves we labelled them as incorrigible animals) did not even understand the rudiments of our business. How can people like us, who shun any official position like the plague, fit into a "party"? What good to us is a "party," in other words a gang of asses who swear by us because they think us people of their own ilk, when we spit at popularity and would be untrue to ourselves if we began to become popular? In fact it is no loss if we are no longer regarded as the "true and adequate expression" of the unintelligent boors with whom we have been thrown together in recent years.[29]

Meanwhile, what of Düsseldorf, and later Berlin? Lassalle was going from strength to strength; in August 1854 a settlement had even been arranged, through his good offices, between Countess Hatzfeldt and her husband; she was now a rich woman and Lassalle himself prosperous and independent with an income for life. He traveled — to Paris, for instance, or the East (Marx even complained that Lassalle had not paid him a visit in London when he passed via Paris).[30] Marx was full of suspicion, if not fury. He was only too ready to believe rumors that the Düsseldorf workers had complained about high life in the Villa Hatzfeldt; the tales of one of Lassalle's associates named

Gustav Levy — later treasurer of the "Allgemeine Deutsche Arbeiter Verein" (German General Workers Union, ADAV) — were hailed without question as representing the "workers' " views. After all — at about this time Marx had been arrested in London on his way to the pawnshop with valuable family silver inherited by his wife (the police could not believe that a set of 400-year-old silver with the crest of one of the most distinguished families in the country belonged to this unkempt, shaggy-bearded foreigner).[31] Levy had in fact no authority from anyone; he was simply vexed that Lassalle had refused him a loan.[32] Then came an obscure "Colonel Touroute" with stories of the spendthrift existence led by Lassalle and the Countess in their magnificent mansion.[33] Everything was now calculated to make Marx infuriated with Lassalle. He took note of what suited him; he lapped up complaints about Lassalle's "industrial chivalry" and "petticoat diplomacy."[34] He closed his ears, however, to reports that the Düsseldorf workers had sent solemn declarations hailing this house of luxury and profligacy as a haven of fearless and determined support for their party and that Eduard von Müller-Tellering, hitherto a highly esteemed member of the staff of the *Neue Rheinische Zeitung* and now on the run, had been taken into hiding there.[35]

This was the beginning of that phase in the relationship between the two men which was destined to last until Lassalle's death; it was a phase of double-tongued insincerity that even Franz Mehring calls "unpleasant."[36]

Apart from one or two essays and articles Marx had nothing in print. The contract concluded with Leske, the publisher, in February 1845 for a book of "critique of politics and political economy" was not honored except for the payment of the substantial advance of 1,500 francs; the book does not exist. The valuable *Theses on Feuerbach* were simply notebook entries. So little notice was taken of his overvoluminous assault on Bruno Bauer, *The Holy Family or Critique of Critical Criticism,* that no publisher could be found for his next book, *The German Ideology.* The political and linguistic masterpiece of the *Communist Manifesto* was largely unknown; it was no more than a party "circular" without widespread influence. No one was interested in the various émigré quarrels and pamphlets. No one in Germany knew about the American articles — which were mostly drafted by Engels. Here was the beginning of the situation later bemoaned by German politicians such as Bebel, Liebknecht, and Bernstein — the "two patriarchs" were foreign to the German scene.

Lassalle's writings, on the other hand, had a colossal circulation; his activities were on everyone's lips. Whatever he did, whether applying for a residence permit for Berlin, being deported, publishing something — all was "publicity." And the worst of it all was that Marx needed him: "I had asked Lassalle whether he could look out any literary business for me in Germany since in view of my reduced receipts and increased expenses I must take things seriously."[37]

Lassalle proposed a scheme, to be worked out via his cousin Friedländer, for work on a newspaper, but it came to nothing. Lassalle's persistence in his efforts to help Marx was remarkable, but on Marx's side the only result was suspicion; a further proposal, again through the cousin's good offices, that Marx should write for the *Wiener Presse* he did not follow up, though in this case on plausible political grounds — that he did not like the paper's pro-English line. When Lassalle now announced publication of a two-volume book on Heraclitus, an early effort interrupted by the Hatzfeldt affair, Marx lost his temper. It was now almost ten years — since publication of the *Eighteenth Brumaire* — since he had had a single word in print. On economics, the subject which everyone was awaiting, there had been nothing since the pre-March period, since his anti-Proudhon pamphlet *The Poverty of Philosophy*. The announcement of the book on Heraclitus, therefore, produced nothing but fury; Engels reacted similarly, expressing anger and regret that their criticisms were not proving very valid. In a letter in which he uses the habitual opening "Dearest Mohr" for the first time, Engels says casually:

Herewith Lassalle's letter returned. The *silly Jew* through and through. It will be a collection of fine tales scratched together and the thing that will "set things alight" and about which he is being so secretive. We know, of course, that the fellow is useless but it is difficult to find a positive reason for breaking with him, particularly since we have heard nothing more from the Düsseldorf workers.[38]

Marx at once sensed what was really going on — in fact Lassalle had updated an old book in order to "launch off" into new ideas, into the science of economics! Retribution and revenge against the unborn child now became the order of the day. Marx's mere phraseology shows how disconcerted he was; from now on Lassalle became "that fellow," "the Yid," "clever Izzy," "Baron Izzy," "a completely vulgar scoundrel," "the brute," "a pompous ape," "wily Ephraim."[39]

Marx thought Lassalle's statement that he had begun this book in 1846 to be a lie; at the same time, however, he found it "obsolete Hegelian" and therefore possibly originating from that period. He even fumed about the COD price which he said would ensure the book "a very bad reception,"[40] as if that was Lassalle's fault. Even before laying hands on the book he was already jeering at the "comic vanity of the fellow who is determined to become famous and for no good reason writes 75 pages on Greek philosophy."[41] Then came the publication of *The Philosophy of Heraclitus the Dark of Ephesus,* which, according to Lassalle's offensively bombastic statements, was to take away the breath of Berlin's scholastic world. Marx "thumbed the thing through"[42] and went into the attack — but only in letters to Engels; in those to Lassalle it was quite the reverse. To Engels he mocked at this "feeble compilation" and the "enormous exhibition of erudition" — "But every expert knows how easy it is, when one has time and money and, like Mr. Lassalle, can have the Bonn University library sent direct to his home whenever he likes, to put together this sort of exhibition of quotations."[43] While, therefore, he had no good word to say for "Yid Braun's" *Heraclitus the Dark*, at the same time Marx was writing to the author:

During my illness I have thoroughly studied your "Heraclitus" and find the reconstruction of the system from scattered remnants to be masterly, as I did the perspicacity of the polemics. The points I have to criticize are primarily formalities only.[44]

On the very same day he wrote to Engels: "I have at last written to Lassalle. You must give me absolution for the eulogies I was compelled to award to 'Heraclitus the Dark.' "[45]

The case was like that of Ferdinand Freiligrath. Only it was far more momentous, for Lassalle had said himself that he was working on a treatise on political economy and that he hoped to finish by the middle of the following year. Lassalle knew as well as Marx that politics were no longer conceivable without economics. But how thoughtless, how brazen! This was the book for which the world was waiting from him, Karl Marx, and here comes a man, seven years his junior, who has everything Marx lacks — fame, money, political influence, social standing — and talks almost casually about his impudent intrusion into this inner sanctum. It was an intolerable insult.

For precisely at this time Marx was thinking that his own economic studies were far enough advanced to be ready for publication. Moreover, Lassalle knew this. Not only did he know it but he had been asked by Marx to find a publisher. This was what Marx was alluding to in his letter to Engels of December 22, 1857, when he referred to the fellow possibly being useful in hunting up booksellers — a letter full of suspicion and menace against his potential competitor. And eight weeks later to the day he was asking that competitor to intervene for him: "You would of course oblige me if you could see whether a taker is to be found in Berlin."[46]

Lassalle found a publisher. Franz Duncker was prepared to sign a contract, was prepared to publish the book in separate parts (since in fact Marx had no manuscript ready), was prepared to pay an unusually high fee. The fuzzy-haired Yid, the Polish Samuel, the fellow who made a repulsive dirty impression[47] had functioned; Marx wrote with a sigh of relief to Weydemeyer: "It is only thanks to Lassalle's extraordinary zeal and powers of persuasion that Duncker has been persuaded to take this step."[48]

A year went by. The contract was dated March 1858 but the manuscript of

Part 1 was only dispatched to Berlin in February 1859. Now it was expected to be set up, printed, and on sale forthwith; Marx was infuriated that the firm, which had had to wait a year for a manuscript, should now be so slow in sending proofs.[49] There could be only one, one sole explanation — an agent, a saboteur was at work! Lassalle! All his life Marx was well-nigh obsessed by ideas of malice, treachery, and intrigue. The counterpart of the disparaging, arrogant cynicism characterizing his opinion of practically everybody whom he met or was in contact with politically was fear of being the victim of secret machinations. But he could see through them all, in other words could see them everywhere. These were not simply the misgivings of the "Chosen One" seeing his Promethean task made impossible for him by inferior beings — inferior both morally and intellectually. The reason was that suspicious, egocentric irritability bordering on sentimentality against which his horrified father had invariably warned him. The era of the "salaried provocateur," of the "agent," had begun.

The final clue: Lassalle was living in Duncker's house. This information was passed on with the same unctuous satisfaction as the news of an assault on Lassalle when he had been beaten with his own walking stick — "a relic bought in Paris, Robespierre's stick"[50] — the same *schadenfreude* with which the story of Lassalle's involvement in some theater scandal was regaled: "The fellow had better keep someone to give him a box on the ears once a year so that people talk about him, if he can't achieve this through his own Jewish impudence. Meanwhile he still has a remarkable aptitude for getting himself beaten up and thrown out of places."[51]

Precisely four weeks earlier Marx had written to Lassalle: "I thank you for your efforts with Duncker."[52]

But no further manuscripts arrived. Lassalle inquired. Marx promised Part 2 for December. It did not arrive. Lassalle inquired. Marx promised it for 1860, then for 1861. Marx then wanted another publisher. Lassalle arranged for Brockhaus. Marx had no manuscript. Even Engels's reiterated questions as to "how things stood with the book" remained unanswered. *Das Kapital. Volume 1* appeared twenty-two years after Marx's contract with Leske. The *Critique of Political Economy* (Part 1 published by Duncker) was not continued in this form. The main reason Marx gave was the wretchedness of his existence — a liver complaint, cholera, shortage of money. The latter was the subject of his well-known letter to Engels in which he requested him, please, to send money for the postage since otherwise he could not send off the manuscript and adding: "I do not think anyone has ever written about 'money' while suffering from such a shortage of money."[53] To Lassalle he wrote:

As far as delay in dispatch of the manuscript is concerned, I was first prevented by illness and then had to catch up with other hackwork. The real reason, however, is

that: the material lay before me; it was only a question of the form. But in everything that I wrote I could detect an illness of the liver. And I have two reasons for not allowing this script to be spoilt on medical grounds:
1. It is the result of fifteen years' research, in other words the best years of my life.
2. It represents the first attempt at a scientific presentation of an important view of social relationships. I owe it to the Party, therefore, that the thing should not be disfigured by the dull wooden style associated with an illness of the liver.[54]

Again and again one is reminded of his father's imploring letters admonishing his student for his ridiculous plaintiveness and irresponsibility, for turning every little attack of diarrhea into cholera and every feeling of dizziness into a heart attack. Lassalle wrote artlessly to say how pleased he had been to hear from a mutual friend who had visited Marx of his glowing health and how plump and well he looked. Marx was deeply hurt.[55] Another typical instance of Lassalle's tactlessness — practically an attack on his health.

Far more serious was the crippling silence that greeted Duncker's publication of the book. Reviews did not even appear in the specialized periodicals. The book was neither understood nor noticed. Its advent had been announced for years and now — was that all? Elard Biscamp, editor of the London émigré newspaper *Das Volk* (later taken over by Marx), asked in disillusionment: "What good is that?" Wilhelm Liebknecht burst into tears of disappointment[56] — and of course was at once described as an ass, a boor, and a brute:

What does such an ass really want? As if he couldn't see from the first three lines of the preface that this first part must be followed by at least fifteen others before coming to a final conclusion. Naturally the solutions to the tricky questions of money, etc., are so much muck to Liebknecht since for him these problems do not exist. But one might at least expect such a blockhead to note at least those points which suit his little purposes. Anyway what does Sunday mean to a cow.[57]

With Lassalle things were even worse. Tactlessly he combined his congratulations on Marx's book with the announcement of a brochure of his own.[58] Marx replied diplomatically: "No praise for my book has given me so much pleasure since it comes from a competent judge."[59] He certainly did not mean it. Lassalle had written with that enthusiasm for his own affairs which Marx found so trying to the nerves — "how can a man be so stupid as to put down something like that in black and white"[60] — Lassalle had said that he had written all night in an attempt to construct "an edifice of logic and fire which could not fail to have its effect on people."[61]

And what now? The "fellow" was clearly indefatigable and inexhaustible, for something else now appeared. Lassalle had written a play, *Franz von*

Sickingen, which again gave rise to all sorts of correspondence between London, Manchester, and Berlin.

Lassalle sent scripts simultaneously to Marx and Engels. In his letter to Engels he assured him that this would be his only theater piece but that he had *had* to write this; it had been "ordered from on high" and was to be regarded as a critical, or more precisely self-critical, exposition of the failure of the revolution. Marx seized upon this interpretation at the outset of his letter in reply: "The intended collision is not only tragic but is the tragic collision which rightly spelled the doom of the revolutionary party of 1848/49."[62]

Lassalle's play told the story of the German warlord Franz von Sickingen, presenting him as the classless revolutionary who had divorced himself from his own class ideologically but not existentially, but who was unable to look upon the masses, the potential standard-bearers of revolution, as anything other than the object of liberation, not as the subject of action. A "revolution from above," therefore. The conflict was set out by Lassalle in an article "On the tragic concept" of the play which he attached to his letter to Marx.

Significantly, though not surprisingly, Marx was in full agreement with Engels, who wrote to Lassalle four weeks later. His severest criticisms were two-fold: the idealization of an individual after the style of Schiller (and therefore Kant), in other words the buildup of an individual tragedy instead of a revolutionary drama on the lines of a Shakespearian plot bringing elements of the lower orders into the play; second and connected therewith, failure to emphasize the typically plebeian nature of the opposition as opposed to its Lutheranism and chivalry. Marx demanded more action by representatives of the peasantry and revolutionary elements in the towns. As Lassalle said in his reply, this was tantamount to asking for a new play. Engels, as usual the more explicit, stressed that it was immaterial whether any link between Sickingen and the peasantry could be proved historically.

Lassalle went to the root of the argument, fully realizing that this was the start of a fundamental debate unconnected with this particular occasion; he attempted to draw the line beyond which an author — and a historian too — could not go in his selection of historically important material: "He cannot attribute to his hero *any* views which lie beyond the horizon of the *entire period* in which he lived. Should he do this, he becomes unhistorical, tendentious in the worst sense of the word. . . . The invention of actual happenings in the historical field I regard as definitely *inadmissible.*"[63]

The question raised in this play was the relationship between truth and reality. Lassalle made use of a comprehensible historical situation in order to distill from it a basic concept of the tragedy of revolution, to highlight a conflict by no means confined to one specific revolution, to present, as he himself said, the "central, ever-recurring conflict between revolutionary action and its necessity — in short the tragedy of *the* formal revolutionary concept par excellence.''

Whereas Lassalle wished to extract his version of the truth by interpreting actual happenings, by highlighting movements and trends in the real world, Marx and Engels wished to clamp their version of the truth on to reality interpreted along their lines, to inject into reality a pattern of action and lines of progress springing from a half-formed quasi-posthumous concept. For them realism was not the exaggerated description of what should inevitably have happened in a given situation but the descriptive exaggeration of it.

Here is another illustration of Lassalle's completely different concept of politics, of his conception of revolution. For him revolution was the replacement of an old principle by a new one, a better one but not an entirely different one; the hierarchical structure remained. This, after all, was the basis of all his political agitation — and it was also the basis of his disagreement with Marx.

Nevertheless, communications with Lassalle were not severed. Marx marked time, he used Engels as go-between, asking him to give a partial explanation why he was sometimes so intolerant, pointing out that it must be understood how preoccupied he was with the Vogt affair and his difficulties with Freiligrath and that his "temper was occasionally soured."[64] The reason was simple — under no circumstances did Marx wish to lose his link to Berlin.

At this moment a highly opportune inquiry arrived from Lassalle. Friedrich Wilhelm IV had died and Wilhelm I had declared an amnesty. The ever-active Lassalle's first idea was a new *Neue Rheinische Zeitung*. A letter was dispatched to London on January 19, 1861: "How much capital is required here to float a newspaper. . . . Who of the former editors of the *Neue Rheinische Zeitung* might possibly return here for such a purpose?"[65]

The old, eternal, ever-recurring idea — a newspaper! It is almost pathetic that neither of the two — neither Marx nor Lassalle — knew what it would cost. Countess Hatzfeldt! She had money after all; her fortune was said to amount to 300,000 taler. Even Marx was dazzled by so many noughts. Then came Engels's sober warnings that that was nothing like enough for a daily paper and that the lady would certainly not employ her capital, merely the interest, and so money would inevitably soon run short — could they not confine themselves to a weekly paper? Here was the Manchester businessman, whose firm's crest was an angel, warning against acting without thinking. Remarkably enough, however, Marx never passed on these admonitions. Instead he went to Berlin — with a forged passport in the name of Bühring.[66]

VISIT TO BERLIN

It was one of the most significant, but at the same time most peculiar, journeys of Marx's life. Engels, the friend with whom he normally discussed the most trivial paralipomena, was only told of the plan in a single laconic sentence.[67] A week later Marx was staying with his uncle Philips in Zalt-Bommel, Holland, and from there he wrote to Lassalle: "As I wrote to you earlier, I propose to travel from here to Berlin in order to discuss with you personally possible common political and literary enterprises but more especially in order to see you again."[68]

The big difficulty was that Marx had no passport. He was stateless. Since his voluntary renunciation of Prussian citizenship he had been existing on a piece of paper of doubtful value, the old French deportation certificate of 1849. His application to resume his citizenship had been turned down by the Prussian government in 1849. He now asked Lassalle whether and how he could cross the frontier without trouble and get to Berlin, also how he could legally resume residence in Prussia.

It is clear that for Marx the problem of the newspaper or periodical was merely a pretext. The grounds on which he eventually let the project drop are not the explanation; Lassalle had demanded to be one of the editors and, in the event of Engels joining them as third editor, to have a right of veto, since otherwise Marx and Engels would in practice be in sole control of the paper. How right he was and how comprehensible his attitude. Lassalle, after all, was going to provide the money, acting not as some banker's puppet but as a politician. An expensive journey to the Continent, however, was not necessary to find all this out. The fact is that Marx wanted to return to Germany. He wanted to be there for two reasons: to make use of his influential and in some respects powerful friend's contacts and at the same time to cast an eye over the lion's den:

I arrived in Berlin last Sunday morning [May 17]. . . . Lassalle, who lives in a very beautiful house on one of the most beautiful streets of Berlin, had made all preparations for my reception and welcomed me with extraordinary friendliness. After we had whiled away the first few hours in talk and a little rest and refreshment had banished the fatigue of the journey, Lassalle took me straight to Countess Hatzfeldt's house; as I soon discovered, she dined with him every day at 4:00 P.M. and spent her evenings with him.[69]

During this stay in Berlin Marx lived a double-track existence. He was both able and willing to enjoy the good things of life and he found his environment amusing, pleasant and enjoyable. He missed nothing — the Countess's makeup, her elegance, her aristocratic *laisser-aller* with no trace of a bluestocking attitude, her hair, her eyes, her face, lined but beautiful — "twenty and twenty make fifty-seven."[70] He was even prepared to carry on a mild flirtation with her.

He enjoyed the dinners given "in honor of my return,"[71] the term which, oddly enough, he was already using to describe his visit; with some satisfaction he enumerated the dignitaries assembled round him — General von Pfuël, Bleibtreu, the painter of battle scenes, Förster, the historian and Privy Councillor who even proposed a toast to him. At table he sat between the hostess and a niece of Varnhagen von Ense. They went to the opera where they had a box and, moreover, one near that of the King.

What must Marx's thoughts have been? In London he lived in a house full of squalling children, pregnant women, ulcers, and illness, besieged by creditors demanding payment, with never a bottle of port unless it was a present from Manchester; he was plagued by liver troubles, carbuncles, loss of appetite, and insomnia; he had no neighbors, no friends, no crony, no stag parties, no social life; and, above all, his book did not progress. Everything in Berlin was the exact opposite — fame, splendor, influence, political prestige, wealth, an aristocratic way of life, and membership of the highest social circles.

Marx had never been so bitterly mortified in his life. He never forgave Lassalle his welcome and his help. Hardly had he returned to London than he wrote to Engels a letter full of animosity:

. . . Lazarus, the leper, is therefore the prototype of the Jew and Lazarus-Lassalle. . . . His original illness was secondary semi-cured syphilis. . . . To the detriment of his health our Lazarus now lives as luxurious a life as his opposite, the rich man. . . . He has become altogether too superior and would think it a waste of his time, for instance, to go into a beer tavern. . . .[72]

Only two days earlier he had written to Lassalle with the conventional civilities thanking him for his friendly reception and hospitality. Marx still needed Lassalle, for Lassalle was still working energetically to recover Marx his citizenship; Marx, in fact, asked him to proceed and was impressed by the self-assurance with which he made personal approaches, even to the highest authorities. All his efforts were fruitless, however. If Marx could have had his own way, he would now have returned to Germany for good. He sensed "an atmosphere of decay and catastrophe everywhere."[73] Although — or perhaps because — he knew that in that case he would never have time to finish his great book, that a newspaper and the day-to-day political wranglings would put an end to that, he allowed Lassalle to continue his efforts. Jenny, however, was the one who had no wish to return under any circumstances. Marx's children had become British; they knew German but they spoke and wrote in English. Under no circumstances, moreover, did Jenny von Westphalen wish to live near "this person," as she called Countess Hatzfeldt. She had her own very definite ideas about social behavior. She did not, for instance, accept Friedrich Engels's common-law marriage with his working-class girl — when he produced her one day at some public function she turned ostentatiously away and refused to shake hands with either of them.[74] Similarly she could not forgive Lassalle his scandalous relationship with the Countess.

Lassalle made the unpardonable mistake of failing to grasp this. He did something even worse: he offered to take one of Marx's daughters as companion to the Countess in Berlin. This happened when he paid a return visit to London in July and August 1862. He had had friendly letters from Marx including all sorts of requests and instructions. He had had charming letters from Jenny Marx, in which she was apparently quite frank with him. Over and over again he had put up money for them; he had helped with exchange transactions; he had arranged for potential correspondents for the newspaper; and he was trying to settle the wretched business of Marx's citizenship. He could not suspect that they hated or even disliked him, nor did he know details of Marx's domestic and financial situation. It was no fault of Lassalle's that Marx — still both downcast and impressed by his stay in Berlin — forced his wife to get all their silver out of pawn and have visiting cards printed showing "Jenny Marx, *née* Baronesse Westphalen."

The visit must have been an almost grotesque affair. Jenny's recollections of it read like a rough translation of one of Marx's barrages of invective; she even uses phrases like "nigger" or "the workers' Messiah," Marx having referred to "the rabble's Redeemer."[75]

Just at this time Marx was working out his theory of income and he was infuriated by the time-wasting, flamboyant manners and conceit of "this greatest of scholars, deepest of thinkers and most brilliant of investigators," as also by the "collossal appetite and wanton lust of this 'idealist.' "[76] Marx was not balanced enough to find all this merely entertaining — the odd little story told to Eduard Bernstein, for instance: Marx was showing Lassalle round the British Museum and pointed out the Rosetta Stone to him, whereupon Lassalle replied, "What do you think? Should I spend six months making my mark as an Egyptologist?"[77]

Marx now overstepped all bounds of reason. "The brute" now turned into "the Jewish nigger"[78] — and this was no mere random invective but a well-considered insult.

It is now quite clear to me [he wrote to Engels] that, as the shape of his head and the texture of his hair show, he is descended from the Negroes who followed Moses' train out of Egypt (unless his mother or grandmother on his father's side interbred with some nigger). Well then — this combination of Jewish and German descent with a basic Negroid background is bound to produce something peculiar. The fellow's importunity is also Negroid.[79]

The reason, however, was not some dramatic psychological difference. Politics, scientific politics, were of course at the bottom of it.

ENEMY INSTEAD OF PARTNER

On April 12, 1862, Lassalle had given an address on the democratic significance of the working class to a workmen's union in the suburb of Oranienburg where were assembled mainly workers from the great engineering works of northern Berlin. This speech, subsequently published with the title "Workers' Program," is regarded as the beginning of the story of the modern Prussian-German workers' movement, in fact the starting point of the social-democrat movement in Germany.[80] It marked the transition from all previous theory to agitation, the first attempt to impart material force to theory in that, for the first time it expounded theory to the masses — the *Communist Manifesto* as a forensic feat, so to speak.

Lassalle succeeded in producing a brilliant interpretation of Marx's ideas with his own special combination of oratorical agility, erudite allusions, and political militancy. As always he conceived his own role as a transcendent one:

After all these explanations, gentlemen, you will realize the true significance of the famous brochure issued by Abbé Sieyès in 1788, the year preceding the French Revolution; it may be summarized in these words: "What is the Third Estate? Nothing. What should it be? Everything."[81]

The "Workers' Program" was naturally intended to be the legitimate successor to the "famous brochure" — and to a certain extent it was. It was a scintillating attack on the three-tier voting system and an inspiring call to the workers to develop consciousness of their own estate — class consciousness. Marx and various critics have accused Lassalle of invariably using the indefinite term "workers' *estate,*" but this is not true. Actually in the "Program" the term "class" is used repeatedly and throughout; it is employed, as being of similar meaning, both alongside and as an alternative to the word "estate." In Lassalle's eyes the difference was clearly terminological; no political sleight of hand was involved. He referred to improvement of the workers' lot "as a class," to improving their "classless state";[82] he also referred, though in other terms, to precisely that process which Marx was later to call the "development of a class as such into a class of its own," in other words not merely *being* a working class but *knowing* that it was one.

The speech created a sensation. In December 1862 Lassalle received a letter from Leipzig as follows:

We, your three friends undersigned, . . . consider that there is only one man in Germany whom we would wish to see at the head of so important a movement, only one man capable of accomplishing so difficult a task, only one man in whom we place such complete confidence that we would willingly subordinate ourselves to him as leader of the entire movement — and that man is you. . . .

We cannot do other than ask you to place yourself at the head of the movement and take charge of the direction of it yourself. We can and should add that the majority of those who have read your brochure think as we do. When read here it produced wild enthusiasm and it will have the same effect on the workers throughout Germany; all will gladly and confidently recognize you as the leader . . . Otto Dammer, F. W. Fritzsche, Julius Vahlteich.[83]

With some justifiable exaggeration this may be called the document on which the ADAV was founded. It was precisely what Lassalle wanted — and it was precisely what Marx wanted too. But no one had asked him; he was not known at all. He had laid the intellectual foundations and now along came this "Izzy" and reaped the harvest. This incident illustrates the *unique* relationship (in the strictest sense of the word) between Marx and his ideas. He regarded them as his *property*. The case was similar to that of Henry Myers Hyndman: instead of being relieved that someone had succeeded in popularizing his complex scientific concepts and building an organization on a foundation constructed by him, he felt that he had been plagiarized and robbed.

Lassalle, however, never denied that he was a disciple of Marx. In some respects Marx might have said of Lassalle what Hegel is supposed to have said on his deathbed: only one man understood me and he misunderstood me. Lassalle regarded himself as Marx's "interpreter," the loudspeaker either for his political genius or his terminology — for instance when he said that property was something alien to the proletariat. Lassalle was not an observer but a man of action, not that he despised theory and doctrine but he wished to *make use* of them. In his reminiscences Liebknecht said of Marx that "Politics for Marx was a study . . . politics is theoretical";[84] for Lassalle it was exactly the opposite — practice. Marx's unjustified rancor against Lassalle, however, raises the question whether his restriction of politics to theory was not a self-imposed method of evasion; this reading of the situation is supported by his perennial laments about his "book of shit" and its wretchedly arid material on the one hand and his desperate attempt to return to

Berlin and his immediate plunge into active political organization after Lassalle's death on the other. In Lassalle's case, however, the choice between the two alternatives was a deliberate one.

Lassalle's "Open Letter of Reply," debated in the ADAV constituent assembly on May 23, 1863, by representatives from eleven cities and therefore rightly held to be the basic document of German social democracy,[85] is a logical exposition of this viewpoint. It is a document of inspiring oratorical ability and political determination — Lassalle's creed. It sets out the core of his political concept, giving a preview of everything implicit in his vast and increasing activity as an agitator. It highlights the two fundamental points in his doctrine: the demand for state-subsidized production cooperatives and the abolition of the "immutable law of wages." Ever since then the battle for and against Lassalle has raged round these two central ideas. Lassalle asked quite logically why it was that state subsidies in the form of interest guarantees were invariably only granted to "big business" (without them there would not be a single railway on the entire Continent); the same resources, he said, could be used with equal justification to create and maintain major industries owned by the workers. This was by no means a sudden idea propounded for purposes of agitation; it was the result of fundamental economic thinking. This is proved by his correspondence with Rodbertus, the Grand Old Man of political economy; here, for instance, Lassalle explains why he has been careful to avoid talking of improving the lot of the working class, also why he is careful to refrain from putting forward his proposal for cooperatives as the *solution* of the social problem. He wishes it be looked upon as a transitional solution.[86] Moreover, alongside the demand for universal suffrage, he regards abolition of private property in land and capital as the "central core" of his ideas.[87] That this was by no means to be regarded as a method of propping up the state or conformism is shown by the correspondence with Rodbertus, who treated Lassalle with respect but warned him imploringly against embarking on the path of revolution.[88]

This courteous argument with Rodbertus emphasizes that it is perfectly possible for two theorists to embark on a discussion even if they are only partially in agreement.[89] This was something of which Karl Marx was incapable. Anyone who deviated in the slightest degree from his theories or proposals was an enemy, generally in the pay of someone else. When Marx later learned of Lassalle's almost pathetic negotiations with Bismarck this was for him and for Engels the final proof that Lassalle was "a common rogue."[90]

He now accused Lassalle (behind his back; Marx no longer wrote to him) of two things: that Lassalle had copied everything from him (Marx) and that his theory of the "immutable law of wages" was extracted from the ultra-reactionary theories of Malthus and Ricardo. Marx was in such a jealous rage that he did not even perceive this glaring inconsistency. Franz Mehring was the first to draw attention[91] to the malice and inequity with which Marx wrote off Lassalle's writings either as a sixth-former's plagiarisms (if he had read them) or as schoolboy ruminations not worth reading (if he had not read them) when in fact they deserved to be taken very seriously and had led to the creation of a gigantic workers' movement.

In her reminiscences even Jenny Marx refers to Lassalle's shameless plagiarizing and makes spiteful fun about the "fanatical admiration of the rabble and the tramps for their new Messiah" whom they thought worthy of incense, flag-waving and laurel wreaths even beyond the grave.[92]

In fact Lassalle's paragraphs about the "immutable law of wages" are surprisingly applicable today. He starts, for instance, by demolishing the argument that the lot of the workers has demonstrably improved over the centuries; human happiness, he maintains, must be considered *within* its own time span; the human or inhuman lot of a certain class cannot be judged by comparing it with the animals in the primeval forest or the Negroes in Africa or the medieval serfs. The savage who has never seen soap does not feel deprived by its absence, nor did the worker living before the invention of printing notice his lack of books to read — "Consequently the situation of any class can only be judged by comparison with the situation of another class of the same period."[93] The "Open Letter" is in fact a document of intellectual integrity, political explosiveness, and high oratorical quality.

Marx's sneer, "How is it then . . . that the main passages in this were actually textually familiar to me"[94] is incredibly small-minded. Admittedly there was much in Lassalle's concept which could be criticized, particularly his idea of state-subsidized and state-financed "popularly owned concerns." Lassalle's loyalty to the state and the monarchy is undeniable; it was the cornerstone of his political thinking. On this point a "Marxist" critic had good grounds for argument. But Marx did not argue; he preserved an indignant silence.

The vanity which Marx imputed to Lassalle undoubtedly provided the impulse for some of his actions but it was certainly not his sole motive. He had precise ideas about his aims — so precise that he submitted them to Bismarck. The notorious "conspiracy" with Bismarck never took place; there was an official exchange of letters and telegrams but their walks together along Berlin's crowded Friedrichstrasse while arguing their points of view can hardly be distorted into "secret meetings." Lassalle's misjudgment of his own political position and the practicability of his concept of an officially authorized "revolution" stands out clearly in the covering letter which he sent Bismarck with the statutes of the newly formed ADAV, on June 8, 1863.

Bismarck regarded these meetings and letters with somewhat supercilious amusement, though he was not without respect for Lassalle as a man. He looked upon politics as a horse-trading business and knew that "the poor devil" Lassalle had nothing to offer him; he was a general without an army, not a man to do business with.

The storybook end to Ferdinand Lassalle's life was almost logical — death in a duel about an overdramatized and actually trivial love affair conjures up a picture of a cavalier mode of life combined with lofty pretensions; it also illustrates his compulsive tendency to error. Engels jeered that a better solution to the problem would have been to have thrown the girl on the bed in his lodging and duly taken her — she was not after his fine intellect but only his Jewish energy.[95] In a typically paradoxical comment Marx called "the pretext for his death . . . one of the many tactless acts which he committed in his life."[96] Behind this facade of frivolity, however, lay genuine sorrow. Engels's initial reaction was not merely one of shock but of genuine appreciation of a man who was "politically . . . undoubtedly one of the most important fellows in Germany."[97] Marx wrote to Countess Hatzfeldt to say how astonished, dismayed, and shocked he had been at Lassalle's death:

He was one of those for whom I had a great affection. . . . Be convinced that no one can feel deeper grief than I at his being torn away. And above all I feel for you. . . . I hope, my dear Countess, that with your brave lofty spirit you will withstand this blow of fate and will remain always convinced of the totally steadfast devotion

Of your sincere friend
Karl Marx[98]

Three weeks after this letter Marx founded the International. Was he really its founder?

CHAPTER EIGHT

THE INTERNATIONAL

"A SILENT FIGURE ON THE PLATFORM" —
INAUGURATION WITHOUT THE LEADER

Marx regarded the International Workers Association, known to history as the First International, as his life's work; two decades later, in 1883, when assembling material for a biography of Marx, Engels said that "without the International Mohr's life would be a diamond ring with its biggest gem missing."[1] But Marx did not create it; it was a product of history, almost an accident.

Throughout Europe the restoration period was one of economic boom; the course of events was revolutionary. From 1850 capitalist industrialization advanced by leaps and bounds. The foundations of industrial production methods had been laid in the 1840s with the introduction of the mechanical loom, construction of railways, and the change from wood to coke firing in blast furnaces. The length of the German railway network, for example, rose from 469 kilometers in 1840 to 5,856 in 1850.[2] Now, however, came an explosion; in the three decades from 1850 to 1880 the figure for steam-produced horsepower in England rose from 1.3 to 7.6 million, that in France from barely 0.4 to nearly 1.3, and that in Germany from 0.26 to 5.1 (in 1831 12 percent of looms were still worked by hand, 82 percent by water-power and only 6 percent by steam). Coal and steel production shot up similarly; with a total of 12 million tons, German steel production had increased twelvefold during this period, though it was still less than half the British figure of 25 million tons.

Not only were vast fortunes made but a vast army of industrial proletarians grew up. They had no political organization. In 1852 Marx had disbanded the League of Communists both in England and on the Continent as being "no longer suited to the times";[3] the émigrés were quarreling among themselves; many of the 1848 revolutionaries had gone overseas.

Up to the first economic crisis of 1857 there was no organization capable of initiating a strike. The first nationwide German trade union was that of the cigar-makers, formed in 1865; the printers followed a year later.[4] In England, however, as early as June 8, 1847 the Chartists had pushed through a factory law restricting working time for women and juveniles to eleven hours, and from May 1, 1848, to ten hours. This was not at all to the liking of the manufacturers, who were worried about their young people's morals and exposure to vice; instead of being immured for a whole twelve hours in the cozy, clean, moral atmosphere of the factories, they were now to be loosed an hour earlier into the hard, cold, frivolous outer world. Certain managers even drafted petitions that they caused their workers to sign: "As parents your petitioners believe that an additional hour of leisure can have no result other than the ruin of their children's morals, idleness being the root of all evil."[5]

In France too one of the most important results of the 1848 revolution had been the introduction of the twelve-hour day, which "as demanded by Robert Owen forty years ago, has been stigmatized by the ruling classes and the ruling scientific doctrine as an atheistic crime against the 'Christian' virtue of work and held up to ridicule as utopian."[6]

Owen's school of thought, however, had bogged down in religious free-thinking; the Chartists were thinking in terms of wage battles and social advantages, not of the abolition of capitalism. The London building workers' strike of 1859 elicited the first grant of the right of association; in France association was still banned — nearly 4,000 workers were sentenced for belonging to such forbidden associations between 1853 and 1866. In Germany, as even Marx conceded,[7] Lassalle had reawakened the workers' movement after fifteen years of slumber. The French situation was especially typical of the conflicting tendencies and developments; two separate but parallel sets of ideas were at work, those of Blanqui and his concept of a surprise attack by a resolute minority and those of Proudhon, with his hope of appeasement by enriching the poverty-stricken. Proudhon was an opponent of strikes and it almost seems as if Napoleon III — "the imitation Caesar"[8] — was not altogether immune to the powerful influence of Proudhon, opposed to the Emperor though he was; his attempt to synthesize the bourgeoisie and the working class under the Second Empire amounted to a permanent appeasement policy: concessions to the trades unions but no political concessions.

Napoleon financed — in fact organized — the dispatch of a workers' delegation to the World Exhibition in London in 1862. He instituted a selection system for the two hundred delegates; the imperial and municipal treasuries each donated 20,000 francs for the journey and financed the printing and distribution of the resultant reports. The lament by the Paris Prefect of Police that the Emperor might just as well repeal the anti-combination laws was understandable.[9]

In fact this apparently innocent excursion by ship to England marked the genesis of a very different "combination" — the First International.

Not only was increased interest being taken in international contacts but they had become a necessity. Garibaldi, the father-figure of the Italian struggle for independence, had been feted in London. A monster meeting held in the crowded St. James's Hall in March 1863 — one of the few public demonstrations which Karl Marx attended — prevented Palmerston from going to war on the side of the South in America; it was a demonstration of solidarity with Lincoln and the abolitionists. A further French delegation was present at a mass meeting held in July 1863 in support of the Polish insurgents — freedom for Poland and an end to her three-fold partition had always been regarded as synonymous with the advance of the workers' movement; a free united Poland would have implied victory over Russian hegemony.

During 1863 Marx was intensely preoccupied with the Polish rising; for the first six months he was working on an essay "The Polish Question"[10] (only published in 1961) inspired by his hatred of Russia and his conviction that Prussia's dependence on Russia was the result of her anti-Polish policy. A certain Colonel Capinski, with whom he frequently conferred, tells of a nocturnal drive in a cab following a visit to Alexander Herzen, during which Marx suggested raising a legion of 1,000 men and even promised that, via a friend, he could persuade the deposed Prince Karl of Brunswick to finance them.[11]

A committee of English workers under the chairmanship of George Odger, Secretary of the London Trade Union Council, drafted an address of welcome to their French colleagues; officially it was said to be an expression of gratitude for their participation but it was actually an urgent appeal for international solidarity — reciprocal support for strikes, stoppage of the import of cheap "foreign labor," which upset the wages and prices structure, and systematic mutual contacts were all demanded. The address had been translated by Professor Edward Spencer Beesly, the London historian, and it created great excitement in the Paris "workshops." A further meeting was called for September 28, 1864, in St. Martin's Hall near Covent Garden, for the formal exchange of this address of welcome and the French address of thanks. Beesly made a short welcoming speech in the smoke-filled hall that was full to bursting, with 2,000 people present. The German workers' choir sang. Odger then read the English message. Henri-Louis Tolain, an engraver who had been a member of both the previous delegations and had gained prominence at the Paris elections with a socialist manifesto as his platform, read the French reply. He only referred to the Polish rising briefly at the beginning; the speech was a lengthy version of the call "Workers of all countries, unite."

The man who had propagated this idea sat "as a silent figure on the platform";[12] Karl Marx had only been invited a few hours before the long-prepared meeting opened. A newspaper report quotes his name at the bottom of the list.[13]

Le Lubez, one of the French delegates, had contacted Marx early on — but only to ask his advice. He was asked to propose a German delegation but he was not invited himself. How out of touch Marx initially was with all these movements and political organizations is shown by a letter to Engels in which he refers to Odger as President of the London Trade Union Council and to one of the delegates as a mason when he was in fact a carpenter.[14] His proposal that Johann Georg Eccarius, an honest, mediocre tailor from Thuringia who had already been a member of the League of the Just and the League of Communists, be elected was accepted; Eccarius fulfilled the condition that only "real" workers could be delegates. Initially Marx's interest in all this seems to have been somewhat distant, and these workers organizations were clearly something strange to him. He had buried himself for years in his theoretical work and had first to become accustomed to the idea of the "possibility of transition." His letter to Weydemeyer is couched in somewhat hesitant terms — "not without significance," "might possibly have a significant effect." "Workers" are referred to in inverted commas; this was not his creation; initially he was an observer.

At this first conference Le Lubez had put forward an organizational plan and this was expanded by resolutions and additional proposals from the British trade unionists. It was decided to form a central Commission with Subcommissions in the European capitals and a Central Committee — the later General Council; statutes were also to be drawn up. Individual countries were to be represented by Corresponding Secretaries appointed by the countries themselves. All this machinery was later to prove very complex to operate.

In the Central Committee, however (initially numbering 34 and rising to 50 with coopted members), were two Germans — Eccarius and Marx. His proposal that the Corresponding Secretary for Germany be nominated by the German Workers' Education Association was an astute political move, since he had thereby outmaneuvered the most powerful political grouping in Germany, Lassalle's ADAV; had he not done this, the ADAV would certainly have nominated Lassalle. Moreover Marx was the only nonworker. Here is another illustration of his conflicting, overlapping motivations; he shrinks from the "threat" of practical action but at the same time is tempted by it; his lamentations about his wearisome work in the British Museum and the "economic shit"[15] are now counterbalanced by complaints about the "incubus" of the International, which "I would be glad to be able to shake off."[16] The urge to participate in the creation of a great international workers organization, to help determine its course, is inhibited by obvious contempt for his comrades-in-arms and a secret, but none the less clear, desire to operate *in Germany*.

A year after formation of the International Marx attempted to create local groups in Germany consisting of individual members in Köln, Berlin, Magdeburg, Solingen, and Stuttgart — using for the purpose ex-members of the ADAV who had resigned from it.[17] It was a clear attempt to organize a German opposition party.

First, however, he had to consolidate his position in the General Council. Once again there was the same hesitancy, the same probing, waiting attitude; he left the first session of the General Council ahead of time. He was not even present when he was elected to the nine-man drafting committee to draw up the statutes. He was not present at the second session, nor at the third. Though Cremer, the Secretary-General, wrote asking for his help, Marx was not among those present at the fourth session. Either he gave illness as an excuse — though in a letter to Weydemeyer he said that he was "pretty well cured" — or he sulked in a letter to Engels, saying that he had not been told of the "rendezvous" in time[18] — though his faithful Eccarius went along and left for the meeting from Marx's house. It was all reminiscent of the similar situation when the *Communist Manifesto* was being drafted.

On this occasion moreover Engels was missing. There is no question here of the orthodox Marx/Engels combination gulping over the grammar; until he moved to London in 1870 Engels's attitude to the International was one of aloofness, if not skepticism. He refused to become one of its correspondents; there was no Manchester group. The "Inaugural Address" and "Provisional Rules" stem not from Marx/Engels but from Marx.

On October 18, 1863, when Marx first attended a sitting of the General Council, he was horrified by the jargon of a badly written, prolix, crude preamble, "pretending to be a declaration of principles . . . crusted over with the vaguest tags of French socialism."[19]

A subcommittee was formed and it assembled in Marx's house; just as in Brussels in 1847/8, he was handed the material; postponements, delays in completion, and finally the rejection of the entire declaration of principles were accepted. Apart from the retention of two or three phrases about "duty" and "right," "truth, morality and justice," but "placed in such a way that they can do no harm,"[20] Marx now wrote *his* text. Together with the "Provisional Rules" it became the most important document of the nineteenth-century workers' movement after the *Communist Manifesto*. The statutes are written in a hymnlike staccato, almost a canticle, a synthesis of harshness and lyricism — "Considering: That the emancipation of the working classes must be conquered by the working classes themselves."[21]

To seduce the reader into following its line of thinking, the "Inaugural

Address" presents itself as a plea in court, as the case for the prosecution; it is a call to disobedience, analytically deduced. Apart from the trumpet call of the opening words, "Working Men!,"[22] anyone expecting magic formulae or inflammatory appeals will be disappointed; the style is argumentative, highlighting primarily the fact that here is an author who has profound politico-economic studies behind him. It is a classic example of authorship from the man who lectured on economic science to the German laborers in Brussels shortly before the revolution or to the Vienna workers at the height of the revolution. Never before had anyone translated economic terms so directly into a political pamphlet. In the "Address" Marx was clearly not only introducing ideas from *Capital* but even quoting material which he had extracted for his book — for instance the famous and notorious "Blue Books," the official publications of the British Parliament and Foreign Office issued ever since the seventeenth century. Marx's "Address" possessed the transparent logic of a mathematical equation. Against a background of misery, hunger, sickness, want, and infant mortality, Marx, with dates quoted, holds up the fact that "about 3,000 persons divide amongst themselves a yearly income of about £25,000,000 sterling" and "death by starvation rose almost to the rank of an institution during this intoxicating epoch of economic progress in the metropolis of the British Empire." The central phrase in the "Address," pondering on the prospects of the working class's winning political power, is a calculating one: "One element of success they possess — numbers; but numbers weigh only in the balance if united by combination and led by knowledge."[23]

Then, with a sharp change of atmosphere, the text switches from percentage figures to emotionalism, from import quotas to the abolition of child labor, still a rousing reveille, never a song of melancholy.

From this cold, embittered picture, however, of well-deserved though not immutable wretchedness of life on this earth, there is built up a vision of another world; but, as always with Marx when he is trying to enunciate a prophecy, set forth aims, or make the new ideas comprehensible, all that emerges is nebulous lyricism: "like slave labor, like serf labor, hired labor is but a transitory and inferior form, destined to disappear before associated labor plying its trade with a willing hand, a ready mind and a joyous heart."[24]

OPPOSITION PARTY TO THAT OF THE "COMMONPLACE BLOCKHEAD" LIEBKNECHT

So Marx became Corresponding Secretary for Germany in the International. He never occupied any other official position, though he occasionally allowed himself to be coopted by other national splinter groups and consequently signed documents as Secretary for Holland or, oddly enough, for Russia.[25]

Links to Germany, however, were tenuous, almost nonexistent. Franz Mehring refers to the colored spectacles through which Marx looked at conditions in Germany.[26] The color seems to have been mainly yellow — jaundiced hatred of the Lassalleans even after his rival's death. From the traditional Marxist rewriting of history there emerges a picture of a traitorous German party deviating from the right (or rather left) road dictated by Karl Marx. As Mehring observed, however, this was an old story but neither a true nor an agreeable one.[27] Both Bernhard Becker, who took over the ADAV immediately on Lassalle's death, and Johann Baptist von Schweitzer, the President from 1865, behaved correctly, in fact as friends and allies. They offered Marx the most important post available, the succession to Lassalle as President of the ADAV. Interestingly this produced two divergent reactions; on October 4 Marx wrote to a Solingen friend, the metal worker Carl Klings, an ex-member of the League of Communists and one of the leaders of the anti-Lassalle opposition in the ADAV, to say that he did not wish to accept but set much store by being elected nevertheless; he thought that it would make a good impression on the public.[28] Who this "public" was Marx explained quite frankly in the next sentence — the newly formed International! In that case he would, of course, have carried a very different weight there. At any rate Marx did not receive a single vote at the Solingen election.

On the other hand in another letter (to Liebknecht) and one, moreover, written *before* the formation of the International, Marx declared himself ready to accept the presidency of the ADAV on certain conditions.[29]

From the outset the International was *also*, in Marx's eyes, a platform from which to attack the most powerful workers' party in Germany. Shortly after its formation he had said in a letter to Kugelmann that "I prefer a hundred times over my agitation here through the International Association"[30] to working in or for the ADAV; only two months after the meeting in St. Martin's Hall he had written to Carl Siebel, a relative of Engels: "You understand that the adherence of the ADAV will only be of use initially vis-à-vis our opponents here. Later the entire apparatus of this union must be destroyed since its whole basis is wrong."[31]

One of Marx's first moves was a studied one — a letter to Abraham Lincoln who, moreover, replied in polite measured terms; it was one of the early prestige victories for the Secretary for Germany.

The legend that Schweitzer was an agent of Bismarck and that the ADAV closed its doors to the International belongs to the realm of impious fable; it is an anti-ADAV fairy tale. In fact Schweitzer published the "Inaugural Address" in one of the first issues of his *Social-Demokrat,* its first appearance in German and the first time many German workers had ever read anything

written by Karl Marx. He also accepted Wilhelm Liebknecht on to the editorial board, something which he was under no compulsion to do, and gave
instructions that only Liebknecht should edit news about the International.
He asked both Marx and Engels to cooperate; on February 15, 1865, he
wrote to Marx that he was preparing a resolution in which the ADAV would
declare its full agreement with the principles of the International and that
they would send delegates to every annual congress (official adherence was
banned under the German anti-combination laws). Schweitzer received no
answer to this letter.

Instead Marx and Engels amused themselves by attacking Schweitzer as a
homosexual (in their correspondence of 1864, 1865, and 1866 the word
"capital" appears only in parenthesis, terms such as "work," "scientific reading," or "the book" are rarely used but intense interest is shown in "clap,"
"cocks," and "cunts"). Their strictures reeked of stuffy petit-bourgeois re-
spectability — "we poor old-timers with our childish predilection for
women";[32] they shuddered at perversion, filth, and (God forbid) theory or
criminal law reform. Anyone so obviously happy to be addressed as "General" would obviously make allowances for crimes of passion; Schweitzer,
however, who was trying to popularize Marx in Germany, even to the extent
of dramatizing Das Kapital, was of value only to provide material for black-
mail.

At the same time, however, Marx was undecided, in two minds, dissatisfied
with his own activities and their results. He plunged into a whirl of meetings
and conferences, forcing himself to conform to the rule that "one must say B
as soon as one has said A";[33] a whole week was often taken up in discussions, decision-making, and drafting of resolutions.[34] At the same time he
was writing to Engels that the worst of such agitation was that it was boring
and burdensome as soon as one became involved.[35] Marx's personnel policy
was to recruit only followers of mediocre caliber, old fighters such as Lessner,
Eccarius, or Schapper, the generally respected but ineffective veteran who got
on everyone's nerves with his reminiscences of his old campaigning days.[36]
This may have been helpful to Marx's backstage diplomacy, as Engels recalled in old age;[37] it was less helpful in building up an efficient centralized
organization. As early as April 1866 Marx wrote: "I must say to you frankly
that things are going very wrong with the International."[38]

In fact the Corresponding Secretary for Germany had had no success either
in building up any movement worthy of the name or in arranging any close
affiliation between the London émigrés and the British workers' movement.
In August 1866 he lamented that Liebknecht had not succeeded in founding
"even a six-man branch in Germany"[39] and in later years Marx referred
quite bluntly to "the German workers' party's purely platonic relationship to
the International."[40] Equally Engels later referred to "the theoretical charac-

ter of the movement" as being "very confused . . . among the masses."[41] Triumphant announcements about large-scale cooperation with the British or imminent amalgamation with the trade unions are indications of revolutionary impatience rather than appreciations of the political situation. On October 13, 1866, Marx wrote to Kugelmann: "The London Council of the English Trade Unions (its Secretary is our President Odger) is just discussing whether it should call itself the British Section of the International Association. If that is done, then in a certain sense we shall have control of the working class here and we can push on the movement very much."[42]

But it did not happen; the Trade Union Council had no such idea in its head; it even refused to allow a representative of the International to be present at its meetings. Marx's dream of holding all the strings of power in his hand was never realized. The more precisely Marx described it, the further away it was: "Things are moving. And in the next revolution, which is perhaps nearer than it appears, we (i.e., you and I) will have this powerful engine *in our hands*."[43]

While Marx was singing songs of triumph to Engels the General Council's office in London was expropriated for arrears of rent. Not a single industrial trade union had joined the International; the heavy industry workers remained reticent. Mazzini, Italy's most influential socialist politician, had kept himself and his organization aloof from the International, which he regarded as being under the influence of the destructive and ambitious Marx.[44] The French, who provided the strongest contingent, were Proudhonists — the only link between them and Marx was a full year's feuding. They caviled at the "nonworker" and blocked his initiatives, even one directed against Russian tyranny, saying why battle against *Russian* tyranny as if there was none anywhere else.

Marx was eventually squandering so much of his time in similar hectic intrigues — he must anticipate this attack and damp down that protest — that any meaningful action by the International was almost pushed into the background. He was angry with Odger — the post of Secretary-General should be abolished. He was angry with the London French — he might have the seat of the General Council moved to Geneva. He was angry with "those asses of Proudhonists," with "the Belgian idiocy," with "the Italian heretic Pope," with "the Russian (Bakunist) adventurers," with "the insolent little Wilhelm" (Liebknecht). Small wonder that Franz Mehring's view of the entire political dreamland in which Marx and Engels moved was:

The international vantage point which permitted them a general view of the whole, at the same time prevented them from penetrating into the details characteristic of the individual countries. Even their most enthusiastic admirers in England and France have admitted that they never succeeded in mastering all the details of

English and French life like natives and, once having parted company with Germany, they never succeeded in reestablishing their former thorough and familiar touch with German conditions. This was true even of the German party questions proper in which their judgment was clouded by their undiminished mistrust of Lassalle and everything Lassallean.[45]

Marx's relations with the leaders of the German workers' movement were by no means smooth; the fact that Bebel could describe a visit to London as a "journey to Canossa"[46] illustrates the attitude of superiority, suspicion and aloofness prevalent there. Wilhelm Liebknecht records with some pride in his reminiscences[47] that he had often argued with Marx but quarreled with him only twice; he did not know Marx's opinion of him, however: it was harsh to the point of contempt. As early as the 1850s Marx was referring to him as a commonplace fellow, "his uselessness as an author being equaled by his unreliability and weakness of character"; he had only avoided well-deserved relegation to the back room because he, Marx, proposed to use him one day as a scarecrow.[48] So it went on for years. Matters got worse when Liebknecht returned to Germany in 1862 and busied himself in building up a party — "Schweitzer is right on one point, that is Liebknecht's incapacity"; "Liebknecht's little rag displeases me in the highest degree"; "Liebknecht has a knack of collecting around him the stupidest people in Germany"; "the fellow is really too impertinent"; "Liebknecht has once more had the luck of the stupid"; "the brute";[49] "the commonplace blockhead." This final crescendo came in a letter to Engels of almost unparalleled severity — an overall squaring of the account?

This was not friendly mockery on the part of a great politician who would later shake hands with a smile; when Marx wrote like that, he meant it. It was the tone he invariably adopted when some personal *and* political vexation was in the offing, in other words when the central authority was under fire. The date of the letter, May 16, 1870, explains why a politician, to whom other contemporaries such as Eduard Bernstein ascribe unequaled political ability, should be so totally condemned in such humiliating terms; in the autumn of the previous year Liebknecht and Bebel had succeeded in creating a major political party out of the various groups and unions dominating the German scene. A party rally had been held at Eisenach from August 7 to 9, 1869 (its temporary headquarters had been an inn with the sign "Zum Mohren" [The Moor(!)]), and the German Social Democratic Workers' Party had been formed. This most important development in the German workers' movement was *not* approved by Karl Marx; neither by word nor deed was he involved. The name Eisenach never once appears in his letters of this period. News of the preparations was received with ill-humored mockery; a lengthy letter from Liebknecht was dismissed in a single sentence — "Enclosed a letter from little Wilhelm."[51] From this time on he followed developments — but with rage. Marx took Liebknecht's request that he pay a visit to the Congress as an order from a superior and reacted against it violently: "I *must* come to their August Congress, I *must show myself* to the German workers . . . I *must* fuck around with the Communist Manifesto."[52]

Moreover the letter sets out precisely the reason for this rage. The new party is only acceptable if it adheres to the International. Marx regards *his* organization as the superior one and *his* should be the command authority to prevail. The German party appeared to be taking on the character of a people's party, than which Marx wanted nothing less — "If we went there now we should have to speak against the people's party"; his concept was of a cadre party. His language now became crude.

From now on Liebknecht was simply a target for attack. Engels refused to accept the "imperious tone" of Liebknecht's letters (they did not, in fact, contain any such thing) but nevertheless continued in the same letter:

You must be confusing London with Crimmitschau and think that, with a flick of the fingers, one could found a "Friend of the Citizenry and Peasantry" here as well. You ought to know, however, that, London being larger than Crimmitschau, the difficulties of setting up a newspaper and the claims made upon it are that much greater. If you can place about £10,000 at our disposal, then we are at your service.[53]

Liebknecht was taken to task even for his friendly offer to obtain for Engels a mandate from the Social Democrats of Saxony for the London Conference of the International in September 1871; "*I* need no authority," Engels replied, adding that he would be delegate for Italy and Spain.[54] The same letter includes a blunt refusal to suggest additional Christian names, required for official registration, for Liebknecht's son Karl, born on August 13, 1871 (Liebknecht had asked Marx and Engels to be godfathers): "Marx and I do not secretly make up Christian names; we each only have one" (which was not true).

Suspicion of Liebknecht did not stem from personal animosity; it was directed against the party, the "artisans" organization which they did not themselves control. As a result of some triviality, failure to dispatch free copies of brochures, for instance, not only was Liebknecht hauled over the coals[55] (he had already refused to accept such rudeness) but the "Party" itself was put in the dock: "I cannot conceal from you that the treatment which we have received from the 'Party' definitely does not encourage us to put anything more into its hands. . . . For the last time I demand that this crude procedure should cease."[56]

The nicknames "General" and "Soldier" (the latter was Liebknecht's) seem to have become a sort of violin key, setting the tone. Estrangement and remoteness were obvious but it was primarily the political developments in

Germany from which the "two old ones" were estranged and remote — the aggressively didactic tone that they used with Liebknecht they also used to the German workers' party. Bebel and Liebknecht, later also Kautsky and Berstein, were not willing to be taught their business, to submit to "remote control." Quite soon Liebknecht was saying that it was "a crazy procedure for a workers' party to barricade itself in a theoretical ivory tower over the workers' heads."[57] He was a pragmatist and realized that peace, not war, with the Lassalleans must be the order of the day. The efforts to align the two, promoted by Liebknecht and culminating in the Gotha Party Rally of 1875 when the two parties united to form the German Socialist Workers' Party, meant an immediate and final breach with Marx and Engels.

They read about it in the newspaper;[58] they had not been informed. Marx and Engels did all they could to stop the plan for union; they were particularly critical of the program: "It is of such a character that, if it is accepted, Marx and I can *never* give our adherence to a *new* Party established on this basis and shall have very seriously to consider what our attitude toward it — in public as well — should be."[59]

The most striking document dealing with this affair, the now-famous *Critique of the Gotha Program,* was not published in Marx's lifetime. Engels handed over the manuscript to Kautsky only in 1891 for publication in the *Neue Zeit,* having first "indicated" that he could just as easily get it published by Adler in Vienna — "published it will be in any event."[60] Engels declared that he was "completely indifferent" to further pin-pricks from disgruntled Lassalleans or from within that wing of the party — "If they want, I am quite prepared to tell them that I am not accustomed to asking permission from them. It is all one to me whether they approve this publication or not."[61]

The subject was a letter from Karl Marx to Wilhelm Bracke dated May 5, 1875, covering "Marginal Notes to the Program of the German Workers' Party"; these were to be brought to the notice of Bebel, Liebknecht, and others. Almost two decades later and eight years after Marx's death, Engels discovered that Bebel had never seen this criticism of the Gotha Program by Marx![62]

The fact that it was possible for one of Karl Marx's most important effusions to "disappear" is further proof of remoteness and estrangement. Liebknecht was determined to have his political alliance at any price and he clearly dismissed the "Marginal Notes" as one of the superfluous lectures issued by the theorists in their ivory tower. In fact they were something very different. The two Londoners' vexation — "I cannot forgive him for never telling us a *single word* about the thing"[63] — was far more than mere injured pride on the part of army commanders whose troops were taking independent action. It was sheer horror at the theoretical cancer that had eaten into their political structure. Despite the shrill tone typical of Marx's arrogance, the

"Marginal Notes" illustrate his overwhelming intellectual superiority. After the *Manifesto* and the "Inaugural Address" they are his most systematic exposition of theory and politics. They include the phrase "dictatorship of the proletariat"; they set out the difference between the value of labor and the value of labor power; they define the aim of a communist society — from each according to his ability, to each according to his needs.[64]

Marx sweeps aside the high-sounding conceptual inaccuracies clearly culled by Liebknecht from Lassallean thinking. The Program opens with the words: "Labor is the source of all wealth and all culture," to which Marx replies: "Labor is *not the source* of all wealth. *Nature* is just as much the source of use values." The Program "improves upon" the Statutes of the International laying down that "the emancipation of labor must be the act of the working class," to which Marx replies: " 'Labor'? Let him understand who can." The Program proposes to "pave the way" gently for the solution of the social question and "call into being" cooperative societies; Marx says: "This is worthy of Lassalle's imagination that one can build a new society by state loans just as well as a new railway!"

Marx writes with the fury of a man whose repeated message has been "all you needed to do was to read the works of one man — myself"; he analyzes the imprecisions in thinking contrasting them with certain clear-cut ideas — his own. For the first time he deals with the problem of the new state:

But one man is superior to another physically or mentally and so supplies more labor in the same time or can labor for a longer time; and labor, to serve as a measure, must be defined by its duration or intensity, otherwise it ceases to be a standard of measurement. This *equal* right is an unequal right for unequal labor. It recognizes no class differences because everyone is only a worker like everyone else; but it tacitly recognizes unequal individual endowment and thus productive capacity as natural privileges. *It is therefore a right of inequality in its content, like every right.*[65]

Marx states that these defects — different individuals being also unequal individuals — are inevitable in the first phase of communist society. Only when the antithesis between mental and physical labor has vanished can the rule be established: "from each according to his ability, to each according to his needs." But this state of affairs must be achieved, or rather it must be fought for: "Between capitalist and communist society lies the period of the revolutionary transformation of the one into the other. Corresponding to this is also a political transition period in which the state can be nothing but the *revolutionary dictatorship of the proletariat.*"[66]

So there it is — the specter that was to haunt Europe from now on. There is also something else which we have already seen at similar periods, or rather turning points, of Marx's life — unbending determination after the loss of a battle. It was in evidence after the end of the *Rheinische Zeitung,* after the failure of the *Neue Rheinische Zeitung* "Party," and after the suppression of the Paris Commune. Terror was then the watchword — force as the counter to force.

When Karl Marx wrote that sentence with its unequivocal call to a "counterdictatorship," the nature of which he did not specify, the mechanics of which he did not explain, the duration of which he did not even indicate, when he set out this panacea, later rewritten as a charter, something else had also come to an end, and irrevocably so: by its humiliating disregard of its fifty-seven-year-old mentor the German party had indicated that he was not essential as one of its founding fathers. Moreover *his* Party, the First International, had foundered. In practice it ceased to exist after 1871.

Once more Marx was both right and wrong. Like all his "Critiques" his *Critique of the Gotha Program* was brilliant; the Party, however, was successful with *their* program. Social democracy scored an overwhelming victory at the Reichstag elections of 1877.[67] And Marx's great essay, his attempt to translate his philosophy into practical organizational terms, had not been a success. No initiatives were taken apart from welfare campaigns during strikes, support for workers locked out, or occasional demonstrative mass meetings. The annual conferences of the International in London, Geneva, Lausanne, Brussels, or Basel were the scene of resolutions and counterresolutions, quarrels and ill-humor. Marx practically did not participate at all. He was regarded as the "backroom" leader and the theoretical brain. Primarily, however, it was the Italians who refused to do obeisance to him; they were continually putting forward proposals or demanding votes directed almost openly against him. Marx sighed: "With the intrigues of the Proudhonists in Paris, of Mazzini in Italy, of the jealous Odger, Cremer and Potter in London, with Schulze-Delitzsch and the Lassalleans in Germany!"[68] All this may perhaps have given the International the unenviable reputation of a dangerous secret society; no one knew precisely what they were really up to, or when, where, how, or by whom they were directed. Sometimes there was talk of fresh branches in Spain and Italy and then of imminent proscription in France. They were thought to be both omnipotent and ubiquitous, to have provided the fire-raisers even for the great Chicago fire of 1871. Wavering between revulsion and admiration, the public looked upon them as a half-Jesuit, half-Freemason association, a secret society with limitless funds, a headquarters, and a magician in command. The *Times* estimated the membership at two and a half million and capital at several million pounds; at the Hague Conference the arrival of delegates at the station was watched by a fearful and horrified crowd and they were followed to their hotels; children were told: "If you go out don't take with you anything they could steal."[69]

Rumors about Marx turned him sometimes into Bismarck's private secretary, sometimes into a corpse; he was gazed at like a Negro among Eskimos — so that man with white hair and flowing beard, in a smart dark tailor-made suit, with an eyeglass, was the Red Czar. Meanwhile, after the Hague Congress, Marx went quietly off to Scheveningen to take the waters. A Paris police informer's report[70] describes him dutifully taking his baths and listening to concerts in the evening with his family on the terrace of the Grand Hotel.

Even the papal Encyclical of 1879, "*Quod apostolici muneris,*" refers to the gentlemen of the International as the real enemies of God and mankind. The truth was very different. In the General Council's till in 1869/70 was £50; hardly any of the several hundred membership cards sent to Germany by Marx were returned; in late 1871 there were 385 members,[71] 254 of them in England. The British trade unions did keep in close touch with the General Council but remained entirely independent in their political activities; fewer and fewer trade unions joined; the members of the International were primarily craftsmen. One of them, Eugène Pottier, wrote the anthem of which everyone thinks today when the word "International" is mentioned; it may have contributed to the misconception about a vast army of members with power and influence. It was first sung in 1888 and remained unknown in Germany until 1910.

Marx was naturally aware that the International had the reputation of a secret conspiratorial organization; he also knew that he was pictured as the string-puller of a "Red Orchestra." He very seldom gave interviews, but in July 1871 was questioned by an American journalist:

"People talk of secret instructions from London and even of financial support. Can it be maintained that the ostensible public activities of the association exclude the possibility of any clandestine links —" Dr. Marx: "Has there ever been an association which could carry on its work without having both confidential and open communications? But talk of secret instructions from London as if they were decrees on matters of faith and morality issued by some intriguing headquarters with papal authority would indicate total misappreciation of the nature of the International. It would presuppose a centralized form of government in the International; in fact, however, the organization of the International guarantees the utmost latitude to local initiative and independent action. In fact the International is definitely not a government of the working class; it is an association rather than a command organization."[72]

Marx himself, however, was largely responsible for the impression which he deprecated on this occasion; it resulted primarily from two personal campaigns, his vehement support for the Paris Commune which had nothing whatsoever to do with socialism, and his world-famous, perennial, and devious battle with Bakunin.

PACT OF FRIENDSHIP WITH THE
OLD ENEMY BAKUNIN

"Bakunin sends you greetings."[73] This was the surprising sentence with which Marx announced to Manchester that he had met Bakunin in London. It was their first encounter for sixteen years. It took place six weeks after Marx had sent his condolences to Countess Hatzfeldt on the death of Lassalle — "Rejoice over one thing. He died young, in triumph, like Achilles"[74] — and three days after he had submitted the "Inaugural Address" to the Committee of the International Workers' Association in St. Martin's Hall, intended to be his most important political organization. The meeting with Bakunin should be viewed in this historical context, for the initiative came from Marx. For many years no one knew how it had actually come about. In the intervening period Bakunin had stayed in London but the two had never met. The intermediary was only discovered in 1913 by D. Ryazanoff, the outstanding expert on Marx, editor of the great Moscow edition of his works. The answer was that Marx and Bakunin used the same tailor: "Dear Marx, We are at present making suits for the great Bakunin who, as far as I know, will only be here for a short time. Should you want his address, I can get it for you. . . . Your friend, Fred. Lessner."[75]

Marx got in touch *that very day,* for Bakunin's somewhat condescending reply is dated the day after Lessner's letter: "Dear Marx, It would give me great pleasure to see an old acquaintance again. I am always at home until 1:00 A.M. . . ."[76]

They met a week later, on November 3, the day before Bakunin's departure for Italy. Marx was very pleased and wrote to say how much he had liked him, better than formerly, and that he was one of the few people whom he found to have developed forwards instead of backwards after sixteen years.[77] The same letter also contains the cryptic sentence: "I also talked over the Urquhart denunciations with him."[78]

Various interreacting developments illustrate the special peculiar feature of the involved relationship between these two men. Bakunin admired Marx's achievements in matters of theory but did not trust him personally. Marx regarded Bakunin as a muddleheaded pan-Slav agitator whom one could well use at times but who could become dangerous if he carried too much weight or gained overmany adherents. Marx's opinion of him tallied with that of the revolution's Police President in Lyon during the Commune, who made the famous remark: "What a man! On the first day of a revolution he is a perfect treasure; on the second he ought to be shot."[79]

At this point it was still "the first day"; the International, Marx's political life's work, was being formed. This was why he went to Bakunin and attempted to recruit him for the Italian section of the International. He gave Bakunin the Statutes and the "Inaugural Address" (he later sent further copies as well). Years later, at the time of the great showdown with Bakunin, Marx referred to his enthusiasm but maintained that he had never done anything thereafter. On his side Bakunin has a somewhat different recollection of their meeting:

> . . . he arrived and we had a discussion; he swore that he had never done or said anything against me but on the contrary had always felt genuine friendship and great respect for me. I knew that he was not speaking the truth but I no longer harbored any real resentment against him. . . . In short we parted as ostensibly very good friends, though I did not return his visit.[80]

Denunciations, untruths, ostensibly good friendship — there is a story behind this relationship and it goes back a long way. It fluctuates between suspicion, loyalty, half-truth, and ultimate brutality but it is by no means a "talc." The struggle between the two lies at the very heart and core of all debates about the history of the workers' movement even to the present day; if the story be traced back the question inevitably arises whether there is not a "built-in" inhumanity in the great picture of the new socialist mankind. There is no way of evading the answer; for a hundred years now men have been in two minds. Marx and Bakunin=Stalin and Trotsky

When Bakunin left Russia for Germany as a young aristocratic officer in 1840, he had no idea whither developments would take him. He studied in Berlin and published articles in Ruge's *Deutsche Jahrbücher* using the pseudonym Jules Elysard. His article "Die Reaktion in Deutschland" (Reaction in Germany) signified his conversion to a degree of radicalism and demonstrated that he was siding with the Young Hegelians in their battle against Schelling; even its style was reminiscent of Engels's article "Schelling und die Offenbarung" (Schelling and the Revelation).

Bakunin evolved no theory of his own. The great process of fermentation produced the germ of one great idea — away with the state which contained, or gave rise to, everything evil. No state, no misery; no state, no serfdom. He went to Dresden; he went to Paris; he moved in "revolutionary salon" circles; he was to be seen with Louis Blanc and Felix Pyat, with Proudhon, George Sand, and Turgenev; he wrote articles about Belgian Jesuits in the *Constitutional;* he visited "Les Ouvriers," the association of socialists and communists. But he held aloof "from all political enterprises until 1846."[81] Then came the February revolution — *"la république est proclamée à Paris."* The frenzy, the ecstasy, the enthusiasm increased daily until "at last" he could say: *"On se batte à Berlin. Le Roi est en fuite."*

Bakunin was a salesman of revolution. He had no precise aim, no theory, no political strategy. The lonely peak of disciplined political theory scaled by

Marx, which he was putting into words in the *Neue Rheinische Zeitung* at this time, is all the more striking when compared with this meaningless, ill-considered, fly-by-night activity. Bakunin was in a state of emotional exaltation; his cry was an unthinking "destroy what is destroying you";[82] but noble, glorious emotional reactions are not the stuff of which politics are made. The correspondence between Marx and Bakunin published in Ruge's *Deutsch-Französische Jahrbücher* provides a striking illustration of the difference between emotionalism and political rationalism.

This is also the difference that makes political veering and hauling possible, that enabled the Nazi and Communist parties to take combined action in crisis-torn Berlin in 1932, that led the French Communist Party to issue a no-strike call in 1968 while Daniel Cohn-Bendit's students were plastering the walls, that led all the postulates enunciated in *The State and Revolution* to be thrown overboard ten days later when its author, Lenin, had seized power.

"ONE CANNOT ENTRUST EVERYTHING
TO THE RUSSIANS"

On July 6, 1848, about the time that Bakunin was describing himself as "consumed with revolutionary fervor, the deepest red of all red republicans and democrats,"[83] Marx published a dispatch from Paris in the *Neue Rheinische Zeitung* denouncing Bakunin as a Russian spy, an agent of the Czar. Bakunin later said that the article had hit him as if a copingstone had fallen on his head and that it should clearly be regarded as retribution by Marx for the fact that someone had plucked up courage to put into practice ideas differing from his own; according to the article the source of the rumor was — George Sand. Shortly afterward, as a result of an urgent appeal from Bakunin, the famous woman issued a *démenti* saying that not only had she never made a statement of this nature but also that Bakunin's loyalty and character were not in doubt.

This affair has never ceased to cast its shadow over Marx. Whole libraries were filled with "explanations" — he had known nothing about it; he had been away; he had wanted to help Bakunin by the publicity which would be increased by official *démentis;* he even gave vent to severe condemnation of such destructive strategy. The last great battle of words in this affair took place in 1913 between Ryazanoff and Franz Mehring. At this time Mehring had already become the official historian of Social Democracy; four years later he was one of the co-founders of the German Communist Party together with Karl Liebknecht and Rosa Luxemburg, and he was the editor, authorized by Marx's daughter Laura, of Marx's papers. Yet even he dismisses with magisterial sarcasm the sacrosanct hero cult built up around Marx, the "Marx theology" that turns every casual remark into a revelation and suppresses anything disreputable:

Now the Bakunin problem is not a Party problem; it is a question of propriety and honesty. . . . Of course, if the Bakunin problem is only a question of propriety and honesty, the fact that they are unable to give a proper answer to it may seem all the more serious for the Marxists.[84]

Here is the point: it is not whether some stupid gossip was inadvertently peddled — nothing in the *Neue Rheinische Zeitung* was printed "inadvertently" — the point is whether denunciation and calumny are legitimate weapons with which to "eliminate" a political opponent. Can tactics involving secret information and insinuation help to bring about the birth of the "new man"? What leader, what Secretary-General, what Central Committee decides? What court deals with the case? Admittedly it is questionable whether flaws in the character of one individual of genius can produce defects in the theory or practice of a body of doctrine which has molded our world for over a hundred years. But may not the theory that men are tractable, disposable, and malleable be perverted until it ends by breaking the man who refuses to be guided and educated? That "man is good" can be an evil hypothesis under certain circumstances. Someone lays down what is good; someone defines the purpose of utopia. The line dividing this from illusion is a thin one. The relationship between illusion and utopia is similar to that between sentimentality and emotion. Sentimentality implies disregard of others, ultimately, in fact, implies cruelty. It will be remembered that in his days as Chief Editor Marx's best joke over the evening glass of wine was "I will destroy you." When Bakunin and Marx met in Berlin a month after the denunciation, Marx said: "Do you know that I am now at the head of such a well-disciplined communist secret society that, if I were to say to one of its members: 'Go and kill Bakunin,' he would kill you?"[85]

Mexico, the icepick . . .

Intolerance as part and parcel of the great theory of the liberation of mankind? Is the case of Lassalle a Bakunin case or a Trotsky case? It was Lenin who coupled the names of Trotsky and Lassalle, Lenin who, like Marx, could not bear to lose a game of chess (Gorky records how vexed and miserable Lenin was if he lost;[86] Liebknecht records that Marx was so cross and intolerable after being beaten at chess that Jenny asked him not to play chess with Marx again in the evenings).[87] Again Lenin once said to Gorky: "And despite this Trotsky is not one of us. He is with us but he is not one of us. There is something wrong about him, stemming from Lassalle."[88]

In this context too should be viewed Lenin's comment, which has been quoted over and over again as an illustration of his remarkable humanity; carefully read, however, it instils fear into the reader because behind it lies the implication of force, the arrogance of power, the prerogative of decision. It is Lenin's remark on listening to a Beethoven sonata:

I know of nothing better than the "Appassionata"; I could listen to it every day. It is astounding, superhuman music. I always think with some pride, which is perhaps naïve of me: What miracles men can achieve. . . . But I cannot listen to music very often; it plays on the nerves; one would like to say stupid tender things, to stroke the heads of the men who live in a revolting hell and yet can create something beautiful. But today one must not stroke anyone's head; you would get your hand bitten off. One must beat the heads, beat them mercilessly, although according to our ideals, we are opposed to the use of force against people.[89]

And supposing the man who does the head-beating is wrong? Supposing the man who slices heads off has arrogated to himself an alleged right to do so? Injustice stemming from eschatology? There was a prelude to Lenin's remark: "Should the communist society, however, one day find itself compelled to regulate the production of men as it has regulated the production of things, it will be this society and this alone which does it without difficulty."[90]

This was written, not by Malthus, but by Friedrich Engels.

Bakunin's reply to the curious form of apology selected by Marx to atone for a case of crude slander was one of superb indifference, typical of him: "I replied that if [his] secret society had nothing else to do than kill people whom he disliked, it could only be a society consisting of minions or ridiculous braggarts. . . ."[91]

This misses one point, however: Marx never had such an organization available. So much the worse. Desires are at least as indicative as facts. Bakunin realized, however, that this was no mere accident, no journalist's gaffe, not a piece of false information unfortunately passed on inadvertently. In Bakunin's eyes the thread of despotism and dirigism in Marx's character was a facet of the theory of "*ruling, educating and organizing* the masses according to the ideas of that theory. . . . Marx . . . has a passionate desire to see the victory of his ideas, of the proletariat and so of himself. . . . The disease lies in the search for power, the love of domination, the thirst for authority and Marx is contaminated through and through with this disease."[92]

Antagonism was therefore two-fold; its basis was factual as well as personal. Marx's violent rejection of Bakunin as a "theoretical cipher" whose program was "a hodge-podge of superficial ideas collected right and left"[93] was balanced by aversion to his king-size personality. Contemporaries describe Bakunin as an imposing apparition with the devil in his bones. Herzen called everything about him gigantic, "his ability, his appetite, the whole man";[94] Byelinsky describes him as follows: "Michael is often guilty and sinful but there is something in him which outweighs all his deficiencies — that is the eternally active principle which lives deep within his spirit."[95]

The following story gives an example of the feats ascribed to him: during a rising in Pisa he was in a house surrounded by soldiers but simply walked out through them; not one of them dared touch him.[96] He had an obvious naughty-boy streak about him as well, however; when he was once asked what he would do if the world were ever arranged entirely to his liking, he displayed the anarchist's skepticism by saying: "Then I should pull it all down again."[97]

Bakunin had taken part in the Dresden rising, had escaped in a mailcoach together with Richard Wagner, had been arrested by Prussian troops and condemned to death in Olmütz. The Russian government intervened and Bakunin was deported; he spent years in solitary confinement in various Russian prisons and was eventually "reprieved" by Alexander II and exiled to Siberia, whence he escaped in 1861.

Even this period in Siberia provided material for the rumormongers. For the rest of his life Bakunin raged against the fairytales told about his period of arrest and exile;[98] he was no prisoner in a fortress, he would say, but a gay spark who was given a cheerful welcome by Czar Nicholas and had a good time with wine and women.

It may be that Bakunin owed this leniency, which eventually enabled him to escape to America, to something else: in the first year of his arrest in the Peter-Paul fortress he had written a "Confession" or plea for clemency to Czar Nicholas I. This document never saw the light of day in his lifetime and was not found until 1916, in the safe of the Head of Section III in the Czar's Chancellery. Bakunin referred to it only once, in a letter to Herzen,[99] and then never again. He realized that, had his act of obeisance become known, it would have ended his political career in Europe and destroyed his personal credibility. During the years of his battle with Bakunin Marx made desperate efforts to lay hands on "this extremely servile letter";[100] it would have been a triumph for him and would have saved him having to have recourse to trivial, dubious subterfuges.

At this point, however, something bordering on farce occurred and it ruined forever the relationship between Marx and Bakunin. This is the "incident" referred to by Marx in his letter to Engels telling of his meeting with Bakunin in London after the latter's escape. While Bakunin was moldering in various prisons — and his Siberian "penny dreadful" was giving rise to all sorts of rumors abroad — an article appeared in a London newspaper accusing him of being a Russian spy. The old story all over again. The article was signed "F.M.," the abbreviation used by a man named Marx.

But — it was another Marx. However incredible it may sound, Karl Marx had nothing whatsoever to do with the charge that appeared in the *Morning Advertiser* of August 29, 1853; the author was a landowner named Francis Marx. Not a soul believed that, however. Two days later the newspaper, which had close connections with David Urquhart, the reactionary British politician, published a letter from Ruge pointing out that Marx had already been guilty of a similar calumny — in the *Neue Rheinische Zeitung.* To the end of his days Alexander Herzen was convinced that this malicious sniping against a defenseless prisoner came from Marx.[101]

This was what Marx was referring to when he visited Bakunin and *this* was what Bakunin was referring to when he noted, "I knew that he was not telling the truth." Bakunin was convinced that Marx was making a second attempt on his political life — and he was never dissuaded from this conviction. This was understandable since no official correction of the report was ever issued; the *Morning Advertiser* did not print Marx's counterblast.[102]

Henceforth relations between the two men were dictated by tactical considerations, but they became increasingly hostile. Marx wanted to recruit Bakunin for the International. Bakunin did in fact join but took no action; he did not even answer letters. Once again it was Marx who pressed for statements of some sort, even declarations of friendship. They came, but were they entirely sincere?

You ask whether I am still your friend. Yes indeed, more than ever, my dear Marx, because I understand better than ever how right you were to carry on and summon us forth, to stride ahead along the great path of economic revolution and to reprimand those who had been side-tracked into nationalist or ultimately political by-ways. . . . My fatherland is now the International, of which you are one of the principal founders. You therefore see, dear friend, that I am your disciple and proud of being so.[103]

In the years preceding this letter — 1865, 1866, and 1867 — nothing; hardly a word, hardly any participation in the International. Bakunin went his own way, leaving Marx offended and suspicious: "After years during which one has heard nothing from him he turns up again in Switzerland. Yet he does not attach himself to the International but to the League for Peace and Freedom."[104]

During this period there occurred an irritating incident that clearly hurt and offended Marx: he sent Bakunin a signed copy of *Capital* which had just appeared — and Bakunin did not reply! Once again one is tempted to label as a typical accident the fact that Bakunin's essay on his "Relations with Marx" breaks off at precisely this point:

It was at the Geneva Peace Congress that the old communist Philipp Becker handed me on Marx's behalf the first, and so far only, volume of an extremely important, learned, profound, though very abstract, book entitled *Das Kapital*. Then I made a colossal error; I forgot to write to Marx to thank him. Some months later . . .[105]

Many critics — Ryazanoff for instance — have tried to play this incident down and write it off as insignificant. But this implies disregard of all that Marx did to promote his book — including even faking critiques under different names[106] and being prepared for the first time in his life to take out British naturalization papers in order to obtain a passport for a trip to Paris without which there would be no French edition of the book.[107] Two letters from contemporaries confirm the importance attached by Marx to reaction or nonreaction to his book. One is from Jenny Marx, of all people, and it illustrates the tone in which Bakunin was referred to in the Marx household:

Have you seen and heard nothing of Bakunin? As he was an old Hegelian my husband sent him his book — but no word from near or far. One can't entrust everything to the Russians; they may not hold with the "Little Father" in Russia but they do hold with or are held by Little Father Herzen, which comes to the same thing. Hop, skip and jump.[108]

So the same story over and over again; either he was a spy or he was in the pay of Alexander Herzen, the millionaire and administrator of a fund for revolution. Denouncement was despatched by the same mail, so to speak, as the signed copy of *Capital*. Becker, the recipient of this letter from Jenny Marx, said at once to Bakunin: "What! You've not yet written to him! Marx will never forgive you that."[109]

He was right. It is odd that Bakunin should have disregarded something which he had recognized and put into words more clearly than anyone else:

Marx is extremely conceited, so conceited as to descend into dirt and lunacy. Anyone who has the misfortune, however innocently, to offend his morbid, permanently susceptible and permanently touchy vanity becomes his irreconcilable enemy; then he considers any methods permissible and will in fact employ the most disgraceful and impermissible methods to smear such a man in the eyes of the public. He lies, invents and takes pains to spread the meanest slanders.

He will never forgive a personal offense; to be liked by him one must worship him, turn him into an idol; to be tolerated by him one must at least be afraid of him. He likes to go around with little people, lackeys and flatterers.

Marx's entire circle is a sort of mutual contract between the vanities on which he exists. In it Marx is the main distributor of honors; at the same time, however, he is perfidious, malicious, never frank or open, always the instigator of some campaign against people of whom he is suspicious or who have had the misfortune to fail to defer to him to the extent expected of them. As soon as he has decreed a campaign against someone he will shrink from no villainy, no ignominy.[110]

Marx did not reply to his "disciple's" flattering letter; it was too late. But to repeat: this was not merely a case of a personal quarrel, of irritability or of pique; there was a simultaneous and equally weighty disagreement on political concepts.

Bakunin saw in Marx a sort of Red Bismarck, a pan-Germanist Kaiser[111] who wished to set up state-organized socialism under Prussian-German hegemony, everything in fact against which he had fought all his life. Bakunin did not like the Germans (any more than the Jews); to him they were sinister and horrifying. Moreover he wanted to abolish the state — not create a new one but to have no state at all. To him Marx's pattern of political organization was as alien as it was suspect.

In the same year in which he had written his letter of allegiance to Marx, Bakunin formed the Alliance de la Démocratie Socialiste in Geneva; it was planned as an international anarchist organization and was clearly a counter to the International. It evoked a great response in Italy, Spain, the Swiss Jura, France, and Holland, in other words from countries in which socialist groupings are still characterized today by marked anarchist and syndicalist tendencies. Although the Alliance refused to accept the International's main ideological tenets[112] (instead of class warfare Bakunin proclaimed equality of classes and instead of organized struggle for power the abolition of the state), it asked for affiliation. The General Council of the International agreed, subject to the conditions that it disband itself as an independent international organization, become a section of the International, and recognize its statutes.

This took place in 1869, the year in which the great combined rally of all working-class unions was held in Eisenach, an achievement for which Liebknecht and Bebel were primarily responsible. Marx, however, refused Liebknecht's invitation to attend this Congress from which the German Social Democrat Party emerged. He insisted that every "heretical" influence — in other words, the spirit of Lassalle — must first be eliminated, and that this must be done as if it were "a spontaneous act by the workers themselves."[113]

Marx was on the defensive everywhere. The first Congress held with the Alliance resulted in victory — for Bakunin. On one side-issue, the question of the right of inheritance, the meeting cast only one-quarter of its votes *in favor* of the London Committee. Marx had not been present; he had gone off to Germany on a holiday trip with his daughter Jenny; his secretary Eccarius ran round wringing his hands saying: "Marx will be extremely displeased."[114]

In Germany matters were clearly taking their own course. Marx had to accept a reprimand from Liebknecht and Bebel to the effect that he no longer had an overall view of the German scene; he was certainly not the ruling authority. He was the wiseacre, the oracle to whom pilgrimage was made —

but the pronouncements of the oracle were by no means invariably followed. In Basel his followers were voted down. Moreover, as before, hardly any notice was being taken of his book; in England, where he had lived for almost two decades, no one knew about it (it was never translated into English during Marx's lifetime).

Marx girded his loins for a counterblast — and the man who knew all about it was Bakunin:

It may be, however, and probably will be that I shall have to involve myself in a battle with him, not about some personal insult but about a question of principle, that of state communism assiduously championed by him and the party he runs, both the British and the German. That, however, will be a battle, not for life but to the death. But all in good time and the time for this has not yet come.[115]

The tone is one of self-assured politeness, but unfortunately Bakunin himself was not so fastidious. A serious political struggle was looming; both sides knew it and both made their preparations after their own fashion. In December 1868 Bakunin had written to Marx that there was no longer any degree of solidarity between him and Herzen; they were no longer even in personal touch. Now, a year later, he wrote this letter prophesying battle — to Herzen. And he had very clear ideas on the tactics, even stratagems, with which he hoped to defeat Marx.

To a large extent, moreover, this was also a defensive battle. Over and over again rumors about Bakunin the "agent, the Russian spy, the informer," raised their heads and were broadcast. Over and over again they originated from Marx's — Karl, not Francis — immediate entourage. There were veiled references in all sorts of newspapers, hints about political meetings — and all this came to Bakunin's ears.[116] Finally he managed to nail down a rumor-monger by name, but it was a name unknown to him — Wilhelm Liebknecht — and he arrived as a delegate to the Basel Congress. Here was a wonderful opportunity to crush once for all the serpent of calumny's head. So a court of honor was held in the wings of the Basel Congress and it turned into Bakunin's second great triumph and victory. The source of rumor could not be tracked down to Marx, so no *démenti* was to be expected from him; he preserved a deafening silence; he lifted not a finger to help his fellow-member of the International.

Liebknecht was compelled to make a public apology, in writing. Then Bakunin, the Russian aristocrat, the international anarchist, and the permanent refugee, made an unforgettable gesture: he shook Liebknecht's hand, took the paper on which the apology was written, and lit a cigarette with it. Then he departed for Italian Switzerland to translate into Russian the book of which he had such a high opinion, of which he possessed a signed copy for which the grudging author had never received an acknowledgment — *Das Kapital.*

A Russian publisher had offered him a fee of 1,200 rubles with 300 in advance. Early in January 1870, however, there appeared in Switzerland a young Russian named Netchayev, an anarchist who had had to go into hiding for murdering a suspected traitor (he was extradited to Russia in 1872). He implored Bakunin not to bury himself in translation but to pursue his revolutionary activities. Bakunin stopped work (and never resumed it). Netchayev promised to square matters with the publisher. This he did, but his method was both puerile and criminal: he wrote a threatening letter on the notepaper of some mysterious committee with dagger, ax, and revolver as its crest; the letter was couched in terms typical of an illiterate blackmailer and stated that any demand for repayment of the advance was tantamount to a death sentence. Bakunin knew nothing about it. When he found out — and also about other childish political plots such as a plan to attack the Simplon mailcoach — he severed all relations with Netchayev and hurriedly dispatched a receipt acknowledging that he was in debt to the amount of the advance. All in all this was not an incident of vast political significance and would certainly not have been thought so by Karl Marx, whose own relations with publishers were not always of the smoothest.

But — at the latest since the Basel Congress Marx and Engels had been on the lookout for evidence, any evidence, which might incriminate Bakunin. This is the period at which the "extremely servile letter" is mentioned in their correspondence; embezzlement was considered but rejected as an argument; Engels dismissed as utterly ridiculous a charge that Bakunin had misused a certain sum of money for his escape instead of paying his taxes with it.[117]

But now Bakunin was in league with "one of the most unscrupulous terrorists,"[118] a criminal rather than a politician, a blackmailer and an embezzler. Marx actually contrived to obtain the letter from St. Petersburg; oddly enough he did so from the man who eventually translated *Capital* into Russian, the writer and economist Nikolai F. Danielson. The battle was now on.

As always Marx waged war on two levels: by political polemics he tried to undermine his opponent's theoretical position; from these polemics he distilled his own, and generally superior, theoretical position. It was a procedure peculiar to him, defined as follows by Ricarda Huch: "Everything he undertook he subjected to his reasoning and thereby turned it into a corpse; what he dealt with was past, even if it was also future."[119] Over and over again, half mockingly, half contemptuously, Bakunin had described the sword of Damocles hanging over him as "Marx's habitual weapon, a heap of filth";[120] in addition he had pointed out Marx's total lack of following or influence in England, although all his politicoeconomic theories were based on the situation in England — Marx's failure ever to master this situation culminated in his bitter attacks on the English working class at the Hague Congress. Bakunin had also drawn attention to certain decisive gaps in Marx's thought pattern:

He fails to take into account other ingredients of history, for instance the obvious repercussions of political, juridical and religious institutions on the economic situation. . . .

Herr Marx also totally fails to appreciate one highly important factor in the historical development of mankind: every race and every people has a particular temperament and character which are of course themselves the product of a multiplicity of ethnographic, climatic, economic and historical causes but which, once established, exert considerable influence on the destiny of any country irrespective and independent of the economic field and which even influence the development of its economic forces.[121]

Here we reach the most sensitive point. Two decades later Engels was given to think by similar objections to his own ideas. Here we touch the *nervus rerum* — and if the dispute with anarchism has still not been settled to this day, the reason is this disquiet, the question whether it is advisable and right to eliminate the subject and subjectivity so completely, to erect so perfect a screening system against all imponderables that writers can one day be regarded merely as "engineers of the human soul."

As soon as the program of Bakunin's Alliance appeared Marx began to talk of "this shit" that was trying to compensate for the "idealism" missing in his own organization, "Russian idealism," something particularly abhorrent to the Russophobe Marx. He saw the threat of Russian leadership looming larger than he had ever imagined.[122] During the Commune rising Bakunin had placed himself at the head of a senseless, though heroic, enterprise; *he* had been the man summoned to Lyon by the revolutionaries on September 26, 1871; there the Commune had seized the town hall, abolished the administrative and governmental machinery of the state, and set up a federal commune. Bakunin was taken prisoner, released, and escaped to Switzerland late in October. He was now in Locarno, too poor to buy a cup of tea and full of "hatred against the revolutionary propaganda carried on by Marx . . . because he thought it chiefly responsible for the indecisive attitude of the proletariat."[123]

Marx collected evidence against Bakunin wherever he could. He knew that the next Congress, which he had suggested should assemble in Holland, would be a "life and death matter for the International";[124] in fact Marx already knew that he would be resigning from it.[125] For this reason he made a personal appearance at the Hague Congress in September 1871. The meeting was submerged in papers and documents in French, Spanish, Russian, and German. The Congress remained undecided. It set up a commission to enquire into the charges against Bakunin. On September 7 it produced a report to the effect that the Alliance was *not* to be regarded as a semi-independent organisation within the International. Whereupon Marx stepped forward in person — and produced the famous Netchayev letter. Bakunin was "annihilated." He was expelled. He sent a statement, scornfully referred to by Engels as his "political death sentence," to the *Journal de Genève:* "I withdraw. From now on I shall not bother anyone and I only ask to be left in peace."[126]

The Congress decided to publish all the evidence and it was handed over to Marx and Engels. Between April and July 1873, helped by Paul Lafargue, they wrote a memorandum entitled "The Socialist Democratic Alliance and the International Workers Association"; Franz Mehring describes it as providing no historical evidence and being simply a biased speech for the prosecution, one of the meanest attacks ever published by Marx and Engels: "It does not deal at all with the internal causes responsible for the decline of the International. Although it caused Bakunin to withdraw from the struggle, it did not touch the movement which bore his name."[127]

Further damage had been done by the fact that in March 1870 Marx had personally dispatched a *"communication privée"* in German and French to all German Party offices and their adherents, warning them against "Bakunin the Russian and his machinations." At the time Bakunin was working on the translation of *Capital*. He knew nothing at all about this "confidential communication," which was read at Party conclaves everywhere from Berlin to Leipzig and was inevitably taken as a ukase — without authority Marx had issued it on the official notepaper headed "Working Men's International Association Central Council. London." Various statements such as "serious and subterranean activities,"[128] which at the very least were "misleading," ultimately led to various political and legal complications. In particular Marx was accused of having misused his Party position in a personal or ideological dispute that did not justify any executive measures.

By a small majority the Hague Congress agreed to a proposal from Marx and Engels that the seat of the General Council be transferred to New York.

NO WORD ON THE PARIS COMMUNE

The International, however, was not torn apart merely by the battle between two political saurians. The central reason, the historical — or rather, unhistorical — reason that inevitably brought about its end, was strikingly illustrated in the Franco-Prussian War.

Once more the dichotomy peculiar to Marx was in evidence: his analysis of the causes of the war and of the true historical forces opposing each other was impeccable, but his political "instructions" missed the mark; they by-passed reality and enunciated only possibilities. The International's influence upon events both in France and Germany was nil. This dichotomy between the correct starting point and the illusory aim, in which his imagination took refuge as it were, is detectable in the "First Address of the General Council of the International Working Men's Association on the Franco-Prussian War" written by Marx between July 19 and 23, 1870, at the General Council's behest. The vital paragraph reads:

If the German working class allows the present war to lose its strictly defensive character and to degenerate into a war against the French people, victory or defeat will alike prove disastrous. All the miseries that befell Germany after her war of independence will revive with accumulated intensity. The principles of the International are, however, too widely spread and too firmly rooted among the German working class to apprehend such a sad consummation.[129]

This clear call for a defensive war stems directly from his hope that the workers would come to realize certain definite things and in this he was doing exactly that of which Bakunin for one had accused him, underestimating the force of nationalist emotion. It is noteworthy that Engels took an entirely different view on this point. When Marx wrote "the French need a thrash-ing"[130] he meant that a German victory would lead to centralization of the German workers' movement and give them preponderance over the French. Bismarck would, at one blow as it were, sweep away the influence of Blanqui and Proudhon.

He, *Marx,* was to be the victor of Sedan and the vanquished not so much Napoleon III as that group which had always opposed him in the Interna-tional: "For my part I would like to see the Prussians and French beat each other in turn but the Prussians finally emerge as victors — as I expect."[131]

The Prussian victory at Sedan, the capture of Napoleon III, and the estab-lishment of the Third Republic proved Marx right with his "death-knell of the Second Empire" announced in the "First Address"; nationalistic frenzy in Germany, however, proved that he was wrong in his hope that the war would remain defensive. Between September 6 and 9, 1870, again at the behest of the General Council, Marx wrote the "Second Address of the General Coun-cil on the Franco-Prussian War" (and signed it as Secretary for Germany and Russia). Early in this "Address" comes the sentence: ". . . we were not wrong in our apprehension lest the German war should 'lose its strictly defen-sive character and degenerate into a war against the French people.' "[132]

But that was *not* what the "First Address" — of which no fewer than 30,000 copies had been printed with the help of the Peace Society — had said; it had said exactly the opposite. In it Marx had said that the principles of the International were too widely spread and too deeply rooted for anyone to fear that the war would turn out as in fact it had done. He had had no such fear himself and had brushed any such fear aside on the grounds that the international proletariat in the Reich had reached a certain stage of enlightenment. Either Marx was counting upon the short memories of his contemporaries or he was unconsciously correcting himself but — whether consciously or unconsciously — this textual correction entailed the withdrawal of his previous pronouncement. The discrepancy is a measure of the divorce between his wishful thinking and reality, a divorce characteristic of his whole attitude to the Paris Commune.

Paris surrendered on January 28, 1871. Contrary to all forecasts and exhortations not a syllable of protest came from the German proletariat, still less any action against the annexation of Alsace-Lorraine. The five million gold marks which France had to pay as war reparations were welcomed and accepted. The attempt by Thiers, the new Minister-President in Paris, to disarm the National Guard led to rioting and fraternization with the troops ordered to confiscate their weapons. Civil war broke out. Thiers fled to Versailles. On March 26 the National Assembly was elected by universal, equal, and direct suffrage; it called itself "Commune de Paris" after that of 1792. A merciless battle — similar to that of June 1848 — flared up and raged for two months to the day. By May 28 the last Communard was dead, including Gustave Flourens, one of whose letters Jenny Longuet concealed from the police and for whom Jenny Marx wrote her touching obituary.

Karl Marx hailed the Commune with enthusiasm — in retrospect. Not a word came from the General Council; for two months it remained silent. Marx did propose that there should be an address and was commissioned to write it. But he did not do so. On the contrary, a week later he declared that he now thought it inopportune.[133] In a letter he said that inadequate information on events in Paris, particularly from the Paris Section, prevented a statement being made.[134] This is one of the two extant letters written by Marx on matters directly connected with the Commune. After the letter to Leo Frankel in late April he attended three sessions of the General Council but did not write an address. His complaint about inadequate information is justified and also revealing: of the ninety-two members of the Commune Council only seventeen were adherents of the International; the majority was Blanquist; even the "hard core" was recruited primarily from adherents of Proudhon. Both factions stood aloof from the International; Proudhon loathed it, calling it pure dogma, unproductive and burdensome.[135] From this time Marx pleaded the excuse of severe illness. He did not go to another meeting and produced no manuscript — an odd contrast to his own statement that he had "written several hundred letters . . . to every corner of the world"[136] on the subject, and even more to Engels's description of his glowing health at this time.[137]

Marx was forced to realize that this was not "his" revolution. It was a rising, a revolt — sincere but senseless. The tributes he paid to it in letters were to a heroic gesture — "history has not a like example of a like greatness"[138] — something that he spurned, even despised, an attitude not confined to Bakunin's hoisting of the Red Flag over Lyon and his declaration that the state was abolished. The hopelessness of the enterprise was clear to Marx from the outset;[139] in a letter to Liebknecht describing the defeat of the Commune he deliberately uses the word "*honnêteté*"[140] in a disparaging sense and says that the "fault" lay with the Communards. On May 30, 1871, two days after the Commune had been finally suppressed, Marx produced the long-awaited "Address of the General Council of the International Working Men's Association" — on this occasion signing as Secretary for Germany and Holland. But — the addressee was dead; it was an obituary.

This forty-page brochure, first published in English, was an immediate and sensational success; three editions were printed in rapid succession and it was translated into many languages. It is a polemic written after a lost battle, in fact a lost war.[141] It is one of the most blistering, most committed, and most brilliant of Karl Marx's writings, spiteful, sparkling with anger, disillusionment, and hate. This thin volume entitled *The Civil War in France* is still regarded today as a textbook of the communist theory of revolution and government; Lenin refers to it copiously in *The State and Revolution*. Both its style and its moral content are reminiscent of Marx's article on the June rising — to which he himself refers;[142] in that article he showed himself pitiless as regards the casualties on the government side and now he justifies a spectacular murder of hostages laid at the door of the Communards; the Archbishop of Paris was among the victims but Marx calls Thiers "the real murderer" because he had refused to exchange Blanqui, who had been taken prisoner.[143] The public gasped at such savagery, but Marx rejoiced. His shattering comment to his friend Kugelmann sounds like the essence of that negative dialectic which, by meticulous analysis, turns a defeat into a murder-story post festum: "I have the honour to be at this moment the best calumniated and the most menaced man of London. That really does one good after a tedious twenty years idyll in my den."[144]

The giant roaring and flexing his muscles — *ad majorem gloriam Marxi?* Marx's assertions that here, as everywhere in the class war, his Association had had a hand, that this rising was the work of "our party," are simply not true. His trumpet call against the victorious foe who bewailed the Commune's intention to abolish property, the basis of all civilization — "Yes, gentlemen, the Commune intended to abolish that class of property. . . . It aimed at the expropriation of the expropriators"[145] — was not even a "dream of the future"; it was not a dream at all but pure invention. The Commune did not want to abolish anyone's property or expropriate anyone (except the churches insofar as they were property-owning bodies); certainly not. The "constitution" stage was never reached; the steps taken by the Commune were neither socialist nor communist but reformist. It stated that the bureaucracy should be elected, and fixed an upper limit for their salaries; it demanded free education for all, temporary rent rebates, and abolition of night work in the bakeries; it stopped all sales of goods held in municipal pawnshops (and on April 30 decreed the abolition of all pawnshops). These measures are similar to the social, but by no means socialistic, demands which Marx later subjected to such devastating criticism in his *Critique of the Gotha Program.*[146] Franz Mehring puzzled over the contradiction between Marx's flights of fancy and his "real" ideas, in the *Communist Manifesto,* for instance.[147] Marx enveloped his opponents in poisoned shrouds of mockery and scorn until they were in a state to be digested by the Orcus of history. But his hate was directed against people; he white-washed the past. Monsieur Charles Marx's Madame Tussaud's gallery displayed a row of specters — hunchbacks, cripples, murky figures. There was Thiers, the "monstrous gnome," the "master in small state roguery, a virtuoso in perjury and treason, a craftsman in all the petty strategems, cunning devices and base perfidies"; there was Jules Favre, the Foreign Minister, a forger "living in concubinage with the wife of a drunken resident of Algiers" and a legacy-hunter "in the name of the children of his adultery"; there was Ernest Picard, Minister of the Interior, brother of a swindler on the Bourse convicted of stealing a vast fortune. In contrast to them were pictured shining figures, "the real women of Paris . . . heroic, noble and devoted, like the women of antiquity." If these nonexistent figures had made nonexistent history, what did the prospect for the future look like?

The crux of the matter lay in the question how the new state was to be created. Since this question could be answered neither by Marx in his brochure on the civil war nor by anyone else, this was why the First International had outlived its usefulness; there was no consensus of opinion on theory. The Commune provided no concrete pattern for the structure of the new state; similarly there was no ideological unity inside the International. In his brochure Marx held up the Commune as an example of "workers' rule," but it was not; Leo Frankel to whom he wrote, for instance, a Hungarian refugee who became Minister of Labor under the Commune, was a well-read goldsmith. Marx was well aware of that at the time — not ten years later when he admitted that the Commune had not been socialist.[148] Even now the central paragraph of his brochure reads like the defense of a nonexistent theory: "The working class . . . have no ideals to realize but to set free the elements of the new society with which old collapsing bourgeois society itself is pregnant."[149]

Here was the point — without "utopias and ideals," in other words without a political theory, revolution inevitably degenerated into revolt. That Marx, whose life's work was theory, should defend this vacuum in theory makes the inconsistency even more striking. It shows — as does his silence during those two months — that in the last analysis Marx could make little use of the Commune apart from honoring it posthumously. By its very nature it was Bakunist. After all it was Bakunin, not Marx, who had been called for and feted (and released after his arrest in Lyon). In the eyes of the Commune Marx as a personality was as nonexistent as his ideas. Bakunin promptly jeered that, although the Commune had overthrown all Marx's ideas, he had doffed his hat to it in violation of all logic and was now hurriedly adopting its program and its aims as his own.[150] Twenty years later Engels wrote: "Well and good, gentlemen, do you want to know what this dictatorship looks like? Look at the Paris Commune. That was the Dictatorship of the Proletariat."[151] There are only two possible explanations: either the commune was being evoked as being something which it definitely was not, or the words "Dictatorship of the Proletariat" mean something today which they did not mean at that time. Neither the genesis nor the aims of the Commune can be brought into harmony with the actual theory of Karl Marx; here was an unprepared rising sweeping away the state, and the purpose of this copybook anarchist action was merely reform. The oft-quoted example of the Commune's workers' cooperatives is in fact an example of their exact opposite; orders were issued that all workshops and factories *which had been closed* should be made over to cooperatives. The real purpose of this, however, was to enable the fugitive owners to return or at least reopen their businesses.

The fact that today an entire gallery in the Marx-Engels Museum in Moscow is devoted to the memory of the Communards is a monument of misconception. In a glass case, alongside a photograph of Marx, is a small strip of red material — the ribbon of the flag that flew over the last of the Paris barricades on May 28, 1871. Another photograph of Marx with his signature and the words "*Salut et Fraternité*" carries the dates 1818 to 1883 — added in Lenin's handwriting. There are three other signatures and a date difficult to explain at first sight: October 13, 10:45 A.M. They are the landing time and names of the crew of the first multiseater Soviet spaceship, Voskod 1; the photograph went with them into space. But this combination of tribute to Soviet achievements and appeal to the traditions of the Commune is based upon an artificial interpretation of history. The flag of the Commune hangs in the Institute founded by Giangiacomo Feltrinelli, the Italian millionaire and anarchist revolutionary who lost his life in mysterious circumstances; it would make more sense to drape that flag over his coffin — he at least bought it. So the wheel came full circle. Marx's battle with Bakunin had never been a mere quarrel with a man he did not like; it was a dispute with a political concept that he thought wrong. For the first and only time Marx had available the great organization for which he had longed, fought, and worked; revolution had broken out where he had always prophesied that it would. But it had been a Bakunist rising.

It was *this* for which Bakunin had to pay the price. And the International, which could neither solve nor overcome this internal and tactical contradiction, had become superfluous. Marx knew as much before he went to The Hague; on July 29 he wrote to Kugelmann: "It will be a matter of life and death for the International and, before I retire, I want at least to protect it from disintegrating elements."[152] But it had slipped out of his hands; even the faithful Eccarius had turned against him and was now "a pure blackguard, in fact canaille."[153] The British, hitherto Marx's most reliable allies, had been enraged by one of his sarcastic remarks — when discussing mandates someone said that a certain member was "not a recognised English workers' leader," to which Marx jeered that that was a distinction rather than the reverse.

On the penultimate day Engels presented the discomfited, astounded, and silent assembly with the proposal that the General Council be moved to New York. Even the voting machine seemed unwilling to do his bidding — New York was agreed to only after an interminable procedural debate and by the very narrow majority of twenty-six votes to twenty-three, with nine abstentions. A leaflet distributed next day in The Hague read: "Called upon to do its duty, the International collapsed. It fled from the revolution over the Atlantic Ocean."[154] This had been produced by the indignant French. This was also the sixth and final day, on which Marx "dealt with" Bakunin. It was his final great show of malice and his last effort at practical action. Henceforth, for the rest of his life he put into practice his ideal — politics as theory.

·CHAPTER NINE·

"CAPITAL"

SHORTAGE OF MONEY, ILLNESS, QUARRELS —
EXCUSES FOR EVADING THE "ECONOMIC SHIT"?

For Karl Marx these years of hectic intrigue also covered the birthpangs of his love-hate child, *Das Kapital*. It took almost twice as many years to see the light of day as a baby does months. This book was his life's work, not just the crowning achievement of his life but his "main business" from the outset. *Das Kapital*'s Book of Genesis is also Karl Marx's intellectual biography. It was his self-imposed task, the focus of his existence, but it was also the burden under which he collapsed, both his goal and his doom.

All through the literature on Marx there runs the erroneous statement and the erroneous belief that Marx only became interested in problems of political economy in later life. Rosenberg, for instance, finds nothing on this discipline in the list of books read by Marx while a student in Berlin[1] and Ernest Mandel thinks similarly;[2] Engels's letter to Mehring saying that "he [Marx] knew absolutely nothing of economics"[3] is also quoted as a source. In fact, voluminous unpublished extracts from his early reading material (preserved in the Instituut voor Sociale Geschiedenes, Amsterdam) show that young Marx had even gone back to the ancient philosophers for some of his ideas; the mere list of books from which he made excerpts covers 100 manuscript sheets.[4] A striking illustration is a passage in Aristotle's *Politics* in which one need only substitute the word "capitalist" for "trader" or "usurer" and one would think that one was reading Marx; it even includes the distinction between the use-value and exchange-value of goods, later claimed by Marx as one of his most important discoveries.[5]

Marx's inordinate, agonizing preoccupation with Hegel, mentioned in letters to his father while a student, clearly formed part of his critical search for a structure of economic ideas. Marx was certainly not interested in Hegel merely as the philosopher who had once celebrated the outbreak of the French Revolution with Schelling and Hölderlin in Tübingen and who refused to lecture in Berlin University on July 14 each year so that he might celebrate the storming of the Bastille over a glass of red wine; he was interested in

Hegel as a theorist who had used the word "class" in his lectures in Jena as early as 1803/4 and had done so almost in a Marxist context — "Industrialists and manufacturers base their very existence on the misery of a class."[6] One of Hegel's essays dating back to 1799, which has vanished and exists only in summary form, was a commentary on a British politicoeconomic document.[7] His famous dialectical antithesis between master and servant was no mere exercise in philosophical thinking but a phrase used to describe the discrepancy between the economic situations of two sets of people — though Hegel regarded emancipation of the servant as an *intellectual* not an *actual* possibility. In Hegel's view alienation was natural to mankind and its elimination postulated change in the makeup of the individual, not change in the structure of society. The servant could be intellectually more free than his master, but he was still a servant. Hegel, however, was aware of the concept of alienation and he perceived the contradictions inherent in bourgeois society. A paragraph in his *Philosophy of Right* reads like a preview of Marx's theory of accumulation in *Capital:*

The accumulation of riches is increased through the universalization of interdependence between men that results from their requirements and universalization of the methods of assembling and producing the resources to meet those requirements . . . on the one hand; similarly on the other hand there remains the isolation and confinement of specialized work and therefore the dependence and poverty of the class restricted to this work. . . .[8]

It is greatly to the credit of Georg Lukacs that in his study *Der junge Hegel und die Probleme der kapitalistischen Gesellschaft* (Young Hegel and the Problems of Capitalist Society) he has drawn attention to the influence of Hegel's *economic* thinking on Marx's general scheme of ideas. Jürgen Habermas then pointed out, quite logically, that Schelling also had already referred to the "alien being whose province was work and the product of work."[9]

Even the excerpts Marx made in Kreuznach,[10] though taken from obscure sources such as the *Gazette de France* and J. Fievée's *Correspondence politique et administrative* or the 109 extracts from Montesquieu's *De l'esprit des lois*, prove that economics were in the forefront of Marx's interests; his quotations from Leopold von Ranke's *Deutsche Geschichte im Zeitalter der Reformation* (German History of the Reformation Era) about the position of the financiers or from Thomas Münzer deal with the quality of the human being as a commodity. For Marx, excerpts formed part of his colossal digestive process and he regarded himself as harnessed into a paper-processing factory ultimately throwing up paper on to the dunghill of history and leading him to amass books ranged by countries and subjects.[11] The process is vividly described by Paul Lafargue:

His method of work often involved him in tasks the magnitude of which is hardly to be conceived of by the readers of his books. For instance, in order to write the twenty-odd pages of *Capital* dealing with English factory legislation, he had worked through a whole library of Blue Books containing reports by special Commissions of Enquiry and English and Scottish factory inspectors. As the numerous pencil markings show, he read them from cover to cover.[12]

Marx's appetite for reading (he practically copied out books he thought important — 547 pages from Botta and Schlosser's *World History*, 356 pages from J. B. Jukes's *Student's Manual of Geology*),[13] this thirst for print and ink, was also a form of evasion. He circled round his work on "the book" but again and again he tried to set off down tracks leading him away from the center of the circle. The story of the unfinished *Capital* is one of perpetual advance and retreat, the story of a work of art.

The "artistic whole,"[14] as Marx wished his book to be and to be thought to be, was his nightmare, "the damned book," "economic shit."[15] The prospect made his head swim and he swam away from it. As early as 1845 he had signed a contract with Leske, who sent increasingly frosty and reproving letters from Darmstadt demanding either delivery of the promised book or repayment of the 1,500-franc advance; at precisely the same time Marx was writing to his Russian friend Annenkov in Paris, sometimes a source of financial support, that he would have liked to send him his book on political economy but unfortunately could not find a publisher. This was a lie. Leopold Schwarzschild summarizes the situation in one terse sentence: "He had a publisher but no book on economics; he spread the story that he had a book on economics but no publisher."[16]

On August 1, 1846, he promised the publisher the first volume for the end of November, adding that "Volume 2 can follow quickly."[17] The manuscript was never dispatched. Marx was forever finding fresh sources, books, scientific treatises, and he literally took refuge in study of them. This period also produced entreaties from Engels, who implored his friend to finish:

Now be sure that the material you have assembled is soon loosed upon the world. It is damned well high time. . . . So work hard and get into print quickly.
　Try to be finished with your book on political economy. Even you are dissatisfied with much of it, that does not matter; opinion is ripe and we must strike while the iron is hot. . . . Now, however, it is high time. Be sure that you are finished *before* April; do as I do; set yourself a time by which you are *positively determined to be finished* and ensure that it is printed quickly . . . it must be out soon.[18]

Yet five years later, when Marx reached London in August 1849, there was still no "book on economics." After a further two years boredom and reluctance to start were making him want to "pitch into another science."[19]

Instead of being finished in five weeks — a gross underestimation of his own book — for six months he never went near the library. Then he buried himself there for six months, from 9:00 A.M. to 7:00 P.M., and then for a whole four years, from 1853 to 1856, never entered the place. Not until 1857 was "the book" referred to again, when his hopes began to rise that the great crisis and with it the revolution was now approaching: "I am working like mad all night on a synthesis of my economic studies so that at least I can have the outlines clear before the deluge."[20]

This statement, repeated ten days later in the "nightmare" letter ("I am working quite colossally, generally till 4:00 A.M."),[21] is horrifying when one thinks that, although Marx had begun his book thirteen years before, the outlines were not yet there. Under the pressure of the anticipated revolution (which never occurred), urged continuously by his friend from Manchester, implored by his exhausted wife who copied out the manuscript, and admonished by Lassalle who had arranged a highly favorable contract with Duncker in Berlin, Marx despatched something to Berlin early in 1859; but it was not what he had promised nor what his friends expected. Arnold Künzli puts it epigrammatically:

It consisted merely of the first two of the planned three chapters of the first section of the planned four sections of the first volume of a treatise planned to consist of six volumes, in other words merely the beginning of the beginning of the beginning.[22]

Duncker in Berlin was told that this book, *Critique of Political Economy,* was the first part of a work of which there would be many subsequent sections. The subsequent sections never appeared. There remained, nevertheless, a vast manuscript covering fifty printed pages and entitled *Grundrisse der Kritik der politischen Ökonomie* (Contribution to the Critique of Political Economy); it was published in Moscow between 1939 and 1941 and in East Berlin in 1953. The difficulties on which the great ambitious plan primarily foundered were both personal and material. Marx dealt with them in his famous preface, written in a defensive tone:

The enormous material for the history of political economy which is accumulated in the British Museum, the favorable vantage point afforded by London for the observation of bourgeois society and finally the new stage of development upon which the latter appeared to have entered with the discovery of gold in California and Australia, determined me to begin afresh from the very beginning and to work through the new material critically. These studies led partly of themselves into apparently quite remote subjects on which I had to dwell for a longer or shorter period. Especially, however, was the time at my disposal curtailed by the imperative necessity of earning my living. My contributions, during eight years now, to the first English-American newspaper, the *New York Tribune*, compelled an extraordinary scattering of my studies, since I occupy myself with newspaper correspondence proper only in exceptional cases. However, articles on striking economic events in England and on the Continent constituted so considerable a part of my contributions that I was compelled to make myself familiar with practical details which lie outside the sphere of the actual science of political economy.[23]

This was only half the truth, however. Marx's book suffered from a basic constructional error, from something approaching dishonesty of authorship; in fact it was by no means merely an inexhaustible thirst for knowledge that caused him to submerge himself in this flood of material; Marx quite deliberately inflated his books in order to satisfy the German public's predilection for fat volumes. As early as 1851 the wily Engels had advised him to adapt himself to the rapid production tempo of "Germany's wretched mediocre men of letters" and produce something scholarly and fundamental — but voluminous as well.[24] Jenny Marx records that Marx quite deliberately "added much historical material since nowadays Germans only believe in voluminous books."[25] He himself took courage from a motto in his beloved *Divine Comedy:*

> Here all suspicion needs must be abandoned,
> All cowardice must needs be here extinct.

Suspicion and cowardice, however, were permanent accompaniments of his work, even leading him to alter the essential content of his book with an eye on the public and the market.

And there was a further factor. Marx did not want to write a purely theoretical book. He wanted to submit an investigation that would both make the march of historical events comprehensible and also serve as a recipe-book for action. His method and his purpose, however, prevented any rapid conclusion of the process of analysis, since the course of historical events did not run as Marx thought it ran — or rather, wished to make it run. The mistaken prophecies of crises for 1852, 1853, and 1855 were no incidental errors. They were empiric proof that his theories of "automatic mechanisms" could not be right and that his economic calculations — the period required for reproduction of constant capital, for instance — were wrong.[26]

A further eight years were to pass before the first volume appeared, but for Marx it was a direct sequel:

The work, the first volume of which I now submit to the public, forms the continuation of my "Contribution to the Critique of Political Economy," published in 1859. The long pause between the first part and the continuation is due to an illness of many years' duration that again and again interrupted my work.[27]

Is that true? It is a ticklish subject, obscured by legends about Karl Marx's illnesses and material privations. The truth is otherwise.

Marx was totally ruthless, vis-à-vis both the outside world and himself. It is possible to stand in awe of so great and independent a spirit; it is also possible to detect a moral *horror vacui*. There remains, however, a tangle of forces, qualities, contradictions, and tensions making up a character quite out of the ordinary. Even an analysis of his handwriting refers to his "totally arbitrary attitude with regard to money," to his "complete absence of a sense of time," and to his "disregard of the day-to-day demands of his environment."[28] It continues:

He had difficulty in concluding anything, in planning a book and could barely restrain himself from starting new ventures; in addition to his commitment to the "higher intellectual plane" a degree of inflexible determination may have exerted some influence; his pronounced egoism, moreover, meant that he was determined to need or be dependent upon no one; his main pleasure lay in the dispute with the world which he had taken upon himself and its pursuit with the sharp, pungent weapons of his mind. . . . This also, however, enabled him to "switch off" and so (despite his susceptibility) to become impervious to much, to disregard many things, sometimes disdainfully, sometimes with comparative moral generosity; his peculiar personal reaction to anything disillusioning was one of scorn.[29]

This terminological patchwork — "dependent on no one," "impervious," "disdainful," "disregard" — is the outcome of an examination of samples of Marx's handwriting from different periods; at the same time it reveals a clear pattern of behavior. The mixture of generosity and disdain with which Marx brushed aside money-earning problems, for instance, or the possibility of leading an orderly domestic existence, meant that he was continually heading for the rocks: his income was never as low as that of thousands of proletarian families, but nevertheless he lived in actual poverty for years. He was often unable to leave the house because his shoes or his coat were at the pawnbroker's. He could not even send his manuscript to Duncker because he had no money for the postage: "The wretched manuscript is ready but cannot be dispatched because I have not a farthing to frank and insure it."[30]

Things were not always that way, however. Again and again Marx was able to lay claim to contributions and legacies, sometimes of considerable size, only to plunge back — as if in relief — into chaos and disorder as soon as the eddies resulting from the previous period had subsided. The graphological memorandum refers to a sado-masochistic side to his character, a retreat into dirt and disorder. An informer's report, which by a quirk of fate found its way to his brother-in-law in Berlin, His Excellency Ferdinand von Westphalen, Prussian Minister of the Interior, emphasizes this curious, almost suicidal tendency to a chaotic way of life contrasting so sharply with his efforts to preserve a respectable exterior with his expensive suits and his eyeglass for instance:

He is an extremely untidy person; he manages his affairs badly and leads the life of the bohemian intelligentsia. . . . It is a rare thing for him to wash or comb his hair or change his linen. He drinks too much. Often he lounges about doing nothing for days on end but, if there is anything which must be done, he works day and night with tireless energy. He has no notion of keeping regular hours.[31]

Marx did not *want* to be practical; he even despised the word. Werner Sombart makes some severe comments on the subject: "For any objective observer there can be no doubt that Marx's failures in life must largely be ascribed to *his personal incapacity* to master life. Marx was in the highest degree what is described as an 'unpractical' character."[32]

To Marx himself the word meant exactly the opposite; he gave it a new connotation:

I laugh at the so-called "practical" men and their wisdom. If one chose to be an ox, one could of course turn one's back on the agonies of mankind and look after one's own skin. But I should really have regarded myself as *unpractical* if I had pegged out without completely finishing my book, at least in manuscript.[33]

The fate of the subsequent volumes of *Capital* provided further cause for anxiety. From 1869 Marx was drawing a very generous £350 pension from Engels who, moreover, was always "improving" it by additional financial contributions. From 1870 Engels was living in London and took almost the entire international correspondence off Marx's shoulders. Marx was now free to complete his book: he was in the prime of life, prosperous and independent; he still had sixteen years to live. But he did not write the book. Between 1870 and 1877 he never touched the manuscripts. He even refused to speak of them. The terse reply to Kautsky's friendly inquiry, saying that the younger generation were eagerly awaiting the second volume, was "So am I."[34] He left even Friedrich Engels completely in the dark about the progress of the work, its degree of completion, and the state of the manuscript. Remarkably enough Engels was not conversant with Volume 1 — although he had been writing about it for decades, although he had sent out letters resembling questionnaires asking for advice from industrialists who were expected to give Marx information on the running of their businesses, a question on which he was totally ignorant, although he had been indefatigable in dis-

patching cases of port and many, many pound notes. The fact remains that
Friedrich Engels never saw the manuscript of Volume 1 of *Capital*. He
received from Marx one of those emotional letters[35] which should invariably
be treated with some suspicion; the book was dedicated to a somewhat distant friend, Wilhelm Wolff, who had died in 1864! Marx wanted to dedicate
the English translation to Darwin who, however, turned down the offer with a
polite but reserved letter dated October 13, 1880. Marx was pertinacious in
his efforts to establish a closer relationship. The two men lived only twenty
miles from each other, but they never met. Marx read the *Origin of Species* a
year after it was published, in December 1860; together with Liebknecht he
attended a series of six lectures on Darwin given by Thomas Huxley in the
autumn of 1862. In the autumn of 1873 he sent Darwin, then aged sixty-four
(Marx was fifty-five at the time) a copy of the second edition of *Capital*; the
covering letter has been lost but the book is signed by Marx as Darwin's
"sincere admirer."[36] This was intended as far more than a form of greeting; it
was meant to establish a link between the authors of two epoch-making
books. From Darwin came a short acknowledgment in two sentences; to
anyone familiar with English ways they would have implied that the writer
neither wished to discuss the book nor have any further contact with its
author.[37] Seven years then passed without contact between the two. Darwin
clearly took no stock of Marxism or even of socialism — he characterized the
efforts of German Social-Darwinists to establish a connection between socialism and his theory of development as "foolish."[38] He did not read Marx's
book; pages 105 to 822 in his copy were uncut (the footnotes referring to
him were on pages 352 and 385–386).[39]

Marx must have approached him once more. Marx's letter has so far not
been found; Darwin's polite but reserved reply, in which he characterizes anti-
Christian or atheist propaganda as detrimental to freedom of thought,[40] does
not indicate clearly *what* Marx wished to dedicate to him; it may have been
the English translation of Volume 1 of *Capital* or Volume 2. Neither in fact
existed at the time.

Volume 2 did not appear. Engels had issued his warning — "Now be sure
to push on with the second volume"[41] — exactly as twenty-three years before. The publisher pressed him; Liebknecht inquired; Engels wrote over and
over again, imploring, admonishing, sometimes showing impatience:

I should think that it must by now be clear to you that, if only for the sake
of your second volume, a change in your style of life is essential. If such interrup-
tions are to be repeated for ever, you will never be finished; if you take a little
more open-air exercise, which will free you of your carbuncles, you will finish
sooner or later.[42]

Here it was — reason number two for noncompletion, the reason always given by Marx when anyone asked him for effort or work: illness.

In fact Karl Marx was a sick man all his life. Illness plays its part even in his correspondence with his father; the good man anxiously warned his student son against overwork but eventually his forebodings came true — Marx turned into an unemployed, sickly philosopher. Even in his early years, however, there appeared a curious phenomenon: he could work himself sick or become sick through vexation — "From vexation over Jenny's illness and my fruitless intellectual efforts in the past, from consuming anger . . . I became sick."[43]

Scientifically, psychosomatics is an insufficiently explored discipline to be able to produce irrefutable statements and results; one can only study the parabola of sickness in Marx's life. If the work parabola be drawn simultaneously in a different color, the results are remarkable.

Marx suffered from disorders of the liver and spleen; later he was afflicted for years on end with boils and obviously terribly painful carbuncles, for which at the time there was really no medical remedy. In the closing years of his life a semi-chronic bronchitis was a further trial. Tuberculosis, for which he was rejected as totally unfit for military service, was never referred to again in his later years; this was probably a discreetly arranged form of evasion of service urged on him by his mother, who even proposed bribery. Two of his brothers and sisters, however, did die of tuberculosis of the lungs. The parabola showing the relationship between work and sickness, however, shows something else: Marx became ill, almost to the very day, when some serious work "threatened"; inflammatory leaflets, polemics or scurrilous pamphlets such as "Die grossen Männer des Exils" (The Great Men in Exile) or "Herr Vogt" were never interrupted by illness. The most complex aspect of the phenomenon, however, was that he was no *malade imaginaire* taking refuge between the sheets; on these occasions Marx *was* ill, in most cases seriously.

Autumn 1851: the *New York Daily Tribune* offers him regular work at a good salary and he is in financial distress — Marx becomes ill. Engels has to write the articles — "If it were possible for you to let me have an article on conditions in Germany written in English by Friday morning."[44]

Winter 1851: Joseph Weydemeyer asks him to contribute to the periodical *Die Revolution* which he had started in America — "My husband has been very sick all week, in bed most of the time. . . . Karl is too weak to write to you."[45]

Winter 1853: Bangya, the intermediary to whom Marx (then aged thirty-five) had entrusted his manuscript "Die grossen Männer des Exils," is discovered to be an Austrian government agent; Marx's book on the communist trial in Köln is confiscated in Germany — "This week I was within an ace of pegging out from an inflammation of the liver, or at least I only just escaped it. . . ."[46]

Summer 1857: offer of a fee for an article in the new American encyclopedia — "For the last three weeks I have been filled to the brim with medicine and pills . . . as a result of my old, and I think hereditary, liver complaint."[47]

Spring 1858: Lassalle has arranged the contract with Duncker and the manuscript *must* be produced — "I am so unwell with this spleen business that this week I have been unable to think, read, write or do anything save the articles for the *Tribune*. These can naturally not be neglected since I must be able to draw on the rascals *as soon as possible*. This indisposition is disastrous, however, since I cannot start to work on the thing for Duncker until I feel well and have some vigour and grasp in my fingers again."[48]

Summer, autumn, and winter 1858: Lassalle, Duncker, and Engels are all pressing him but Marx is ill the whole year — "I have never had so violent an attack of my liver complaint";[49] "agony in my 'nut' ";[50] "run down physically";[51] "Indisposed . . . so that any writing requires extraordinary effort";[52] "devilish toothache."[53]

At the same time Marx himself realized that he was being a hypochrondriac;[54] his wife put matters quite clearly:

Much of the deterioration in his condition is due to mental disquiet and excitement which is naturally greater now after conclusion of the contract with the publisher and which increases daily since it is simply impossible for him to bring this work to conclusion.[55]

Decades later Engels, standing dumbfounded in front of the jumble of unfinished manuscripts, showed that he knew these illnesses to be evasion and subterfuge:

Well now, we are more or less used to these excuses for noncompletion of the book. He was always very depressed when his health did not allow him to deal with his work and he was only too glad to find some theoretical excuse why the book was not yet finished. In his time he used all these arguments *vis-à-vis de moi*; they seemed to salve his conscience.[56]

When it finally appeared, initial reactions to the *Critique of Political Economy* were not encouraging; Liebknecht wept tears of disappointment over the mouse to which the mountain had given birth; even Engels described this first part of the book as "very abstract indeed. . . . I often had to search with difficulty for the dialectical trains of thought."[57] Marx spewed out his rage and mortification in his own violent earthy phraseology; he spewed out bile

— and not only in the figurative sense. He "retched from morning to night";[58] yet once more he was too weak to write a line, was "as feeble as a fly from vomiting which has now lasted for two consecutive days."[59] The fiasco of his completed work made him as sick as working upon it. Moreover, knowing that *this* was not the book he had promised himself and the world, instead of a sense of liberation and relief his condition deteriorated. He himself once said: "My sickness always originates from the head";[60] nevertheless he must have suffered real tortures from his festering abscesses, boils in the tenderest spots, and ulcers that broke no sooner were the old ones healed.

Even the most medically ignorant layman knows that skin complaints have something to do with mental overstrain. One of the most reputable dermatologists in Hamburg University Hospital would not exclude a cause-and-effect relationship in the case of boils, though naturally without precise diagnostic data nothing can be proved.[61] Whether Marx really regarded illness as a means of nonidentification, self-alienation in other words, and whether gastrointestinal disorders can be considered as the direct effect of some existential problem cannot be stated with scientific certainty. What is certain, however, is that Marx can be described as a neurotic and a hypochondriac, a man who took refuge in the idiosyncrasies of which his father complained, a man who never spared himself but was always descending into querulous self-pity. "This time it is the skin"; "abdominal phthisis"; "fit for the knacker's yard."[62] A whole list of such exaggerated statements could be compiled — a solar system taking pleasure in being ill. Another well-known doctor in Hamburg University Hospital puts it this way: "A neurotic takes the easiest way out to avoid a decision. . . . Illness shields the neurotic . . . from the real decision. In addition for him illness has the advantage that it arouses the sympathy of his fellowmen, provides an excuse both to himself and those around him and so removes from him the necessity for decision."[63]

Not until 1867, when at last "the filthy book,"[64] Volume I of *Capital*, was finished, was the nightmare removed. The last postponement was due to "carbuncles on the backside and near the penis,"[65] but a week later the manuscript was taken to Hamburg. Almost from the moment when Marx settled down in the train in order to hand it in person to Meissner, the Hamburg publisher, he felt better. The following days, spent staying with Kugelmann in Hannover, were almost gay. Engels, who had received the announcement of completion with a "Hurrah" and had also sent Marx his journey money[66] — £35 in bisected £1 notes as always, the second halves following on receipt of the first — summarized the situation:

It has always seemed to me that this damned book, on which you have labored so long, has been the root cause of all your misfortune and that you could and would never emerge until you had shaken it off. This eternally unfinished thing oppressed you physically, mentally and financially and I can very well understand that now, having rid yourself of this nightmare, you seem to yourself like a totally different person.[67]

He did not know that this was destined to be only an interim statement of account, that Karl Marx would never complete his life's work.

Marx had left his friend completely in the dark regarding the state of the book; he had even given numerous hints that his studies were nearing conclusion or that a final text was imminent, giving the impression that a systematically planned book would emerge fully complete. As it subsequently proved, however, for the last fifteen years of his life following publication of Volume 1 Marx hardly, if at all, worked on *Capital*. The information given by Engels in his prefaces to Volumes 2 and 3 was almost sensational: the manuscripts he found among Marx's papers had clearly been written between 1864 and 1867, in other words *before* Volume 1 had been published.[68] Moreover, Marx had not been prevented from completing his book by illness or debility. Arthur M. Prinz, the American expert on Marx, calls the "obligate story" of the terrible illnesses which kept Marx from finishing his book "a myth . . . he could have finished *Das Kapital* had his heart really been in it."[69] Letters show that Marx actually ran away from this book, that he definitely looked for excuses; a school report would have said: "Is easily sidetracked." He delved into such problems as the chemistry of nitrogen fertilizers, agriculture, physics, and mathematics. His book of excerpts of 1878[70] is full of tables and sketches, on atmospheric temperature for instance, or drawings of sea shells and fossils; whole pages are covered with chemical formulae; on page after page whole lines are carefully erased with a ruler. Methodical labor for no good purpose. This time-wasting in senseless and extreme precision was a method of evasion; even in the early days Engels had warned him: "As long as you have some book you think important lying in front of you unread, you will never get down to writing."[71] And there were always sufficient books lying unread to satisfy the appetite of this gargantuan devourer of paper — studies on differential calculus, a Danish theory of the state, or Russian grammar. Marx immediately wrote a treatise on differential calculus and various other mathematical manuscripts; he learned Danish; he learned Russian. Among his papers Engels, who knew only too well the defenses behind which Marx barricaded himself, found "over two cubic meters of books on Russian statistics alone."[72] The word "excuse" appears even in a letter from Marx himself to the Russian translator of *Capital*; in it he counts himself lucky that publication in Germany is prevented by anti-socialist legislation and that fortunately fresh material from Russia and the United States provides him with the excuse he is looking for to continue with his research instead of finishing the book and publishing it.[73]

Even this "excuse," however, does not stand up to examination. In fact the Prussian police regarded "this printed matter as social-democratic or rather socialistic or communistic" but "nevertheless there is no evidence in it of incitement on the above-named lines to overthrow of the existing state or social order." There seemed no reason to ban it therefore. Dr. von Schultzendorff, the Prussian police expert, reported that, for these same reasons, *Das Kapital* did not come under Paragraph 6 of the law on socialism; capitalists and property-owners, he said, were depicted "in a by no means rosy light" but the book dealt only with people "in so far as they personified economic categories."[74]

The fact that Marx's life's work remained fragmentary, therefore, cannot be laid at the door of external circumstances. Since, apart from his great polemics or works of criticism and shorter inflammatory writings, everything remained uncompleted, the question arises whether this was due to some fundamental tendency. Marx could not resist the temptation to rework completely anything that he had left on one side even if only for a month; he himself called this "a peculiarity."[75] Paul Lafargue records that Marx loathed the idea of publishing anything that had not been worked over again and again, that he could not bear to produce anything incomplete or imperfect.[76] He would rather burn his manuscripts, he said, than leave them behind unfinished. But this is exactly what he did. Engels's letter to August Bebel of August 1883 gives a picture of his consternation at the piles of notebooks and "jumble" of papers left by Marx:

Alongside certain parts which had been fully worked through were others which were mere outlines; everything was in rough copy apart from some two chapters. Quotations to serve as illustrations were in no order, simply thrown together and assembled for later selection. In addition there was the handwriting — only just legible even to me and that with difficulty.[77]

Even in 1885, in the Preface to Volume 2 which he edited, Engels was still referring to the careless style, the colloquial, often rough and humourous expressions, interspersed with English and French jargon, the hodgepodge of material, barely arranged, still less fully worked over, incoherent sentences — ideas in shorthand, not a book in manuscript.[78]

A most interesting recent study[79] points out that there is a link between the fragmentary nature of Marx's book and the Romantics. Marx's own early poems were written under the influence of the Romantic trend; a further indication was his interest in folksongs, the folksongs he collected for Jenny, for instance — with excerpts from Herder and Byron. Jenny's father, his beloved Ludwig von Westphalen, introduced him to Romantic literature and his lifelong enthusiasm for Shakespeare dates from the same period; his studies under August Wilhelm von Schlegel in Bonn, under Steffens and Ritter, both pupils of Schlegel, in Berlin and finally his familiarity with Friedrich Schlegel's ideas clearly exerted some influence. Marx, after all, not only subsequently described his own writings as an artistic whole, but invariably proclaimed that the world he foresaw and hoped to see would be peopled by richly endowed, profound, perceptive beings. In fact, he moved entirely in the sphere of the Romantic concept of generic genius and all-around craftsmanship. Friedrich Schlegel says this: "A truly free and cultured man must be able to attune himself, as he wishes, to the philosophical or philological, the critical or the poetic, the historical or rhetorical, the ancient or the modern — quite arbitrarily, at any time and to any degree, just as one tunes an instrument."[80]

The affinity with this fundamental Romantic concept can be detected everywhere in Marx's book.[81] The Romantics considered the conduct of bourgeois society to be iniquitous since it prevented man developing his full potentialities; they considered the Philistine's ethos of work to be deadening since it created a world in which man was perverted into avarice instead of being led upward to true life. In his "Lucinda" Friedrich Engels writes: "Industry and profit are the angels of death with flaming swords barring man's return to paradise."[82]

His background development, his character traits, his methods of work, and his acquired knowledge are all factors in this problem of why Marx's book remained a great limbless torso. Clearly the Romantic school of thought influenced Karl Marx; it may not have led him to hope for the "return to paradise" but it did lead him to hope for a future; his sense of elitism, of himself as the (irreplaceable) prophet and leader, predestined him for creative activity per se, almost for artistry; his methods of research were artistic rather than scientific; he tried to materialize what he had already finalized in his head.

In this context Werner Sombart uses the terms naïve and sentimental or else introduces Marx's two linked words, practical and unpractical. In addition, always supposing that men can be divided into two groups, he differentiates between those who live *in* the world and those live *against* the world. Those who adapt themselves can achieve anything; those who live in a state of permanent tension with the world, in other words who do not adapt themselves, live in permanent mental turmoil. Instead of finding solutions, they stumble over contradictions; they deal in the general, not the particular. Sombart calls such men "artistic" and arrives at the final conclusion: "Socialist thinkers all belong to the artistic category of mankind."[83]

In any case Marx never conducted any empirical research. His sole attempt was a questionnaire on "General Statistics of the Working Class," which the

General Council of the International was intended to answer. Nothing ever came of it. The fundamental principle on which Marx worked was what Engels called an *a priori* procedure[84] — in other words, he worked up the available material as "proof" of previously finalized theories. Karl Jaspers accurately describes this procedure:

The style of Marx's writings is not that of the investigator, in other words he does not quote examples or adduce facts which run counter to his own theory but only those which clearly support or confirm that which he considers the ultimate truth. The whole approach is one of vindication, not investigation, but it is vindication of something proclaimed as the perfect truth with the conviction, not of the scientist, but of the believer.[85]

This is perhaps the main reason for the bookworming avidity with which Marx pounced over and over again on fresh material to prove his point — he was conducting a case, a case against history, the evidence for which filled a whole filing cabinet. And Karl Marx was King's Evidence, prosecutor, attorney, judge, and jury all in one. He had to find proofs of the misdeeds of history, *all* the proofs; as long as a single one was missing he could not make his speech in court nor pass judgment.

NO REACTION, NO SUCCESS, NO EFFECT?

One further thing, however, clearly held him back from completing the book. This was the reaction to Volume 1; initially, and for years afterwards, it was disappointing. Marx waited tremulously for some reaction, for criticism or agreement; he might have been a budding novelist rather than a renowned scholar — Proust, not Darwin. Only two months after publication he wrote to Engels that the "silence" concerning the book made him "fidgety; I neither see nor hear anything."[86] The book had barely appeared, review copies and publicity handouts were still in the post when the author began to write a series of feverish letters: who had had copies, to which newspapers had they been supplied, which critics might review it and when, where, and how?[87] The object was simply to "bang the drum," no matter how and without reference to fundamentals.[88] All his friends were alerted — Liebknecht, Kugelmann, Engels. There was no time to lose; he could not possibly wait until potential reviewers had actually read the book.[89] What was to be done? Engels, as usual, had the answer: he wrote all the critiques himself, not minding for whom, for which newspaper, or what view he took, whether for or against.[90] It was an incredible procedure, or at least unique in the history of world literature: using various pseudonyms and also some real names (Kugelmann's reviews were written by Engels!), in every conceivable newspaper the author and his closest associate published critiques they had written themselves; for socialist papers they were laudatory, for bourgeois papers scathing.[91] When Engels was eventually at a loss, writing, "I can still write another 4–5 articles about your book from various points of view but I do not know where to send them," Marx had the answer:

Send your reviews for the German papers here. I will have them copied and find the most suitable placements. At least to some extent they will even have a *double emploi* since Meyer is asking for something of the sort for people over there and will make use of them. As soon as Germany has been supplied — and that is the most important since affairs here depend largely on what happens there — you must write a critique for the *Fortnightly Review*. Beesly will have it inserted.[92]

Eventually even this procedure proved too complicated, primarily because Engels himself could barely understand the book.[93] They then agreed upon the "logical" answer: Marx wrote the reviews, Engels signed them, sometimes using a nom de plume, and sent them to the distribution agencies recruited by Marx. Naturally the publisher was not allowed to know what was going on. In fact Marx and Engels anticipated and put into practice the slogan used by an Americanized best-seller agency: "Even bad publicity is good publicity." The book had become a commodity. Kugelmann even went so far as to offer a photograph and biography of Karl Marx to the *Gartenlaube*, which Marx thought too much of a joke. Be that as it may, out of nineteen reviews so far discovered, nine originated from Engels and one from Kugelmann.[94] Marx recommended that one review might perhaps begin by saying that, irrespective of its general trend, the book "did honor to the German intellect"[95] and the phrase promptly appeared in a review of the second edition.[96]

A second edition was not required very quickly. The general reaction ranged from sheer incomprehension to shoulder-shrugging disinterest. Even Engels, treading with caution, wrote that the book's great drawback was its abstract quality and its difficult sequence of thought, which did not facilitate understanding by "a very large class of readers."[97] The solitary great tribute to it came from that mortal enemy J. B. Schweitzer of all people; he wrote a report on "Das Werk von Carl Marx," published as a series of twelve articles in the *Social-Demokrat* from January 22 to May 6, 1868. When Marx's friends later urged him to finish Volume 2, his daughter Eleanor defended him with the acid comment that the great German nation had not yet even condescended to read Volume 1.[98] An "eyewitness," J. P. Mayer, editor of the first edition of Marx's *Frühschriften* (Early Writings) tells how he handed the first two volumes to Otto Wels, the Social-Democrat leader, in Berlin in 1932:

He looked at the volumes and said: "They are impressive but I suppose I should never be able to understand them. But perhaps", he continued, "I shall tell you a little story: as a young man I travelled with August Bebel to the Party Congress in Jena; during the train journey I confessed to August that I could not understand *Das Kapital*. I had stopped . . . very near to the beginning. 'Never mind, Otto', August Bebel replied; 'I have not read further myself'."[99]

Karl Kautsky, too, emphasized on several occasions[100] that Marx's book was neither read nor understood in its author's lifetime. The first edition's 1,000 copies lasted five years; Marx did not live to see a translation in England, his second home. A laconic notice in the *Saturday Review of Politics, Literature, Science and Art* admitted that the book possessed logic, rhetorical force, and a certain charm in the treatment of arid material — "although we regard the author's views as pernicious."[101] When writing his biography of Marx, Franz Mehring called on Rosa Luxemburg for help in the presentation of Volumes 2 and 3; Section 3 of Chapter 12 of his book was written by her.

THE GREAT DISCOVERY —
THE DARWIN OF ECONOMICS

Marx himself was partially responsible for his book's reputation for obscurity; immediately following his *démenti* in the Preface — "With the exception of the section on value-form, therefore, this volume cannot stand accused on the score of difficulty" — there follows the warning that he naturally presupposes readers who are willing to think for themselves.[102] In the Preface to the second edition in 1873 he admitted that he had "coquetted" here and there with Hegel's modes of expression, in other words had introduced a certain mystification and a number of provisos.[103] At the same time he explained that his method was the exact opposite of Hegel's;[104] the method of presentation differs from the method of inquiry. In his method of presentation the end result of his investigations comes at the beginning, not at the end. As a result, the book presents certain specific difficulties. Marx himself redrafted the section on value-form four times during the thirteen years from 1859 to 1872, so it can hardly have been easily comprehensible. The book carries the reader along at varying tempos; at times its pathos is compelling and passionate and it is almost amusing to read, at others it is dry as dust. It possesses the well-known verve of the polemicist — "The English Established Church, e.g., will more readily pardon an attack on 38 of its 39 Articles than on $\frac{1}{39}$th of its income"[105] — but it also shows the caution and dignity of the diagnostic who has no wish to attack *ad personem*, whose targets are conditions, not individuals:

To prevent possible misunderstanding of a word, I paint the capitalist and the landlord in no sense *couleur de rose*. But here individuals are dealt with only in so far as they are the personifications of economic categories, embodiments of particular class-relations and class-interests. My standpoint, from which the evolution of the economic formation of society is viewed as a process of natural history, can less than any other make the individual responsible for relations whose creature he socially remains, however he may subjectively raise himself above them.[106]

The book illustrates both the modesty and the arrogance of Karl Marx, the modesty of the man who had already refused to take credit for being *the* discoverer of the existence of classes in modern society or of the struggle between them, saying that bourgeois historians had described these developments long before him,[107] the arrogance of the man who concluded his Preface to *Capital* with Dante's motto: "Follow your path and let the people say what they will."[108] Nevertheless he wanted to talk *to* the people; the famous letter to Kugelmann shows that Marx was only too well aware of the difficulties presented by the reading of his book — the letter was also an instructional manual "for the ladies" on how to read it: "Will you tell your wife that the most immediately readable sections are those on 'The Working Day', 'Cooperation', 'Division of Labour', 'Machinery' and finally 'Primitive Accumulation'. You will have to give explanations of incomprehensible terminology."[109]

In his study of *Capital*[110] Karl Korsch has expanded and amended Marx's reader's guide; he has examined the book section by section, rearranged it to make it more comprehensible, and highlighted the three most striking parts. He takes first the chapter recommended by Marx himself, Chapter X, "The Working Day," which he considers "represents in many respects the climax of Marx' entire book on capital";[111] he then takes Chapters XIX–XXI on "Wage-labor," "Time-wages," and "Piece-wages"; finally he deals with Part VIII, "The So-called Primitive Accumulation," which is "rightly renowned for its breath-taking tempo and compelling verve. In fact this part, which is easily readable, together with its appended Chapter XXXIII on 'The Modern Theory of Colonization,' in reality forms the third climax of Marx' book."[112]

An even clearer summarization of the book existed; this was a four-page blurb clearly written by Marx himself for the second edition of *Capital,* which he had considerably amended; it has, however, been lost; although at least 4,000 copies were printed, it has so far not been found.[113]

The central theory, the discovery emphasized by Marx himself as the most important result of his labors, is that in the world of commodities there is a specific commodity hitherto not recognized as such — labor: "The best points in my book are: (1) *the double character of labour,* according to whether it is expressed in use value or exchange value (*all* understanding of the facts depends upon this; it is emphasised immediately in the *first* chapter)."[114]

Saint-Simon, one of Marx's most important theoretical predecessors, had not perceived this; not only was he convinced of an industrialized society's potentiality for progress, but he saw no reason for antagonism between employer and worker. The one was the protector of the other; even the *"classe de prolétaires"*[115] had an opportunity to acquire property and become rich. A treatise he proposed to write about this class of society, however, never progressed beyond a two-and-a-half-page draft.[116] As early as the 1840s — proof of the continuity of work and interest between the "early" and the "later" Marx — he had taken extracts from the most abstruse sources on this general theme; from this period too come the first indications of his preoccupation with François Villegardelle, a disciple of Fourier.[117] This method — auto-didactic and didactic simultaneously — so aptly described by Louis Althusser as "reading aloud,"[118] finally led him to new classifications peculiar to Marx. He developed them logically, one from another.

Every commodity has two qualities. It can be a product that is used. In the strict sense of the word it is then no longer a commodity but an object for use. It is made solely to be used. Its value is its utility — from Neanderthal man's wooden club to the coach of state. In a society based on commodity production things are brought into a relationship with each other since not everyone makes his club or his coach for himself and his own use; objects are exchanged. The place where this exchange is made is the market, whether it is the village square or Wall Street. Since at the moment of exchange objects become divorced from their original purpose, the market requires a regulator — money. In primitive societies money is unnecessary. The "unit of reckoning" may be sheep or camels or vegetables or agricultural products. Even in our highly developed society such units of reckoning come back into play in times of crisis; in the war and postwar periods, for instance, it was cigarettes; in an inflationary period it may be objets d'art; in 1946 a fur coat could be exchanged for a packet of Chesterfields or a tiled stove for a hundredweight of onions; in 1975 one could "acquire" a country house with a Picasso or a car with a copy of Bacon. Marx quoted Aristotle — "5 beds = 1 house"[119] — in order to demonstrate fluctuations in the expressions of value — money or commodities as "money-form."

The use-value of a thing is therefore removed, alienated, changed in purpose when it is "marketed"; its meaningful use-value becomes a meaningless, extrasensory exchange-value. The alienated object becomes a commodity deprived of its purpose. The fact that the price of a new car can be paid for a certain registration plate in London is "extrasensory" in Marx's sense of the word. At this point he introduces the notion of the "fetish character" of certain commodities:

A commodity appears at first sight a very trivial thing and easily understood. Its analysis shows that it is, in reality, a very queer thing, abounding in metaphysical subtleties and theological niceties. So far as it is a value in use, there is nothing mysterious about it, whether we consider it from the point of view that by its properties it is capable of satisfying human wants or from the point that those properties are the product of human labour. It is as clear as noon-day that man, by his industry, changes the forms of the materials furnished by nature in such a way as to make them useful to him. The form of wood, for instance, is altered by making a table out of it. Yet for all that the table continues to be that common everyday thing, wood. But as soon as it steps forth as a commodity, it is changed into something transcendent. It not only stands with its feet on the ground but, in relation to all other commodities, it stands on its head and evolves out of its wooden brain grotesque ideas far more wonderful than "table-turning" ever was.[120]

Marx's inquiry was now directed toward "capital," the money that creates money. The question of how it originates is not answered by his description of a (possibly absurd) process of exchange. If the products exchanged are of equal value, there will be no profit. Someone who exchanges a coat for ten pounds of tea has not necessarily earned anything. The question posed by Marx, therefore, was this: how can a possessor of money (the owner of a coat or the owner of a Picasso) buy a commodity for what it is worth and sell it for what it is worth — in other words, exchange goods of equal value — and still extract a sort of third value from them, his profit?

Marx's discovery was that a certain commodity existed in the market that could be acquired and that itself produced value — labor-power.

Only the acquisition of *this* commodity and its utilization (or exploitation) created capital. The special characteristic of *this* commodity was that it created value and, furthermore, more value than it cost. The wages received by the worker were admittedly adequate to maintain him — to feed him, clothe him, and maintain his family. They did not correspond, however, to the value of the product that he created. Some part of his working time, however long or short it might be, was taken by the employer. This slice of unpaid work was the employer's profit. If he were to pay the worker precisely the value which the product he manufactured represented or could bring on the market, that which formed the basis of capital would not arise — surplus value. Marx's definition of "capitalism" as a social condition was a logical equation: the sale of labor-power as a commodity created dependents who did not own what they produced. The man who did own it did not produce it himself; he not only received the product but also claimed for himself the difference between the wages he paid and the real value of the product. Marx consequently arrived at the classic statement "We know that the value of each commodity is determined by the quantity of labour expended on and materialised in it, by the working time necessary, under given social conditions, for its production."[121]

The historical development of wage-labor and commodity production, Marx maintained, created two types of law, two types of morality, two different classes — the "free worker," free to sell himself and his labor-power and "free" from the result of his labor, which did not belong to him; in the literal sense of the word he did not belong to himself. On the other side stood the nonworking employer, pictured in Marx's rogues' gallery as a cross between slaveowner and bloodsucker.

The ring of humanitarian wrath is unmistakable, references to sources and to his predecessors are clear. His theoretical achievement is inconceivable without the moral impulse; yet in Marx's case even this outcry against mercilessness and inhumanity was "read aloud."

He quotes a report of the official Children's Employment Commission:

". . . but it seems likely not [to be] equal in money-value to the waste of animal power now going on in glass-houses throughout the kingdom from growing boys not having enough quiet time to eat their meals at ease, with a little rest afterwards for digestion." And this in the year of progress 1865! Without considering the expenditure of strength in lifting and carrying, such a child, in the sheds where bottle and flint glass are made, walks during the performance of his work 15-20 miles in every 6 hours! And the work often lasts 14 or 15 hours! In many of these glass works, as in the Moscow spinning mills, the system of 6 hours' relays is in force. "During the working part of the week six hours is the utmost unbroken period ever attained at any one time for rest, and out of this has to come the time spent in coming and going to and from work, washing, dressing and meals, leaving a very short period indeed for rest and none for fresh air and play, unless at the expense of the sleep necessary for young boys, especially at such hot and fatiguing work. . . . Even the short sleep is obviously liable to be broken by a boy having to wake himself if it is night, or by the noise if it is day." Mr White gives cases where a boy worked 36 consecutive hours; others where boys of 12 drudged on until 2 in the morning and then slept in the works till 5 A.M. (3 hours!) only to resume their work. "The amount of work", say Tremenheere and Tufnell, who drafted the general report, "done by boys, youths, girls and women in the course of their daily or nightly spell of labour is certainly extraordinary." Meanwhile, late at night perhaps, the "self-denying" Mr Glass-Capital, primed with port wine, reels out of his club homeward droning out idiotically "Britons never never shall be slaves!".[122]

Marx quotes theorists, political economists, ancient philosophers and the Bible; he scythed around, hurling missiles of hate, calling down the death and destruction due to the unjust. *This* is the towering characteristic of this book, not that it summarized everything that political and economic theorists had worked out before him, not that it was a brilliant summary of previous writings; its fascination lies in its change of tempo, in its juxtaposition of breathless onslaught and crystal-clear proof. Calligraphy like the thought-diagram attached to a letter to Engels[123] is tantamount to a system of coordinates on squared paper.

A system of coordinates for a new humanism rescued from the men whom Marx accused of manhunting? He had earlier written an article for the *New York Daily Tribune* accusing the Duchess of Sutherland of instituting a system of slavery, and its publication created a sensation when Harriet Beecher Stowe, the goodwill ambassador for the American Negro slaves, was welcomed to London by the Duchess. This piece of journalistic polemics was now turned into the central paragraph in the section on "Accumulation of Capital":

As an example of the method obtaining in the 19th century, the "clearing" made by the Duchess of Sutherland will suffice here. This person, well instructed in economy, resolved, on joining the government, to effect a radical cure and to turn the whole country, whose population had already been reduced, by earlier processes of a like kind, to 15,000, into a sheep-walk. From 1814 to 1820 these 15,000 inhabitants, about 3,000 families, were systematically hunted and rooted out. All their villages were destroyed and burnt, all their fields turned into pasturage. British soldiers enforced this eviction and came to blows with the inhabitants. One old woman was burnt to death in the flames of the hut which she refused to leave. Thus this fine lady appropriated 794,000 acres of land that had belonged to the clan from time immemorial. She assigned to the expelled inhabitants about 6,000 acres on the sea shore — 2 acres per family. The 6,000 acres had until this time lain waste and brought in no income to their owners. The Duchess, in the nobility of her heart, actually went so far as to let these at an average rent of 2s 6d per acre to the clansmen who for centuries had shed their blood for her family. The whole of the stolen clan-land she divided into 29 great sheep farms, each inhabited by a single family, for the most part imported English farm hands. By 1835 the 15,000 Gaels had already been replaced by 131,000 sheep. The remnant of the aborigines flung on the sea shore tried to live by catching fish. They became amphibious and lived, as an English author says, half on land and half on water and withal only half on both. . . .

The spoliation of the Church's property, the fraudulent alienation of the state domains, the robbery of the common lands, the usurpation of feudal and clan property and its transformation into modern private property under circumstances of reckless terrorism, were just so many idyllic methods of primitive accumulation. They conquered the field for capitalistic agriculture, made the soil part and parcel of capital and created for the town industries the necessary supply of a "free" and outlawed proletariat.[124]

This example is illustrative of the basic difference between Marx's attitude and the horror evinced by the general public, for revulsion at the rapacious mechanism of capitalism in the raw, with its exploitation and disregard of human beings, was general. At the same time as Marx was working on his book Baudelaire, for instance, was writing his *Fusées;* it was never finished, but in it he referred to the prevailing moral and spiritual laws as inexorable, he denounced technocracy as the harbinger of a spurious progress leading to starvation, and he forecast that those who were trying to oppose the brutality that seemed to be sweeping all before it would find themselves faced by rulers prepared to make unscrupulous use of their resources — "we shall die from precisely that on which we think to live."[125] In his *Life without Principle*, published in 1861, Thoreau described the jungle law prevalent in society, when a child who fell out of a window was mourned as a loss — to the business world — when anyone going for a walk was looked upon as an idler, and when a man seen making notes in the open was naturally assumed to be calculating his wages.[126] Emile Durkheim, the sociologist and one of the most perspicacious analysts of capitalist culture, anticipated the modern slogan about the suicidal society by calling his book *Le Suicide;* in it he says: "Society is becoming a disorganized ant-heap of individuals."[127]

The hallmark of Marx's great book is its tone of indictment and appeal; the impetus of the book derives from the examples, differing widely in time and place, of mechanized inhumanity; he quotes, for instance, Adam Smith's assertion that in the mid-eighteenth century mental defectives were preferable employees on certain functions that were business secrets.[128]

It is worth noting here that the flame of Marx's anger was lit by — paper. Never in his life had he seen a workman doing his job; he did not know any workers; he did not live among them; he had never set foot in a factory; he had not accepted the opportunity offered him by his closest friend — an employer in one of the toughest and most rapidly expanding branches of industry[129] — to inspect such a concern; he never entered Engels's factory in Manchester. Marx's sympathy was purely intellectual.

But Marx did not stop there. He pursued two parallel lines of argument in his book: a description, amounting to a colossal indictment, of the "How," the state of injustice and humiliation, paralleled by an attempt to analyze the "Why." Marx's answer to the question "Why" was to change the "How." As a result, alongside the impetus of the humanitarian appeal, the book presents the dialectic of a theoretical exercise. This is why, after flaying the Duchess of Sutherland, he can turn to the accumulation of capital and, after describing the child market in Bethnal Green, where nine-year-olds were hired out to the London silk factories, he turns to the theory of surplus value.[130] Both are central to Marx's theory of political economy.

As a result of alteration in the nature of objects through diversion from their original purpose, the change from use-value to exchange-value, they become commodities. As exchange-values commodities are units of measure for the working time expended on them. Parts of this working time — the "unnecessary" working time — are filched from the worker. Surplus value is surplus work. The value is appropriated by the man who should consequently be called the *recipient* of work instead of the *giver* of work. But in an industrialized society the worker can no longer do without him.

So commodities — and primarily the commodity "labor-power" — are transformed into money and money into capital; with the assistance of capital increased value is created from which again increased capital is made. The terms "surplus value," "surplus produce," and "surplus labor" had already been linked by Adam Smith. As Marx himself emphasizes,[131] they were the main theme of Ricardo's arguments; Vygodsky, the Soviet expert on Marx, points out[132] that these terms had also been used by other Ricardo specialists such as William Thompson. None of them, however, had analyzed one specific factor: the originating process of capital.

There is no need to quote the nursery rhyme

> *When Adam dug and Eve span*
> *Who was then the gentleman?*

in order to arrive at the question: where, when and how does capital originate? It must, after all, have been there before this capitalist cycle began, since without capital there can be no capitalism. Marx puts the question succinctly:

The whole movement, therefore, seems to turn in a vicious circle, out of which we can only get by supposing a primitive accumulation, an accumulation not the result of the capitalist mode of production, but its starting point.[133]

This primitive accumulation — "primitive" because the term implies an early historical period, the origin of capital and the production methods arising therefrom — springs, in Marx's view, from the breakup of feudalism's social and economic structure in face of capitalism. The one emerged from the other. The relevant section of *Capital* is a fiery essay, an excursion through history, using — and quoting at length from — historical sources intended to illustrate the transformation of the independent small farmer or smallholder into the large landowner and thence into the possessor of capital.

Reduction in density of the independent, self-sufficient agricultural population was the counterpart to the increase in density of the industrial proletariat. This vast industrial reserve army was "kept down" both in its material standard of living and its prospects of human happiness; as international competition intensified and monopoly agreements were concluded, it would be driven even deeper into poverty. In such a society Marx can see no prospect of improvement in this terrible picture of tortured mankind.

At this point Marx pursues three overlapping trains of thought. First, the capitalist's struggle for profit is not a "personal" characteristic of the individual employer, whose private life may be perfectly honorable; it is law of society. This law governs the next train of thought: that a pernicious cycle exists — overproduction, falling profit rates, sales crisis, unemployment. The employer cannot employ his workers because he cannot sell his products; he cannot sell his products because he has no customers. Labor-power then becomes easier and cheaper to obtain and the next cycle begins. This development, however, leads to the third train of thought, something new: consciousness. The proletariat is no longer a stolid mass, a "class as such," but realizes its situation and becomes a "class of its own." This clarifies Marx's entire dialectical and historical concept: capitalism is an alliance of a few powerful men against many impotent men, injustice per se and therefore reprehensible. Capitalism, however, carries within itself, in fact produces, the germ of a new phase and to that extent it is to be welcomed. Since without the capitalist phase there would be no proletariat, initially stolid but later conscious and organized, it is a historically positive phase of history.

The entire book culminates in this raging passage:

One capitalist always kills many. Hand in hand with this centralisation, or this expropriation of many capitalists by few, there develops on an ever-extending scale the cooperative form of the labour-process, the conscious technical application of science, the methodical cultivation of the soil, the transformation of the instruments of labour into instruments usable only in common, economy of all means of production by their use as means of production of combined, socialised labour, the entanglement of all peoples in the net of the world market, thus producing the international character of the capitalistic regime. Along with the constantly diminishing number of the magnates of capital, who usurp and monopolise all advantages of this process of transformation, grows the mass of misery, oppression, slavery, degradation, exploitation; but with this too grows the revolt of the working class, a class always increasing in numbers and disciplined, united, organised by the very mechanism of the process of capitalist production itself. The monopoly of capital becomes a handicap to the method of production which has sprung up and flourished along with and under it. Centralisation of the means of production and socialisation of labour at last reach a point where they become incompatible with their capitalist framework. The framework is burst asunder. The knell of capitalist private property sounds. The expropriators are expropriated.[134]

And then what?

MANKIND AS A RACE OF ANTS — HISTORY AS
THE CHIPS OF WOOD THEY DRAG AROUND

This passage in particular illustrates the lacunae that confront us over and over again in the works of Karl Marx: the analysis is brilliant and correct, the conclusions drawn are vague or erroneous. This book too was originally intended to have a "critique" title; the decision to call it *Capital* instead of "Critique of Political Economy" was taken by Marx in late 1862.[135] In this case the changeover comes in the middle of the paragraph; up to the words "usurp and monopolize" it could be a treatise written in 1975; starting from the words "grows the mass of misery" it is pure nineteenth-century daguerreotype, not a blueprint for socialism. The "knell of capitalist private property" has not yet sounded in any single highly industrialized country in the world.

If the conclusions are wrong, however, can the diagnosis be entirely right? Criticism of the falsity of Marx's theory started very early — with Engels. A paragraph in one of his reviews cannot be read any other way: "This book will greatly disillusion many a reader . . . he gives only very obscure indications of what should exist after the social upheaval."[136]

Engels gave vent to numerous, perfectly astounding, utterances of this nature — "we have no final aim; we are evolutionists"[137] or "Marx's entire world concept is no doctrine but a method. It provides no ready-made dogma but indicates starting points for further investigations and the method of these investigations."[138]

This interpretation is supported by the terribly unfinished state of the great draft; it never became an "artistic whole" but remained unbalanced. The various complex overlapping stages and drafts[139] and the mighty limbless torso that was Marx's legacy show that he himself was by no means sure of his theories and conclusions; as one of the drafts shows, he regarded the "Theories of Surplus Value" merely as a section of a chapter, a historical digression belonging to the part "The Production Process of Capital."[140] Even Engels, who had wrestled with the 1,500 pages of manuscript and wished to expunge many of them,[141] was unable to collate them all; Karl Kautsky edited them between 1905 and 1910.

Rosa Luxemburg must be regarded as the most profound critic of the defects in Marx's thinking and writing. She plunges in at precisely the point where the gap in the argumentation is at its widest, where airy-fairy hopes and exclamation marks take the place of detailed argument. Marx's description of the accumulation of capital, to which reference is made in Volume 2, she regards as worse than merely unfinished: "In particular the analysis of accumulation of capital, which is the point here, though being the last chapter of the manuscript, has emerged as the worst; it comprises only a bare 35 pages in a volume of 450 pages and breaks off in the midst of the argument."[142]

Rosa Luxemburg's critique is taboo today in orthodox Marxist circles; a furious attack on it was published by *Vorwärts* as early as February 16, 1913. The central point that worried her was that, if you followed Marx's scheme of things, you went round in a circle. Since accumulation of capital relies upon the fact that the capitalist does *not* use for himself the major part of the surplus value (all the rivers of champagne, mountains of caviar, and fleets of Rolls-Royces notwithstanding), for whom, and above all *what,* does the remainder of the surplus value produce? Clearly something for another section of the population, for an increased number of consumers who, precisely on the basis of this law of capitalist production discovered by Marx, develop increased requirements — and receive increased means of satisfying these requirements.[143] As a result, Rosa Luxemburg insists on posing the question that overshadows any discussion of this subject: how is it that *despite everything* people in capitalist societies are better off? Her summing up is lapidary: "The society to which the hypotheses in Volume 2 of *Capital* relate exists nowhere in the world of reality."[144]

The dispute that rages inexorably today, employing all the weapons of denunciation, the argument started by and peculiar to Rosa Luxemburg is two-fold: if the system of diagnosis used by Marx in *Capital* is defective on certain decisive points, is it invalid? Second, is Marx's picture of the New World, admittedly presented only in vague outline, a practical proposition or has it already materialized?

There is no serious Marx expert who will answer the second question in the affirmative. Whether it be Ernest Mandel, Louis Althusser, Henri Lefebvre, Ernst Bloch, Karl Korsch, Adam Schaff, Leszek Kolakovski, or Paul Mattick, the Yugoslav "Praxis" group, or the Italian "Il Manifesto" group, none of them regard the "socialist reality" as real socialism.[145]

The ever-recurring present day workers' riots, in Warsaw or East Berlin for instance, are sparked off by precisely the problem analyzed by Marx, surplus work and increased norms. East German economic theorists of course tried to explain to the workers that conveyor belts set to run at a greater speed represented a new factor in that, under socialism, labor-power had ceased to be a commodity and the resulting profit would serve to satisfy social requirements. That is correct if applied to schools, universities, hospitals, social services, or rent reduction. It is not right if applied to the quality of life in the broader sense. "We can never win anyone in the West over to socialism," an East Berlin radio mechanic lamented at a Party conference, "if the tapes here always run quicker and over there they insist on longer cadence signals."[146] Even the long-despised piped music was introduced into Wolfen, the East German film concern, in order to produce "maximum psychological stimulus." Since 1965 the American MTM (Methods–Time Measurement) procedure has been introduced into numerous popularly owned industries, though condemned by the West German Communist Party as the ultimate monstrosity of capitalist exploitationist methods and generally nicknamed "Must Try More," "Make Thousands More," or "Mit Teuflischen

Mitteln" (with devilish methods). Under MTM thousands of basic movements — grasp, lift, carry, fetch — in a work process are dissected by means of slow-motion pictures and then, by adding up the individual timings, a table of timing norms is prepared. The East German industrial directory lists some one hundred cadre personnel authorized to instruct workers in the avoidance of inefficient movements. Dr. Winfried Helms, one of the staff of the West German MTM agency, reports that her firm recently conducted a training course in the Central Institute for Manufacturing Technique in Karl-Marx-Stadt and "since then our procedures have become fairly widespread over there."[147] The semi-symbolic ritual phrase "Work makes men free," Lenin's incantation as he swept out a Kremlin courtyard with his own hands on May 1, is therefore purely metaphorical.

Even Marxist economic theorists are unable to detect any new quality in work in the nationalized industries.

Paul Mattick, for instance, who is fully aware that the period of prosperity in certain countries after World War II is no compensation for the frightful poverty and misery prevalent in most of the world,[148] says quite frankly that the revolution forecast by Marx[149] has so far taken place nowhere in the world but that Marx never intended a state capitalist system to arise as has happened in that part of the world that calls itself socialist.[150] In his view there is no qualitative change when the domination of capital over labor is replaced by the domination of controllers over the controlled.[151]

If that is so, the validity of the theory can be questioned on broader grounds; in fact it is no longer merely a matter of surprise that nowhere should Marx have defined the term "class" or set out the mechanics of his new-model state; in that case there is a vacuum central to the whole theory and that vacuum is — man.

Man as an idea, as a peg on which to hang hopes, as "the people," "the proletariat," or a "class," or as an object of pity and sympathy — in that sense man is to be found in Marx's writings. But man as an *individual* entity, with *individual* hopes, *individual* limitations, and *individual* finite qualities — in that sense man is not to be found in Marx's writings. One of the finest, and at first sight most illuminating, passages in *Capital,* a source of socialist forward thinking until the time of Brecht's poems, says reflectively:

A spider conducts operations that resemble those of a weaver and a bee puts to shame many an architect in the construction of her cells. But what distinguishes the worst architect from the best of bees is this, that the architect raises his structure in imagination before he erects it in reality. At the end of every labour-process, we get a result that already existed in the imagination of the labourer at its commencement. He not only effects a change of form in the material on which he works, but he also realises a purpose of his own that gives the law to his modus operandi and to which he must subordinate his will.[152]

This is Hegel upside down, but Hegel nevertheless — reason as the governing spirit of the world, brain-power endlessly expandable and limitless, as the mainspring of history. Is that correct? Are men limitlessly tractable and changeable without destroying some deep-seated structures? Can human societies be solely and exclusively designed according to the dictates of the brain cells?

It is not the case among animals, as is now known. The disconcerting experiment made by John P. Calhoun, the American behavioral research expert,[153] to set up a sort of "communist" mouse colony ended in debacle. Cages and nesting-boxes were given the best possible environment; food and water were provided in unlimited quantities; there were no natural enemies, no diseases, no agitating external factors; temperature was kept at a pleasant level. In short, conditions of life were ideal. Initially a flourishing and rapidly increasing colony developed Then, however, it became apparent that wealth and status symbols have a part to play even in a society of mice. A status symbol was the possession of one of the lower nesting-boxes, from which access to the food was easier; nesting higher up necessitated expenditure of greater energy, and "in a mouse colony energy is the equivalent of income, in other words is the economic factor."[154] The first "settlers" occupied all the space available and there were battles between succeeding generations for territory and wives. The older males wore themselves out and died off. The females became aggressive. The social structure of the mouse colony was thrown into confusion because the traditional patterns of behavior had become reversed. Calhoun's conclusion from his experiment was: "If a society can no longer provide an adequate social role for its individuals, aggressiveness increases correspondingly; finally the establishment collapses completely."[155] After two and a half years the animals had become increasingly passive, dejected rather than aggressive. They never played, displayed no sexual activity, and barely left their nests except to eat. Matings ceased and within a few months the colony died out. All that remained were some fifteen elderly females of an age equivalent to a human centenarian. Numerous other similar experiments prove irrefutably that rearing animals under artificial conditions does not eliminate certain existential mechanisms or *innate* patterns of behavior.[156]

Animals, however, are not human beings. This was precisely the point Marx wished to make. Nevertheless the question remains whether man does not possess certain definite instincts that are immutable — for instance, he wants "his" place whether around the camp fire or in the underground or even in the lunatic asylum.

Karl Marx does not examine the problem of the value of individuality, of love and death for instance; he regards men as such as the executors of history, industrious ants understanding and grasping a chip of history — and this means that he remains undeniably a disciple of Hegel. His topsy-turvy statement that human anatomy was a key to the anatomy of the ape[157] was intended as something more than a pungent repudiation of Spencer's theory of development; it reduced mankind to the level of a historical factor. In Hegel's view it was the nation that was united, formed in fact, by the human spirit working through history — a theory given a humorous twist by Karl R. Popper, who commented that one might just as well say that in Hegel's view a nation was a collection of men united by a communal misconception regarding their history.[158]

Even in his early writings Marx regarded particular personal qualities as identical with social qualities; the community, the totality, society invariably only became real to him if the individual were *merged* into them. For Marx, the truth about the individual was discoverable only in numbers of individuals. A person was a species idea — a section of people.[159] Accordingly the social order — in short, the state — was the superior level; if need be, as laid down by Lenin, the Party, as truly representing this social order, constituted this superior level. This approximates closely to Hegel's ideal of the State. In his *Critique of the Philosophy of Right,* Marx's central purpose had been to reconcile the State and bourgeois society, that world of isolated individuals.

The points of overlap are closely related. In Hegel's view the nature of man is governed by his relationship to the outside world. He finds his true self by "translation of himself from the night of possibility into the day of the present."[160] This self-generative process is one not so much of the actual man as of the absolute, abstract intellect, a "super-human" development. Hegel writes in the abstract, divorced from the sensory world; the idea, as an absolute, is the motive force of history. The development of history is a development of thought. History is reduced to logic.

At this point Marx, who described logic as the currency of the mind, enters with his criticism. This is the point at which there begins the now famous process of adjusting Hegel's ideology from head to foot.

Nevertheless he does not cut totally loose from Hegel's entire concept of the world. He fills in the details differently; once again for Marx consciousness forms the "foot." Auguste Cornu's description of the two concepts as "totally antithetical"[161] is an overrigid interpretation. It can nevertheless be supported by Marx's statement:

My dialectical method is not only different from the Hegelian but is its direct opposite. To Hegel the process of thinking which, under the name of "The Idea", he even transforms into an independent subject, is the demiurgos of the real world, which is only its external manifestation. With me, on the contrary, the ideal is nothing else than the material world reflected by the human mind and translated into forms of thought.[162]

Cornu considers that Hegel's view of the relationship between man and nature is confined exclusively to the level of consciousness and Marx's view to the level of concrete active existence. This is not correct. The example of the bees in *Capital,* for instance, shows that no such clear-cut distinction can be made; the concept of work as a self-generative act on the part of man carries the imprint of Hegel.[163] Marx admitted as much in his critique of Hegel, which was focused primarily on the *Phenomenology*.[164] He "added" that the factor of alienation was missing in Hegel's concept of work. A "consciousness" factor therefore?

It is almost a vicious circle; when Marx diverges from Hegel, at the same time his train of thought invariably overlaps, with certain nuances, with that of Hegel. The entire intellectual and political biography of Karl Marx testifies to the fact that it was ideas to which he attributed any formative energy, ideas which could destroy, build, or support a state. Material power only emerged when the *theory* had been grasped by the masses. All his life, even during the period of the International, theory was more important to Marx than any practical political work or "meetings quelconque."

That there is no contradiction here is clear from Friedrich Engels's triumphant announcement of his idea of the State: "Well and good, gentlemen, do you want to know what this dictatorship looks like? Look at the Paris Commune. That was the dictatorship of the proletariat."[165] In the same concluding section of his introduction to Marx's *Civil War in France* he takes issue with Hegel's philosophical notion of the State as "the realization of the idea" and calls this State "nothing but a machine for the oppression of one class by another."[166] The trouble is that this is precisely what he is proclaiming himself — the realization of an idea, a machine for the oppression of one class by another, the dictatorship of the proletariat.

Marx was not simply "coquetting with Hegel"; his writings bore the stamp of a real deep-rooted affiliation to Hegel's pattern of thinking. And this applies to *Capital* too. Ever since the appearance of the book the never-ending critical dispute about it has mostly revolved around its remarkable lack of consideration of individual capabilities, of specific individual human qualities.

The statement, apparently purely politicoeconomic though it is, that as exchange-values all commodities are definite units of measure of the working-time expended on them is perhaps indicative of the crux of the problem. To take a further example, how is the value of *Guernica* to be established when it has no use-value anyway? It is obvious that Marx's closed circle dealt only in quantities; quality, either of the manufacturing process or of the manufactured product, was a factor that did not enter into the calculations. The theory of labor-value deals only with one aspect of the many ingredients contributing to the production of value. In forming an opinion of (or condemning) nations, Marx took no account of the formative imponderables such as climate, temperament, and national traditions; similarly, in forming an opinion of production processes he left out of account the individual human ingredients such as aptitude, agility of mind, and even qualitative physiological differences. In considering this point one must not confine oneself to the "upper crust" products — from Velázquez to Joyce, where a scale of values established by time-measurement is clearly inapplicable. It is equally inapplicable to a shoe, a house, or a fatted calf. Further, there are values that simply are not measurable by work, either quantitatively or qualitatively. Even though a silver mine, a coal seam, an oil well, or a high-speed current can be *marketed* as a result of work, they are values in themselves and may be valued at entirely different rates at different historical periods — the wealth represented by a country's coal reserves is not the same in 1870, 1930, 1950, and 1980. This is so although — or perhaps because — at certain stages this wealth is not touched by human hand.[167]

It is perhaps remarkable, and it is comparatively unknown, that Karl Liebknecht was extraordinarily critical of Marx's theory of value. His objections revolve around precisely the point we have been considering — whether in fact there are not certain defects in the diagnostic system of Marx's book. If this is true, then the "mistakes" or "mistaken developments" of the twentieth century are no such thing. They are *consequences* of the doctrine.

Liebknecht calls Marx's term "work" a "mystical 'it,' a transcendental occult entity, a morass of mysterious power. . . . In fact it is only a word instead of a notion, a dialectical verbal stunt instead of a solution."[168] He describes Marx's theory of value quite frankly as unsatisfactory; he considers the emergence of surplus value as deduced by Marx to be the product of a basic economic generative process.[169] His reasoning is that something is missing which should have closed the gap in the logical argumentation — a clear factual relationship between the value of labor-power and the value of its output:

In Marx's view the worker receives full payment for his labor-power as such; but in the labor process an allegedly mystical attribute (capability) of this labor-power is used up, the ability to produce more than is necessary for its reproduction.

This interpretation of exploitation is invalidated by its great obscurity, in fact by a serious and central contradiction: if labor-power really has the capacity to produce more than is necessary to reproduce itself, has the employer who engages that labor-power engaged and paid for only that part of it which is necessary for its own reproduction or has he not also engaged the remainder, the rest of it, this occult power, this mystical "it," this value-producing ability over and above the power required to reproduce itself? By what authority can it be maintained that a relationship of any sort should be established between the value of wages (the purchase price of labor-power) and that of labor-power's self-reproductive ability? Labor-power is engaged and paid for as it is with all its attributes, just as the purchase price of a flower includes not only the stalk, leaves, etc., but also its ability to smell or give pleasure by its shape or color. How could such a restricted acquisition of labor-power be delimited in practice? What sense is there in this restriction to the reproductive part of labor-power only?

Wherein lies what is called "exploitation" if the whole of the labor-power is paid for and a full equivalent for the value of that labor-power is provided?[170]

Again and again Liebknecht points out that "value" is not a capitalistic notion but existed before capitalist society and will exist after it,[171] that the productivity of labor is not the prerogative of *one single* class — not even of the working class — but of all social forces.[172] He also shows that, as occasion served, Marx twisted facts and figures, sometimes introducing empirical findings into his argumentation when they could not be proved, at others excluding them "to the point of irrealism in the solution."[173] Moreover Liebknecht's description of the basic contradictions in Marx's theory culminates in an explicit reference to precisely that lacuna to which reference has been made so often and of which various illustrations have been quoted: Marx did not take account of man as he is, "the historic moral factor"[174] in Liebknecht's words.

This is no side-issue, however. It is the whole basis of the criticism that, if the line of thinking be pursued, reduces Marx's book on economics to a gigantic fresco — an artist has painted a picture of the nineteenth century's economic history with passion and explosive ardor. But Géricault's colors, lines, even his ideology, cannot be "inherited"; they offer no solution to present-day painters. From Charles Bettelheim to Louis Althusser (who referred to "Marx' theoretical antihumanism")[175] to Werner Becker the argument always revolves round this problem. Liebknecht puzzled over the social answer to an economic problem; Werner Becker rightly asked what was the economic background to the criticism of the exchange-value/use-value relationship. If one reads Becker's analysis of the counterarguments, it is clear that he is talking of the same thing as Rosa Luxemburg, the same flaw, the same yawning gap:

What gives Marx the right, based on his discovery and perception of objective economic laws, to talk of "exploitation," etc., of the labor-power of wage-laborers by the owners of capitalist means of production? He cannot possibly take his stand upon the notion that exploitation of the workers emanates from the psychological, and therefore subjective, malevolence of the proprietors of capitalist means of production.

This much can be said, however: none of the chapters of *Capital* dealing with the origin and function of surplus value gives any explicit reasoning for the *economic injustice* of the exchange-value/use-value ratio of labor. However great the detail in which Marx describes the "Production of absolute surplus value," there is an absence of *economic reasoning* for the critical attitude which, to judge from the sense and the presentation, should be associated with the analysis of capitalist surplus value.[176]

The question remains: Marx's gigantic achievement, his brilliant compendium of criticism of developing capitalism — can it form a model, is it a force for the future, is it a practical guide to action?

CHAPTER TEN

THE LAST YEARS

PRIVATE GENTLEMAN BY THE FIRESIDE WITH
HIS SHERRY AND HIS BOOKS

There was one person who knew only too well that *Capital* raised more questions than it answered — Karl Marx. This can be the only explanation for the fact, referred to by Engels as almost inconceivable, that Marx to all intents and purposes "concealed" large, fully drafted parts of further manuscripts; those on which Engels had to labor had largely been written by 1860.[1] Marx's omnivorous appetite for more and more and yet more material had given rise to a mountain of heterogeneous unprocessed material bristling with factual errors,[2] a "brouillon" — and all this he had left largely untouched for one and a half decades.[3] Shortly before his death Marx realized that he was bound to leave it to Engels to "make something of it."[4] Engels's labor on all this was almost superhuman; all the statistical material — whether originating from Russian, Polish, or Turkish sources — had to be checked. In addition, there was the misery of deciphering Marx's almost totally illegible handwriting, which almost cost Engels his eyesight. When Volume 3 had appeared eleven years after Marx's death, Engels, then aged seventy-four, gave up:

And then Vol. 4. Now of that there is a *very* rough manuscript, of which up to now it is impossible to say how much can be used. I myself cannot again undertake to unravel it and dictate the whole as I did Vol. 2 and 3. My eyesight would break down completely before I was half through. I found that out years ago and tried another dodge. I considered it would be useful to have one or two intelligent men of the younger generation broken in to read Mohr's handwriting. I thought of Kautsky and Bernstein. K was then still in London (some 6 or 7 years ago). I asked him and he assented; I said I would pay one hundred pounds for the complete "fair copy" of what there is and assist him where he could not decipher. Then he left London, took one folio with him and for years I heard no more. He was too busy with the *Neue Zeit*, so I had manuscripts and copy returned, as far as the latter went — perhaps ⅛ to ⅙ of the whole. Bernstein too is not only very busy but suffers from overwork, has not yet completely overcome his neurasthenia and I hardly dare ask him. I shall see whether Tussy will; if he volunteers, all well;

if not, I do not intend to run the risk of having it said that I brought on a relapse of his illness by overloading him with work.

That is my position: 74 years, the which I am beginning to feel, and work enough for two men of 40. Yes, if I could divide myself into the F.E. of 40 and the F.E. of 34, which would be just 74, then we should soon be all right. But as it is, all I can do is to work on with what is before me and get through it as far and as well as I can.[5]

There is clearly a contradictory situation here; nevertheless the feverish nervous energy expended by Marx in hunting up evidence and proofs testified at the same time to a form of satiety. He preferred to lick the newborn child clean rather than risk the expenditure of further creative energy. When Meissner, the Hamburg publisher of *Capital,* asked for a second edition in 1871 — offering a fee of 500 taler — Marx plunged into revision of the book, and spent eighteen months doing it. From 1867 he was negotiating for a French translation; this was initially undertaken by Jean-Jacques Elisée Reclus, the anarchist, and then by Joseph Roy, translator of Feuerbach, but Marx was not satisfied with the latter's work. Marx worked more intensively on these negotiations, on checking the translation and on the complexities of the contract, than he ever did on writing anything new; he admitted that revision of the French translation alone had given him "more trouble than if he had rewritten the entire book in French."[6] He had in fact rewritten the entire book and it differed substantially from the German version.[7] When the 1875 edition appeared, Marx financed it himself; he bore the cost of the publisher's contract; his uncle in Amsterdam, usually so full of goodwill, friendly and ready to help, had refused, saying he was ready to help his friend and relative at any time in an emergency but he had no wish to assist the book's political and revolutionary purposes.[8]

The first foreign-language edition appeared in 1872, in Russia of all places; it was translated by Nikolai F. Danielson, the nationalist, who undertook this complex work in the evenings since he worked in a bank by day. Marx meanwhile knew enough Russian to follow the work closely. Most unexpectedly the book was not confiscated; the authorities regarded it as so incomprehensible that hardly anyone would read it and practically no one would understand it.[9] Nevertheless both its impact and its sales were many times greater than in Western Europe. The book was passed on like contraband goods, often in a New Testament binding. Historically this was something of a coincidence, since at about the same time Marx almost allowed an important business deal to crash because he refused to take the oath on the Bible. Lafargue, Marx's son-in-law, had become a refugee in London from the Commune and had founded a photolithography and engraving firm in which Marx became a partner — naturally financed by Engels. Lafargue filed a lawsuit against one of his partners over a patent problem, and Marx, the new partner, ultimately took over the case. To avoid the embarrassment of a public appearance in court by an ex-Communard and the leader of European socialism, the case was submitted to an arbitrator who records the incident in his memoirs as follows:

Before they gave evidence I required them in due form to be sworn on the Bible, as the law required for legal testimony. This filled both of them with horror. Karl Marx protested that he would never so degrade himself. Le Moussu said that no man should ever accuse him of such an act of meanness. For half an hour they argued and protested, each refusing to be sworn first in the presence of the other. At last I obtained a compromise, that the witnesses should simultaneously "touch the book" without uttering a word. Both seemed to me to shrink from handling the sacred volume, much as Mephistopheles in the Opera shrinks from the Cross. When they got to argue the case, the ingenious Le Moussu won, for Karl Marx floundered about in utter confusion.[10]

From Engels's famous graveside oration to Louis Althusser's studies on Marx, emphasis has always been laid on the fact that Marx had discovered the law of history;[11] but the underestimations of historical potentialities for development should be remembered. Marx's interpretation of historical trends was warped by revolutionary impatience and so he almost invariably arrived at false prognostications. In fact he did exactly that of which he had accused Hegel — allowing actual history, by means of a conjuring trick, to appear as the expression of ideal history. He too scorned the "usual empiricism" and raised it to the level of idealism; but he called it materialism. Admittedly he invariably investigated definite, concrete, material structures of society — but then soared up away from them, above them. History never obeyed his "had to be."

From this too stemmed his total misappreciation of German developments, his alienation and aloofness from the German workers' movement, and the inactivity of his last fifteen years. For instance, he disregarded the fact that, in the efforts at unification between the Lassalleans and the Eisenachers, it was the Lassalleans — written off by him as a moribund sect — who adopted a critical viewpoint, and it was *his own* critical viewpoint. The Eisenachers raised no objection to the draft of the unification program, but at the "West German Workers' Rally" the Lassalleans put forward criticisms tallying largely with those he himself made a little later. "Marx was quite wrong," Franz Mehring says; "there could be no more fundamental misjudgment of the matter."[12] From this point onward until his death Marx was the scholar in retreat, the man of private means, almost without contact with the outside world of reality: "What you write about the Germans does not surprise me in the least. It is just the same here. Engels and I have accordingly withdrawn totally from the crew (and so had Lessner). The only exception is a German worker who is a friend of mine but whose name for the moment escapes me. . . ."[13]

To his wife's relief the domestic turmoil caused by the Communard refugees had ceased and he lived in a mixture of idleness, comfort — and suspicion. He only "received" unwillingly and with decreasing frequency; German visitors had to present their credentials in writing before they were allowed in. Engels was the only permanent visitor. He generally arrived about noon, the time at which Marx's working day ended. They lunched together; after lunch Marx would lie down and then go for a walk. Engels would frequently return in the afternoon for interminable argument and discussion of what they had read; Marx, for instance, read Aeschylus afresh every year. Owing to his lack of appetite and liver complaint Marx liked dinner to consist of highly seasoned food — caviar, smoked fish, heavy wines and champagne. Then he would sit with Engels till midnight over a bottle of rum.

Even with Engels conversation seldom turned to Germany. When Engels later visited Germany (in 1893) he was forced to admit how totally strange, novel, and surprising he found Berlin; it was by no means a poverty-stricken city but economically booming, with a large, well-organized workers' movement that, again to his astonishment, had won certain rights and privileges. Bismarck's social legislation had already established disability and old age insurance for workers and a fairly comprehensive "Workers' Sickness Insurance."[14]

The Kaiser had been forced to promulgate and sign these laws almost under pressure from Bismarck; Eugen Richter, leader of the left-wing Liberals, had called the draft of the accident insurance law "no longer socialist but communist."[15] Bismarck had to use the authority of the Kaiser, who was forced to send a personal message to the Reichstag in 1881 recommending the law. This did not help (the law was only passed in amended form) nor was the Kaiser really behind it. "The soup tureen is now full," he said, with the same moral insensitivity that led Wilhelm II to say on the outbreak of World War I: "I have not willed it."[16] All this went on entirely uninfluenced by the author of *Capital*. Werner Richter, Bismarck's biographer, writes:

If government circles in Berlin knew about Marx at all, they did so only because in some astounding way he, a Jewish petit bourgeois and grandson of a rabbi, had succeeded in marrying the daughter of the ultraconservative Prussian Minister von Westphalen and carrying her off to a dismal bohemian existence. After his death in 1883 he became a totally uninteresting figure and was quickly forgotten. At this period no one would have dreamed that his fantasies would one day acquire world-shaking potential.[17]

Gone were the days when Jenny Marx, clearly alluding to Engels and Lafargue, had lamented: "Unfortunately someone is always coming to bother

Mohr; one could hate them for it."[18] Now he lived in a small circle, respectably and pleasantly.

Marx's study with its lovely view over the park, its walls lined with books, its fireplace, the leather sofa on which he used to rest, his cigars, pipe-cleaning gear, photographs of his family, Engels, and Wilhelm Wolff, and the inevitable piles of matches from his cigars or pipes which were always going out ("*Capital* will not bring in enough money to pay for the cigars I smoked when I was writing it")[19] was the comfortable workroom of a scholar who had made his name.

As far as the general company he kept was concerned he was undiscriminating and capricious; he himself found it strange that "one cannot well live altogether without company and that, when you get it, you try hard to rid yourself of it."[20] The curiosity that the "Red Terror Doctor" had excited ever since his support for the Commune, he found flattering but at the same time tiresome. He took no part in demonstrations or meetings. When, however, at the instance of Queen Victoria's eldest daughter, wife of the German Crown Prince, Sir Mountstuart Grant Duff, the M.P., invited him to the exclusive Devonshire Club, he accepted with alacrity. The report by his distinguished and curious host gives a picture of a well-dressed private gentleman:

He is a short, rather small man with grey hair and beard which contrasts strangely with a still dark moustache. The face is somewhat round; the forehead well shaped and filled up — the eye rather hard but the whole expression rather pleasant than not, by no means that of a gentleman who is in the habit of eating babies in their cradles. . . . His talk was that of a well-informed, nay learned man — much interested in Comparative Grammar which had led him into the Old Slavonic and other out-of-the-way studies. . . . It was all very *positif*, slightly cynical — without any appearance of enthusiasm — interesting and often, as I thought, showing very correct ideas when conversing on the past and the present, but vague and unsatisfactory when he turned to the future. . . . It will not be Marx who, whether he wishes it or not, will turn the world upside down.[21]

"Private gentleman" was the way Marx described himself on his first trip to Karlsbad.[22] For years his friend Dr. Gumpert had been ordering him off to all sorts of seaside resorts and spas — primarily Harrogate — and he had now finally recommended Karlsbad. Independently of Gumpert, Dr. Myrtle, the Scottish watering-place doctor, had also urgently advised Karlsbad for Tussy, who was near a nervous breakdown, even more than for Marx himself. So in autumn 1874 they set forth for the spa, then still in Austria. In the Karlsbad list of visitors in 1874 entry 220 reports the arrival of Wilhelm Marx, Austro-Hungarian Police President of Vienna, with his wife Louise; he took rooms in the Union, facing the gardens. Immediately below this entry comes "Herr Ivan Turgenev," writer from Russia, who took rooms in the King of England on the Schlossplatz.

Camouflage? In fact no. This was one of the curious coincidences which history *too* can provide; in fact the police potentate of the same name arrived a few days before Marx, a coincidence that was to be repeated annually. Turgenev never set eyes on Marx, although he was also living on the Schlossplatz and they could have seen each other through the windows. On August 10 Marx had written to Kugelmann: "I cannot start from here before the 15th August (Saturday) and shall take about four days to get to our destination, since Tussy must not exert herself too much. Salut."[23]

This was destined to be the last letter Kugelmann ever received from Marx. As in other cases this much-trumpeted friendship with the Hannover doctor was a curious relationship. Marx had come to know him through Freiligrath, who had recommended Kugelmann to him on December 3, 1862, as "an intelligent, aspiring man, full of energy and goodwill."[24] They became pen friends; Kugelmann was a fervent admirer of Marx and possessed the only complete collection of all Marx's writings, which Marx himself and later Engels also had to borrow since they had failed to keep many pamphlets and brochures. Kugelmann turned into a sort of correspondence bureau in Germany; for years German contacts were routed through him and he gave Marx reports on political and economic developments in Germany. Marx graciously accepted his extravagant adoration, installed the bust of Jupiter which Kugelmann presented to him in his study, and hung over the chimney-piece the piece of wallpaper rescued for him by Kugelmann when Leibniz's house in Hannover was pulled down. Marx even spent his first "vacation" after delivery of the manuscript of *Capital* with the Kugelmann family in Hannover and his letters show that he was relaxed, almost gay, and was enjoying being fussed over.

At the same time, however, Kugelmann got on his nerves. He found Kugelmann's behavior at home, where he was half family dictator and half reformist revolutionary, repellent. There was, however, another more conclusive cause of irritation: in the autumn of 1866 Marx had asked Kugelmann for money or, alternatively, whether he could make discreet arrangements for a favorable loan of some 1,000 taler;[25] Kugelmann passed this on to his friend Engels who was better off, never suspecting that Engels was the permanent standby; Marx, who obviously intended this contribution to be *additional* to those of Engels and made without his knowledge, reacted with extreme irritation and hauled Kugelmann over the coals. He never forgave Kugelmann this "presumption." Thenceforth he made use of Kugelmann for all sorts of menial services but there could be no further question of friendship.

One of these little services was to find rooms in Karlsbad. Kugelmann arrived a few days ahead, a fact that did not seem to fill Marx with enthusiasm, took rooms in the Haus Germania, and awaited "with fervent passion" the arrival of his adored master. Among the entries for Sunday August 22, 1874, in the "Carlsbad Visitors List," is the following, number 238: "13 316 — Herr Charles Marx, private gentleman, with daughter Eleanor, from London — residing: "Germania" — Schlossberg, arrived 19 August."[26]

Although not one of the smarter hotels like Turgenev's, it was still too expensive for Marx; he solaced himself, however, with the thought that a "better address" might mollify the police. It was, in fact, a modest hotel-pension, very different from the Olympia Palace Hotel that now occupies the site at 11 Zamecky vrch; a plaque records the great man's visit, however. To his vexation he found that, having registered as "private gentleman," he had to pay a double rate of tax for his cure. Perhaps the view from their two rooms was some compensation; looking out at the back across the slope the white Hubertusberg was visible, and on sunny afternoons the ladies who worked there could be seen driving out in two-horse cabs for their walk along the Tepl, gaily dressed and with brightly colored parasols.[27]

The cure did Karl Marx good. He studiously obeyed all the orders — drinking the spring water, going for a walk, cutting down his drinking. During this first visit, as on subsequent occasions, he lived the comfortable, leisurely life of a retired, highly educated senior civil servant. His letters are contemplative — "there are no birds in the woods here. Birds are healthy creatures and do not like the mineral-laden atmosphere";[28] the letters are also full of malicious tittle-tattle, which Marx always liked. During one year's visit his letters contained little other than gossip about the youngest of Liszt's three illegitimate daughters, whose mother was the same Countess d'Agoult with whom Herwegh had gone about in Paris; her name was Cosima and she had divorced Hans von Bülow, the Munich conductor, and recently married Wagner:

One is everywhere plagued with the question: What do you think of Wagner? He is entirely characteristic of these upstart Prussian-German court musicians; a harmonious foursome lives together in Bayreuth — Wagner, his wife (recently divorced from Bülow), the cuckolded Bülow and Liszt, father-in-law to both of them; they hug, kiss, worship each other and have a good time. When one also remembers that Liszt is a Catholic monk and that Madame Wagner (christian name Cosima) is his "natural" daughter by Madame d'Agoult (Daniel Stern), one could barely dream up a better operatic libretto for Offenbach than the patriarchal relationships of this family group. The affairs of this group — like the Nibelungen — could be presented in a tetralogy.[29]

Marx went about with cultured bourgeois with whom he went for his regulation walks or conversed over wine in the evenings; there was Otto

Knille, the historical painter, originator of patriotic frescoes and friezes and well endowed with official commissions; there was Simon Deutsch, who had once quarreled with Marx because he had rejected the radical ideas of 1848 (he was now a banker and they made it up); there was Professor Herrmann Friedberg from Breslau and W. A. Freund, the gynecologist from Silesia who had been called William Alexander after the Humboldt brothers; there was Moritz Traube, the famous chemist and discoverer of the Traube cells, the links between organic and inorganic life. Marx later asked him for certain information for Engels' *Dialectics of Nature*.[30] It was a life of cultured academic conversation, easygoing but malicious gossip, and mild flirtations, one of which was clearly between Eleanor and the son of the spa doctor, Professor Leopold Fleckles. Both father and son were doctors but they also dabbled in the literary field and Eleanor found them "really very witty";[31] Fleckles Senior edited the popular *Sprudelsteine,* a collection of articles on Karlsbad "affairs"; Fleckles Junior edited *Sprudel, Allgemeines deutsches Badejournal* (General German Spa Journal). In this, on August 30, 1874, appeared a "denunciation" that alerted the police to the presence of Marx: "(Telegram from Sprudel). Marx, for years Head of the International, and the Polish Count Plater, leader of the Russian Nihilists, have arrived in Carlsbad for a cure."[32]

Marx took this as rather a joke, particularly "since I have the municipality's receipt showing tax for the cure as paid";[33] this appears in the same letter to Engels in which he complains of the vexatious Kugelmann's continual fault-finding and boorish ways. In the following year the cry had become: "I find the absence of my personal physician Kugelmann very beneficial to my health."[34] The "identification" given in this ridiculous rag did in fact result in Marx's being put under police surveillance (of which he knew nothing) — the "Magic Mountain" as a Punch and Judy show with its villainous policeman. On September 1, 1875, a report was dispatched from Karlsbad by "Veith, Austro-Hungarian Regency Counsellor and District Headman" to the "Senior Austro-Hungarian Regency Presidium in Prague," starting "Ref: Behavior of Charles *Max* present here for a cure" (in the file someone had corrected "Max" to "Marx" in pencil).[35] The dreaded Head of the International and bloodthirsty leader of the Commune was credited with peaceable behavior giving rise to no serious suspicions. Nevertheless Prague admonished the worthy Counsellor:

While taking note of the report of 1 September ult, J.Z81/praes, concerning the presence in Karlsbad of Dr. Charles Marx from London, I request Your Excellency to keep the behavior of the above-named under unobtrusive but continuous observation during his stay particularly in so far as his habitual social contacts are concerned and to report to me forthwith in the event of any noteworthy developments.[36]

But there was little occasion for further comment. During his third stay in Karlsbad in 1876 it was officially reported that Marx was not concerned in any conspiratorial conclave. On the contrary, in the previous year a major biographical article had appeared in the *Sprudel,* in its different way as silly as the earlier "Telegram." Marx, however, was flattered, as he was later in December 1881 when Ernest Belfort Bax's first full biography appeared and was announced on large placards all over London's West End. This was clearly the publication to which Tussy was referring in a letter to Liebknecht written shortly before her suicide: "Mohr spoke of a very good article . . . perhaps M.O. in D can tell us more about it."[37] At the time Liebknecht did not know that "M.O. in D" meant Max Oppenheim, a manufacturer with whom Marx had become friendly during his time in Karlsbad and who had addresses in Prague and Dresden; he also did not know that she was in fact referring to a leaflet entitled "Carl Marx" published in *Sprudel* on September 29, 1875 by Julius Walter. Julius Walter was the pseudonym of Tussy's "spa boy friend," Dr. Ferdinand Fleckles Junior.

Every comedy has its punch line. When Marx could no longer travel to the Continent owing to Bismarck's policy, he nevertheless hoped that his wife, who was seriously ill, might go to take a cure. In November 1880 he indicated as much in a letter to Dr. Fleckles,[38] to whom he had sent a signed copy of the French edition of *Capital.* A few months later, on July 8, 1881, there arrived at the Germania on the Schlossplatz "Frau Cäcilie Marx from London, wife of a rabbi, with daughter Zillach."

But again it was no camouflage. Jenny, the Prussian aristocrat, had no more registered herself as the wife of a rabbi than Karl Marx, the descendant of rabbis, had camouflaged himself as a Police President. The fact that they were namesakes was purely coincidental. Jenny Marx, who had been suffering from a severe liver complaint for years, never saw Karlsbad. Six months after this "mistake" she was dead.

"MANKIND IS SHORTER BY A HEAD"

The last ten years of Karl Marx's life have rightly been described as a slow death. The house was empty, with two daughters living in Paris. All Laura Lafargue's three children were dead; Charles, her firstborn, nicknamed "Schnaps," had only reached the age of three. Jenny Longuet's first child, also named Charles after his grandfather, had died in July 1874 aged only ten months. Eleanor was moody, depressed, and striving for a career of her own. Politically Marx was so completely isolated that the German Party very nearly refused to publish Engels's most important polemic, his "Anti-Dühring." Eugen Dühring was a dubious but clearly fascinating figure among the socialistically inclined Berlin intelligentsia of the 1870s. He was a freelance lecturer who had lost his sight early, half sectarian leader, half social prophet, and an amorphous audience of political radicals gathered around his rostrum. In his public lectures he paid tribute to Marat, Babeuf, and the Commune — and brushed aside Fichte and Hegel, Marx and Lassalle. He proclaimed "last-resort truths" apparently pointing the way for the social-democrat movement which, in view of its increasing practical achievements, could afford to disregard theory or "hair-splitting."

Marx was already so far divorced from developments in Germany that he took no notice of Dühring's attacks on him and made light of warnings from Liebknecht that his ideology was in danger of adulteration; he refused to take issue with Dühring on the grounds that the whole matter was too trivial. Engels, on the other hand, launched an attack on the Berlin lecturer's "system-creating truths" in a series of articles, the first of which appeared in *Vorwärts*. At the General Socialist Congress held in Gotha from May 27 to 29, 1877, however, a statement was issued that "Articles as for example Engels' criticism of Dühring published in recent months are without interest for the majority of readers of *Vorwärts* and in the future must stay out of the Party's central organ."[39] An interminable debate ensued on the utility or futility of such "professorial quarrels," and the tone of Engels's articles was censured. Bebel eventually produced a compromise.[40]

Liebknecht, though singled out for special attack by Engels — he "adds insult to injury"[41] — defended him; in view of his position and achievements Engels could hardly be dictated to regarding the length of his articles. A compromise was reached that the second and third sections should be published in the scientific supplement to *Vorwärts*. This was in fact the most important treatise on scientific socialism and exerted far more influence than *Capital*. Engels subsequently cut it down, selecting three chapters from the original, which had appeared with the sarcastic title *Herr Eugen Dühring's Revolution in Science*. The chapters were translated by Paul Lagargue and appeared in the *Revue socialiste* in the spring of 1880; in the same year they were published as a brochure, *Socialisme utopique et scientifique*. A German edition did not appear for another two years. From the Preface[42] — written by Marx for the French edition and Engels for the German — it is quite clear that Marx did *not* contribute to this book.

Marx's capacity for work had gone. His wonderful brain was no longer functioning properly. The voice that had once called so vigorously for vengeance and appealed for the use of force was now indistinct. He complained to Engels about a "clouding of the mind";[43] his letters were no longer written in his usual current slang but in ungrammatical German: "I hope that Tussy will not finally frivol away her health, that my Cacadou, alias little

Laura, is still blooming because she is subjected to so much bodily exertion. From Paris still no answer to me."[44]

The fact that Marx clearly realized the state he was in leaves an eerie impression on the reader; he even described it — but making exactly the same mistakes as those described: "Mon cher, you like other family members, will have noticed my mistakes in orthography, construction and bad grammar; in my very bewildered state I always notice them, but only *post festum*."[45]

The helplessness and loneliness of his letters from Algeria, the piteous tone of his descriptions of his ailments or of the countryside — Marx had never been particularly interested in scenery — were all signs of decline, bottle post.

Illness had been gnawing at his wife for years and Jenny suffered increasingly intolerable pain. When this was diagnosed as incurable cancer of the liver, the doctors abandoned the struggle and even allowed her one more journey to Paris to see her daughters. In the summer of 1881 the parents made their last "excursion" together, from which Marx returned very ill with pleurisy, bronchitis, and inflammation of the lungs. Eleanor describes the two of them, both aware that the end was near: "Moor once more got the better of his illness. Never shall I forget the morning when he felt strong enough to go into mother's room. When they were together they were both young again — she a young girl and he a loving youth, both on the threshold of life, not an old man devastated by illness and an old dying woman parting from each other for ever."[46]

Marx was so weak that he did not even go to his wife's funeral; her last wish had been that she be buried without ceremony. He had watched her sinking slowly but in remarkable peace, "her eyes fuller, more beautiful, lighter than ever."[47] Her last words, oddly enough spoken in English, were addressed to her Karl. On that December 2, 1881, Engels, the family friend said at Jenny Marx's graveside: "Moor is also dead."[48]

Little more than a year remained to Karl Marx, and it was a year of aimless wandering, searching for the life that was gone. His time too was running out. He felt himself "doubly crippled,"[49] morally by the loss of his wife and physically by his increasing breathing troubles with thickening of the pleura and inflammation of the windpipe; in fact he was in an advanced stage of tuberculosis. In January 1882 he took refuge in the Isle of Wight, but his bronchial catarrh became worse and Eleanor, who went with him, was in such low water that he was looking after her. She summoned a female friend, which Marx found hurtful. Jenny was overwhelmed with anxiety about her marriage, which was becoming increasingly fragile, and she was afflicted by cancer of the bladder and tuberculosis. Laura was too selfish to bother about her father. Marx took pains to keep Engels somewhat at a distance, writing even at this stage: "Good old Fred may easily kill someone out of love."[50] The lonely odyssey went further — to Algiers. But instead of spring sunshine and sea breezes he spent two and a half months in cold and rain. Only during the very last weeks did it become so warm that Marx had his hair cut short and his beard shaved; unfortunately he had his photograph taken *before* "sacrificing his prophet's beard and his wig on the altar of some Algerian barber."[51] The whole trip was slightly unreal, like an oriental fairytale — a comfortable journey from Marseille, first class on a ship of the "Paquebots à vapeur des Postes Françaises," arrival in the high-class d'Orient Hotel (later the Algiers Town Hall), the strange company. He described it all to Engels:

A superb position here; my chamber looks out on to the bay of the Mediterranean and Algiers harbor with villas mounting the collines amphitheatre-like (*des ravines au dessous des collines, d'autres collines au dessus*); further away the mountains; among other things one can see the snow-capped peaks behind Matifou, *sur les montagnes de Kabilie, des points culminants du Djurdjura.* (All consist of the above-mentioned limestone collines). At 8 in the morning there is nothing more magical than the panorama, the air, the vegetation — a wonderful mélange of Europe and Africa. Every morning — 10 or 9 — 11 thereabouts my promenade through *des ravines et les collines situées au dessus de la mienne.*[52]

Nevertheless, from his "exile" he made proper fun of Engels, saying that he, after all, had advised him to take the trip "in a fit of African enthusiasm although he knew nothing particular about the place."[53] In fact twenty-five years earlier Engels had written the article on Algeria in the *New American Cyclopaedia.* Jewish humor with a shrug of the shoulders at the futility of everything can often be detected in Marx's confused letters; he took people's advice but put no faith in it. The same attitude of mind is to be seen in a little *"conte drolatique"* that he recorded for his daughter Laura:

A boat man was holding a little skiff ready on a turbulent river. A philosopher, who wanted to get to the opposite bank, got in and the following dialogue took place:
Philosopher: "Boatman, do you know history?" Boatman: "No."
Philosopher: "Then you've wasted half your life." And then: "Have you studied mathematics?" Boatman: "No."
Philosopher: "Then you've wasted more than half your life."
No sooner had the philosopher said this than the wind capsized the boat and both were hurled into the water, the philosopher and the boatman.
Boatman: "Can you swim?" Philosopher: "No."
Boatman: "Then you've wasted the whole of your life."[54]

From Algeria, with his health no better, Marx went to Monte Carlo for a month and in early summer to Argenteuil to stay with the Longuet family;

from there he went to Enghien for the sulphur baths and then to Vevey on
Lake Geneva with Laura, whom he had managed to persuade "to accompany
the old man of the mountains."[55] Laura Lafargue subsequently based her
arguments with Engels about Marx's legacies on this period they spent together and the talks they held. The three months spent in Argenteuil must
have done Marx good, mentally at least, for he was with the family, children
and all three daughters; Eleanor had arrived from London with Lenchen
Demuth to look after Jenny, who was pregnant. The visit could not be too
prolonged, however, for Eleanor and Laura did not get on and the Longuet
marriage was not harmonious; although Jenny was ailing and had four children to look after, her mother-in-law was continually making scenes and
reproaching her for not going out to work to clear the household's debts.

Back in London Marx's health temporarily improved, but fog and damp
soon drove him back to Ventnor in the Isle of Wight — where he again met
fog and damp. Interminable lonely walks only made him sicker and more
melancholy. There could be no thought of work. The final blow came on
January 11, 1883, when Jenny Longuet died at the age of thirty-eight, his
firstborn and the mother of his only grandchildren. Eleanor hardly knew how
to break the news to him: "I felt that I was bringing my father his death
sentence. I racked my brain all the long anxious way to find how I could
break the news to him. But I did not need to; my face gave me away. Mohr
said at once: 'Our Jennychen is dead.' "[56]

Marx's will to live had gone. He was suffering from laryngitis, bronchitis,
and a lung abscess, but he bore it all with stoic equanimity. He took mustard
baths for his cold feet; he swallowed down the loathsome warm milk, a liter a
day, with a quarter bottle of brandy; he dutifully drank some light soup or ate
some other dish lovingly prepared for him by Lenchen; he read French novels. But he grew thinner daily. Comforting words from his doctor caused
Engels to hope that he might get on his feet again.[57] But once more this was
hoping against hope. Three days later Engels was standing in front of the
famous armchair:

Yesterday afternoon at 2:30 — which is the best time for visiting him — I arrived
to find the house in tears. It seemed that the end was near. I asked what had
happened, tried to get to the bottom of the matter, to offer comfort. There had
been only a slight haemorrhage but suddenly he had begun to sink rapidly. Our
good old Lenchen, who had looked after him better than a mother cares for her
child, went upstairs to him and then came down. He was half asleep, she said; I
might come in. When we entered the room, he lay there asleep but never to wake
again. His pulse and breathing had stopped. In those two minutes he had passed
away peacefully and without pain.[58]

Karl Marx was dead.
He had lived life to the full, drained it to the dregs, can one say? He had

marched on to the end, beyond the end, can one say? Study of this man's life with its great promise and its meager fulfillment leads to questions but hardly to answers. Perhaps "Marxism" is merely continuous questioning.

Here again, if one adds it all up, the two aspects are closely allied — the positive and the negative. Today half the globe professes this man's doctrine and so he is inferior in influence only to Christ and Mohammed. But the doctrine itself has become fragmented. Marxism in the second half of the twentieth century should be referred to in the plural.

These are the unanswered questions that make it possible for guns to be pointing at each other along the Chinese-Soviet frontier, for communists to be moldering in prison in Arab states supported by the Soviet Union, for two official communist parties to exist in the "American colony" of Israel, one of them with several seats in parliament, for "putschists" like Fidel Castro and Ché Guevara to call themselves Marxists, for "communists" like Rudi Dutschke to write one of the most penetrating and most fundamental books against Lenin and therefore against the state of affairs in the Soviet Union, for Louis Aragon, one of the best-known communist writers, to call the invasion of Prague by the Warsaw Pact countries a "Biafra of the spirit."

The world has developed differently from the way Marx foretold. Without his whole structure of thinking, however, it might have developed in yet another way. Few people had grasped that at the time of his death.

This man, as "renovated" by Brecht,[59] was neither a splendid fellow nor a gallant comrade-in-arms nor a fighter by nature; he had neither a lion's heart nor a lion's mane; for the biographer he was entrenched behind a barricade of trivialities rather than a desk in his library, though there were no trivialities on the desk; he was neither a prizefighter nor a heroic orator; his money-making efforts were no better than those of a small, permanently bankrupt duchy; he was no Jupiter *tonans;* he was dead. Those who accompanied him on his last journey were few — two old comrades-in-arms, two friends, two relatives, and Wilhelm Liebknecht.[60] The London *Times* carried a short and erroneous report from its Paris correspondent; Reuter's was the first agency to cable the news round the world. The grave, to which hundreds make pilgrimage today and which was daubed and vandalized as late as 1974, was not in its present-day location. Highgate cemetery was a paupers' cemetery and rows of graves were leveled. On several occasions Karl Marx's grave was similarly threatened until eventually, after an offer of transfer to Moscow in 1956, the great-grandchildren arranged a relocation.

His alter ego made the graveside speech; his phrase that "just as Darwin discovered the law of development of organic nature, so Marx discovered the law of development of human history"[61] has been immortalized as testimony to the sixty-five years of a life that interpreted and changed the world like few others. Yet even this law of evolution of history, this alteration of history, was not proof against Karl Marx's skepticism. After a heated argument, first humorous then serious, as to who would do the chores in the state of the future, the lady of the house asked him: "I cannot picture you in an egalitarian period since your inclinations and habits are thoroughly aristocratic." "Neither can I," Marx replied; "those times must come but we must be gone by then."[62]

NOTES ON CURRENCIES

It would have been of interest to give the reader some idea of the size of income that Karl Marx had during his lifetime. An accurate table of rates of exchange cannot be drawn up for this period (1818–1883), however, since there is no method of calculating a rate of exchange applicable to the whole of Germany earlier than 1875. It would be necessary to have precise data of the coinage in which Marx received the sums mentioned in this book since at the time the value of coinage was calculated according to its refined silver content.

A legal rate of exchange was only established by the currency laws of 1871 and 1873 for the two main currencies valid in Germany, the Prussian taler introduced in the eighteenth century (it became the Union taler in 1857) and the South German guilder. The rates fixed were: 1 taler = 3 marks and for the South German guilder "the value of 1 5/7 marks."

On September 22, 1875 — to take effect on January 1, 1876 — the Reich gold currency was introduced into Germany with the mark as the unit of calculation. This superseded the currencies valid in the cities and princedoms which were based on the gold or silver content of the coinage in circulation.

The first quotations of rates of exchange in Berlin were as follows:

3 January 1876	1 pound sterling	20.30 marks
3 January 1876	100 French francs	80.85 marks
3 January 1876	100 Dutch guilder	80.75 marks
16 June 1877	100 Dutch guilder	169.00 marks

It is striking that the value of the Dutch guilder should have more than doubled in a period of barely eighteen months

The following were the rates of exchange quoted in 1885:

In London	1 pound sterling	20.40 marks
In Paris	100 French francs	80.77 marks
In Amsterdam	100 Dutch guilder	168.92 marks

From March 17, 1887, to the end of that year, 100 U.S. dollars could be exchanged for 419.48 marks.

On the basis of the 1975 cost of living index, the sum of RM 1,000 calculated by Willy Haas in 1932 (see p. 124) must be increased to about DM 3,000 (very roughly £ 500 or $1,000).

NOTES

[TRANSLATOR'S NOTE: The German original makes frequent reference to the two major German-language editions of Marx's and Engels's works and correspondence:

Karl Marx, Friedrich Engels "Werke," published by the Institute for Marxism-Leninism, East Berlin, 1956–1968, referred to as MEW,
Karl Marx und Friedrich Engels "Historisch-kritische Gesamtausgabe. Werke/Schriften/Briefe," Leningrad and Moscow, 1927–1935, reprinted 1970, referred to as MEGA.

There is as yet no comparable work in English, though Lawrence & Wishart are producing *Karl Marx, Frederick Engels — Collected Works.* At the time of translation (1976) only vols. 1–6 were available. In particular there is no comprehensive English edition of Marx's and Engels's correspondence.
Wherever possible reference has been made to:

Karl Marx, Frederick Engels Collected Works (above), referred to as ME.
Marx & Engels Selected Works (3 vols.), Moscow: Progress Publishers, 1970, referred to as MESW.
Karl Marx Selected Works (2 vols.), London: Lawrence & Wishart, 1942, referred to as MSW.
Marx & Engels Correspondence 1846–95, London: Lawrence & Wishart, 1934, referred to as *Correspondence.*
Frederick Engels, Paul and Laura Lafargue — Correspondence (3 vols.), translated Yvonne Kapp, Moscow: Foreign Languages Publishing House, 1959, referred to as *Lafargue Correspondence.*
The translation of *Das Kapital* used has been that by Samuel Moore and Edward Aveling, edited by Frederick Engels, Chicago: Charles H. Kerr & Co., 1926.]

· CHAPTER I ·

1. On this subject see Heinz Monz, *Karl Marx. Grundlagen der Entwicklung zu Leben und Werk* (Trier, 1973), p. 242 et seq.
2. Arnold Künzli: *Karl Marx. Eine Psychographie* (Vienna, 1966), p. 58.
3. Monz, op. cit., p. 243 n.17.
4. Ibid., p. 227 et seq.
5. Auguste Cornu, *Karl Marx et Friedrich Engels. Leur vie et leur oeuvre* (Paris, 1954), vol. 1, pp. 53–54.
6. On this subject see Eleonore Sterling, *Er is wie Du. Aus der Frühgeschichte des Antisemitismus in Deutschland (1815–1850)* (Munich, 1956), p. 30.

7. Ibid., pp. 130, 37.

8. Ibid., p. 132.

9. Monz says: "See Submission No. 146/1819 dated 1 October 1819 by Johann Matthias Zell and Bochkoltz, notaries, in State Archives, Koblenz, Section 587, 40 No. 52 and Trier Almanac for 1820." Op. cit., p. 257 n.15.

10. Karl Marx, "Werke und Schriften. Bis Anfang 1844 nebst Briefen und Dokumenten," in *Karl Marx, Friedrich Engels 'Historisch-kritische Gesamtausgabe. Werke/Schriften/Briefe'* (henceforth referred to as MEGA), pt. I, vol. 1, 2nd half-vol., p. 192.

11. Monz refers to "Master Allotment List of owners of and revenues from real estate and buildings in the District of Mertesdorf, Articles 14 and 286 in State Archives, Koblenz, Section 442, No. 872." Op. cit., p. 252 n.74.

12. Cf. Monz, op. cit., p. 255.

13. Ibid., p. 256.

14. Eleanor Marx-Aveling to Wilhelm Liebknecht in Liebknecht, "From Reminiscences of Marx," in *Karl Marx Selected Works* (henceforth referred to as MSW) (London, 1942), vol. 1, p. 130.

15. Ernst Matheus, "Der humanistische Ansatz des jungen Marx," in *Festschrift* (1961), p. 75.

16. Robert Wilbrandt, *Karl Marx. Versuch einer Einführung*, p. 9.

17. Monz (op. cit., p. 241) says: "Numbers of Jews resident in the district (*Regierungsbezirk*) of Trier were:

1816	2819
1823	3330
1834	4280
1843	4781."

18. Monz, op. cit., p. 251 et seq.

19. Eleanor Marx-Aveling: "Karl Marx," in *Mohr und General. Erinnerungen an Marx und Engels* (Berlin, 1964), p. 273.

20. Karl Marx to François Lafargue, Nov. 12, 1866, in *Karl Marx, Friedrich Engels "Werke"* (henceforth referred to as MEW) (East Berlin, 1956–1968), vol. 31, p. 536. The editorial note 548 (op. cit., p. 688) plays the matter down, saying: "Marx's father previously owned a small vineyard on the Moselle." There were in fact several vineyards, they were not small, and he did not own them "previously." His entire holding of land was shown in his estate with his other property. For details see Monz, op. cit., p. 270 et seq.

21. Heinrich Marx to Karl Marx, Nov. 9, 1836, in *Marx Engels Collected Works* (henceforth referred to as ME) vol. 1, p. 663.

22. Monz gives "Submission No. 560/1839 of 8 Nov 1839 and No 436/1840 of 2 Aug. 1840 by Franz Georg Funck, notary in Trier, in State Archives, Koblenz, Section 587, 40 Nos 477–8." Op. cit., p. 281 n.50.

23. Ibid., p. 285.

24. Ibid., p. 97.

25. Künzli, op. cit., p. 68.

26. Monz, op. cit., p. 55 et seq.

27. Ibid., p. 262, nn.18, 19.

28. Ibid., nn.20, 21.

29. Werner Sombart, *Der proletarische Sozialismus* (Jena, 1924), vol. 1, p. 60.

30. Monz, op. cit., p. 261, nn.15, 16; Cornu, op. cit., p. 59; Wolfgang Schwerbrock,

Karl Marx privat. Unbekannte Briefe (Munich, 1962), p. 11 et seq.

31. Franz Mehring (ed.), *Aus dem literarischen Nachlass von Karl Marx, Friedrich Engels und Ferdinand Lassalle. Gesammelte Schriften von Karl Marx und Friedrich Engels 1841 bis 1850*, vol. 1 (March 1814–March 1844), p. 5.

32. Karl Marx to Friedrich Engels, Sept. 17, 1878, MEW, vol. 34, p. 78.

33. Monz, op. cit., p. 229.

34. For school-leaving essay see ME, vol. 1, pp. 7–9; for "Union of Believers," MEGA, pt. I, vol. 1, 2nd half-vol., pp. 171–174.

35. Karl Marx to Friedrich Engels, May 18, 1859, *Marx & Engels Correspondence 1846–1895* (London, 1934), (henceforth referred to as *Correspondence*) p. 123.

36. Karl Marx, "Theses on Feuerbach," *Karl Marx, Frederick Engels Collected Works* (henceforth referred to as MESW) (Moscow, 1970), vol. 1, p. 14. The "Theses" were not published during Marx's lifetime. They appear in his notebook for 1844–1847 under the heading "*1. ad Feuerbach.*"

37. Karl Marx, "The German Ideology," MESW, vol. 1, p. 32.

38. Plato, *Republic*, translated by B. Jowett (Oxford, 1888).

39. Paul Lafargue, "Reminiscences of Marx," MSW, vol. 1, p. 82.

40. From an unpublished graphological memorandum, No. 13615, dated June 12, 1974, written at the author's request by Hans Lamp'l, the Hamburg expert in forensic graphology.

41. Heinrich Marx to Karl Marx, Nov. 8 and 18, 1835, ME, vol. 1, pp. 645, 647–648.

42. Henriette Marx to Karl Marx, Nov. 29, 1835, ibid., pp. 648–649.

43. Heinrich Marx to Karl Marx, Nov. 18–29, 1835, ibid., p. 647.

44. Heinrich Marx to Karl Marx, Mar. 19, 1836, ibid., p. 653.

45. Ibid., pp. 652, 656.

46. Ibid., p. 658.

47. Karl Marx to A. von Brüningk (draft), Oct. 18, 1852, MEW, vol. 28, p. 556.

48. Karl Marx to Ferdinand Lassalle, June 10, 1858, *Correspondence*, p. 111.

49. ME, vol. 1, p. 665

50. Leopold Schwarzschild, *The Red Prussian* (London, 1948), p. 31.

51. ME, vol. 1, p. 704.

52. Mehring, op. cit., p. 11.

53. Henriette Marx to Karl Marx, Sept. 16, 1837, ME, vol. 1, p. 683.

54. Heinrich Marx to Karl Marx, Mar. 2, 1837, ibid., p. 672.

55. Ibid., p. 670.

56. Henriette Marx to Karl Marx, Feb. 10, 1838, ibid., p. 693.

57. Heinrich Marx to Karl Marx, Aug. 12, 1837, ibid., p. 675.

58. Heinrich Marx to Karl Marx, Nov. 17, 1837, ibid., p. 684.

59. Marx himself took these unhappy efforts at inept poetry as a joke; when Laura Lafargue passed them to Franz Mehring, she added: "I should tell you that my father treated these verses with scant respect; whenever my parents spoke of them they laughed outright at these youthful follies." Mehring, op. cit., p. 25 et seq.

60. ME, vol. 1, p. 23.

61. Mehring, op. cit., p. 26 et seq.

62. ME, vol. 1, pp. 525–527.

63. Karl Marx to Jenny Marx, Dec. 15, 1863, MEW, vol. 30, p. 643.

64. Monz, op. cit., p. 231.

65. Ibid., p. 328.

66. Maxim Kovalevsky, "Erinnerungen an Karl Marx," in *Mohr und General*, p. 394.

67. ME, vol. 1, p. 27.
68. Ibid., p. 28.
69. Heinrich Marx to Karl Marx, Feb. 3, 1837, Dec. 28, 1836, ME, vol. 1, pp. 664–665.
70. Jenny von Westphalen to Karl Marx, undated, in Internationaal Instituut voor Sociale Geschiedenes, Amsterdam, catalogue number 3290, letter No. 14. Numbers 3289–3312 in the catalogue cover the period 1836–1843. A letter numbered 14 under catalogue number 3290 is therefore undoubtedly from the early period.
71. Karl Marx to Heinrich Marx, Nov. 10, 1837, ME, vol. 1, p. 10.
72. Ibid., pp. 17–18.
73. Friedrich Engels, "Ludwig Feuerbach and the End of Classical German Philosophy," in K. Marx & F. Engels, *Selected Works* (henceforth referred to as MESW), (Moscow, 1970) vol. 3, p. 337 et seq. In the preface (p. 336) Engels refers to full recognition of Feuerbach's influence as "an undischarged debt of honour."
74. Moses Hess to Berthold Auerbach, Sept. 2, 1841, MEGA, pt. 1, vol. 1, 2nd half-vol., p. 261.
75. Henriette Marx to Karl Marx, Feb. 15/16, 1838, ibid., p. 230.
76. Franz Mehring, *Karl Marx. The Story of his Life* (London, 1936), p. 19.
77. Ibid., p. 23.
78. Henriette Marx to Karl Marx, Oct. 22, 1838, MEGA, pt. 1, vol. 1, 2nd half-vol., p. 233.
79. Bruno Bauer to Karl Marx, Mar. 1, 1840, ibid., p. 237.
80. MEW, Supp. vol. 1, p. 215.
81. ME, vol. 1, p. 85.
82. Ibid., p. 705.
83. See D. Ryazanoff, foreword to MEGA, pt. 1, vol. 1, 1st half-vol., p. xxx. David Baumgardt in his study "Uber den 'verloren geglaubten' Anhang zu Karl Marxens Doktordissertation" (in *Gegenwartsprobleme der Soziologie* [Potsdam, 1949]) contests Ryazanoff's theory and reconstructs the layout of the dissertation.
84. Ryazanoff, op. cit., p. xxxiv; ME, vol. 1, p. 106.
85. Henriette Marx to Karl Marx, May 29, 1840, MEGA, pt. 1, vol. 1, 2nd half-vol., p. 244.
86. Karl Marx to Arnold Ruge, July 9, 1842, ME, vol. 1, p. 389.
87. Henriette Marx to Karl Marx, May 29, 1840, MEGA, pt. 1, vol. 1, 2nd half-vol., p. 244 et seq.
88. Bruno Bauer to Karl Marx, Apr. 12, 1841, ibid., p. 251 et seq.
89. Bruno Bauer to Karl Marx, July 25, 1840, ibid., p. 244.
90. ME, vol. 1, p. 175.
91. Manfred Kliem (ed.), *Karl Marx. Dokumente seines Lebens 1818–1883* (Leipzig, 1970), p. 242.
92. Ibid., p. 121.
93. Mehring, *Life*, p. 37.
94. D. Ryazanoff, foreword to MEGA, pt. 1, vol. 1, 1st half-vol., p. LXII.
95. Ibid.
96. Ibid., p. LXIII.
97. ME, vol. 1, p. 283.
98. Mehring, *Life*, p. 48.
99. ME, vol. 1, pp. 215–221.
100. Karl Marx to Arnold Ruge, Nov. 30, 1842, ibid., pp. 394–395.
101. Ibid., p. 393.
102. *Rheinische Zeitung*, Dec. 23, 1842.

103. Karl Heinzen, "Erlebtes," in Mehring, *Gesammelte Schriften* (Berlin, 1961), vol. 4, p. 423 et seq.

104. *Mannheimer Abendzeitung*, Dec. 28, 1843, MEGA, pt. 1, vol. 1, 1st half-vol., pp. 152–153.

105. Karl Marx to Ludwig Kugelmann, Jan. 11, 1868, *Letters to Kugelmann* (London, 1941), p. 58.

106. Heinzen, op. cit., p. 429.

107. "Unmasking the Stalin Terror" — text of Khrushchev's speech to the Twentieth Congress of Communist Party of USSR, Feb. 25, 1956, issued by Eastern Bureau of German Social Democrat Party, 1956, p. 46.

108. Report dated Mar. 2, 1843, MEGA, pt. 1, vol. 1, 1st half-vol., p. 151.

109. Karl Marx to Arnold Ruge, Mar. 13, 1843, ME, vol. 1, p. 399.

110. Betty Lucas, "Ein Erinnerungsblatt aus London," in *Leipziger Sonntagsblatt*, Sept. 14, 1862.

111. Marriage contract between Karl Marx and Jenny von Westphalen, June 21, 1854, ME, vol. 3, p. 572.

112. *Internationaal Instituut voor Sociale Geschiedenes*, Amsterdam, catalogue No. I F/139.

113. Karl Marx to Friedrich Engels, June 26, 1854, MEW, vol. 28, p. 371.

114. Karl Marx to Arnold Ruge, Jan. 25, 1843, ME, vol. 1, pp. 397–398.

115. Bruno Bauer, *Vollständige Geschichte der Parteikämpfe in Deutschland* (Berlin, 1847), vol. 1, p. 151.

116. "Kreuznach Notes" (1843), in MEGA, pt. 1, vol. 1, 1st half-vol., p. 98. They refer to: Heinrich, *History of France*; Ludwig, *History of Last Fifty Years*; Daru, *Venice*; Lacretelle, *History of France*; Rousseau; Bailleul, *Madame de Staël*; Brougham, *Poland*; Montesquieu; Russell, *History of British Government*; Lappenberg, *History of England*; Schmidt, *History of France*; Chateaubriand; Lancizolle, *July Days*; Wachsmuth, *History of France*; Ranke, *Reformation*; Ranke, *Contemporary History and Politics*; Lingard, *History of England*; Geijer, *Sweden*; Pfister, *History of Teutons*; Moser, *Patriotic Fantasia*; Jouffroy, *Principle of Heredity*; Hamilton, *North America*; Machiavelli.

117. Karl Marx to Arnold Ruge, Mar. 13, 1843, ME, vol. 1, pp. 398–399.

118. Karl Marx to Ludwig Feuerbach, 1843, 20 (?), Oct., ME, vol. 3, pp. 350–351.

119. This seems likely from the date of Feuerbach's letter (Oct. 25, 1843). Marx moved to Paris at the end of October.

120. *Deutsch-Französische Jahrbücher*, Karl Marx to Arnold Ruge, May 1843, ME, vol. 3, p. 134.

121. Ibid., p. 138.

122. Ibid., p. 145.

123. Ibid., p. 144.

124. Ibid.

125. Ibid., p. 142.

126. Ibid., pp. 142–143.

127. Ibid., p. 175. The phrase "opium *for* the people" is often used in trite atheist propaganda, but it is not to be found in Marx's writings; the distortion postulates a dispensing hierarchy, and this Marx did not intend.

128. Ibid., p. 182.

129. Ibid., p. 154.

130. Ibid., p. 156.

131. Ibid., p. 167.

132. Ibid., p. 169.
133. Sterling, op. cit., p. 39. Simon Dubnow, *Weltgeschichte des jüdischen Volkes* (Berlin, 1926), vol. 3, p. 73.
134. ME, vol. 3, p. 174.
135. Künzli, op. cit., p. 209 et seq.
136. Ibid., p. 212 et seq.

· CHAPTER 2 ·

1. See comparison of passport details and contemporary descriptions in Manfred Kliem (ed.), *Karl Marx. Dokumente seines Lebens 1818–1883* (Leipzig, 1970), p. 15 et seq.
2. Mayall's records disappeared. In the late nineteenth century his heirs sold one or two photographs of Marx to the Photographische Gesellschaft Charlottenburg, which was registered as copyright holder until the 1920s.
3. Paul Nerrlich (ed.), *Arnold Ruges Briefwechsel und Tagebuchblätter aus den Jahren 1825 bis 1880* (Berlin, 1886), vol. 1 (1825–1847), p. 343.
4. Nerrlich, op. cit., vol. 2 (1848–1880), p. 346.
5. Walther Victor, *Marx und Heine. Tatsache und Spekulation in der Darstellung ihrer Beziehungen* (Berlin, 1951), p. 44.
6. Karl Marx to Friedrich Engels, May 8, 1856, MEW, vol. 29, p. 53.
7. Heinrich Heine to Moses Moser, Apr. 22, 1829, in *Heinrich Heine, 'Briefe,'* ed. Friedrich Hirth, vol. 1, p. 272.
8. See F. H. Eisner, "Ein Aufsatz Heines in 'Le Globe', Februar 1832?" in *Zeitschrift für deutsche Literaturgeschichte*, 1959 issue, pp. 421–425.
9. Heinrich Heine, *Sämtliche Werke*, ed. Hans Kaufmann (Munich, 1964), vol. 8, p. 107.
10. Cf. Leo Kreutzer, *Heine und der Kommunismus* (Kleine Vandenhoek Series 322). This piece of research is noteworthy since it is the first account and analysis of the events outlined here.
11. "Gegen Carl Heinzen," in *Deutsche Brüsseler Zeitung*, Oct. 28, 1847, MEW, vol. 4, p. 341.
12. Heine, *Sämtliche Werke*, vol. 11, p. 243.
13. Ibid., p. 162.
14. Kreutzer, op. cit., p. 17.
15. See H. H. Houben (ed.), "Erinnerungen von Alex. Weill," in *Gespräche mit Heine*, p. 465: "I was an honest republican. When I saw, however, how the scum of my party, cobblers and fellows who mended chamber pots, mangled me in their filthy pamphlets, used the familiar 'du' with me, cursed me for a traitor and a Jew and were only waiting to drag me to the guillotine as soon as these dullards came to power; when I found this brood of frogs creeping out of hedges and marshes, listened to them croaking in the undergrowth and realised that their republican cackle was far more valuable and enduring than my nightingale songs — then I turned away in disgust and supported the constitutional monarchy which is more than enough for me." Quoted from Auguste Cornu, *Karl Marx et Friedrich Engels*, vol. 3, p. 29.
16. Heinrich Heine, *Works* (Heinemann, 1893), vol. 5, pp. 96–97.
17. Kreutzer, op. cit., p. 19.
18. Heine, *Works*, vol. 8, pp. 10–11.

19. Heine, *Sämtliche Werke*, vol. 13, p. 245 et seq.
20. Cornu, op. cit., p. 2 et seq. The prospect of an 1,800-franc annual income was enough for Marx to move to Paris with his family.
21. Anold Ruge to his mother, Nerrlich, op. cit., vol. 1, p. 349.
22. Arnold Ruge to Fröbel, June 4, 1844, ibid., p. 358.
23. Arnold Ruge to his mother, ibid., p. 349.
24. Arnold Ruge to Fröbel, ibid.
25. Karl Marx, "Letters from the *Deutsch-Französische Jahrbücher*," ME, vol. 3, p. 144.
26. Ibid., p. 133.
27. Ibid., p. 145.
28. Ibid., p. 144.
29. Ibid., pp. 201–202.
30. Karl Marx, "Critical Marginal Notes," ME, vol. 3, p. 197.
31. Friedrich Engels, "On the History of the Communist League," MESW, vol. 3, p. 178.
32. Friedrich Engels to Franz Mehring, Sept. 28, 1892, MEW, vol. 38, p. 480 et seq.
33. Probably all the parts have not been published yet; the Marx-Engels Institute in Moscow has admitted that it has not published all the extracts. On this subject see David J. Rosenberg, *Die Entwicklung der ökonomischen Lehren von Marx und Engels in den vierziger Jahren des 19 Jahrhunderts* (Berlin, 1958), p. 83.
34. In particular Moses Hess, *Einundzwanzig Bogen aus der Schweiz* and *Über das Geldwesen*; Wilhelm Schulz, *Die Bewegung der Produktion.*
35. Karl Marx, "Economic and Philosophic Manuscripts," ME, vol. 3, pp. 269 et seq., 294.
36. Ibid., p. 304 et seq.
37. Karl Marx, "Critical Marginal Notes," ME, vol. 3, p. 189.
38. Ibid., p. 205.
39. Arnold Ruge to K. M. Fleischer, July 9, 1844, Nerrlich, op. cit., vol. 1, p. 359.
40. Friedrich Engels to Karl Marx, early Oct. 1844, MEW, vol. 27, p. 8.
41. Friedrich Engels to Karl Marx, Jan. 20, 1845, ibid., p. 16.
42. Friedrich Engels to Karl Marx, ibid.
43. See Cornu, op. cit., vol. 3, p. 247 et seq.
44. Arnold Ruge to K. M. Fleischer, May 27, 1845, Nerrlich, op. cit., vol. 1, p. 395.
45. Ibid.
46. Arnold Ruge to Fröbel, Nov. 1844, ibid., p. 379.
47. Quoted from Cornu, op. cit., vol. 1, p. 250.
48. Friedrich Engels to Karl Marx, Nov. 19, 1844, MEW, vol. 27, p. 9.
49. Secret State Archives, folio 77, No. 500, quoted from Cornu, op. cit., vol. 1, p. 7.
50. Heinrich Börnstein, *Fünfundsiebzig Jahre in der Alten und Neuen Welt. Memoiren eines Unbedeutenden* (Leipzig, 1881), vol. 1, p. 357.
51. Karl Marx to Johann Baptist Schweitzer, in *Sozial-Demokrat* 1865, Nos. 16, 17, 18, *Correspondence*, p. 171.
52. Franziska Kugelmann, "Kleine Züge zu dem grossen Charakterbild von Karl Marx," in *Mohr und General*, p. 297.
53. Pierre-Joseph Proudhon to P. Ackermann, Nov. 23, 1843, in *Lafargue Correspondence*, vol. 2, pp. 112 et seq.
54. Karl Marx, "Communism and the *Augsburg Allgemeine Zeitung*," ME, vol. 1, p. 220.
55. Karl Marx, "Critical Marginal Notes," ME, vol. 3.

56. Karl Marx to Johann Baptist Schweitzer, in *Social-Demokrat* 1865, Nos. 16, 17, 18, *Correspondence*, p. 175.
57. Karl Marx to P. W. Annenkov, Dec. 28, 1846, *Correspondence*, p. 372.
58. Maxim Kovalevski, "Erinnerungen an Karl Marx," in *Mohr und General*, p. 402.
59. Karl Marx to P. W. Annenkov, Dec. 28, 1846, *Correspondence*, p. 6.
60. Cornu, op. cit., p. 7 et seq.
61. Ibid., p. 254.
62. Jenny Marx, "Kurze Umrisse eines bewegten Lebens," in *Mohr und General*, p. 205 et seq.
63. Karl Marx to Heinrich Heine, Feb. 1, 1845, quoted from Victor, op. cit., p. 59.

· CHAPTER 3 ·

1. ME, vol. 4, p. 676.
2. Archives of the Belgian Sûreté Publique, Karl Marx dossier, Enclosure 10. Marx's statement reads: "To obtain permission to reside in Belgium I agree to pledge myself on my word of honour not to publish in Belgium any work on current politics. Dr. Karl Marx." French version in Luc Somerhausen, *L'Humanisme agissant de Karl Marx* (Paris, 1946), p. 77; English version in ME, vol. 4, p. 77.

On the same day the Chief of Police wrote to the Burgomaster of Brussels: "Should it come to your knowledge that he has broken his word or is taking any other action prejudicial to the Prussian government, our neighbour and ally, I request you to report to me forthwith." French version: Enclosure 13, and Somerhausen, ibid. Quoted from Auguste Cornu, *Karl Marx et Friedrich Engels*, vol. 4, p. 210 et seq.
3. Karl Marx to Burgomaster Görtz, Oct. 17, 1845, ME, vol. 4, p. 678: "Your Excellency: I most respectfully request you to obtain for me from the esteemed Royal Government administration in Trier a certificate for emigration to the United States of North America. My discharge papers from Royal Prussian military service are to be found in the office of the Chief Burgomaster in Trier or of the Royal Government administration there. Your Excellency's most obedient servant, Dr Karl Marx."

Karl Marx to Burgomaster Görtz, Nov. 10, 1845, ibid., p. 679:
"Your Excellency: In reply to your esteemed letter of 8th of this month I hereby state that my request of the 17th of the previous month for release from citizenship of the Kingdom of Prussia for the purpose of emigration to the United States of North America related solely to my own person but, *if it should be necessary for granting consent*, I request that the release should be extended to cover my family as well. Brussels, 10 November 1845. Your Excellency's most obedient servant, Dr. Karl Marx."
4. Karl Marx to Friedrich Engels, May 15, 1847, MEW, vol. 27, p. 83.
5. Karl Marx, *Poverty of Philosophy*, ME, vol. 4, p. 182. The phrase comes from George Sand's historical novel *Jean Ziska*.
6. Golo Mann, *The History of Germany Since 1789* (London, 1968), p. 88.
7. "When, in the spring of 1845, we met again in Brussels Marx had already developed his materialist theory of history in its main features from the above-mentioned basis" — Friedrich Engels, "History of the Communist League," MESW, vol. 3, p. 178.
8. Franz Mehring, *Karl Marx. The Story of His Life*, p. 110.

9. Karl Marx and Friedrich Engels, *The German Ideology*, ME, vol. 5, p. 49.
10. Ibid., p. 47.
11. MESW, vol. 3, p. 335.
12. Ludwig Feuerbach, *Essence of Christianity*, trans. Marian Evans (London, 1893), p. 271.
13. Karl Marx to Arnold Ruge, Mar. 13, 1843, ME, vol. 1, p. 400.
14. Karl Marx to Ludwig Feuerbach, Aug. 11, 1844, ME, vol. 3, p. 354.
15. Ludwig Feuerbach to Karl Marx, Oct. 25, 1843, MEGA, pt. 1, vol. 1, 2nd half-vol., p. 317.
16. MESW, vol. 3, p. 335.
17. Ibid., pp. 92, 93, 95.
18. Paul Lafargue, "Reminiscences of Marx," MSW, vol. 1, p. 81.
19. Karl Marx, "Bekenntnisse," in *Mohr und General*, p. 607 et seq.
20. Friedrich Engels, "Bekenntnisse," ibid., p. 609 et seq.
21. Franziska Kugelmann, "Kleine Züge zu dem grossen Charakterbild von Karl Marx," in *Mohr und General*, p. 303.
22. Wilhelm Blos, "Karl Marx als Mensch," in *Die Glocke*, Anno 6, vol. 1 (Issue 5 of 1918), p. 159.
23. Quoted from Werner Sombart, *Der proletarische Sozialismus* (Jena, 1924), vol. 1, p. 67.
24. Quoted in Carl Vogt, *Mein Prozess mit der Allgemeinen Zeitung*, p. 151.
25. Sombart, op. cit., p. 63.
26. Lafargue, op. cit., MSW, vol. 1, pp. 83–84.
27. Ibid., p. 87.
28. Eleanor Marx-Aveling, "Karl Marx. Löse Blätter," in *Mohr und General*, p. 274.
29. Wilhelm Liebknecht, "From Reminiscences of Marx," MSW, vol. 1, p. 121.
30. Louis Fischer, *The Life of Lenin* (London, 1964), p. 65.
31. Wilhelm Blos, *Denkwürdigkeiten eines Sozialdemokraten*, vol. 2, p. 38.
32. Wilhelm Liebknecht, "Karl Marx zum Gedächtnis," in *Mohr und General*, p. 103.
33. D. Ryazanoff (ed.), *Karl Marx. A Symposium*, p. 234.
34. Karl Marx to Friedrich Engels, Nov. 7, 1867, MEW, vol. 31, p. 380.
35. "My wife has unfortunately given birth to a girl, not a boy." Karl Marx to Friedrich Engels, Apr. 2, 1851, MEW, vol. 27, p. 229.

    "Because yesterday . . . my wife was delivered of a bona fide traveller — unfortunately of *the* sex *par excellence*. Had it been a male child, things would be better." Karl Marx to Friedrich Engels, Jan. 17, 1855, MEW, vol. 28, p. 423.

    "*Vivat* the little cosmopolitan. *Il faut peupler le monde des garçons*." Karl Marx to Jenny Longuet, Aug. 19, 1879, MEW, vol. 34, p. 388.

    ". . . as far as I am concerned, I prefer the 'male' sex in children." Karl Marx to Jenny Longuet, Apr. 29, 1881, MEW, vol. 35, p. 186.
36. Wilhelm Liebknecht, in *Mohr und General*, p. 170.
37. Internationaal Instituut voor Sociale Geschiedenes, Amsterdam, catalogue entry D 3303.
38. Karl Marx to Friedrich Engels, July 31, 1851, MEW, vol. 27, p. 293.
39. Karl Marx to Joseph Wedemeyer, Aug. 2, 1851, *Letters to Americans*, p. 24; to Friedrich Engels, June 21, 1854, MEW, vol. 28, p. 370; to Friedrich Engels, Oct. 30, 1856, MEW, vol. 29, p. 81; to Friedrich Engels, Apr. 9, 1857, ibid., p. 123; to Friedrich Engels, July 15, 1858, ibid., p. 340; to Friedrich Engels, Apr. 9, 1863, MEW, vol. 30, p. 340.

40. Karl Marx to Friedrich Engels, Nov. 30, 1868, MEW, vol. 32, p. 217.
41. Karl Marx to Friedrich Engels, June 21, 1854, MEW, vol. 28, p. 370, and Feb. 22, 1858, MEW, vol. 29, p. 284.
42. Liebknecht, "From Reminiscences of Marx," MSW, vol. 1, p. 120.
43. Bert Andreas, *Briefe und Dokumente der Familie Marx aus den Jahren 1862–1873 nebst zwei unbekannten Aufsätzen von Friedrich Engels* (Hannover, 1962) p. 219.
44. Karl Marx to Friedrich Engels, May 7, 1867, MEW, vol. 31, p. 296.
45. Karl Marx to Friedrich Engels, Oct. 19, 1867, ibid., p. 368.
46. Karl Marx to Friedrich Engels, Nov. 24, 1851, MEW, vol. 27, p. 370.
47. See Arnold Künzli, *Karl Marx. Eine Psychographie* (Vienna, 1966), p. 323.
48. The text of the obituary is given in Andreas, op. cit., pp. 245 et seq. Marx's daughter Jenny also wrote an obituary of Flourens in April 1871 using her pseudonym J. Williams. Ibid., p. 247.
49. Jenny Marx to Ferdinand Lassalle, May 5, 1861, in Ferdinand Lassalle: *Nachgelassene Briefe und Schriften*, vol. 3: *Der Briefwechsel zwischen Lassalle und Marx* (Berlin, 1922), p. 359.
50. Karl Marx to Jenny Marx, June 21, 1856, MEW, vol. 29, pp. 532, 535.
51. Liebknecht, in *Mohr und General* op. cit., p. 135.
52. Karl Marx to Ludwig Feuerbach, Aug. 11, 1844, ME, vol. 3, p. 357.
53. Karl Marx, "Herr Vogt," MEW, vol. 14, p. 439.
54. Friedrich Engels, *History of the Communist League*, MESW, vol. 3, p. 176.
55. Ibid.
56. Ibid.
57. Quoted from Martin Hundt, *Wie das "Manifest" endstandt* (Berlin, 1973), p. 23.
58. Arnold Ruge to K. M. Fleischer, July 9, 1844, in Paul Nerrlich (ed.), *Arnold Ruges Briefwechsel und Tagebuchblätter* (Berlin, 1886), vol. 1, p. 359.
59. Wilhelm Weitling. *Garantien der Harmonie und Freiheit*, prologue to 3rd edition, pp. x–xiii, quoted in *Der Bund der Kommunisten. Dokumente und Materalien* (Berlin, 1970), vol. 1, p. 86.
60. Friedrich Engels, *History of the Communist League*, MESW, vol. 3, pp. 177–178.
61. Draft of an address by Karl Schapper on common ownership, *Der Bund der Kommunisten*, p. 102.
62. Wilhelm Weitling to Karl Marx, Friedrich Engels, and Moses Hess, Sept. 22–27, 1845, ibid., p. 253.
63. *Richtlinien Wilhelm Weitlings für die Aufnahme in den Bund der Gerechten* (1842), ibid., p. 135.
64. Wilhelm Weitling, '*Garantien der Harmonie und Freiheit* (1842), ibid., p. 149.
65. Künzli, op. cit., p. 634 et seq.
66. ME, vol. 3, p. 187.
67. Jacob in his blessing said, "Judah is a young lion" and Marx refers to "proletarian lions" — Karl Marx, "*Die Junirevolution*," MEW, vol. 5, p. 134. This article opens with an emphatic statement twisting reality into *his* interpretation of it: "The Paris workers have been *suppressed* by superior force but they have not *succumbed* to it. They have been *beaten* but their opponents have been *vanquished*."
68. Hermann Kriege to Karl Marx, June 9, 1845, quoted in *Der Bund der Kommunisten*, p. 241.
69. Friedrich Engels, *History of the Communist League*, MESW, vol. 3, p. 179.
70. Leopold Schwarzschild, *The Red Prussian* (London, 1948), p. 130.
71. Friedrich Engels, *History of the Communist League*, MESW, vol. 3, p. 181.
72. Ibid., p. 180.

73. Report by P. W. Annenkov on session of Communist Correspondence Committee in Brussels 1846, quoted in *Bund der Kommunisten*, p. 303 et seq.
74. Franz Mehring, *Life*, p. 116.
75. Circular from Communist Correspondence Committee, Brussels, attacking the *Volks-Tribun* edited by Hermann Kriege, May 11, 1846, quoted in *Bund der Kommunisten*, p. 322.
76. Letter from Communist Correspondence Committee London, to Karl Marx in Brussels, June 6, 1846, ibid., p. 347.
77. Letter from Communist Correspondence Committee, London, to Communist Correspondence Committee, Brussels, July 17, 1846, ibid., p. 380.
78. Hundt, op. cit., p. 103.
79. Extracts from record of addresses by Karl Marx and Friedrich Engels to Communist Workers Education Association, London, Nov. 30 and Dec. 7, 1847, quoted in *Bund der Kommunisten*, p. 622.
80. Ibid., p. 623.
81. Karl Marx to Georg Herwegh, Oct. 26, 1847, MEW, vol. 27, p. 470.
82. "When Engels and I first joined the communist secret society we did so only on condition that anything tending to promote superstitious worship of authority be removed from the statutes." Karl Marx to Wilhelm Blos, Nov. 10, 1877, MEW, vol. 34, p. 308.
83. For both statements see Hundt, op. cit., p. 91.
84. See primarily Andreas, op. cit.
85. Friedrich Engels to Karl Marx, Oct. 25/26, 1847, MEW, vol. 27, p. 98.
86. Helmut Gollwitzer, *Forderungen der Freiheit* (Munich, 1962), p. 175.
87. Friedrich Engels to Karl Marx, Oct. 25/26, 1847, *Correspondence*, p. 21.
88. Friedrich Engels to Karl Marx, Nov. 24, 1847, *Correspondence*, p. 20.
89. Hundt, op. cit., p. 215 et seq.
90. Decision of Central Agency of "League of Communists," Jan. 24, 1848, quoted in *Bund der Kommunisten*, p. 654.
91. Mehring, *Life*, p. 148.
92. MESW, vol. 1, p. 127.
93. "By bourgeoisie is meant the class of modern capitalists, owners of the means of social production and employers of wage labour. By proletariat the class of modern wage labourers who, having no means of production of their own, are reduced to selling their labour power in order to live." Ibid., p. 108.
94. Ibid., pp. 189–190.
95. Friedrich Engels to Friedrich Adolph Sorge, May 4, 1887, *Letters to Americans*, p. 185.
96. Mehring, *Life*, p. 149.
97. Rossana Rossanda, *"Die sozialistischen Läander: Ein Dilemma der westeuropäischen Linken,"* in *Kursbuch*, Dec. 30, 1972, p. 28.
98. "[W]e do not deny that there are countries such as America, England and I might perhaps add Holland if I was better acquainted with your institutions, where the workers may be able to achieve their aim by peaceful means." Karl Marx, "Speech at the Hague Congress," MESW, vol. 2, p. 293.

• C H A P T E R 4 •

1. Jenny Marx, "Kurze Umrisse eines bewegten Lebens," in *Mohr und General Erinnerungen an Marx und Engels*, p. 207.

2. ME, vol. 6, p. 649.
3. Karl Marx to editor of *La Réforme*, Mar. 8, 1848, MEW, vol. 4, p. 537 et seq; Jenny Marx, op. cit., p. 207 et seq.
4. Jenny Marx, op. cit., p. 208.
5. Karl Marx to editor of *La Réforme*, Mar. 8, 1848, MEW, vol. 4, p. 537.
6. See L. Somerhausen, *L'Humanisme agissant de Karl Marx* (Paris, 1946), p. 241.
7. MEW, vol. 5, p. 3 et seq.
8. Ibid., p. 4.
9. Quoted in Martin Huber, *Der grosse Maggid und seine Nachfolger*, p. 180.
10. See Karl Marx, "Herr Vogt," MEW, vol. 14, p. 439 et seq.
11. MESW, vol. 3, p. 176.
12. Friedrich Engels to Karl Marx, Apr. 25, 1848, MEW, vol. 27, p. 125.
13. See Mehring, *Life*, p. 160.
14. Stephen Born, *Erinnerungen eines Achtundvierzigers* (Leipzig, 1898), p. 198.
15. MESW, vol. 3, pp. 165–166.
16. Ibid., p. 167.
17. Minutes of meeting of "Workers Association" committee, Jan. 15, 1849, MEW, vol. 6, p. 579.
18. MESW, vol. 3, p. 167.
19. The "General Common Law of the Prussian State" of 1794 was a compendium of the Civil Code, trade, currency, maritime, and insurance law together with the penal, church, state, and administrative codes; it was in general valid until introduction of the Civil Law Book in 1900.
20. Mehring, *Life*, p. 155.
21. After Ferdinand Cohn-Blind's assassination attempt, Bismarck had stated at a sitting of the Reichstag on March 31, 1886, that of course he did not know whether Marx had trained murderers but that Cohn-Blind was a pupil of Marx. Laura Lafargue and Eleanor Marx-Aveling both signed a statement published in the *Sozial-Demokrat* on April 15, 1886, and in the French *Le Socialiste* on April 25, 1886, protesting against this "infamy."
22. Laura Lafargue to Friedrich Engels, Apr. 13, 1886, in *Friedrich Engels, Paul and Laura Lafargue "Correspondence"* (referred to hereafter as *Lafargue Correspondence*), vol. 1, p. 348.
23. Karl Marx, "Sieg der Kontre-revolution zu Wien," in *Neue Rheinische Zeitung*, Nov. 7, 1848, MEW, vol. 5, p. 457.
24. Karl Marx, "Die Junirevolution," in *Neue Rheinische Zeitung*, June 29, 1848, MEW, vol. 5, p. 136 et seq.
25. Karl Marx, "Die Freiheit der Beratungen in Berlin," in *Neue Rheinische Zeitung*, Sept. 17, 1848, MEW, vol. 5, p. 405 et seq.
26. Gottschalk, "An Herrn Karl Marx," quoted in Hans Stein, *Der Kölner Arbeiterverein (1848–1849). Ein Beitrag zur Frühgeschichte des rheinischen Sozialismus* (Köln, 1921), p. 96.
27. Arnold Ruge, diary entry of May 7, 1849, in *Arnold Ruges Briefwechsel und Tagebuchblätter aus den Jahren 1825–1880*, Nerrlich, ed. (Berlin, 1886), vol. 2, p. 85.
28. Friedrich Engels to Laura Lafargue, June 11 and 28, 1889, in *Lafargue Correspondence*, vol. 2, pp. 275, 282.
29. Interview with *Le Figaro* reproduced in *Le Socialiste* of May 20, 1893, and reproduced in full in *Lafargue Correspondence*, vol. 3, p. 382 et seq.
30. MEW, vol. 6, p. 176.

31. On this subject see Louis Fischer, *The Life of Lenin* (London, 1964), p. 634 et seq.
32. Ibid., p. 639.
33. Vladimir I. Lenin, "The Question of Nationalities or Autonomisation," in Lenin, *Collected Works*, vol. 36, p. 605.
34. Lenin, "Little Better but Better," in *Pravda*, Mar. 4, 1924.
35. Fischer, op. cit., p. 670.
36. MEW, vol. 5, p. 332.
37. Friedrich Engels, "Der dänisch-preussische Waffenstillstand," MEW, vol. 5, p. 394.
38. Albert Brisbane, *A Mental Biography* (Boston, 1893), p. 273.
39. *Neue Rheinische Zeitung*, Sept. 19, 1848.
40. Karl Marx to Friedrich Engels, Nov. 29, 1848, MEW, vol. 27, p. 131.
41. Friedrich Engels to Karl Marx, undated, ibid., p. 133.
42. Karl Marx, "Keine Steuern mehr!" in *Neue Rheinische Zeitung* Nov. 17, 1848, MEW, vol. 6, p. 30.
43. Quoted from Wilhelm Blos, *Denkwürdigkeiten eines Sozialdemokraten*, vol. 1, p. 165.
44. Acting Police Director Wilhelm Arnold Geiger to Karl Marx, Aug. 3, 1848, MEW, vol. 5, p. 383.
45. MEW, vol. 6, p. 234.
46. Ibid.
47. Friedrich Lessner, "Erinnerungen eines Arbeiters an Friedrich Engels," in *Mohr und General*, p. 264 et seq.
48. MEW, vol. 6, p. 580.
49. Gerhard Becker, *Karl Marx und Friedrich Engels in Köln 1848–1849. Zur Geschichte des Kölner Arbeitervereins* (Berlin, 1963), p. 206.
50. Karl Marx, "Die revolutionäre Bewegung," in *Neue Rheinische Zeitung*, Jan. 1, 1849, MEW, vol. 6, p. 150.
51. Karl Marx: "Verteidigungsrede," in *Neue Rheinische Zeitung*, Feb. 2, 1849, ibid., p. 257.
52. See Stein, op. cit., p. 99.
53. Manfred Kliem (ed.), *Karl Marx. Dokumente seines Lebens 1818–1883* (Leipzig, 1970), p. 256.
54. See MEW, vol. 36, p. 807 et seq., n.523.
55. See *Karl Marx. Biographie* issued by Institute for Marxism-Leninism under authority of Central Committee of Soviet Union Communist Party.
56. Engels mentions eight rifles with bayonets and 250 live rounds in the editorial room. Friedrich Engels, "Marx and the *Neue Rheinische Zeitung*," MESW, vol. 2, p. 171.
57. Ibid.
58. Karl Marx, "Die standrechtliche Beseitigung der *Neuen Rheinischen Zeitung*," in *Neue Rheinische Zeitung*, May 19, 1849, MEW, vol. 6, p. 505.
59. Karl Marx to Friedrich Engels, June 7, 1849, MEW, vol. 27, p. 137.
60. Karl Marx to Joseph Weydemeyer, Aug. 1, 1849, *Letters to Americans*, p. 16.
61. Jenny Marx, in *Mohr und General*, p. 211.
62. Karl Marx to Joseph Weydemeyer, Aug. 1, 1849, *Letters to Americans*, p. 16.
63. Karl Marx to Friedrich Engels, Aug. 23, 1849, MEW, vol. 27, p. 142.
64. Ibid.

· C H A P T E R 5 ·

1. Karl Marx to Heinrich Marx, Nov. 10, 1837, ME, vol. 1, p. 19.
2. MEW, suppl. vol., p. 190.
3. Karl Marx, "Werke und Schriften bis Anfang 1844 nebst Briefen und Dokumenten," in MEGA, pt. 1, vol. 2, p. 504.
4. Ferdinand Freiligrath, "*Aus Spanien*," in *Morgenblatt für gebildete Stände*, no. 286,
   Nov. 1841; Georg Herwegh, "*An Ferdinand Freiligrath*," in *Rheinische Zeitung*,
   Feb. 27, 1842.
5. Georg Herwegh to Ferdinand Freiligrath, early 1842, in Wilhelm Buchner, *Ferdinand Freiligrath. Ein Dichterleben in Briefen*, vol. 1, p. 427 et seq.
6. For instance Ferdinand Freiligrath to Levin Schücking, Nov. 23, 1842, ibid., p. 340.
7. Ibid.
8. Ibid., vol. 2, p. 46 et seq.
9. Ferdinand Freiligrath to Minister Eichhorn, undated, ibid., p. 125.
10. Ferdinand Freiligrath to Karl Buchner, Feb. 11, 1844, ibid., p. 99.
11. Ferdinand Freiligrath to Levin Schücking, Feb. 3, 1844, ibid., p. 97 et seq.
12. Quoted from Buchner, ibid., p. 114.
13. Quoted from Manfred Häckel, *Freiligraths Briefwechsel mit Marx und Engels*,
    vol. 1, p. XXXI.
14. Ibid., p. XXX.
15. Buchner, op. cit., vol. 2, p. 142.
16. Karl Marx to Joseph Weydemeyer, Jan. 16, 1852, *Letters to Americans*, pp. 32–33.
17. Ferdinand Freiligrath to Karl Buchner, Feb. 12/16, 1846, in Buchner, op. cit.,
    p. 172 et seq.
18. Ferdinand Freiligrath to Lina Schwollmann, Apr. 17, 1848, quoted from Häckel,
    op. cit., p. XLIII.
19. *Neue Rheinische Zeitung*, June 29, 1848, MEW, vol. 5, p. 133.
20. *Neue Rheinische Zeitung*, Oct. 12, 1848, ibid., p. 416.
21. Quoted from Häckel, op. cit., p. LIV et seq.
22. Karl Marx to Friedrich Engels, Aug. 23, 1849, MEW, vol. 27, p. 142.
23. Quoted from Häckel, op. cit., p. LXI.
24. Karl Marx to Friedrich Engels, Aug. 1, 1849, MEW, vol. 27, p. 139.
25. Ibid.
26. Karl Marx to Friedrich Engels, Aug. 25, 1851, MEW, vol. 27, p. 320.
27. Karl Marx to Hermann Ebner, second half of Aug. 1851, ibid., p. 572.
28. Alexander Herzen, *Mein Leben. Memoiren und Reflexionen 1852–1868* (Berlin,
    1962), p. 190.
29. Cf. Karl Marx to Friedrich Engels, May 3, 1851, MEW, vol. 27, p. 244; Friedrich
    Engels to Karl Marx, Sept. 7, 1852, MEW, vol. 28, p. 126.
30. Franz Mehring (ed.), *Aus dem literarischen Nachlass von Karl Marx, Friedrich
    Engels und Ferdinand Lassalle. Gesammelte Schriften von Karl Marx und Fried-
    rich Engels 1841 bis 1850*, (Stuttgart, 1913), vol. 1, p. VIII.
31. Herzen, op. cit., p. 39.
32. Herzen tells an illuminating story about Ruge: "A year later Ruge gave a series of
    lectures in London on the philosophical movement in Germany. The lectures were
    bad. . . . Ten people came to the second lecture and only about five to the third —
    among them Worcell and I. Ruge came up the empty hall and as he passed
    us squeezed my hand hard saying: 'Poland and Russia have come but Italy is

missing. I won't let Mazzini and Saffi forget that when the people rise next time.' As he moved on, angry and grumbling, I cast a glance at Worcell's sardonic smile and said to him, 'Russia inviting Poland to lunch.' 'It's the end of Italy,' Worcell remarked, shaking his head, and we went."

33. Karl Marx to Friedrich Engels, May 25, 1851, MEW, vol. 27, p. 269.
34. Quoted in Mehring, *Life*, p. 198.
35. Herzen, op. cit., p. 196.
36. Ibid., p. 195.
37. Cf. Ferdinand Freiligrath to Karl Marx, undated, in Häckel, op. cit., pp. 43, LXXI.
38. Ferdinand Freiligrath to Karl Marx, undated, ibid., p. 42.
39. The communist trial in Köln from October 4 to November 12, 1852, was a case against eleven members of the League of Communists staged mainly by Prussian police agents. The indictment was based primarily on forgeries and stolen documents. Seven of the accused were sentenced to three to six years of fortress arrest. Marx drew attention to the forgeries mainly in his brochure: *Enthüllungen über den Kommunisten-Prozess zu Köln* (Revelations on the Communist Trial in Köln).
40. Ferdinand Freiligrath to Karl Marx, Dec. 1, 1851, in Häckel, op. cit., p. 29 et seq.
41. Karl Marx to Friedrich Engels, Apr. 16, 1860, MEW, vol. 30, p. 47; Dec. 6, 1860, ibid., p. 123 et seq.; May 7, 1860, ibid., p. 51; June 7, 1859, ibid., vol. 29, p. 448.
42. Karl Marx to Friedrich Engels, June 7, 1859, MEW, vol. 29, p. 448.
43. Jenny Marx to Louise Weydemeyer, Mar. 11, 1861, in *Mohr und General*, p. 261.
44. Karl Marx to Friedrich Engels, May 7, 1860, MEW, vol. 30, p. 51.
45. Karl Marx to Friedrich Engels, Apr. 16, 1860, ibid., p. 47.
46. Quoted from Franz Mehring, *Life*, p. 284.
47. Friedrich Engels to Jenny Marx, Dec. 22, 1859, MEW, vol. 29, p. 636.
48. Karl Marx to Friedrich Engels, Nov. 19, 1859, MEW, vol. 29, p. 513.
49. Friedrich Engels to Karl Marx, Oct. 18, 1867, MEW, vol. 31, p. 367.
50. Friedrich Engels to Jenny Marx, Dec. 22, 1859, MEW, vol. 29, p. 636 et seq.
51. Friedrich Engels to Eduard Bernstein, July 15, 1882, in Helmut Hirsch (ed.), *Eduard Bersteins Briefwechsel mit Friedrich Engels* (Assen, 1970), p. 117 et seq.
52. Ferdinand Freiligrath to Karl Marx, Feb. 28, 1860, in Häckel, op. cit., p. 137 et seq.

· CHAPTER 6 ·

1. Karl Marx to Friedrich Engels, Mar. 7, 1865, MEW, vol. 31, p. 93.
2. Jenny Marx to Joseph Weydemeyer, May 20, 1850, in *Mohr und General*. p. 240 et seq.
3. See Gustav Mayer, "Neue Beiträge zur Biographie von Karl Marx," in *Archiv für die Geschichte des Sozialismus und der Arbeiterbewegung*, Year 10, quoted from Yvonne Kapp, *Eleanor Marx*, vol. 1: *Family Life 1855–1883* (London, 1972), pp. 289–290.
4. Karl Marx to Joseph Weydemeyer, July 13, 1849, MEW, vol. 27, p. 500; Jenny Marx to Joseph Weydemeyer, May 20, 1850, in *Mohr und General*, p. 238 et seq.
5. Karl Marx to Friedrich Engels, Sept. 13, 1854, MEW, vol. 28, p. 391.
6. Karl Marx to Friedrich Engels, Mar. 31, 1851, MEW, vol. 27, p. 226.
7. Franziska Kugelmann, "Kleine Züge zu dem grossen Charakterbild von Karl Marx," in *Mohr und General*, p. 294.
8. Karl Marx to Friedrich Engels, Feb. 15, 1859, MEW, vol. 29, p. 397.
9. Jenny Marx to Louise Weydemeyer, Mar. 11, 1861, in *Mohr und General*, p. 259.

10. Ibid., p. 252. Behind her husband's back Jenny Marx collected money from all sorts of acquaintances — "You cannot think how you have helped me with your prompt contributions" she wrote to Bertha Markheim (Jenny Marx to Bertha Markheim, in Bert Andreas, *Briefe und Dokumente der Familie Marx aus den Jahren 1862–1873 nebst zwei unbekannten Aufsätzen von Friedrich Engels* [special edition by Archiv für Sozialgeschichte]), vol. 2, p. 175.

11. Franz Mehring, *Life*, p. 217.

12. Charles A. Dana to Karl Marx, Mar. 8, 1860, MEW, vol. 14, p. 680 n.1.

13. Quoted from Kapp, op. cit., pp. 57, 123.

14. See MEW, vol. 28, p. 722 n.475.

15. Friedrich Engels to Karl Marx, Dec. 12, 1855, MEW, vol. 28, p. 464.

16. Willy Haas, "Marx und Lenin. Notizen zu zwei neuen Monumentalausgaben," in *Die literarische Welt*, no. 7 (1932).

17. Karl Marx to Friedrich Engels, Oct. 3, 1866, MEW, vol. 31, p. 257.

18. Friedrich Engels to Karl Marx, Sept. 18, 1868, MEW, vol. 32, p. 153.

19. Kapp, op. cit., p. 62.

20. Karl Marx to Ludwig Kugelmann, Mar. 17, 1868, *Letters to Kugelmann*, p. 65.

21. Kapp, op. cit., p. 43.

22. Karl Marx to Friedrich Engels, July 31, 1865, MEW, vol. 31, p. 131 et seq.

23. Kapp, op. cit., p. 190.

24. Karl Marx to Friedrich Engels, Dec. 14, 1867, MEW, vol. 31, p. 409.

25. Karl Marx to Friedrich Engels, July 24, 1857, MEW, vol. 29, p. 157.

26. Karl Marx to Friedrich Engels, Aug. 13, 1868, MEW, vol. 32, p. 136.

27. Karl Marx to Friedrich Engels, Sept. 28, 1852, MEW, vol. 28, p. 147.

28. Kapp, op. cit., p. 74.

29. Karl Marx to Paul Lafargue, Aug. 13, 1866 — see Kapp, op. cit., pp. 298–299.

30. Wilhelm Liebknecht, "Karl Marx zum Gedächtnis," in *Mohr und General*, p. 102 et seq.

31. Ibid., p. 133 et seq.

32. Ibid., p. 39. From Shakespeare's *Julius Caesar*.

33. Paul Lafargue, "Reminiscences of Marx," in MSW, vol. 1, p. 93.

34. See Wilhelm Liebknecht, "Reminiscences of Marx," ibid., p. 122.

35. Ibid., pp. 124–125.

36. See Kapp, op. cit., p. 101; and Internationaal Instituut voor Sociale Geschiedenes, Amsterdam, catalogue no. I/G 187.

37. Kapp, op. cit., p. 59.

38. Ibid., p. 75.

39. Eduard Bernstein, *Aus den Jahren meines Exils. Erinnerungen eines Sozialisten* (Berlin, 1918), p. 173.

40. Karl Marx to Friedrich Engels, Nov. 11, 1882, MEW, vol. 35, p. 110.

41. See Karl Kautsky, "Mein zweiter Aufenthalt in London," in *Friedrich Engels Briefwechsel mit Karl Kautsky*, edited by Benedikt Kautsky, p. 90. Other sources give the remark in French since it was made to Lafargue: "*Ce qu'il y a de certain c'est que moi, je ne suis pas Marxiste.*" See Friedrich Engels to Eduard Bernstein, Nov. 2/3, 1882, MEW, vol. 35, p. 388, and Bernstein, op. cit., p. 218.

42. MEW, vol. 33, p. 727 n.113.

43. Jenny Longuet to Eleanor Marx-Aveling, Apr. 10, 1882, quoted in Kapp, op. cit., p. 240.

44. Jenny Longuet to Eleanor Marx-Aveling, Nov. 8, 1882, ibid., p. 235.

45. Karl Marx to Jenny Longuet, Dec. 7, 1881, MEW, vol. 35, p. 242.

46. Eleanor Marx-Aveling to Olive Schreiner, June 16, 1884, quoted in Kapp, op. cit., p. 229.
47. Karl Marx, *The Eighteenth Brumaire of Louis Bonaparte*, in MESW, vol. 1, p. 398.
48. Andreas, op. cit., p. 200.
49. Eleanor Marx-Aveling to Jenny Longuet, Jan. 8, 1882, in Kapp, op. cit., p. 227.
50. Eleanor Marx-Aveling to Jenny Longuet, June 18, 1881, ibid., p. 224.
51. Eleanor Marx-Aveling to Jenny Longuet, Jan. 15, 1882, ibid., p. 227.
52. Ibid., p. 221.
53. Eleanor Marx-Aveling to Karl Marx, Mar. 23, 1874, ibid., p. 153 et seq.
54. From the unpublished papers of the Aveling family, ibid., p. 257.
55. Edward Aveling, "Charles Darwin and Karl Marx," in *New Century Review* (April 1897).
56. Hesketh Pearson: *Bernard Shaw, His Life and Personality*.
57. Diary entry by Miss Potter, quoted in Kapp, op. cit., p. 284.
58. Eleanor Marx-Aveling to Frederick Demuth, Mar. 1, 1898, quoted in Bernstein, op. cit., p. 178.
59. At any rate since publication of extracts of the relevant letter from Louise Kautsky-Freyberger by Werner Blumenberg (at the time working in the Internationaal Instituut voor Sociale Geschiedenes in Amsterdam) in his monograph *Karl Marx* (Rowohlt Taschenbuch Verlag, 1962).
60. Jenny Marx, "Kurze Umrisse eines bewegten Lebens," in *Mohr und General*, p. 216.
61. Werner Blumenberg to Heinz Monz, January 23, 1964 — see Heinz Monz, *Karl Marx. Grundlagen der Entwicklung zu Leben und Werk* (Trier, 1973), p. 359.
62. See Kapp, op. cit., p. 291.
63. Eleanor Marx-Aveling to Frederick Demuth, Feb. 3, 1898, ibid., p. 297.
64. Eleanor Marx-Aveling to Laura Lafargue, ibid., p. 291.
65. The letter from Louise Kautsky-Freyberger to August Bebel, dated Sept. 2/4, 1898, was examined in the Internationaal Instituut voor Sociale Geschiedenes, Amsterdam. Quoted from Hans Magnus Enzensberger (ed.), *Gespräche mit Marx und Engels*, vol. 2, p. 703 et seq.
66. There was a lively correspondence between Friedrich Engels and Karl Kautsky about the divorce, Engels being emphatically on the side of Louise Kautsky. See *Friedrich Engels Briefwechsel mit Karl Kautsky*, op. cit., pp. 340–348.
67. Werner Blumenberg, *Karl Marx* (monograph), p. 115.
68. Monz, op. cit., p. 361.
69. See *Der Spiegel*, no. 44 (1972), p. 188 et seq.
70. Yvonne Kapp (op. cit., p. 297) says that this was "privately communicated" to her. She does not say by whom.
71. Will dated July 26, 1926, quoted in Kapp, op. cit., p. 294.
72. Ibid. See also Gustav Mayer, *Friedrich Engels. A Biography* (London, 1936), p. 235.
73. August Hermann Ewerbeck to Moses Hess, Nov. 1, 1848, in "Moses Hess' Briefwechsel," edited by Eduard Silberer together with Werner Blumenberg in *Quellen und Untersuchungen zur Geschichte der deutschen und österreichischen Arbeiterbewegung*, vol. 2, p. 207.
74. Friedrich Engels to Eduard Bernstein, Apr. 23, 1883, in *Eduard Bernsteins Briefwechsel mit Friedrich Engels*, p. 206.
75. Werner Sombart, however, does not think that Engels was a socialist "to the bottom of his heart"; instead he regards him as a splendid, gay, sunny personality who turned into an epicurean businessman with an inclination for sport and

hobbies. See Werner Sombart, *Der proletarische Sozialismus* (Jena, 1924), vol. 1, p. 51.

76. Stephan Born, "Friedrich Engels in Paris," in *Ich erinnere mich gern — Zeitgenossen über Friedrich Engels*, edited by Manfred Kliem, p. 77.

77. Edward Aveling, "Friedrich Engels zu Hause," ibid., p. 187.

78. "When anyone arrogantly brushes aside positive Christianity, then I defend this doctrine since it springs from one of the most profound requirements of human nature, the yearning for salvation from sin through the grace of God; whenever, however, there is a question of defending the freedom of the intellect, then I protest against any coercion." Quoted in Hirsch, op. cit., p. 25.

79. Mayer, op. cit., p. 14.

80. Carl de Haas to Adolf Schults and Friedrich Roeber, Mar. 4, 1841, in Friedrich Engels, "Cola di Rienzi. Ein unbekannter dramatischer Entwurf," edited by Michael Knierim, p. 63.

81. Friedrich Engels, "Cola di Rienzi."

82. Friedrich Engels to Laura Lafargue, 30 Dec. 1871, in *Frederick Engels, Paul and Laura Lafargue — Correspondence* (Moscow: Foreign Languages Publishing House, 1959) (henceforth referred to as *Lafargue Correspondence*), vol. 1, p. 35.

83. Quoted from Mayer, *Friedrich Engels. Eine Biographie*, p. 73. (not in English translation).

84. Moses Hess to Berthold Auerbach, ibid., p. 117.

85. Friedrich Engels to Karl Marx, Jan. 15, 1847, MEW, vol. 27, p. 74.

86. Friedrich Engels to Karl Marx, Jan. 20, 1845, ibid., p. 14.

87. Friedrich Engels to Karl Marx, Feb. 22/26, and Mar. 7, 1845, ibid., p. 20.

88. Friedrich Engels to Karl Marx, Nov. 19, 1844, ibid., p. 10.

89. Engels later admitted that the preparatory work for another book had been done with the carelessness of youth; when writing *The Origin of the Family, of Private Property and the State* he had not read all the relevant literature and himself called much of his reasoning "guesswork." Friedrich Engels to Laura Lafargue, June 13, 1891, *Lafargue Correspondence*, vol. 3, p. 76.

90. Karl Marx: "Die revolutionäre Bewegung" in *Neue Rheinische Zeitung*, Jan. 1, 1849, MEW, vol. 6, p. 150.

91. Friedrich Engels to Karl Marx, Dec. 11, 1851, MEW, vol. 27, p. 388.

92. Friedrich Engels to Karl Marx, Mar. 2, 1852, MEW, vol. 28, p. 35.

93. Friedrich Engels: "The European War," in *New York Daily Tribune*, Feb. 2, 1854, MEW, vol. 10, p. 8.

94. Friedrich Engels to Karl Marx, Apr. 14, 1856, *Correspondence*, pp. 83–84.

95. Sources are contradictory regarding the precise origin of this nickname. Eleanor Marx-Aveling, in her article "Ich erinnere mich gern" (Kliem, op. cit., p. 114), says that he acquired it as a result of his articles on the Franco-Prussian War of 1870 in the *Pall Mall Gazette*, in which he predicted with accuracy the battle of Sedan and the annihilation of the French army. Paul Lafargue, on the other hand, gives Marx's daughter Jenny as the "godmother" and also *Le Figaro*, which referred to "General Staff" as if it were a person. In any case this was Engels's nickname to the end of his days — in English as well.

96. Friedrich Engels to Karl Marx, July 4, 1866, MEW, vol. 31, p. 230. The battle of Sadowa took place on July 3, 1866.

97. Friedrich Engels to Eduard Bernstein, Feb. 22/25, 1882, Hirsch, op. cit., p. 85.

98. Friedrich Engels to Karl Kautsky, in *Friedrich Engels' Briefwechsel mit Karl Kautsky*, op. cit., p. 154.

99. Friedrich Engels, Introduction to "The Class Struggles in France," MESW, vol. 1, pp. 190, 191.
100. Ernst Bloch, "Hegel, Praxis, Neuer Materialismus," in *Karl Marx und die Menschlichkeit. Utopische Phantasie und Weltänderung* (Rowohlt German Encyclopaedia, 1969), p. 37.
101. Quoted in Mayer, *Biographie*, p. 262 (not in English translation).
102. Helmut Hirsch, *Friedrich Engels* (Rowohlt monograph, 1942), p. 62.
103. On the death of Engels's father in March 1860 his brothers proposed that he renounce in their favor his rights in his father's firm in Engelskirchen. One of the reasons they gave was that Engels had been living abroad since 1849. To assure his legal and financial position in the firm of Ermen & Engels in Manchester, he was bought out with a sum of £10,000. This enabled Engels later to become co-proprietor of the firm. Apart from the fact that under English law there are difficulties in the transfer to his heirs of a deceased person's rights as co-proprietor of a firm, his brothers' proposal was an infringement of Engels's right of inheritance. Engels did not become co-proprietor of the firm in Manchester until 1864. MEW, vol. 30, p. 744.
104. Friedrich Engels to Karl Marx, Mar. 11, 1857, MEW, vol. 29, p. 109.
105. *Friedrich Engels. Eine Biographie.* Institute for Marxism-Leninism, East Berlin, p. 260 et seq.
106. See also Paul Lafargue, "Persönliche Erinnerungen an Friedrich Engels," in Kliem, op. cit., p. 117.
107. Friedrich Engels to Jenny Marx, May 11, 1858, MEW, vol. 29, p. 558.
108. Friedrich Engels to Laura Lafargue, June 11, 1889, *Lafargue Correspondence*, vol. 2, p. 276.
109. Hellmuth von Gerlach, "Sozialdemokratische Grossen," in Kliem, op. cit., p. 205.
110. Friedrich Engels to Karl Marx, Nov. 29, 1868, MEW, vol. 32, p. 215 et seq.
111. Friedrich Engels to Karl Marx, Jan. 26, 1863, MEW, vol. 30, p. 317.
112. Friedrich Engels to Karl Marx, Aug. 27, 1867, MEW, vol. 31, p. 293.
113. Karl Marx to his daughter Jenny, Mar. 16, 1866, ibid., p. 501 et seq.
114. Karl Marx to Ludwig Kugelmann, Oct. 25, 1866, *Letters to Kugelmann*, p. 44.
115. Karl Marx to Friedrich Engels, Sept. 16, 1882, MEW, vol. 35, p. 95.
116. See MSW, vol. 1, p. 83 et seq.
117. Ibid., p. 84.
118. Karl Marx to Friedrich Engels, Apr. 11, 1868, MEW, vol. 32, p. 58.
119. See Peter Ludz, "Zur Situation der Marxforschung in Westeuropa," in *Kölner, Zeitschrift für Soziologie und Sozialpsychologie* Year 10 (1958), p. 457.
120. Ibid. ("*Passionné, impulsive, rempli d'une colère vindicative.*")
121. J. P. Mayer, "Reflections on Equality," in *The Socialist Idea. A Reappraisal*, edited by Leszek Kolakowski and Stuart Humpshire, pp. 63 et seq., 67. The extracts are to be found in the Internationaal Instituut voor Sociale Geschiedenes, Amsterdam — from Montesquieu, Catalogue No. I/B 16, from Ranke No. I/B 17, from Villegardelle No. I/B 32.
122. See Eleanor Marx-Aveling, "Friedrich Engels," in Kliem, op. cit., p. 108.
123. See Werner Blumenberg, "Ein unbekanntes Kapitel aus Marx' Leben," ibid., p. 55.
124. Friedrich Engels to Karl Marx, July 16, 1858, MEW, vol. 29, p. 345; see also Karl Marx to Friedrich Engels, Mar. 17, 1854, MEW, vol. 28, p. 330.
125. Werner Blumenberg, op. cit.
126. Karl Marx to Friedrich Engels, Sept. 17, 1853, MEW, vol. 28, p. 289; Nov. 23, 1853, ibid., p. 310; May 22, 1854, ibid., p. 362.

127. Karl Marx to Friedrich Engels, about Dec. 12, 1853, ibid., p. 313.
128. Jenny Marx to Karl, unpublished undated letter in Internationaal Instituut voor Sociale Geschiedenes, Amsterdam, Catalogue No. I/D 3312.
129. See Arnold Künzli, *Karl Marx. Eine Psychographie*, p. 386.
130. "If Mohr writes saying that his daughters had cross-examined him as to who Miss Burns really was and Lizzy should happen to find the letter, there would be an interminable argument since Lizzy wants the blessing of the Church on her union. She is indifferent to the State but not to heaven. And when the hither and thither ends with her sobbing quietly, then General puts a piece of paper in front of her headed 'To be read when you have calmed down' and leaves the house." Walther Victor, *General und die Frauen. Vom Erlebnis zur Theorie* (Berlin, 1932), p. 119.
131. Karl Marx to Jenny Marx, Sept. 17, 1878, MEW, vol. 34, p. 344.
132. Karl Marx to Friedrich Engels, Jan. 8, 1863, MEW, vol. 30, p. 310.
133. Friedrich Engels to Karl Marx, Jan. 13, 1863, in Mayer *Biography*, op. cit., p. 172.
134. Friedrich Engels to Karl Marx, Jan. 26, 1863, ibid., p. 173.
135. "No condolences can help in such cases . . . and I do not write to condole but simply because I know it does one good to be shown the sympathy of those from whom one can allow oneself to expect it." Quoted in Kapp, op. cit., p. 49.
136. See MEGA, pt. 1, vol. 3, p. 117.
137. Albert Massiczek refers to this in his study on Marx, *Der menschliche Mensch. Karl Marx' jüdischer Humanismus* (Vienna, 1968), pp. 233, 238.
138. ME, vol. 1, p. 454.
139. See Massiczek, op. cit., p. 159 et seq.
140. This is the way the Jewish scholar Rosenzweig puts it, ibid., p. 371.
141. See for instance Giulio Girardi, "Der Marxismus zum Problem des Todes," in *Concilium* (International Periodical for Theology), Year 10, Issue 4.
142. Karl Marx, "Peuchet. On Suicide," ME, vol. 4, p. 598 et seq.
143. Karl Marx to Friedrich Engels, Aug. 30, 1873, MEW, vol. 33, p. 88 et seq.
144. Karl Marx to Ferdinand Lassalle, July 28, 1855, MEW, vol. 28, p. 617.
145. "I have been through all sorts of misfortune but only now do I know what real unhappiness is. I feel myself broken down." Karl Marx to Friedrich Engels, Apr. 12, 1855, ibid., p. 444.
146. Quoted from Paul Lafargue, "Persönliche Erinnerungen an Friedrich Engels," in *Mohr und General*, p. 487.
147. See Gustav Mayer, *Biographie*, vol. 2, p. 471 (not in English translation).
148. Karl Marx to Friedrich Engels, Feb. 23, 1851, MEW, vol. 27, p. 193.
149. Karl Marx, "Inaugural Address of the Working Men's International Association," MESW, vol. 2, p. 18.
150. Karl Marx to Friedrich Engels, Apr. 6, 1866, MEW, vol. 31, p. 205.
151. Friedrich Engels to Eduard Bernstein, June 17, 1879 (draft), MEW, vol. 34, p. 378.
152. Karl Marx to Eleanor Marx-Aveling, Jan. 9, 1883, MEW, vol. 35, p. 422.
153. Friedrich Engels to Laura Lafargue, Sept. 11, 1892, *Lafargue Correspondence*, vol. 3, p. 191.
154. Karl Marx to Jenny Longuet, Apr. 11, 1881, *Correspondence*, p. 389.
155. Karl Marx to Friedrich Adolph Sorge, Dec. 15, 1881, ibid., p. 397.
156. Eleanor Marx-Aveling, "Karl Marx. Lose Blätter," in *Mohr und General*, p. 270.
157. Karl Kautsky, "Mein erster Aufenthalt in London," in *Friedrich Engels' Briefwechsel mit Karl Kautsky*, op. cit., p. 29.
158. Enzensberger, op. cit., vol. 2, p. 521.

159. Kautsky, op. cit., p. 29: "Madame Jenny is said to have gone further and called Engels Marx's evil spirit. This would be a serious matter but it would put Frau Marx rather than Engels in an unfavorable light. It may be doubted that she did in fact use this expression. She and Mrs. Hyndman were gossiping over tea or coffee and exchanging their domestic worries. She may have let fall a critical comment on Engels which Mrs. Hyndman, who was of no account politically, interpreted God knows how, passed on God knows how and was further exaggerated in Hyndman's imagination."

160. Karl Marx to Friedrich Adolph Sorge, Dec. 15, 1881, *Correspondence*, p. 398.

161. Ernest Belfort Bax, in Enzensberger, op. cit., p. 588.

162. Karl Marx to Friedrich Adolph Sorge, Dec. 15, 1881, *Correspondence* p. 397; Karl Marx to Henry Myers Hyndman, July 2, 1881, MEW, vol. 35, p. 202 et seq.

163. Friedrich Engels to Edward Bernstein, Mar. 31, 1882, MEW, vol. 35, p. 297.

164. Kautsky, op. cit., p. 27.

165. Friedrich Engels to August Bebel, Aug. 30, 1883, MEW, vol. 36, p. 56.

166. On this subject see Heinz Stern and Dieter Wolf: *Das grosse Erbe* (Berlin, 1972).

167. Eleanor Marx-Aveling to Karl Kautsky, Mar. 15, 1898, in Kapp, op. cit., p. 278.

168. Eleanor Marx-Aveling to Laura Lafargue, Mar. 26, 1883, ibid., p. 279.

169. Eleanor Marx-Aveling to Friedrich Engels, June 2, 1883, ibid., p. 279.

170. Paul Lafargue telegraphed to Engels that very day saying that he was coming at once, *Lafargue Correspondence*, vol. 3, p. 482.

171. Friedrich Engels to Laura Lafargue, Mar. 25, 1883, ibid., vol. 1, p. 123.

172. Laura Lafargue to Friedrich Engels, June 11, 1885, ibid., p. 294.

173. Laura Lafargue to Friedrich Engels, June 20, 1883, quoted in Kapp, op. cit., p. 280.

174. Friedrich Engels to Laura Lafargue, June 24, 1883, ibid. Concerning the expression used by Engels, "literary executors," MEW (vol. 36, Note 66) gives the following explanation: "On 28 April 1883, in his article 'On the death of Karl Marx,' Engels noted that Marx by word of mouth had appointed his youngest daughter Eleanor and Engels as his 'literary executors.' "

175. Paul Lafargue to Friedrich Engels, Dec. 24, 1889, *Lafargue Correspondence*, vol. 2, p. 352.

176. Laura Lafargue to Friedrich Engels, Dec. 15, 1886, ibid., vol. 1, p. 403.

177. Friedrich Engels to Paul Lafargue, Sept. 12, 1880, ibid., p. 76.

178. Friedrich Engels to Laura Lafargue, Sept. 13, 1886, ibid., p. 369.

179. Friedrich Engels to Editorial Board of Le Socialiste, Oct. 21, 1885, ibid., pp. 312–313.

180. Laura Lafargue to Friedrich Engels, Oct. 23, 1885, ibid., p. 315.

181. Laura Lafargue to Friedrich Engels, Feb. 11, 1885, ibid., p. 265.

182. Paul Lafargue to Friedrich Engels, Feb. 12, 1891, ibid., vol. 3, p. 32.

183. MEW, vol. 7, p. 553.

184. Friedrich Engels to Jenny Marx, July 25, 1849, *Correspondence*, p. 24.

185. Karl Marx to Friedrich Engels, Aug. 30, 1852, MEW, vol. 28, p. 121.

186. Quoted in *Marx-Chronik. Daten zu Leben und Werk*, compiled by Maximilien Rubel (Munich, 1968), p. 47.

187. Jenny Marx, "Kurze Umrisse eines bewegten Lebens," in *Mohr und General*, p. 212.

188. Wilhelm Liebknecht, *Karl Marx zum Gedächtnis. Ein Lebensabriss und Erinnerungen* (Nuremberg, 1896), p. 59.

189. Friedrich Engels to Joseph Weydemeyer, Apr. 12, 1853, MEW, vol. 28, p. 576.

190. MEW, vol. 8, p. 575.
191. MEW, vol. 7, p. 550.
192. Karl Bittel, *Karl Marx. Neue Rheinische Zeitung–Politisch-ökonomische Revue* (Berlin, 1955), p. 16.
193. Wilhelm Pieper to Friedrich Engels, Jan. 1851, quoted in Blumenberg, op. cit., p. 98.
194. Karl Marx to Friedrich Engels, Apr. 2, 1851, *Correspondence*, p. 36.
195. Karl Marx to Adolf Cluss, Sept. 15, 1853, MEW, vol. 28, p. 592: "Being a continual newspaper-greaser bores. It takes much time, eats one away and ultimately after all is nothing. However independent one wishes to be, one is tied to the paper and its readers, particularly if one is paid cash as I am. Purely scientific work is something totally different."
196. Robert Payne, *Marx* (London, 1968), p. 235.
197. Karl Marx to Jenny Marx, June 11, 1852, MEW, vol. 28, p. 527.
198. Eduard Bernstein, who took the manuscript from Marx's papers, did not publish it; he even erased from the 1913 edition of the Marx-Engels correspondence all passages dealing with it. Not until 1924 did he hand it over to the archives of the German Social-Democrat Party. The book was first published in 1930 in Russian as Vol. 5 of *Marx-Engels-Archiv* by the Marx-Engels Institute, Moscow.
199. Quoted from Manfred Kliem, *Karl Marx. Dokumente seines Lebens 1818–1883*, p. 317 et seq.
200. Their destinies were very different. Heinrich Bürgers became a progressive Reichstag deputy; Wilhelm Becker became Burgomaster of Köln and a member of the Prussian Senate; Nothjung, the journeyman-tailor, and Röser, the cigar-maker, rejoined the workers' movement after their arrest, as did Friedrich Lessner; Wilhelm Joseph Reiff, a laborer, and Karl Wunibald Otto, a chemist, did not return to active political life.
201. MESW, vol. 1, p. 186.
202. An edition in book form, revised by Marx, did not appear in Hamburg until 1869.
203. Victor Hugo, *Napoleon the Little* (London: Vizetelly & Co., 1852), p. 175.
204. Ibid., p. 53.
205. Ibid., p. 40.
206. MESW, vol. 1, p. 398.
207. Ibid., p. 404.
208. Ibid., p. 402.

· CHAPTER 7 ·

1. Franz Mehring, *Life*, p. 177.
2. Shlomo Na'aman, *Lassalle* (Hanover, 1970), p. 12. Na'aman, who has written the most thorough biography of Lassalle, calls him a person of "unchildlike childishness and immature maturity": "As a boy and a youngster Lassalle showed every tendency to become an unstable, scatter-brained, precocious, unbalanced but quick-witted member of society whose antisocial egoism was relieved by no redeeming feature — unless one was taken in by his ingratiating and studiedly polite manner. His uncontrolled, effervescent temper made him even more intolerable as a youngster. . . ." Op. cit., p. 2.
3. Ibid., p. 15.

4. Karl Marx, "Reflections of a Young Man on the Choice of a Profession," ME, vol. I, p. 7.
5. Na'aman, op. cit., p. 13.
6. Ibid., p. 19.
7. Ibid., p. 20.
8. Ibid., p. 27.
9. Heinrich Heine to Karl August Varnhagen von Ense, Jan. 3, 1846, in Heine, *Briefe*, edited by Friedrich Hirth, vol. 3, p. 36.
10. Heinrich Heine to Ferdinand Lassalle, Mar. 7, 1846, ibid., p. 71.
11. Na'aman, op. cit., pp. 57, 129.
12. See Maximilien Rubel, *Karl Marx/Friedrich Engels. Die russische Kommune. Kritik eines Mythos*, p. 286 et seq; also "La charte de la Première Internationale. Essai sur le marxisme dans l'A.I.T." in *Mouvement sociale*, 51 (1965), p. 3 et seq.
13. Karl Marx to Georg Herwegh, Oct. 26, 1847, MEW, vol. 27, p. 470.
14. Mehring, *Life*, p. 177.
15. Na'aman, op. cit., p. 46.
16. Friedrich Engels to Karl Marx, Apr. 25, 1848, MEW, vol. 27, p. 126.
17. Karl Marx to Friedrich Engels, May 18, 1859, *Correspondence*, p. 123.
18. Marx sent Müller-Tellering's envelope carrying this form of address to Adolf Cluss (Karl Marx to Adolf Cluss, May 10, 1852, MEW, vol. 28, p. 521). Eduard von Müller-Tellering was Marx's favorite member of the staff of the *Neue Rheinische Zeitung*; he was the Vienna correspondent and his reports, though aggressively anti-Semitic, were in high favor with Marx — "Your reports are indisputably the best we receive. . . ." (Dec. 5, 1848, MEW, vol. 27, p. 485). Later, when an exile in London, Müller-Tellering became a violent opponent of Marx and wrote the first anti-Semitic pamphlet against him, "Vorgeschmack in die künftige Diktatur von Marx und Engels." On this subject see Werner Blumenberg, "Eduard von Müller-Tellering Verfasser des ersten antisemitischen Pamphlets gegen Marx," in *Bulletin of Internationaal Instituut voor sociale Geschiedenes*, Amsterdam, vol. 6 (1951), p. 197.
19. August Bebel, *Aus meinem Leben* (Berlin, 1964), p. 63 et seq.
20. Karl Marx, "Prozess gegen Rheinischen Kreisausschuss" (speech for the defense), in *Neue Rheinische Zeitung*, Feb. 27, 1849, MEW, vol. 6, p. 256.
21. Quoted in Na'aman, op. cit., p. 184.
22. Wilhelm Liebknecht, "Karl Marx zum Gedächtnis," in *Mohr und General*, p. 60.
23. Hans Magnus Enzensberger (ed.), *Gespräche mit Marx und Engels* (Frankfurt/Main, 1973), vol. I, p. 79 et seq.
24. Franziska Kugelmann, "Kleine Züge zu dem grossen Charakterbild von Karl Marx," in *Mohr und General*, p. 306.
25. See Manfred Kliem (ed.), *Karl Marx. Dokumente seines Lebens 1818–1883*, p. 43.
26. Karl Marx to Friedrich Engels, Feb. 11, 1851, MEW, vol. 27, p. 184 et seq.: ". . . apart from this I am very pleased with the public and genuine isolation in which we two, you and I, find ourselves. It entirely suits our position and principles. We have now finished with the system of mutual concessions, with half-truths admitted for reasons of propriety and with our duty of sharing in the public ridicule of the party with all these asses."
27. Karl Marx to Friedrich Engels, May 8, 1851, ibid., p. 254.
28. Karl Marx to Friedrich Engels, Feb. 4, 1852, MEW, vol. 28, p. 19.
29. Friedrich Engels to Karl Marx, Feb. 13, 1851, MEW, vol. 27, p. 189.

30. Karl Marx to Ferdinand Lassalle, July 28, 1855, MEW, vol. 28, p. 617.
31. Information to Liebknecht from Laura Lafargue in Wilhelm Liebknecht, op. cit., p. 91 et seq.
32. See Mehring, *Life*, p. 251.
33. MEW, vol. 29, p. 665 n.43.
34. Na'aman, op. cit., p. 208.
35. Mehring, op. cit., p. 251.
36. Ibid., p. 315.
37. Karl Marx to Friedrich Engels, Dec. 2, 1854, MEW, vol. 28, p. 415.
38. Friedrich Engels to Karl Marx, May 11, 1857, MEW, vol. 29, p. 134.
39. "Enclosed is a letter (with annex) from the great Lassalle which now positively proves to me that he has in fact seriously begun to be known as a result of his reputation in Berlin. . . . The good Lassalle has pursued philosophy, Heraclitus, as he did the Hatzfeldt case and, if one is to believe him, has finally won his 'case.' . . . However we will look at the thing ourselves and, although it is a gift horse, will look it hard in the mouth — on the express condition, of course, that Heraclitus does not smell of garlic. The fellow may perhaps be useful to us in hunting up booksellers, unless he is afraid that the reputation he is looking for in the economic field might suffer from competition and so he might lose his 'case.' "
    Karl Marx to Friedrich Engels, Dec. 22, 1857, ibid., p. 234.
40. Karl Marx to Friedrich Engels, Jan. 28, 1858, ibid., p. 267.
41. Karl Marx to Friedrich Engels, May 8, 1857, ibid., p. 132.
42. Karl Marx to Friedrich Engels, Feb. 1, 1858, ibid., p. 275.
43. Karl Marx to Friedrich Engels, Feb. 1, 1858, *Correspondence*, pp. 103–104.
44. Karl Marx to Ferdinand Lassalle, May 31, 1858, NEW, vol. 29, p. 561.
45. Karl Marx to Friedrich Engels, May 31, 1858, ibid., p. 330.
46. Karl Marx to Ferdinand Lassalle, Feb. 22, 1858, ibid., p. 550.
47. Friedrich Engels to Karl Marx, Apr. 14, 1856, ibid., p. 43.
48. Karl Marx to Joseph Weydemeyer, Feb. 1, 1859, *Correspondence*, p. 119.
49. Karl Marx to Friedrich Engels, Mar. 10, 1859, MEW, vol. 29, p. 409.
50. Karl Marx to Friedrich Engels, Dec. 10, 1859, ibid., p. 520.
51. Friedrich Engels to Karl Marx, June 25, 1860, MEW, vol. 30, p. 68.
52. Karl Marx to Ferdinand Lassalle, Nov. 6, 1859, MEW, vol. 29, p. 618.
53. Karl Marx to Friedrich Engels, Jan. 21, 1859, ibid., p. 385.
54. Karl Marx to Ferdinand Lassalle, Nov. 12, 1858, ibid., p. 566.
55. Na'aman, op. cit., p. 264.
56. Karl Marx to Friedrich Engels, July 22, 1859, MEW, vol. 29, p. 462.
57. Friedrich Engels to Karl Marx, July 25, 1859, ibid., p. 464.
58. Quoted in Na'aman, op. cit., p. 320.
59. Karl Marx to Ferdinand Lassalle, Sept. 15, 1860, MEW, vol. 30, p. 565.
60. Karl Marx to Friedrich Engels, Aug. 10, 1858, MEW, vol. 29, p. 351.
61. Ibid., p. 432 n.381.
62. Karl Marx to Ferdinand Lassalle, Apr. 19, 1859, ibid., p. 590 et seq.
63. Ferdinand Lassalle to Karl Marx and Friedrich Engels, May 27, 1859, quoted in *Marxismus und Literatur*, edited by Fritz J. Raddatz, vol. 1, pp. 82, 84.
64. Karl Marx to Friedrich Engels, Jan. 28, 1860, MEW, vol. 30, p. 11 et seq.
65. Ferdinand Lassalle to Karl Marx, Jan. 19, 1861, ibid., p. 716 n172.
66. Karl Marx to Friedrich Engels, Feb. 27, 1861, ibid., p. 159. K. J. Bühring, a cabinetmaker living in London, was a member of the League of Communists.
67. Karl Marx to Friedrich Engels, Feb. 27, 1861, ibid.

68. Karl Marx to Ferdinand Lassalle, Mar. 7, 1861, ibid., p. 587.
69. Karl Marx to Antoinette Philips, Mar. 24, 1861, ibid., p. 589.
70. Ibid.
71. Ibid., p. 590.
72. Karl Marx to Friedrich Engels, May 10, 1861, ibid., p. 165 et seq.
73. Karl Marx to Friedrich Engels, May 7, 1861, ibid., p. 162.
74. Enzensberger, op. cit., p. 81.
75. Karl Marx to Friedrich Engels, June 24, 1865, MEW, vol. 31, p. 124.
76. Karl Marx to Friedrich Engels, July 30, 1862, MEW, vol. 30, p. 259.
77. Friedrich Engels to Eduard Bernstein, Nov. 2/3, 1882, in Helmut Hirsch (ed.), *Friedrich Engels' Briefwechsel mit Eduard Bernstein*, p. 152.
78. Karl Marx to Friedrich Engels, July 30, 1862, MEW, vol. 30, p. 257.
79. Ibid., p. 259.
80. See editor's prefatory note, "Zum Arbeiter-Program," in Helmut Hirsch (ed.), *Ferdinand Lassalle. Eine Auswahl für unsere Zeit*, p. 196.
81. Ibid., p. 213.
82. Ferdinand Lassalle, "Arbeiter-Programm," ibid., p. 232.
83. Quoted from Na'aman, op. cit., p. 528 et seq.
84. Wilhelm Liebknecht, in MSW, p. 112.
85. See introduction to "Offenes Antwortschreiben," in Hirsch, *Lassalle*, p. 239 et seq.
86. Ferdinand Lassalle to Johann Karl Rodbertus, May 26, 1863, in Johann Karl Rodbertus, *Gesammelte Werke und Briefe*, pt. 4: *Briefe und Briefwechsel*, p. 83 et seq.
87. Ferdinand Lassalle to Johann Karl Rodbertus, Apr. 24, 1863, ibid., p. 57.
88. Ibid., p. 71.
89. Johann Karl Rodbertus, "Fragmente zu dem Verhältnis zu Lassalle," ibid., p. 115 et seq.
90. Friedrich Engels to Karl Marx, Jan. 27, 1865, *Correspondence*, p. 178.
91. See Mehring, *Life*, p. 312.
92. Jenny Marx, "Kurze Umrisse eines bewegten Lebens," in *Mohr und General*, p. 235 et seq.
93. Ferdinand Lassalle, "Offenes Antwortschreiben," in Hirsch, *Lassalle*, p. 258 et seq.
94. Karl Marx to Friedrich Engels, June 3, 1864, MEW, vol. 30, p. 403.
95. Friedrich Engels to Karl Marx, Sept. 7, 1864, ibid., p. 432.
96. Karl Marx to Friedrich Engels, Sept. 7, 1864, *Correspondence*, p. 158.
97. Friedrich Engels to Karl Marx, Sept. 4, 1864, ibid., p. 157.
98. Karl Marx to Sophie von Hatzfeldt, Sept. 12, 1864, MEW, vol. 30, p. 673.

· CHAPTER 8 ·

1. Friedrich Engels to Laura Lafargue, June 24, 1883, MEW, vol. 36, p. 43.
2. See Auguste Cornu, op. cit., vol. 1, p. 17.
3. Karl Marx to Friedrich Engels, Nov. 19, 1852, MEW, vol. 28, p. 195.
4. See *Geschichte der deutschen Arbeiterbewegung*, published by Institute for Marxism-Leninism, East Berlin, vol. 1, p. 234.
5. See Father Jean-Yves Calvez, *Karl Marx. Darstellung und Kritik seines Denkens* (Breisgau, 1964), p. 220.
6. Wolfgang Abendroth: *Sozialgeschichte der europäischen Arbeiterbewegung* (Frankfurt/Main, 1965), p. 36.
7. Karl Marx to Johann Baptist Schweitzer, Oct. 13, 1868, *Correspondence*, p. 250.

8. Mehring, *Life*, p. 319.
9. Ibid., p. 320.
10. Karl Marx, *Die polnische Frage. Manuskripte über die polnische Frage (1863 bis 1864)*, edited by W. Conze and D. Hertz-Eichenrode.
11. From David McClellan, *Karl Marx. His Life and Thought* (New York, 1973), p. 362 n3.
12. Karl Marx to Friedrich Engels, Nov. 4, 1864, *Correspondence*, p. 160.
13. Mehring, *Life*, p. 323.
14. Karl Marx to Friedrich Engels, Nov. 4, 1864, *Correspondence*, p. 159.
15. Karl Marx to Friedrich Engels, Apr. 2, 1851, ibid., p. 36.
16. Karl Marx to Friedrich Engels, Dec. 26, 1865, MEW, vol. 31, p. 162.
17. See *Geschichte der deutschen Arbeiterbewegung*, p. 232. Even this account, however, is forced to admit that "there were a few small groups adhering to the International." (ibid., p. 233.)
18. Karl Marx to Friedrich Engels, Nov. 4, 1864, *Correspondence*, p. 161.
19. Ibid.
20. Ibid., p. 162.
21. MESW, vol. 2, p. 19.
22. Subsequent quotations are to be found in MEW, vol. 16, pp. 5–13, or MESW, vol. 2, pp. 14–17.
23. MESW, vol. 2, p. 17.
24. Ibid., pp. 16–17.
25. "A funny position for me to be functioning as the representative of young Russia! A man never knows what he may come to or what strange fellowship he may have to submit to. . . . I thought it safer to say nothing about Bakunin." Karl Marx to Friedrich Engels, Mar. 24, 1870, *Correspondence*, p. 287.
26. Mehring, *Life*, p. 332.
27. Ibid., p. 329.
28. Karl Marx to Carl Klings, Oct. 4, 1864, MEW, vol. 31, p. 417.
29. See *Karl Marx. Chronik seines Lebens in Einzeldaten*, collated by Marx-Engels-Lenin Institute, Moscow, p. 230.
30. Karl Marx to Ludwig Kugelmann, Feb. 23, 1865, *Correspondence*, p. 197.
31. Karl Marx to Carl Siebel, Dec. 22, 1864, MEW, vol. 31, p. 437.
32. Friedrich Engels to Karl Marx, June 22, 1869, MEW, vol. 32, p. 325.
33. Karl Marx to Friedrich Engels, Mar. 13, 1865, MEW, vol. 31, p. 101.
34. Ibid., p. 100 et seq.
35. Karl Marx to Friedrich Engels, Dec. 2, 1864, ibid., p. 33. Marx uses the word "bothered."
36. See S. Lewiowa, "Karl Schapper," in *Marx und Engels und die ersten proletarischen Revolutionäre*, pp. 117 et seq.
37. Friedrich Engels to Karl Kautsky, 25 Mar. 1895 in Benedikt Kautsky (ed.), *Friedrich Engels' Briefwechsel mit Karl Kautsky*, p. 427.
38. Karl Marx to Friedrich Engels, Apr. 6, 1866, MEW, vol. 31, p. 204.
39. Karl Marx to Friedrich Engels, Aug. 5, 1866, ibid., p. 136.
40. Karl Marx to Gustav Kwasniewski, Sept. 29, 1871, MEW, vol. 33, p. 287.
41. Friedrich Engels to Friedrich Adolph Sorge, Sept. 12/17, 1874, *Correspondence*, p. 329.
42. Karl Marx to Ludwig Kugelmann, Oct. 13, 1866, in *Karl Marx. Letters to Dr Kugelmann* (London, 1941), p. 43.

43. Karl Marx to Friedrich Engels, Sept. 11, 1867, *Correspondence*, p. 227.
44. Copy of a speech by Engels on Mazzini's relations with the International in *The Eastern Post*, July 29, 1871, MEW, vol. 17, p. 644.
45. Mehring, *Life*, p. 507.
46. August Bebel, *Aus meinem Leben* (Berlin, 1964), p. 746.
47. Wilhelm Liebknecht, *Karl Marx zum Gedächtnis. Ein Lebensabriss und Erinnerungen*, p. 39 et seq.
48. Karl Marx to Friedrich Engels, May 25, 1859, MEW, vol. 29, p. 442 et seq.
49. Karl Marx to Ludwig Kugelmann, Dec. 5, 1868, *Letters to Kugelmann*, p. 82; Friedrich Engels to Karl Marx, Feb. 2, 1868, MEW, vol. 32, p. 28, and Apr. 6, 1869, ibid., p. 295; Karl Marx to Friedrich Engels, Mar. 14, 1869, ibid., p. 278; Friedrich Engels to Karl Marx, June 12, 1869, ibid., p. 396.
50. Eduard Bernstein, *Aus den Jahren meines Exils. Erinnerungen eines Sozialisten* (Berlin, 1918), p. 136 et seq.
51. Karl Marx to Friedrich Engels, Apr. 7, 1869, MEW, vol. 32, p. 296.
52. Karl Marx to Friedrich Engels, July 3, 1869, ibid., p. 331.
53. Friedrich Engels to Wilhelm Liebknecht, July 10, 1871, MEW, vol. 33, p. 242 et seq.
54. Friedrich Engels to Wilhelm Liebknecht, Sept. 11, 1871, ibid., p. 280.
55. Friedrich Engels to Wilhelm Liebknecht, Nov. 4, 1871, ibid., p. 304.
56. Friedrich Engels to Wilhelm Liebknecht, Feb. 12, 1873, ibid., p. 568.
57. Wilhelm Liebknecht, "Karl Marx zum Gedächtnis. Ein Lebensabriss," in *Mohr und General*, p. 63 et seq.
58. Friedrich Engels to August Bebel, Mar. 18/28, 1875, *Correspondence*, p. 332.
59. Ibid., p. 337.
60. Friedrich Engels to Karl Kautsky, Jan. 7, 1891, Kautsky, op. cit., p. 268 et seq. See also Karl Kautsky to Friedrich Engels, Jan. 9, 1891 (op. cit., p. 284 et seq); Friedrich Engels to Karl Kautsky, Feb. 23, 1891, and Mar. 17, 1891 (op. cit., pp. 282 and 288).
61. Friedrich Engels to Karl Kautsky, Feb. 11, 1891, ibid., p. 277.
62. Karl Kautsky to Friedrich Engels, Feb. 6, 1891, ibid., p. 273 et seq.
63. Friedrich Engels to August Bebel, Mar. 18/28, 1875, *Correspondence*, p. 339.
64. All following quotations from MESW, vol. 3, pp. 18–26.
65. Ibid., p. 18.
66. Ibid., p. 26.
67. "By the standard of that time the Reichstag elections of 1877 were a great success for Social Democracy. This was mainly due to the cooperation of the various groups which had hitherto been fighting so violently among themselves. In the first round we scored 486,800 votes against 379,500 in 1874. It must be remembered, however, that the electorate was nothing like so large as it is today." Wilhelm Blos, *Denkwürdigkeiten eines Sozialdemokraten*, vol. 1, p. 213.
68. Karl Marx to Friedrich Engels, Sept. 11, 1867, *Correspondence*, p. 227.
69. H. Gerth (ed.), *The First International. Minutes of the Haag-Congress with related Documents*, p. 539.
70. Manfred Kliem (ed.), op. cit., p. 53.
71. Friedrich Engels to Theodor Cuno, May 7/8, 1872, MEW, vol. 33, p. 461.
72. Notes of an interview, July 3, 1871, MEW, vol. 17, p. 640.
73. Karl Marx to Friedrich Engels, Nov. 4, 1864, *Correspondence*, p. 163.
74. Karl Marx to Sophie von Hatzfeldt, Sept. 12, 1864, MEW, vol. 30, p. 673.
75. Friedrich Lessner to Karl Marx, Oct. 26, 1864, quoted in D. Ryazanoff, "Sozial-

demokratische Flagge und anarchistische Ware," in *Die Neue Zeit*, Oct. 31, 1913.

76. Michael Bakunin to Karl Marx, Oct. 27, 1864, ibid.

77. Karl Marx to Friedrich Engels, Nov. 4, 1864, *Correspondence*, p. 163.

78. Ibid.

79. Quoted from Leopold Schwarzschild, *The Red Prussian* (London, 1948), p. 158.

80. Michael Bakunin: "Persönliche Beziehungen zu Marx (1871)," in *Gesammelte Werke* (Berlin, 1924), vol. 3, p. 215 et seq.

81. Kurt Kersten (ed.), *Michael Bakunin's Beichte aus der Peter-Pauls Festung an Zar Nikolaus I* (Frankfurt/Main, 1973), p. 74.

82. Ibid., p. 91 et seq.

83. Ibid., p. 151.

84. Franz Mehring, "Ein neuer Literatenkrakeel," in *Die Neue Zeit*, Dec. 5, 1913, vol. 32, p. 394.

85. Bakunin, op. cit., p. 406.

86. Maxim Gorky: *Erinnerungen an Zeitgenossen* (Frankfurt/Main, 1962), p. 188 et seq.

87. Wilhelm Liebknecht, in *Mohr und General*, p. 107.

88. Gorky, op. cit., p. 217.

89. Ibid., p. 212 et seq.

90. Friedrich Engels to Karl Kautsky, Feb. 1, 1881, Kautsky, op. cit., p. 13.

91. Bakunin, op. cit., p. 212.

92. Ibid., p. 207.

93. Mehring, *Life*, p. 480.

94. Quoted in Ricarda Huch, *Michael Bakunin und die Anarchie* (Frankfurt/Main, 1972), p. 150.

95. Mehring, *Life*, p. 405.

96. Huch, op. cit., p. 239.

97. Ibid., p. 184.

98. Bakunin, op. cit., p. 407. See also his letter to the Brussels *Liberté*, Oct. 5, 1872, ibid., pp. 221–250.

99. "Michael Bakunins Socialpolitischer Briefwechsel mit Alexander Iw. Herzen und Ogaryov," edited by Michail Dragomanov, in *Bibliothek Russischer Denkwürdigkeiten*, edited by Theodor Schiemann, vol. 6, p. 35.

100. Karl Marx to Friedrich Engels, Feb. 19, 1870, MEW, vol. 32, p. 448.

101. Alexander Herzen, *Mein Leben. Memoiren und Reflexionen 1852–1868*, (Berlin, 1962), p. 200 et seq.

102. Karl Marx to Friedrich Engels, Sept. 3, 1853, MEW, vol. 28, p. 280.

103. Michael Bakunin to Karl Marx, Dec. 22, 1868, MEW, vol. 32, p. 757 n284.

104. Quoted from D. Ryazanoff, "Sozialdemokratische Flagge," in *Die Neue Zeit*, Nov. 14, 1913, vol. 32, p. 228.

105. Bakunin, op. cit., pp. 409, 216.

106. Friedrich Engels to Karl Marx, Oct. 18, 1867, MEW, vol. 31, p. 367.

107. Karl Marx to Friedrich Engels, Mar. 20, 1869, MEW, vol. 32, p. 283.

108. Jenny Marx to J. P. Becker, quoted in D. Ryazanoff, op. cit., p. 228.

109. Quoted from Horst Stuke (ed.), *Michael Bakunin. Staatlichkeit und Anarchie und andere Schriften*, p. 409 n. 2.

110. Bakunin, op. cit., p. 206 et seq.

111. Michael Bakunin's letter to the Brussels *Liberté*, Oct. 5, 1872, ibid., p. 240.

112. Michael Bakunin to the internationalists of the Romagna, Jan. 23, 1872, ibid., p. 188.

113. Karl Marx to Friedrich Engels, July 1, 1869, MEW, vol. 16, p. 359.
114. Quoted from Schwarzschild, op. cit., p. 330.
115. Michael Bakunin, "Brief an Aleksander Herzen," in *Kursbuch*, Dec. 19, 1969, p. 2 et seq.
116. For full details see D. Ryazanoff, op. cit., in *Die Neue Zeit*, Oct. 31, 1913, vol. 32, pp. 150–161; Nov. 14, 1913, pp. 226–239; Nov. 21, 1913, pp. 265–272; Nov. 28, 1913, pp. 320–353; Dec. 5, 1913, pp. 360–375; also Franz Mehring, "Ein neuer Literatenkrakeel," Dec. 5, 1913, pp. 393–396.
117. Friedrich Engels to Karl Marx, Feb. 22, 1870, MEW, vol. 32, p. 451.
118. Karl Kautsky to Friedrich Engels, Sept. 6, 1882, Kautsky, op. cit., p. 61.
119. Huch, op. cit., p. 83.
120. Schwarzschild, op. cit., p. 350.
121. Michael Bakunin's letter to the Brussels *Liberté*, in Bakunin, op. cit., p. 244. As an example, scientific research has shown (see Trevor Beeson, *Discretion and Valour. Religious Conditions in Russia and Eastern Europe*) that the percentage of people going to church in the Soviet Union is greater than in Great Britain and that in socialist Poland Catholicism is more firmly rooted than in any other country in the world.
122. Karl Marx to Friedrich Engels, Dec. 15, 1868, MEW, vol. 32, p. 234.
123. Mehring, *Life*, p. 467.
124. Karl Marx to Ludwig Kugelmann, July 29, 1872, *Letters to Kugelmann*, p. 132.
125. Ibid.
126. Friedrich Engels to Friedrich Adolph Sorge, Nov. 25, 1873, MEW, vol. 33, p. 609.
127. Mehring, *Life*, pp. 497, 499.
128. For details, though in the form of an apologia for Marx, see D. Ryazanoff; op. cit., in *Die Neue Zeit*, Dec. 5, 1913, vol. 32, pp. 360–375.
129. MESW, vol. 2, p. 192.
130. Karl Marx to Friedrich Engels, July 20, 1870, *Correspondence*, p. 292.
131. Karl Marx to Friedrich Engels, July 20, 1870, MEW, vol. 33, p. 126.
132. MESW, vol. 2, p. 195.
133. *Documents of the First International*, issued by Institute for Marxism-Leninism (Moscow, undated), p. 169.
134. Karl Marx to Leo Frankel, about Apr. 26, 1871 (draft), MEW, vol. 33, p. 216.
135. Friedrich Engels, Introduction to "The Civil War in France," MSW, vol. 2, p. 456.
136. Karl Marx to Leo Frankel and Louis-Eugène Varlin, May 13, 1871 (draft), *Correspondence*, p. 311.
137. MEW, vol. 33, p. 218 et seq.
138. Karl Marx to Ludwig Kugelmann, Apr. 12, 1871, *Correspondence*, p. 309.
139. This is what the Austrian socialist Heinrich Oberwinder says in his memoirs, *Sozialismus und Sozialpolitik* (Berlin, 1887), p. 55.
140. Karl Marx to Wilhelm Liebknecht, Apr. 6, 1871, *Correspondence*, p. 307.
141. "The Address certainly gives no critical history of the Commune but that was not its aim. . . . It was written as a polemic and not as a historical judgment." Mehring, *Life*, p. 451.
142. Karl Marx, *The Civil War in France*, MESW, vol. 2, p. 239.
143. Ibid.
144. Karl Marx to Ludwig Kugelmann, June 18, 1871, *Letters to Kugelmann*, p. 126.
145. Karl Marx, *The Civil War in France*, MESW, vol. 2, p. 223.
146. Marx's attacks on the demand for equal, free education for all in his "Marginal

Notes to the Programme of the German Workers' Party" (the *Critique of the Gotha Program*), MESW, vol. 3, p. 28.

147. Mehring, *Life*, p. 453.
148. Karl Marx to Ferdinand Domela Nieuwenhuis, Feb. 22, 1881, *Correspondence*, p. 387.
149. MESW, vol. 2, p. 224.
150. Mehring, *Life*, p. 453.
151. Friedrich Engels, Introduction to *The Civil War in France*, MESW, vol. 2, p. 189.
152. Karl Marx to Ludwig Kugelmann, July 29, 1872, *Letters to Kugelmann*, p. 132.
153. Karl Marx to Friedrich Adolph Sorge, May 23, 1872, MEW, vol. 33, p. 470.
154. Mehring, *Life*, p. 490.

· CHAPTER 9 ·

1. David J. Rosenberg, *Die Entwicklung der ökonomischen Lehren von Marx und Engels in den vierziger Jahren des 19 Jahrhunderts* (Berlin, 1958), p. 35.
2. Ernest Mandel, *Entstehung und Entwicklung der ökonomischen Lehre von Karl Marx (1843 bis 1963)* (Frankfurt/Main, 1968), p. 7.
3. Friedrich Engels to Franz Mehring, Sept. 28, 1892, MEW, vol. 38, p. 481.
4. Cf. Günther Herre's outstanding study, based on profound knowledge of these unpublished sources: *Verelendung und Proletariat bei Karl Marx. Entstehung einer Theorie und ihre Quellen* (Düsseldorf, 1973). Maximilien Rubel has published an initial analysis dealing with the extracts: "Les Cahiers de Lecture de Karl Marx: I, 1840–1853; II, 1853–1856," in *International Review of Social History*, No. 2 (1957), p. 392 et seq., No. 5 (1960), p. 39 et seq.
5. Aristotle, *Politics* (Longmans Green, 1877), p. 134 et seq.
6. G. W. F. Hegel, *Jenenser Realphilosophie*, edited by J. Hoffmeister (Leipzig, 1931), vol. 2, p. 257.
7. Cf. Herre, op. cit., p. 28.
8. Quoted in Mandel, op. cit., p. 154.
9. Jürgen Habermas, *Theorie und Praxis* (Berlin, 1963), p. 154 et seq.
10. Cf. Herre, op. cit., p. 38 et seq.
11. Karl Marx to Friedrich Engels, Dec. 18, 1857, MEW, vol. 29, p. 232.
12. Paul Lafargue, "Reminiscences of Marx," MSW, vol. 1, pp. 91–92.
13. Cf. Arnold Künzli, op cit., p. 280.
14. Karl Marx to Friedrich Engels, July 31, 1865, *Correspondence*, p. 204.
15. Karl Marx to Friedrich Engels, Apr. 2, 1851, *Correspondence*, p. 36; Dec. 18, 1857, MEW, vol. 29, p. 232; Feb. 3, 1866, MEW, vol. 31, p. 178.
16. Leopold Schwarzschild, op. cit., p. 135.
17. Karl Marx to Carl Wilhelm Leske, Aug. 1, 1846, MEW, vol. 27, p. 447.
18. Friedrich Engels to Karl Marx, Oct. 1844, ibid, p. 8; Jan. 20, 1845, ibid., p. 16.
19. Karl Marx to Friedrich Engels, Apr. 2, 1851, *Correspondence*, p. 36: "I have got so far that I could be finished with the whole economic shit in five weeks. And that done I shall work out the economy at home and pitch into another science in the Museum. This is beginning to bore me."
20. Karl Marx to Friedrich Engels, Dec. 8, 1857, MEW, vol. 29, p. 225.
21. Karl Marx to Friedrich Engels, Dec. 18, 1857, ibid., p. 232.
22. Künzli, op. cit., p. 273.

23. MESW, vol. 1, pp. 505–506.
24. Friedrich Engels to Karl Marx, Nov. 27, 1851, MEW, vol. 27, p. 374.
25. Bert Andreas, *Briefe und Dokumente der Familie Marx aus den Jahren 1862–1873 nebst zwei unbekannten Aufsätzen von Friedrich Engels* (Hanover, 1962), vol. 2, p. 181.
26. Ernest Mandel (op. cit., p. 70) has pointed out this vital error in argumentation; it can no longer be regarded as an "external" reason for the delays in the writing of Marx's book.
27. Karl Marx, *Capital*: Author's Preface to First Edition, translation by Samuel Moore and Edward Aveling (Chicago, 1926), vol. 1, p. 11.
28. Hans Lamp'l, "Stichwortartige Hinweise zur Persönlichkeit — aufgrund der Handschrift Karl Marx." Memorandum dated June 12, 1974.
29. Ibid, pp. 4, 5.
30. Karl Marx to Friedrich Engels, Jan. 21, 1859, MEW, vol. 29, p. 385.
31. Quoted from Schwarzschild, op. cit., pp. 218–219.
32. Werner Sombart, *Der proletarische Sozialismus*, vol. 1, p. 65.
33. Karl Marx to Sigfrid Meyer, Apr. 30, 1867, *Correspondence*, p. 219.
34. Karl Kautsky, "Mein erster Aufenthalt in London," in Benedikt Kautsky (ed.), *Friedrich Engels' Briefwechsel mit Karl Kautsky*, p. 32.
35. Karl Marx to Friedrich Engels, Aug. 16, 1867, *Correspondence*, p. 226: "So *this volume is finished*. This has been possible thanks to *you* alone. Without your self-sacrifice for me I could never possibly have done the enormous work for the three volumes. I embrace you, full of thanks!"
36. Ralph Colp, "The Contacts between Karl Marx and Charles Darwin," *Journal of the History of Ideas*, vol. 35, no. 2 (Apr.–June 1974), p. 333.
37. Ibid., p. 334.
38. Ibid., p. 335.
39. Ibid., p. 334.
40. Ibid., p. 335: "Moreover, though I am a strong advocate for free thought on all subjects, yet it appears to me (whether rightly or wrongly) that direct arguments against christianity & theism produce hardly any effect on the public & freedom of thought is best promoted by the ["gradual" added] illumination of ["the" deleted, "men's" added] minds which follow from the advance of science. It has, therefore, been always my object to avoid writing on religion & I have confined myself to science. I may, however, have been unduly biassed by the pain which it would give some members of my family, if I aided in any way direct attacks on religion."
41. Friedrich Engels to Karl Marx, Oct. 2, 1869, MEW, vol. 32, p. 172.
42. Friedrich Engels to Karl Marx, Jan. 19, 1870, ibid., p. 426.
43. MEGA, pt. 1, vol. 1, 2nd half-vol., p. 218.
44. Karl Marx to Friedrich Engels, Aug. 8, 1851, MEW, vol. 27, p. 296.
45. Jenny Marx to Joseph Weydemeyer, Jan. 10, 1852, in *Letters to Americans*, p. 31.
46. Karl Marx to Friedrich Engels, Mar. 10, 1853, MEW, vol. 28, p. 221.
47. Karl Marx to Friedrich Engels, May 22, 1857, MEW, vol. 29, p. 137.
48. Karl Marx to Friedrich Engels, Apr. 2, 1858, ibid., p. 312.
49. Karl Marx to Friedrich Engels, Apr. 29, 1858, ibid., p. 323.
50. Karl Marx to Friedrich Engels, May 31, 1858, ibid., p. 329.
51. Karl Marx to Friedrich Engels, July 15, 1858, ibid., p. 340.
52. Karl Marx to Friedrich Engels, Sept. 21, 1858, ibid., p. 355.
53. Karl Marx to Friedrich Engels, Nov. 2, 1858, ibid., p. 366.

54. Karl Marx to Ferdinand Lassalle, May 31, 1858, ibid., p. 560.
55. Jenny Marx to Friedrich Engels, Apr. 9, 1858, ibid., p. 648.
56. Friedrich Engels to Nikolai F. Danielson, Nov. 13, 1885, MEW, vol. 36, p. 385.
57. Friedrich Engels to Karl Marx, Apr. 9, 1858, MEW, vol. 19, p. 319.
58. Karl Marx to Friedrich Engels, July 22, 1859, MEW, vol. 29, p. 462.
59. Karl Marx to Friedrich Engels, Aug. 8, 1859, ibid., p. 470.
60. Karl Marx to Friedrich Engels, Oct. 19, 1867, MEW, vol. 31, p. 368.
61. Professor Meyer-Rohn of the Dermatological Clinic in University Hospital, Hamburg, in a conversation with the author. Arnold Künzli would seem to exaggerate when he translates carbuncles into leprosy and, having found two passages in which Marx compares himself with Lazarus and Job, characterizes the entire story of Marx's illnesses as an extreme manifestation of his Jewish self-hate (op. cit., p. 465). Otherwise Künzli deals with this problem meticulously, accurately, and cautiously; this statement, however, seems to be supposition.
62. Karl Marx to Friedrich Engels, Feb. 10, 1866, MEW, vol. 31, p. 174; Mar. 30, 1855, MEW, vol. 28, p. 442; Feb. 13, 1866, MEW, vol. 31, p. 178.
63. Arthur Jores, *Vom Sinn der Krankheit* (Hamburg, 1950), p. 9 et seq.
64. Karl Marx to Friedrich Engels, June 22, 1863, MEW, vol. 30, p. 359.
65. Karl Marx to Friedrich Engels, Apr. 2, 1867, MEW, vol. 31, p. 281.
66. Friedrich Engels to Karl Marx, Apr. 4, 1867, ibid., p. 283.
67. Friedrich Engels to Karl Marx, Apr. 27, 1867, ibid., p. 292.
68. See MEW, vol. 24, p. 7 et seq., and vol. 25, p. 7 et seq.
69. Arthur M. Prinz, "Myths, Facts and Riddles about the Literary Estate of Karl Marx," in *Der Friede. Idee und Verwirklichung. Festgabe für Adolf Leschnitzer* (Heidelberg, 1961), p. 408.
70. In archives of Instituut voor Sociale Geschiedenes, Amsterdam. See also Künzli, op, cit., p. 280 et seq.
71. Friedrich Engels to Karl Marx, Apr. 3, 1851, MEW, vol. 27, p. 233 et seq.
72. Friedrich Engels to Friedrich Adolph Sorge, June 29, 1883, MEW, vol. 36, p. 46.
73. Karl Marx to Nikolai F. Danielson, Apr. 10, 1879, MEW, vol. 34, p. 372.
74. See Manfred Kliem, op. cit., p. 424.
75. Karl Marx to Ferdinand Lassalle, Apr. 28, 1862, MEW, vol. 30, p. 622.
76. Lafargue, op. cit., MSW, vol. 1, p. 91.
77. Friedrich Engels to August Bebel, Aug. 30, 1883, MEW, vol. 36, p. 56.
78. Preface to *Capital*, vol. 2.
79. Ernst Eduard Walter Kux, "Karl Marx — Die revolutionäre Konfession" (dissertation, Zurich, 1966).
80. Ibid., p. 74.
81. Many students of Marx have pointed to the Romantic basis of his thinking; Thomas Masaryk, for instance, regarded Marx's amorality and penchant for the aristocracy in this context; Benedetto Croce pronounced: "The author of the Communist Manifesto shows himself as a true son of romantic thinking" (Kux, op. cit., p. 13). Kux points out that Marx derived his theories from aesthetic ideas and views, that he relates his judgments on world trade to those on world literature and draws his theory of money from the romantic theory of the drama (Kux, op. cit., p. 11).
82. Ibid., p. 9.
83. Sombart, op. cit., p. 52.
84. Friedrich Engels, Introduction to "The Class Struggles in France," MESW, vol. 1, p. 187.

85. Karl Jaspers, "Marx und Freud," in *Der Monat*, Issue 26 (1950), p. 142 et seq.
86. Karl Marx to Friedrich Engels, Nov. 2, 1867, MEW, vol. 31, p. 374.
87. Karl Marx to Friedrich Engels, Oct. 4, 1867, ibid., p. 352 et seq.
88. Karl Marx to Friedrich Engels, Oct. 20, 1867, ibid., p. 360.
89. Friedrich Engels to Karl Marx, Oct. 11, 1867, ibid., p. 361.
90. Friedrich Engels to Karl Marx, Oct. 13, 1867, ibid., p. 362.
91. Friedrich Engels to Karl Marx, Oct. 18, 1867, ibid., p. 367.
92. Karl Marx to Friedrich Engels, Oct. 19, 1867, ibid., p. 370.
93. Friedrich Engels to Karl Marx, Oct. 22, 1867, ibid., p. 372.
94. Ernst Czobel published seven of them in his *Marx-Engels-Archiv*, vol. 2, pp. 427–462.
95. Karl Marx to Friedrich Engels, Dec. 7, 1867, MEW, vol. 31, p. 403.
96. See Andreas, op. cit., p. 285.
97 Friedrich Engels to Karl Marx, June 16, 1867, *Correspondence*, p. 220.
98. See Andreas, op. cit., p. 241.
99. Quoted from J. P. Mayer, "Reflections on Equality," in Leszek Kolakowski and Stuart Hampshire (ed.), *The Socialist Idea. A Reappraisal*, p. 72.
100. Karl Kautsky, "Vorgeschichte meiner Beziehungen zu Engels," in Kautsky, op. cit., p. 4. See also Karl Kautsky, "Karl Marx' ökonomische Lehren" — Foreword to first edition (Stuttgart, 1893), p. 7.
101. Kliem, op. cit., p. 332.
102. Karl Marx, Preface to First Edition of *Capital*, op. cit., p. 12.
103. Ibid., p. 25.
104. Ibid., p. 25.
105. Karl Marx, *Capital*, op. cit., vol. 1, p. 15.
106. Ibid.
107. Karl Marx to Joseph Weydemeyer, Mar. 5, 1852, *Correspondence*, p. 57.
108. Karl Marx, Preface to First Edition of *Capital*, op. cit., p. 16.
109. Karl Marx to Ludwig Kugelmann, Nov. 30, 1867, *Letters to Kugelmann*, p. 54.
110. Karl Korsch, Foreword to Marx's *Das Kapital* (Berlin, 1969), vol. 1.
111. Ibid., p. xv.
112. Ibid., p. xvii.
113. Anna Wassilyevna Uroyeva, "Wo ist der Prospekt zum 'Kapital' von Karl Marx?" in *Börsenblatt für den deutschen Buchhandel*, July 10, 1973.
114. Karl Marx to Friedrich Engels, Aug. 24, 1867, *Correspondence*, p. 226.
115. Henri de Saint-Simon, "La Classe de prolétaires," in *Oeuvres*, vol. 4, p. 455, quoted in Herre, op. cit., p. 61.
116. Ibid.
117. Ibid., pp. 82, 88.
118. Louis Althusser and Etienne Balibar, *Lire le Capital* (Paris, 1968), vol. 1, p. 17 et seq.
119. Karl Marx, *Capital*, op. cit., vol. 1, p. 68.
120. Ibid., p. 81.
121. Ibid., p. 208.
122. Ibid., p. 290 n. 1.
123. Karl Marx to Friedrich Engels, July 6, 1863, enclosure to letter, *Correspondence*, facing p. 154.
124. Karl Marx, *Capital*, op. cit., vol. 1, pp. 801–802.
125. Erich Fromm, *Der moderne Mensch und seine Zukunft. Eine sozialpsychologische Untersuchung* (Frankfurt/Main, 1971), p. 191.

126. Carl Bode (ed.), *The Portable Thoreau* (New York, 1947), pp. 631–655.
127. Emil Durkheim: *Le Suicide* (Paris, 1897), p. 449.
128. Karl Marx, *Capital*, op. cit., vol. 1, p. 398.
129. As we know, inventions in the cotton-spinning industry took place about the mid-eighteenth century and in England led to a complete transformation of the industry in a remarkably short time. In that country there were 142 mills with 2,000,000 spindles as early as 1788. By contrast, the mainland of Europe and America remained almost unaffected by the new technique until the end of the Napoleonic wars. (See full details in A. Ure, *The Cotton Manufacture of Great Britain*, Introduction to First Edition). Mechanical spinning was only established outside England in the mid-nineteenth century.

The extent of England's lead even at this period, however, is clear from the following table:

STATE OF THE COTTON INDUSTRY 1851

COUNTRY	NO. OF SPINDLES (MILLIONS)	PRODUCTION (MILLIONS OF KGS)	
		RAW YARN & MATERIALS	HOME CONSUMPTION
England	18	277	73
France	4.5	64	52
Russia		31	30
Austria	1.4	30	96
Germany (Zollverein)	0.9	18	96
Belgium	0.4	10	8
Spain	0.7	10	12.5
Italy	0.7	10	13.5
Switzerland	0.9	9	4
U.S.A.	5.5	110	60
	33.0	569	

Werner Sombart, *Der Moderne Kapitalismus. Historisch-systematische Darstellung des gesamteuropäischen Wirtschaftslebens von seinen Anfängen bis zur Gegenwart*, vol. 3: *Das Wirtschaftsleben im Zeitalter des Hochkapitalismus*, first half-vol., p. 161.

130. Karl Marx, *Capital*, op. cit., vol. 1, p. 433.
131. Karl Marx, *Theories of Surplus Value* (London, 1969), pt. 2, p. 150.
132. Vitali S. Vygodsky, *Die Geschichte einer grossen Entdeckung. Uber die Entstehung des Werkes "Das Kapital" von Karl Marx* (Berlin, 1967), p. 72.
133. Karl Marx, *Capital*, op. cit., vol. 1, p. 784.
134. Ibid., p. 836.
135. Karl Marx to Ludwig Kugelmann, Dec. 28, 1862, *Letters to Kugelmann*, p. 23.
136. Friedrich Engels, Review of Volume 1 of *Capital*, *Düsseldorfer Zeitung*, Nov. 16, 1867, MEW, vol. 16, p. 216.
137. Friedrich Engels, interview with *Le Figaro* published in *Le Socialiste*, no. 140, May 20, 1893, quoted in *Lafargue Correspondence*, vol. 3, p. 392.

138. Friedrich Engels to Werner Sombart, Mar. 11, 1895, MEW, vol. 39, p. 428.
139. See the chapter entitled "Die Ausarbeitung des 'Kapitals,'" in Vygodsky, op. cit., pp. 117–130.
140. See "Plan der 'Kritik der politischen Okonomie' (1858 bis 1862)," Foreword by Institute of Marxism-Leninism, Central Committee of East German Social Unity Party, to Karl Marx's "Theories of Surplus Value" (Vol. 4 of Capital), MEW, vol. 26, p. VI.
141. Friedrich Engels to Eduard Bernstein, Aug. 1884, MEW, vol. 36, p. 204.
142. Rosa Luxemburg: Die Akkumulation des Kapitals (Berlin, 1923), p. 400.
143. Ibid., p. 88 et seq.
144. Ibid., p. 400.
145. Both these two political groupings, "Il Manifesto" and "Praxis," regard themselves as unorthodox, theoretical Marxist "progressives." The fact that the Yugoslav group was proscribed together with its newspaper of the same name — edited by Ernst Bloch among other people — its professors removed from their chairs and its meetings banned shows that the clash between theoretical pronouncements and the nationality problem is as explosive as ever.
146. Der Spiegel, no. 44 (1973), p. 41.
147. Ibid., p. 43.
148. Paul Mattick, Marx und Keynes. Die "Grenzen" des gemischten Wirtschaftssystems (Frankfurt/Main, 1971), p. 343.
149. Ibid., p. 340.
150. Ibid., p. 306.
151. Ibid., p. 306 et seq.
152. Karl Marx, Capital, op. cit., vol. 1, p. 198.
153. Cf. Egmont R. Koch, "Aufstieg und Fall eines Mäusestaates," in Akzent — Bild der Wissenschaft. Daten, Fakten, Analysen, vol. 2, no. 3 (March 1974).
154. Ibid.
155. Ibid.
156. See Irenäus Eibl-Eibesfeldt, Grundriss der vergleichenden Verhaltensforschung. Ethologie, p. 33 et seq; Konrad Lorenz, Uber tierisches und menschliches Verhalten. Aus dem Werdegang der Verhaltenslehre, vol. 1, p. 133.
157. MEW, vol. 13, p. 636.
158. Karl R. Popper, Die offene Gesellschaft und ihre Feinde, vol. 2: Falsche Propheten. Hegel, Marx und die Folgen (Berne and Munich, 1958), p. 74.
159. See Heinrich Popitz, Der entfremdete Mensch. Zeitkritik und Geschichtsphilosophie des jungen Marx (Frankfurt/Main, 1967), pp. 76 et seq.
160. G. W. F. Hegel, Phenomenology of Mind, quoted in Popitz, op. cit., p. 114.
161. Auguste Cornu, Karl Marx et Friedrich Engels, vol. 2.
162. Karl Marx, Capital, op. cit., vol. 1, p. 25.
163. For details on this problem see Heinrich Popitz, op. cit., p. 111 et seq.
164. "Kritik der Hegelschen Dialektik und Philosophie überhaupt," in MEGA, pt. 1, vol. 3, p. 156.
165. Friedrich Engels, Introduction to The Civil War in France, MESW, vol. 2, p. 189.
166. Ibid.
167. Father Jean-Yves Calvez, op. cit., p. 248: "But there are commodities which differ from each other completely in quality, commodities demanding totally different qualities of work. Marx however, true to his concept of 'socially necessary working time,' assumes that work qualified in this or that way is a multiple of simple work.

Moreover he relies on an average degree of productivity in society as a whole. Admittedly this is an attractive idea; how can it be applied, however, so long as there is no possibility of making an effective and experimental comparison between work of different qualities? They cannot be compared on the basis of the products emerging from this work, since the relative value of the products is exactly what we are trying to establish with the aid of the measure of work. Must one say that, in order to compare different types of work, we must rely on what is *valid* in any particular society quite apart from any demonstration of the facts based on experiment? Probably there is no other solution; but this is a long way from *real* proof. In the last analysis socially necessary work is only that work which is recognised as such in society."

168. Karl Liebknecht, *Studien über die Bewegungsgesetze des gesellschaftlichen Entwicklung*, p. 256.

169. Ibid., p. 249.

170. Ibid., p. 257 et seq.

171. Ibid., p. 255. See also p. 253: "Why is class, not society, used as a standard in the measurement of the value of *labor-power*, the standard of individual or partial phenomena, not of the generality (totality), of multiplicity not individuality, of the mutable, empirically and historically transient, not the permanent? Where is the value of the output of this same labor-power, in other words of work, measured by overall social standards? Does not logic demand the inclusion of society overall in an estimate of the value of labor-power instead of fortuitous (though detailed) reliance upon gradation by social class levels in the standard of living?"

172. Ibid., p. 250.

173. Ibid., p. 252.

174. Ibid., p. 248.

175. Louis Althusser, *For Marx* (London, 1969), p. 229.

176. Werner Becker, *Kritik der Marxschen Wertlehre. Die methodische Irrationalität der ökonomischen Basistheorien des "Kapitals"* (Hamburg, 1972), p. 131 et seq.

· CHAPTER 10 ·

1. "It is almost inconceivable how a man who had such tremendous discoveries, such a complete and entire scientific revolution, in his head, could keep it there for 20 years. For the Ms I am working at has been written either before, or at the same time as the *first volume*; and the essential part of it is already in the old manuscript of 1860/62." Friedrich Engels to Laura Lafargue, Mar. 8, 1885, *Lafargue Correspondence*, vol. 1, p. 271.

2. "I am awfully busy; deep in the Rent of Land (Vol. III) which causes me a deal of trouble by Mohr's tables being almost without exception miscalculated." Friedrich Engels to Laura Lafargue, Apr. 11, 1894, *Lafargue Correspondence*, vol. 3, p. 330.

3. Friedrich Engels to Laura Lafargue, May 22, 1883, *Lafargue Correspondence*, vol. 1, p. 134.

4. Friedrich Engels, Preface to *Capital*, vol. 2, translated by Samuel Moore and Edward Aveling (Chicago, 1926), p. 11.

5. Friedrich Engels to Laura Lafargue, Dec. 17, 1894, *Lafargue Correspondence*, vol. 3, p. 348.

6. Karl Marx to Matilda Betham-Edwards, July 14, 1875, MEW, vol. 34, p. 146.

7. Karl Marx, Preface and "Note to the Reader" for the French edition of *Capital*, See *Capital* (George Allen & Unwin, 1887) pp. 841–842.

8. August Philips to Karl Marx, Jan. 26, 1872, in Werner Blumenberg, "Ein unbekanntes Kapitel aus Marx' Leben," *International Review of Social History*, vol. I (1956), p. 111.

9. A. Uroyeva, *For All Time and All Men* (Moscow, 1967), p. 102.

10. F. Harrison, *Autobiographic Memoirs* (London, 1911), vol. 2, p. 33 et seq., quoted from David McClellan, op. cit., p. 414.

11. "Marx opened up for scientific knowledge a new 'continent,' that of *history* — just as Thales opened up the 'continent' of mathematics for scientific knowledge and Galileo opened up the 'continent' of physical nature for scientific knowledge." Louis Althusser, *For Marx*, p. 14.

12. Mehring, *Life*, p. 510.

13. Karl Marx to Friedrich Adolph Sorge, Sept. 27, 1877, MEW, vol. 34, p. 295.

14. See law on disability and old age insurance in *Reichsgesetzblatt* (Official Gazette) 1889, pp. 97–101, and law on workers' sickness insurance, *Reichsgesetzblatt* 1883, pp. 73–76.

15. Werner Richter: *Bismarck* (Frankfurt/Main, 1962), p. 248.

16. Heinrich Mann, *Ein Zeitalter wird besichtigt* (Berlin, 1947), p. 511 et seq.

17. Richter, op. cit., p. 425.

18. Franziska Kugelmann, "Kleine Züge zu dem grossen Charakterbild von Karl Marx," in *Mohr und General*, p. 311.

19. Paul Lafargue, "Reminiscences of Marx," MSW, vol. 1, p. 83.

20. Karl Marx to Jenny Longuet, Apr. 11, 1881, *Correspondence*, p. 390.

21. Sir Mountstuart Elphinstone Grant Duff to Crown Princess Victoria of Prussia, 1879, in *Erinnerungen an Karl Marx*, p. 105 et seq., quoted in McClellan, op. cit., p. 445.

22. The account of Marx's visits to Karlsbad follows that of Egon Erwin Kisch, *Karl Marx in Karlsbad* (Berlin, 1968).

23. Karl Marx to Ludwig Kugelmann, Aug. 10, 1874, *Letters to Kugelmann*, p. 138.

24. Ferdinand Freiligrath to Karl Marx, Dec. 3, 1862, in Manfred Häckel, *Freiligraths Briefwechsel mit Marx und Engels*, vol. I, p. 164.

25. Karl Marx to Ludwig Kugelmann, Oct. 13, 1866, *Letters to Kugelmann*, p. 42.

26. Kisch, op. cit., p. 13.

27. Ibid., p. 16 et seq.

28. Karl Marx to Friedrich Engels, Sept. 1, 1874, MEW, vol. 33, p. 112.

29. Karl Marx to Jenny Marx, early Sept. 1876, MEW, vol. 34, p. 193.

30. Karl Marx to Wilhelm Alexander Freund, Jan. 21, 1877, ibid., p. 246.

31. Eleanor Marx-Aveling to Jenny Marx, Aug. 19, 1876, in Kapp, op. cit., p. 175.

32. Kisch, op. cit., p. 57.

33. Karl Marx to Friedrich Engels, Sept. 1, 1874, MEW, vol. 33, p. 112.

34. Karl Marx to Friedrich Engels, Aug. 21, 1875, MEW, vol. 34, p. 6.

35. Kisch, op. cit., p. 30 et seq.

36. Ibid., p. 33 et seq.

37. Wilhelm Liebknecht, *Karl Marx zum Gedächtnis. Ein Lebensabriss und Erinnerungen*, p. 86.

38. Quoted from Kisch, op. cit., p. 75.

39. MEW, vol. 34, p. 552, n. 98.

40. Ibid.

41. Friedrich Engels to Wilhelm Liebknecht, Apr. 11, 1877, ibid., p. 265.

42. MESW, vol. 3, p. 58 et seq.
43. Karl Marx to Friedrich Engels, Nov. 8, 1882, MEW, vol. 35, p. 105.
44. Karl Marx to Friedrich Engels, Mar. 3, 1882, ibid., p. 47.
45. Karl Marx to Friedrich Engels, Mar. 28/31, 1882, ibid., p. 51.
46. From Wilhelm Liebknecht, "From Reminiscences of Marx," MSW, vol. 1, p. 127.
47. Karl Marx to Jenny Longuet, Dec. 7, 1881, MEW, vol. 35, p. 240.
48. Eleanor Marx-Aveling to Wilhelm Liebknecht, in Liebknecht, "From Reminiscences of Karl Marx," MSW, vol. 1, p. 127.
49. Karl Marx to Friedrich Adolph Sorge, Dec. 15, 1881, MEW, vol. 35, p. 247.
50. Karl Marx to Jenny Longuet, Mar. 16, 1882, ibid., p. 289.
51. Karl Marx to Friedrich Engels, Apr. 28, 1882, ibid., p. 60.
52. Karl Marx to Friedrich Engels, Mar. 1, 1882, ibid., p. 45.
53. Karl Marx to Jenny Longuet, Mar. 16, 1882, ibid., p. 288.
54. Karl Marx to Laura Lafargue, Apr. 13/14, 1882, ibid., p. 311.
55. Karl Marx to Laura Lafargue, June 17, 1882, ibid., p. 331.
56. Quoted from Liebknecht, "From Reminiscences of Marx," MSW, vol. 1, p. 128.
57. Friedrich Engels to Laura Lafargue, Mar. 10, 1883, Lafargue Correspondence, vol. 1, p. 121.
58. Friedrich Engels to Friedrich Adolph Sorge, Mar. 15, 1883, Correspondence, p. 414.
59. See Bertolt Brecht, "Marx-Beschreibungen" in "Schriften zur Politik und Gesellschaft," in Gesammelte Werke, vol. 20, p. 74 et seq.
60. Besides Charles Longuet and Gottlieb Lemke, editor of the Sozialdemokrat, Friedrich Engels gives the following as present: Paul Lafargue, Friedrich Lessner, Georg Lochner, Ray Lankester, and Karl Schorlemmer. Friedrich Engels, "Das Begräbnis von Karl Marx," MEW, vol. 19, p. 339.
61. MESW, vol. 3, p. 162.
62. Franziska Kugelmann, in Mohr und General, p. 288.

BIBLIOGRAPHY

Abendroth, Wolfgang. *Sozialgeschichte der europäischen Arbeiterbewegung*, (edition suhrkamp 106). Frankfurt/Main, 1965.

Adler, Max. *Marx und Engels als Denker*, introduction by Thomas Meyer. Frankfurt/Main, 1972.

Adler, Victor. *Aufsätze, Reden und Briefe*, issued by Party Headquarters of Social-Democrat Workers' Party of German-Austria. Folio 1: "Victor Adler und Friedrich Engels." Vienna, 1922.

Althusser, Louis. *For Marx*, translated by Ben Brewster, Allen Lane. London, 1969.

Althusser, Louis, and Balibar, Etienne. *Lire le Capital*. Paris, 1968.

Andréas, Bert. *Briefe und Dokumente der Familie Marx aus den Jahren 1862 bis 1873 nebst zwei unbekannten Aufsätzen von Friedrich Engels*, special edition from Archiv für Sozialgeschichte. Vol. 2. Hannover, 1962.

Aristotle. *Politics*, translated by W. E. Bollard. London, 1877.

Aus der Frühzeit des Marxismus. Engels' Briefwechsel mit Kautsky, edited and annotated by Karl Kautsky. Prague, 1935.

Bakunin, Michael. *Beichte aus der Peter-Pauls-Festung an Zar Nikolaus I*, edited by Kurt Kersten (insel taschenbuch 29). Frankfurt/Main, 1973.

———. "Brief an Aleksander Herzen," in *Kursbuch*, Dec. 19, 1869.

———. "Persönliche Beziehungen zu Marx (1871)," in *Gesammelte Werke*. Vol. 3. Berlin, 1924.

———. "Social-politischer Briefwechsel mit Alexander Iw. Herzen und Ogarjov," with biographical introduction, annexes and comments by Professor Michail Dragomanov, in *Bibliothek Russicher Denkwürdigkeiten*, edited by Theodor Schiemann. Vol. 6. Stuttgart, 1895.

———. *Staatlichkeit und Anarchie und andere Schriften* (Statehood and Anarchy), edited by Horst Stuke. Frankfurt/Main, Berlin, Vienna, 1972.

Balogh, Elémer. "Zur Kritik des Irrationalismus. Eine Auseinandersetzung mit Georg Lukács," in *Deutsche Zeitschrift für Philosophie*, year 6 (1958), issue 1, pp. 58–76; issue 2, pp. 253–272; issue 4, pp. 622–633.

Bauer, Bruno. *Vollständige Geschichte der Partheikämpfe in Deutschland*. Vols. 1–3. Berlin, 1847.

Baumgardt, David. "Uber den 'verloren geglaubten' Anhang zu Karl Marxens Doktordissertation," in "Alfred Vierkandt zum 80 Geburtstag," *Gegenwartsprobleme der Soziologie*, edited by Dr. Gottfried Eisermann. Potsdam, 1949.

Bebel, August. *Aus meinem Leben*. Berlin, 1964.

Becker, Gerhard. *Karl Marx und Friedrich Engels in Köln 1848–1849. Zur Geschichte des Kölner Arbeitervereins*. Berlin, 1963.

Becker, Werner. *Kritik der Marxschen Wertlehre. Die methodische Irrationalität der ökonomischen Basistheorien des "Kapitals."* Hamburg, 1972.

Beeson, Trevor. *Discretion and Valour. Religious Conditions in Russia and Eastern Europe*, foreword by Sir John Lawrence. Glasgow, 1974.

Berdiajev, Nikolai. *Wahrheit und Lüge des Kommunismus*, Darmstadt, 1953.

Berlin, Isaiah. *Karl Marx. His Life and Environment*. London, 1939.

———. *Aus den Jahren meines Exils. Erinnerungen eines Sozialisten*. Berlin, 1918.

———. *Briefwechsel mit Friedrich Engels*, edited by Helmut Hirsch. Assen, 1970.

Bernstein, Eduard. "Johannes Miquel über Marx und seine Abwendung von ihm," in *Die Neue Zeit*, year 30 (no. 5 of 1914), pp. 188–196.

———. *Ein revisionistisches Sozialismusbild*, 3 lectures, edited and with an introduction by Helmut Hirsch. Hanover, 1966.

———. *Die Voraussetzungen des Sozialismus und die Aufgaben der Sozialdemokratie*, edited by Günther Hillmann (rororo classics 252/54). Reinbek bei Hamburg, 1969.

Bettelheim, Charles. *Über das Fortbestehen von Warenverhältnissen in den 'sozialistischen Ländern'*. Berlin, undated.

Bienek, Horst. *Bakunin, eine Invention* (Reihe Hanser 38). Munich, 1970.

Bienert, Walther. *Der überholte Marx. Seine Religionskritik und Weltanschauung kritisch untersucht*. Stuttgart, 1974.

Birth of the Communist Manifesto, edited and annotated with an introduction by Dirk J. Struik. New York, 1971.

Bittel, Karl. *Karl Marx. Neue Rheinische Zeitung–Politisch-ökonomische Revue*. Berlin, 1955.

———. *Karl Marx und die Menschlichkeit. Utopische Phantasie und Weltveränderung* (Rowohlt's German Encyclopaedia 317). Reinbek bei Hamburg, 1969.

———. *Das Materialismusproblem, seine Geschichte und Substanz*. Frankfurt/Main, 1972.

———. *Philosophische Aufsätze zur objektiven Phantasie*. Frankfurt/Main, 1969.

Bloch, Ernst: *Subjekt-Objekt. Erläuterungen zu Hegel*. Frankfurt/Main, 1962.

———. *Über Karl Marx* (edition suhrkamp 291). Frankfurt/Main, 1971.

———. *Über Methode und System bei Hegel* (edition Suhrkamp 413). Frankfurt/Main, 1970.

Blos, Wilhelm. "Karl Marx als Mensch," in *Die Glocke*, year 6 (no. 5 of 1918), pp. 159–161.

Blumenberg, Werner. "Ein unbekanntes Kapitel aus Marx' Leben," in *International Review of Social History*. Vol. 1. Assen, 1956.

———. *Karl Marx* (rowohlt monograph 76). Reinbek bei Hamburg, 1962.

Bode, Carl (ed.). *The Portable Thoreau*. New York, 1947.

Born, Stephan. *Erinnerungen eines Achtundvierzigers*. Leipzig, 1898.

———. "Friedrich Engels in Paris," in *Ich erinnere mich gern . . . Zeitgenossen über Friedrich Engels*, edited by Manfred Kliem. Berlin, 1970.

Börnstein, Heinrich. *Fünfundsiebzig Jahre in der Alten und Neuen Welt. Memoiren eines Unbedeutenden*. Leipzig, 1881.

Bottigelli, Emile. *Lettres et Documents de Karl Marx (1856–1883)*, Milan, 1958.

Brecht, Bertolt. "Schriften zur Politik und Gesellschaft," in *Gesammelte Werke*. Vol. 20. Frankfurt/Main, 1967.

Brisbane, Albert. *A Mental Biography*, edited by R. Brisbane. Boston, 1893.

Buber, Martin. *Der grosse Maggid und seine Nachfolge*. Berlin, 1922.

Buchner, Wilhelm. *Ferdinand Freiligrath. Ein Dichterleben in Briefen*. Vols. 1 and 2. Lahr, 1881.

———. *Gründungsdokumente des Bundes der Kommunisten (Juni bis September 1847)*, edited by Bert Andréas. Hamburg, 1969.

Der Bund der Kommunisten. Dokumente und Materialien, issued by Institute for Marxism-Leninism under Central Committee of East German Unity Party and Institute for Marxism-Leninism under Central Committee of Soviet Union Communist Party. Vol. 1:1836–1849. Berlin, 1970.

Burckhardt, Jacob: Die Kultur der Renaissance in Italien. Ein Versuch, edited by Werner Kaegi. Berlin and Leipzig, 1930.

Calvez, Father Jean-Yves. La pensée de Karl Marx. Paris, 1956.

Cerroni, Umberto. Marx et il dirilto moderno. Rome, 1963.

Colletti, Lucio. Introduction to Eduard Bernstein, Socialismo e Socialdemocrazia. Bari, 1968.

Colp, Ralph. "The Contacts between Karl Marx and Charles Darwin," in Journal of the History of Ideas, vol. 35 (April–June 1974).

Cornu, Auguste. Karl Marx et Friedrich Engels. Leur Vie et leur Oeuvre. Paris, 1954–1970.

Czóbel, Ernst: Introduction to Friedrich Engels, Sieben Rezensionen über den ersten Band des "Kapital." In Marx-Engels-Archiv. Zeitschrift des Marx-Engels-Instituts in Moskau. Edited by D. Ryazanoff. Vol. 2, p. 427 et seq. Frankfurt/Main, 1927.

Demetz, Peter. Marx, Engels and the Poets. Chicago, 1967.

Dubnow, Simon. Weltgeschichte des jüdischen Volkes. Vol. 3. Berlin, 1926.

Durkheim, Emile. Le Suicide. Paris, 1897.

Eibl-Eibesfeldt, Irenäus. Grundriss der vergleichenden Verhaltensforschung. Ethologie. Munich, 1969.

———. Liebe und Hass. Zur Naturgeschichte elementarer Verhaltensweisen. Munich, 1970.

———. Der vorprogrammierte Mensch. Das Ererbte als bestimmender Faktor im menschlichen Verhalten. Vienna, Munich, Zurich, 1973.

Eisner, F. H.: "Ein Aufsatz Heines in 'Le Globe' Februar 1832?," in Zeitschrift für deutsche Literaturgeschichte, no. 3 of 1959, pp. 421–425.

Friedrich Engels' Briefwechsel mit Karl Kautsky. Vienna, 1955. (Second and more complete edition of Aus der Frühzeit des Marxismus, including Karl Kautsky's letters edited and annotated by Benedikt Kautsky.)

Engels, Friedrich — Paul & Laura Lafargue — Correspondence. 3 vols. Moscow, 1959–1963.

Friedrich Engels. Eine Biographie, issued by Institute for Marxism-Lennism under Central Committee of East German Unity Party. Berlin, 1972.

Engels, Friedrich. Cola di Rienzi. Ein unbekannter dramatischer Entwurf, annotated and with an introduction by Michael Knierim. Wuppertal, 1974.

Enzensberger, Hans Magnus (ed.). Gespräche mit Marx und Engels, (insel taschenbuch 19/20). 2 vols. Frankfurt/Main, 1973.

Erlebte Geschichte. Von Zeitgenossen gesehen und geschildert. Part 1: Vom Kaiserreich zur Weimarer Republik. Berlin, 1968. Part 2: Vom Untergang der Weimarer Republik bis zur Befreiung vom Faschismus. Berlin, 1972.

Fetscher, Iring (ed.). Der Marxismus. Seine Geschichte in Dokumenten. 3 vols. Munich, 1962–1965.

Feuerbach, Ludwig. Philosophische Kritiken und Grundsätze (1839–1846). Leipzig, undated.

———. The Essence of Christianity, translated by Marian Evans. London, 1893.

———. Kleine Schriften (Theorie 1). Frankfurt/Main, 1969.

———. Das Wesen der Religion. Köln, 1967.

The First International: Minutes of the Haag-Congress with related Documents, edited by H. Gerth. Madison 1958.

Fischer, Louis. *The Life of Lenin*. London, 1964.

Förder, Herwig. *Marx und Engels am Vorabend der Revolution. Die Ausarbeitung der politischen Richtlinien für die deutschen Kommunisten (1846–1848)*. Berlin, 1960.

Der Friede. Idee und Verwirklichung. Festgabe für Adolf Leschnitzer. Heidelberg, 1961.

Fromm, Erich. *Marx's Concept of Man*. New York, 1963.

———. *Der moderne Mensch und seine Zukunft. Eine sozialpsychologische Untersuchung*. Frankfurt/Main, 1971.

Garaudy, Roger. *Dieu est mort — Étude sur Hegel*. Paris, 1962.

———. *Karl Marx*. Paris, 1964.

Geschichte der deutschen Arbeiterbewegung in 8 Bänden, issued by Institute for Marxism-Leninism. East Berlin, 1966.

Girardi, Giulio. "Der Marxismus zum Problem des Todes," in *Concilium* (International Periodical for Theology), year 10, no. 4 of 1974.

Girsberger, Hans. *Der utopische Sozialismus des 18 Jahrhunderts in Frankreich*, introduction by Bernd Heymann. Wiesbaden, 1973.

Gollwitzer, Helmut. *Forderungen der Freiheit*. Munich, 1962.

Gorky, Maxim. *Reminiscences of My Youth*. London, 1924.

Gorz, André. *Le Socialisme difficile*. Paris, 1967.

Haas, Willy. "Marx und Lenin. Notizen zu zwei neuen Monumentalausgaben," in *Die Literarische Welt*, nos. 4/5, 6, 7, 8/9, 10, and 11 of 1932.

Habermas, Jürgen. *Theorie und Praxis*. Neuwied and Berlin, 1963.

Häckel, Manfred. *Freiligrath's Briefwechsel mit Marx und Engels*. Berlin, 1968.

Hamann, Joseph. "Bericht über ein Gespräch mit Marx," in *Geschichte der deutschen Zimmererbewegung*, vol. 1. Stuttgart, 1903.

Harich, Wolfgang. "Georg Lukács. Die Zerstörung der Vernunft," in *Deutsche Zeitschrift für Philosophie*, year 3 (no. 1 of 1955), pp. 133–145.

———. 'Heinrich Heine und das Schulgeheimnis der deutschen Philosophie' in *Heinrich Heine. Zur Geschichte der Religion und Philosophie in Deutschland*, edited and with an introduction by Wolfgang Harich, Frankfurt/Main 1966.

———. "Ein Kant-Motiv em philosophischen Denken Herders," in *Deutsche Zeitschrift für Philosophie*, year 2 (no. 1 of 1954), pp. 43–68.

———. *Zur Kritik der revolutionären Ungeduld. Eine Abrechnung mit dem alten und dem neuen Anarchismus*, Basel, 1971.

Hegel, Georg Wilhelm Friedrich. *Ästhetik*, with an introductory essay by Georg Lukács. Berlin, 1955.

———. *Grundlinien der Philosophie des Rechts. Mit Hegels eigenhändigen Notizen in seinem Handexemplar und den mündlichen Zusätzen*, edited and with an introduction by Helmut Reichelt (Ullstein Buch 2929). Frankfurt/Main, Berlin, Vienna, 1972.

———. *Politische Schriften*, postscript by Jürgen Habermas (Theory 1). Frankfurt/Main, 1966.

———. *Vorlesungen über die Geschichte der Philosophie*. Vols. 1–3. Leipzig, 1971.

———. *The Phenomenology of Mind*, translated J. B. Baillie. London and New York, 1931.

———. *Jenenser Realphilosophie*, edited by J. Hoffmeister. Vol. 2. Leipzig, 1931.

Heilmann, Hans-Dieter, and Rabehl, Bernd. "Die Legende von der 'Bolschewisierung' der KPD II," in *Sozialistische Politik*, year 3 (no. 10 of Feb. 1971), pp. 1–37.

Heine, Heinrich. *Sämtliche Werke*, edited by Hans Kaufmann. Vols. 1–14. Munich, 1964.
———. *Works*. Vols. 5 & 6. London, 1892.
Heise, Wolfgang. "Über die Entfremdung und ihre Überwindung," in *Deutsche Zeitschrift für Philosophie*, year 13 (no. 6 of 1965).
Heller, Hermann. *Hegel und der nationale Machtstaatsgedanke in Deutschland. Ein Beitrag zur politischen Geistesgeschichte*. Aalen, 1963.
Henrich, Dieter. *Hegel im Kontext* (edition suhrkamp 510). Frankfurt/Main, 1971.
Herre, Günther. *Verelendung und Proletariat bei Karl Marx. Entstehung einer Theorie und ihre Quellen, Tübinger Schriften zur Sozial- und Zeitgeschichte 2*. Düsseldorf, 1973.
Briefe von und an Georg Herwegh, edited by Marcel Herwegh. Munich, 1898.
Herzen, Alexander. *Mein Leben. Memoiren und Reflexionen 1852–1868*, Berlin, 1962.
"Moses Hess Briefwechsel," edited by Edmund Silberer assisted by Werner Blumenberg, in *Quellen und Untersuchungen zur Geschichte der deutschen und österreichischen Arbeiterbewegung*. Vol. 2. 's-Gravenhage, 1959.
Hirsch, Helmut. *Friedrich Engels* (Rowohlt monograph 142). Reinbek bei Hamburg, 1968.
Horn, András. *Kunst und Friheit. Eine kritische Interpretation der Hegelschen Ästhetik*. The Hague, 1969.
Huch, Ricarda. *Michael Bakunin und die Anarchie* (Bibliothek Suhrkamp 334). Frankfurt/Main, 1972.
Hugo, Victor. *Napoleon the Little*. London, 1852.
Hundt, Martin. *Wie das "Manifest" entstand*. Berlin, 1973.
Institute for Marxism-Leninism, *Documents of the First International*. Vol. 4. Moscow, undated.
Internationaal Instituut voor Sociale Geschiedenes, Amsterdam. Catalogue of Marx-Engels papers. Vol. 1: Marx; vol. 2: Engels, etc., typescript.
Jacoby, Johann. *Vier Fragen beantwortet von einem Ostpreussen*. Mannheim, 1841.
Jaspers, Karl. "Marx und Freud," in *Der Monat*, issue 26, (1950).
Jores, Arthur. *Vom Sinn der Krankheit*. Hamburg, 1950.
Kapp, Yvonne. *Eleanor Marx*. Vol. 1: *Family Life 1855–1883*, London, 1972.
Kautsky, Karl. *Das Erfurter Programm*. Berlin, 1965.
———. *Das Erfurter Programm*. Berlin, 1965.
———. *Erinnerungen und Erörterungen*, edited Benedikt Kautsky. 's-Gravenhage, 1960.
———. "Lassalle und Marx," in *Die Neue Zeit*, year 31 (1912/13), pp. 476–490.
———. "Parteipolemik," in *Die Neue Zeit*, year 31 (1912/13), pp. 838–841.
———. "Ein Vertrauensmann," in *Die Neue Zeit*, year 31 (1912/13), pp. 600–602.
Khrushchev, Nikita S. Speech at Twentieth Party Congress, Feb. 25, 1956, in *Khrushchev Speaks*, edited by Thomas P. Whitney. Ann Arbor, 1963.
Kisch, Egon Erwin. *Karl Marx in Karlsbad*. Berlin & Weimar, 1968.
Koch, Egmont R. "Aufstieg und Fall eines Mäusestaates," in *Akzent*, Bild der Wissenschaft— Daten, Fakten, Analysen, year 2, no. 3 (Mar. 1974).
Korsch, Karl. *Karl Marx*, commissioned by International Institute for Social History, edited by Götz Langkau. Frankfurt/Main, 1967.
———. *Marxism and Philosophy*. London, 1971.
———. Preface to Karl Marx's *Das Kapital*, vol. 1: *Der Produktionsprozess des Kapitals* (Ullstein Buch 4025/28). Frankfurt/Main & Berlin, 1969.
Kotzakowski, Leszek. *Der Mensch ohne Alternative. Von der Möglichkeit und Unmöglichkeit Marxist zu sein*. Munich, 1964.

Krauss, Werner. "Karl Marx im Vormärz," in *Deutsche Zeitschrift für Philosophie*, year 1 (no. 1 of 1953).

Kreutzer, Leo. *Heine und der Kommunismus* (Kleine Vandenhoek-Reihe 322). Göttingen, 1970.

Kuczynski, Jürgen. *Die Geschichte der Lage der Arbeiter in Deutschland von 1789 bis in die Gegenwart.* Berlin, 1954.

———. *Die wirtschaftlichen und sozialen Voraussetzungen der Revolution 1848/49.* Berlin, 1948.

Künzli, Arnold. *Karl Marx. Eine Psychographie.* Vienna, 1966.

Kux, Ernst Eduard Walter. "Karl Marx — Die revolutionäre Konfession." Dissertation, Zurich, 1966.

Lafargue, Paul. *Das Recht auf Faulheit & Persönliche Erinnerungen an Karl Marx*, edited and with an introduction by Iring Fetscher. Frankfurt/Main, 1966.

Landshut, Siegfried. *Einleitung zu Karl Marx "Die Frühschriften"* (Kröner Taschenausgabe 209). Stuttgart, 1953.

Lange, Max G. *Marxismus, Leninismus, Stalinismus. Zur Kritik des dialektischen Materialismus.* Stuttgart, 1955.

Lassalle, Ferdinand. *Gesammelte Reden und Schriften.* Vol. 1: *Der italienische Krieg. Franz von Sickingen.* Berlin, 1919.

———. *Nachgelassene Briefe und Schriften.* Vol. 3: *Der Briefwechsel zwischen Lassalle und Marx.* Berlin, 1922.

Ferdinand Lassalle. Eine Auswahl für unsere Zeit, edited by Helmut Hirsch. Frankfurt/Main, Vienna, Zurich, 1964.

Lenin, Vladimir I. "Little better, but better," in *Pravda*, Mar. 4, 1924.

———. *Collected Works*, Foreign Languages Publishing House, Moscow. Vols. 19, 21, 31, 35, and 36; in particular vol. 21: *Karl Marx* (A brief biographical sketch with an exposition of Marxism), and vol. 19: *The Marx-Engels Correspondence.*

———. *Marx, Engels, Marxism.* London, 1934.

Lessing, Theodor. *Der jüdische Selbsthass.* Berlin, 1930.

Lewiowa, S. "Karl Schapper," in *Marx und Engels und die ersten proletarischen Revolutionäre.* Berlin, 1965.

Lieber, Hans-Joachim. "Zur Situation der Marxforschung. II. Zur Situation der Marxforschung in der Sowjetischen Besatzungszone Deutschlands," in *Kölner Zeitschrift for Soziologie und Sozialpsychologie*, year 10 (1958), pp. 658–673.

Liebknecht, Karl. *Studien über die Bewegungsgesetze der gesellschaftlichen Entwicklung*, edited by Ossip K. Flechtheim. Hamburg, 1974.

Liebknecht, Wilhelm. *Karl Marx zum Gedächtnis. Ein Lebensabriss und Erinnerungen.* Nuremberg, 1896.

Longuet, Jean. *La politique internationale du Marxisme. Karl Marx et la France.* Paris, 1918.

Longuet, Jean, and Silber, Georges. *Dessous de la Police russe. Terroristes et Policiers. Azev, Harting et cie, Étude historique et critique.* Paris, 1909.

Lorenz, Konrad. *Ubertierisches und menschliches Verhalten. Aus dem Werdegang der Verhaltenslehre.* Vols. 1 and 2. Munich, 1965.

Lorenz, Konrad, and Leyhausen, Paul. *Antriebe tierischen und menschlichen Verhaltens.* Munich, 1968.

Lucas, Betty. "Ein Erinnerungsblatt aus London," in *Leipziger Sonntagsblatt*, Sept. 14, 1862.

Ludz, Peter. "Zur Situation der Marxforschung. I. Zur Situation der Marxforschung in

Westeuropa," in *Kölner Zeitschrift für Soziologie und Sozialpsychologie*, year 10 (1958), pp. 446–449.

Lukács, Georg. *History and Class-consciousness*. London, 1970.

——. *Der junge Hegel und die Probleme der kapitalistischen Gesellschaft*. Berlin, 1954.

——. *Der junge Marx. Seine philosophische Entwicklung von 1840 bis 1844*. Pfullingen, 1965.

——. *Marxismus und Stalinismus* (Rowohlt German Encyclopaedia 327/28). Reinbek bei Hamburg, 1970.

——. *Schriften zur Ideologie und Politik*. Neuwied, Berlin, 1967.

——. *Zur Ontologie des gesellschaftlichen Seins. Die ontologischen Grundprinzipien von Karl Marx* (Sammlung Luchterhand 86). Darmstadt, Neuwied 1972.

Luxemburg, Rosa. *Die Akkumulation des Kapitals*. Berlin, 1923.

——. *Politische Schriften*. Vols. 1–3, edited and with an introduction by Ossip K. Flechtheim. Frankfurt/Main, 1966, 1968.

Mandel, Ernest. *Entstehung und Entwicklung der ökonomischen Lehre von Karl Marx (1843 bis 1963)*. Frankfurt/Main, 1968.

Mann, Golo. *The History of Germany since 1789*. London, 1968.

Mann, Heinrich. *Ein Zeitalter wird besichtigt*. Berlin, 1947.

Marcuse, Herbert. "Neue Quellen zur Grundlegung des Historischen Materialismus," in *Ideen zu einer kritischen Theorie der Gesellschaft* (edition Suhrkamp 300). Frankfurt/Main, 1969. First printed in *Die Gesellschaft*, year 7 (no. 9 of 1932).

Marcuse, Ludwig. "Die marxistische Auslegung des Tragischen," in *Monatshefte*, vol. 44 no. 5, (Oct. 1954).

Marx, Karl. *Capital*, translated by Samuel Moore and Edward Aveling, edited by Frederick Engels. Chicago, 1926.

——. *The Cologne Communist Trial*, translated by Rodney Livingstone. London, 1971.

——. *Grundrisse zur Kritik der politischen Ökonomie*, issued by Institute for Marxism-Leninism. Moscow, 1953.

——. *Letters to Dr Kugelmann*. London, 1941.

——. *Die polnische Frage. Manuskripte über die polnische Frage (1863 bis 1864)*, edited by W. Conze and D. Hertz-Eichenrode. 's-Gravenhage, 1961.

——. *Selected Works*. 2 Vols. London, 1942.

——. *Theories of Surplus Value*. London, 1969.

Marx, Karl, and Engels, Friedrich. *Collected Works*. Vols. 1–6. London, 1974–1976.

——. *Correspondence 1846–1895*. London, 1934.

——. *Historisch-kritische Gesamtausgabe. Werke/Schriften/Briefe*, edited by D. Ryazanoff and V. Adoratsky. Frankfurt/Main, Berlin (Leningrad), Moscow, 1927–1935; new impression Glashütten im Taunus, 1970.

——. *Letters to Americans 1848–1895*. New York, 1953.

——. *Selected Works*. 3 Vols. Moscow, 1970.

——. *Über Kunst und Literatur*. 2 Vols. Berlin, 1967.

——. *Werke*, issued by Institute for Marxism-Leninism. Vols. 1–39. East Berlin, 1956–1968.

Karl Marx. Biographie, Institute for Marxism-Leninism under Central Committee of Soviet Union Communist Party. Berlin, 1973.

Karl Marx. Chronik seines Lebens in Einzeldaten, compiled by Marx-Engels-Lenin Institute. Moscow and Frankfurt/Main, 1971.

Marx-Chronik. Daten zu Leben und Werk, compiled by Maximilien Rubel, (Reihe Hanser 3). Munich, 1968.

Karl Marx. Dokumente seines Lebens 1818–1883, compiled and annotated by Manfred Kliem. Leipzig, 1970.

Karl Marx im Kreuzverhör der Wissenschaften, Ring lecture "Marxismus und Wissenschaften," University of Zurich, summer term 1973, edited by Fritz Busser. Zurich and Munich, 1974.

Karl Marx' Ökonomische Lehren, elucidated and annotated by Karl Kautsky. Stuttgart, 1893.

Marx und Marxismus heute, edited by Gerd Breitenberger and Günter Schnitzler. Hamburg, 1974.

"Die Marxismus-Diskussion in Polen," in *Ost-Probleme*, year 9 (no. 1 of 1957.)

Marxismus und deutsche Arbeiterbewegung. Studien zur sozialistischen Bewegung im letzten Drittel des 19 Jahrhunderts, edited by Deutsche Akademie der Wissenschaften, Zentralinstitut für Geschichte. Berlin, 1970.

Massiczek, Albert. *Der menschliche Mensch. Karl Marx' jüdischer Humanismus*. Vienna, 1968.

Matheus, Ernst. "Der humanistische Ansatz des jungen Marx," in *Festschrift FW 6*, 1961.

Mattick, Paul. *Marx und Keynes. Die "Grenzen" des gemischten Wirtschaftssystems*. Frankfurt/Main, 1971.

Maus, Heinz. "Umstrittener Marx," in *Neue Politische Literatur*, year 2 (1957), pp. 1–22.

Mayer, Gustav. *Friedrich Engels. Eine Biographie* 2 vols. Köln, undated.

———. *Friedrich Engels. A Biography*, translated by Gilbert and Helen Highet. London, 1936.

Mayer, Hans. *Karl Marx und das Elend des Geistes. Studien zur neuen deutschen Ideologie*. Meisenheim am Glan, 1948.

Mayer, J. P. "Reflections on Equality," in *The Socialist Idea. A Reappraisal*, edited by Leszek Kozakowski and Stuart Hampshire. London, 1974, pp. 59–73.

McLellan, David. *Karl Marx. His Life and Thought*. London, New York, Dublin, Melbourne, Johannesburg, Madras, 1973.

Mehring, Franz. "Aufsätze zur deutschen Literatur von Hebbel bis Schweichel," in *Gesammelte Schriften*, vol. 11. Berlin, 1961.

———. "Aufsätze zur deutschen Literatur von Klopstock bis Weerth," in *Gesammelte Schriften*, vol. 10. Berlin, 1961.

——— (ed.). *Aus dem literarischen Nachlass von Karl Marx, Friedrich Engels und Ferdinand Lassalle. Gesammelte Schriften von Karl Marx und Friedrich Engels 1841 bis 1850*. Stuttgart, 1913.

———. "Geschichte der deutschen Sozialdemokratie," in *Gesammelte Schriften*, vols. 1 and 2. Berlin, 1960.

———. *Karl Marx. The Story of his Life*, translated by Edward Fitzgerald. London, 1936.

———. "Mein Vertrauensbruch," in *Die Neue Zeit*, year 31 (1912/13), pp. 592–600.

———. "Neue Schriften über Marx," in *Die Neue Zeit*, year 31 (1912/13), pp. 985–991.

———. "Ein neuer Literatenkrakeel," in *Die Neue Zeit*, year 32 (no. 10 of 1913), pp. 393–396.

———. "Ein Parteijubiläum," in *Die Neue Zeit*, year 31 (1912/13), p. 793 et seq.

———. "Uber den Gegensatz zwischen Lassalle und Marx," in *Die Neue Zeit*, year 31 (1912/13), pp. 445–450.

Meyer, Helmut. *Franziska und der Student aus Trier*. Berlin, undated.

Mit Gesang wird gekämpft. Lieder der Arbeiterbewegung. Berlin, 1967.

Mohr und General. Erinnerungen an Marx und Engels. Berlin, 1964.

Monz, Heinz. *Karl Marx. Grundlagen der Entwicklung zu Leben und Werk*. Trier, 1973. (A considerably expanded second edition of his *Karl Marx und Trier*.)

Na'aman, Shlomo. *Lassalle*. Hanover, 1970.

Oberwinder, Heinrich. *Sozialismus und Sozialpolitik*. Berlin, 1887.

Payne, Robert. *Marx*. London, 1968.

Pearson, Hesketh. *Bernard Shaw. His Life and Personality*. London, 1961.

Plato. *The Republic of Plato*, introduced, translated and analysed by B. Jowett. Oxford, 1888.

Popitz, Heinrich. *Der entfremdete Mensch. Zeitkritik und Geschichtsphilosophie des jungen Marx*. Frankfurt/Main, 1967.

Popper, Karl R. *Die offene Gesellschaft und ihre Feinde*. Vol. 2: *Falsche Propheten. Hegel, Marx und die Folgen*. Berne & Munich, 1958.

Post, Werner. *Kritik der Religion bei Karl Marx*. Munich, 1969.

Prinz, Arthur M. "Myths, Facts and Riddles about the literary Estate of Karl Marx," in *Der Friede. Idee und Verwirklichung, Festausgabe für Adolf Leschnitzer*. Heidelberg, 1961.

Proudhon, Pierre-Joseph. *Les Confessions d'un Révolutionnaire pour servir à l'Histoire de la Révolution de Fevrier*. Brussels, 1849.

Raddatz, Fritz J. "Lied und Gedicht der proletarisch/revolutionären Literatur," in *Die deutsche Literatur in der Weimarer Republik*, edited by Wolfgang Rothe. Stuttgart, 1974.

——— (ed.). *Marxismus und Literatur*. Vol. 1. Reinbek bei Hamburg, 1969.

Rathenau, Walther. *An Deutschlands Jugend*. Berlin, 1918.

Reichelt, Helmut. *Zur logischen Struktur des Kapitalbegriffs bei Karl Marx*, foreword by Irlng Fetscher. Frankfurt/Main, 1970.

Reichsgesetzblatt (Official Gazette). Nos. 1–28 (1883), 1–34 (1884), 1–27 (1889), 1–48 (1892). (Those of 1883 contain the laws, ordinances, etc, from Jan. 3 to Dec. 18, 1883, together with an agreement of 1880 and two agreements of 1882. Those of 1884 contain the laws, ordinances, etc., from Jan. 2 to Dec. 8, 1884, together with an agreement of 1882 and several agreements, one ordinance and one proclamation of 1883. Those of 1889 contain the laws, ordinances, etc., from Jan. 2 to Dec. 18, 1889, together with one agreement of 1888. Those of 1892 contain the laws, ordinances, etc., from Jan. 9, to Dec. 22, 1892, together with two agreements of 1890 and twelve agreements of 1891.)

Revolution oder Reform? Herbert Marcuse und Karl Popper. Eine Konfrontation. Munich, 1971.

Richter, Werner. *Bismarck*. Frankfurt/Main, 1962.

Riedl, Manfred. *Bürgerliche Gesellschaft und Staat. Grundproblem und Struktur der Hegelschen Rechtsphilosophie*. Neuwied & Berlin, 1970.

Rodbertus, Johann Karl. "Briefe und Briefwechsel," in *Gesammelte Werke und Briefe*, section 4, compiled on the basis of previous editions, edited with an introduction and bibliography by Th. Ramm. Osnabrück, 1972.

———. "Die Forderungen der arbeitenden Klassen," in *Sozialökonomische Texte*, edited by Professor Dr August Skalweit. Frankfurt/Main, 1946.

Rolfes, Helmut. *Der Sinn des Lebens im marxistischen Denken. Eine kritische Darstellung*. Düsseldorf, 1971.

Rosenberg, David. *Die Entwicklung der ökonomischen Lehren von Marx und Engels in den vierziger Jahren des 19 Jahrhunderts*. Berlin, 1958.

Rosental, M. M. "Die Ausarbeitung des Gesetzes vom Kampf der Gegensätze in Karl

Marx' 'Kapital,' " in *Deutsche Zeitschrift für Philosophie*, year 1 (no. 2 of 1953), pp. 332–349.

Rossanda, Rossana. "Die sozialistischen Länder. Ein Dilemma der westeuropäischen Linken," in *Kursbuch*, Dec. 30, 1972, pp. 1–36.

———. *Wir sind die rote Garde. Sozialistische Literatur 1914–1935*, edited by Edith Zenker. 2 vols. Leipzig, 1957.

Rubel, Maximilien. *Karl Marx. Essai de biographie intellectuelle*, Paris, 1957.

Ruge, Arnold. *Briefwechsel und Tagebuchblätter aus den Jahren 1825–1880*, edited by Paul Nerrlich. Vol. 1: *1825–1847*; vol. 2: *1848–1880*. Berlin, 1886.

Rühle, Otto. *Karl Marx. Leben und Werk.* Hellerau bei Dresden, 1928.

Die russische Kommune. Kritik eines Mythos, edited by Maximilien Rubel. Munich, 1972.

Ryazanoff, D. *Karl Marx als Denker, Mensch und Revolutionär.* Frankfurt/Main, 1971.

———. *Marx und Engels nicht nur für Anfänger*, postscript by Bernd Rabehl. Berlin, 1973.

———. "Sozialdemokratische Flagge und anarchistische Ware. Ein Beitrag zur Parteigeschichte," in *Die Neue Zeit*, year 32 (no. 5 of 1913) pp. 150–161, (no. 7 of 1913) pp. 226–239, (no. 8 of 1913) pp. 265–272, (no. 9 of 1913) pp. 320–333, (no. 10 of 1913) pp. 360–375.

Schaff, Adam. *Marx oder Sartre? Versuch einer Philosophie des Menschen*, (Fischer Bücherei 703). Frankfurt/Main and Hamburg, 1966.

———. *Marxismus und das menschliche Individuum.* Vienna, 1965.

Schmidt, Alfred. *Emanzipierte Sinnlichkeit. Ludwig Feuerbachs anthropologischer Materialismus* (Reihe Hanser 109). Munich, 1973.

Schnabel, Franz. *Deutsche Geschichte im 19 Jahrhundert.* Freiburg im Breisgau, 1965.

Schumpeter, Joseph A. *Kapitalismus, Sozialismus und Demokratie.* Berne, 1946.

Schurz, Carl. *The Reminiscences of Carl Schurz.* London, 1909.

Schwarzschild, Leopold. *The Red Prussian*, translated by Margaret Wing. London, 1948.

Schwerbrock, Wolfgang. *Karl Marx privat. Unbekannte Briefe.* Munich, 1962.

Seiler, Sebastian. *Das Complot vom 13 Juni 1849 oder der letzte Sieg der Bourgeoisie in Frankreich. Ein Beitrag zur Geschichte der Gegenwart.* Hamburg, 1850.

Sève, Lucien. *Marxisme et Théorie de la Personnalité.* Paris, 1969.

Sombart, Werner. *Der proletarische Sozialismus.* Vol. 1: *Die Lehre*; vol. 2: *Die Bewegung*, Jena, 1924. Tenth revised edition of the book *Sozialismus und soziale Bewegung.*

———. "Das Wirtschaftsleben im Zeitalter des Hochkapitalismus," in *Der moderne Kapitalismus. Historisch-systematische Dartellung des gesamteuropäischen Wirtschaftslebens von seinen Anfängen bis zur Gegenwart.* Vol. 3. Munich and Leipzig, 1927.

Somerhausen, Luc. *L'Humanisme agissant de Karl Marx.* Paris, 1946.

"Die sowjetische Marx-Revision," from *Nova Kultura* (nos. 17–19 of 1957), in *Ost-Probleme*, year 9 (no. 22 of 1957), pp. 772–782.

Stein, Hans. *Der Kölner Arbeiterverein (1848–1849). Ein Beitrag zur Frühgeschichte des rheinischen Sozialismus.* Köln, 1921.

Sterling, Eleonore. *Er ist wie Du. Aus der Frühgeschichte des Antisemitismus in Deutschland (1815–1850).* Munich, 1956.

Stern, Heinz, and Wolf, Dieter. *Das grosse Erbe.* Berlin, 1972.

Strey, Joachim, and Winkler, Gerhard. *Marx und Engels 1848/49. Die Politik und Taktik der "Neuen Rheinischen Zeitung" während der bürgerlichdemokratischen Revolution in Deutschland.* Berlin, 1972.

Sue, Eugène. *The Mysteries of Paris.* London and Philadelphia, 1925.

Taubes, Jakob. "Abendländische Eschatologie," in *Beiträge zur Soziologie und Sozial-philosophie*, edited by René König. Vol. 3. Berne, 1947.

Thier, Erich. "Die Anthropologie des jungen Marx nach den Pariser ökonomisch-philosophischen Manuskripten," introductory commentary on Karl Marx in *Nationalökonomie und Philosophie*. Köln and Berlin, 1950.

———. *Das Menschenbild des jungen Marx*. Göttingen, 1957.

Trofimow, P. S. "Fragen der materialistischen Dialektik un Erkenntnistheorie im 'Kapital' von Karl Marx," in *Deutsche Zeitschrift für Philosophie*, year 1 (no. 3/4 of 1953), pp. 579–600.

Uroyeva, A. *For all Time and all Men*. Moscow, 1967.

Victor, Walther. *General und die Frauen. Vom Erlebnis zur Theorie*. Berlin, 1932.

———. *Marx und Heine. Tatsache und Spekulation in der Darstellung ihrer Beziehungen*. Berlin, 1951.

Vogt, Joseph. *Sklaverei und Humanität. Studien zur antiken Sklaverei und ihrer Erforschung*, (Historia Einzelschriften No. 8). Wiesbaden, 1965.

Vygodsky, Vitali S. *Die Geschichte einer grossen Entdeckung. Über die Entstehung der Werkes 'Das Kapital' von Karl Marx*. Berlin, 1967.

Weitling, Wilhelm. *Das Evangelium des armen Sünders. Die Menscheit wie sie ist und wie sie sein sollte*, edited by Wolf Schäfer (rowohlt classics 274/76). Reinbek bei Hamburg, 1971.

Werckmeister, O. K. "Ideologie und Kunst bei Marx," in *Neue Rundschau*, year 84 (no. 4 of 1973).

Westermann, William L. *The Slave Systems of Greek and Roman Antiquity*. Philadelphia, 1955.

Wetter, Gustav A. *Der dialektische Materialismus*. Vienna, 1952.

Wiedmann, Franz: *G. W. F. Hegel* (rowohlt monograph 110). Reinbek bei Hamburg, 1965.

Wilbrandt, Robert. *Karl Marx — Versuch einer Einführung*. Leipzig and Berlin, 1918.

INDEX